Medaka Kuroiwa is Impervious to My Charms

1

Ran Kuze

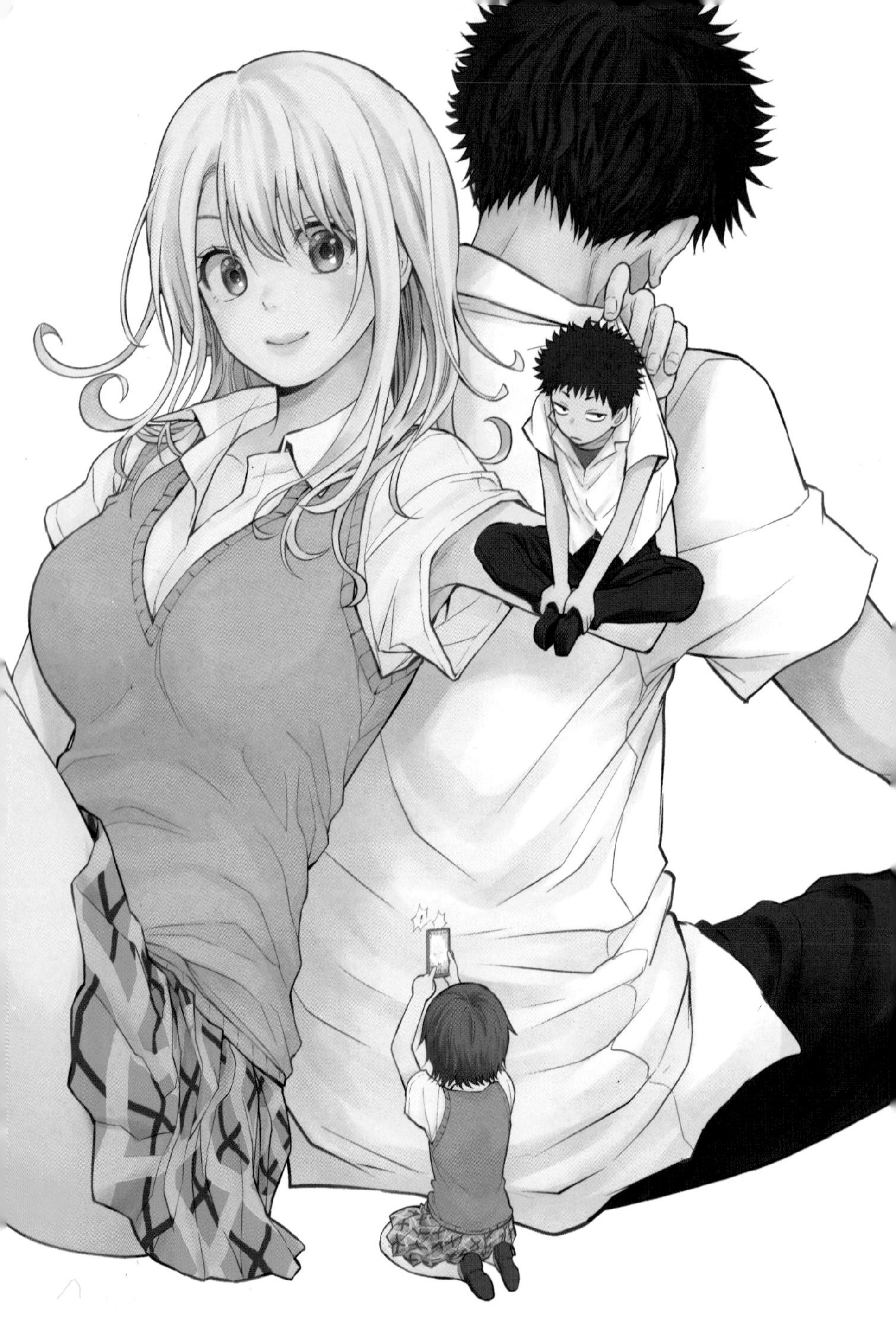

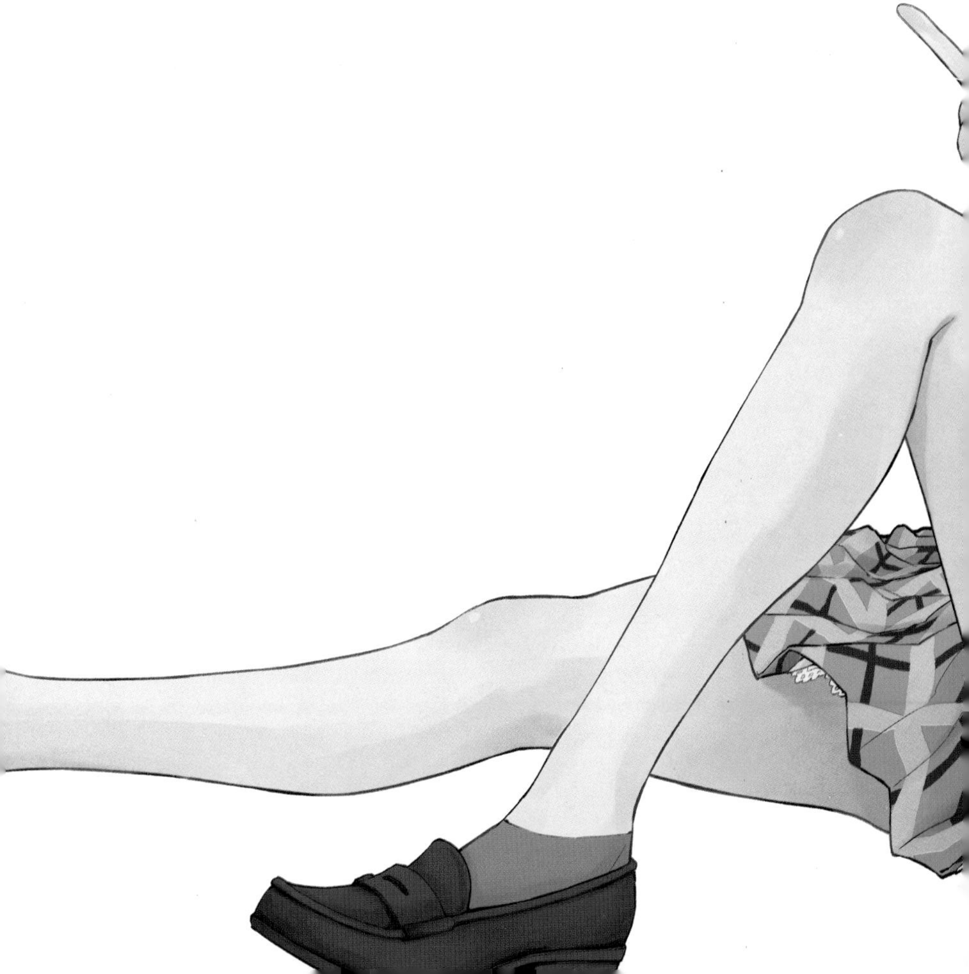

CONTENTS

Chapter 1 The Jerk Who Won't Fall for Me 5

Chapter 2 P.E. with That Jerk 41

Chapter 3 Sketching with That Jerk 67

Chapter 4 That Devilish Jerk 85

Chapter 5 In the Library with That Jerk 99

Chapter 6 "Love" and That Jerk 113

Chapter 7 That Girl and Her Wallpaper 129

Chapter 8 Cosplaying with That Jerk 145

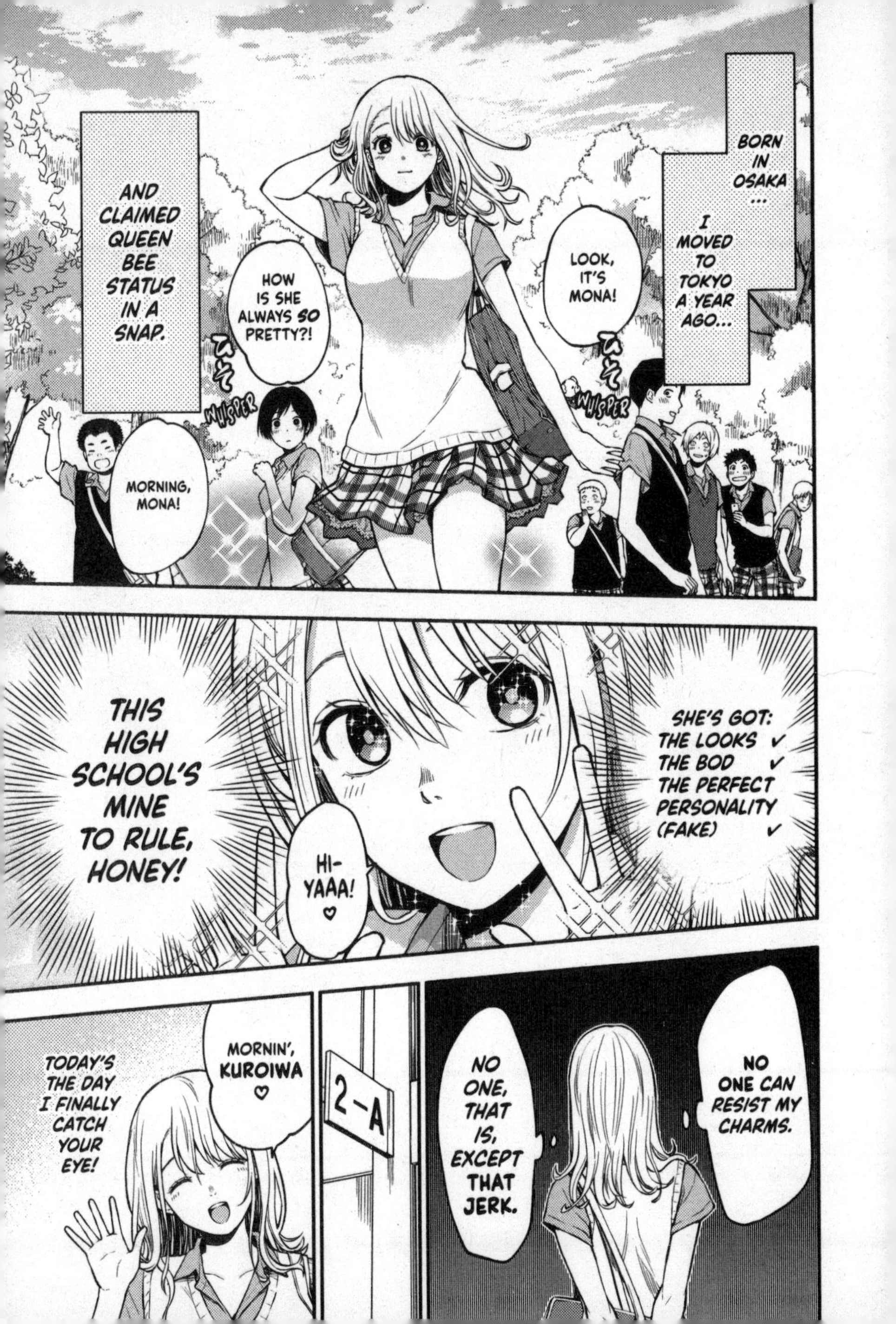
BORN IN OSAKA... I MOVED TO TOKYO A YEAR AGO...
LOOK, IT'S MONA!
ひそ WHISPER
HOW IS SHE ALWAYS SO PRETTY?!
ひそ WHISPER
AND CLAIMED QUEEN BEE STATUS IN A SNAP.
MORNING, MONA!
SHE'S GOT: THE LOOKS ✓ THE BOD ✓ THE PERFECT PERSONALITY (FAKE) ✓
HI-YAAA! ♡
THIS HIGH SCHOOL'S MINE TO RULE, HONEY!
NO ONE CAN RESIST MY CHARMS.
NO ONE, THAT IS, EXCEPT THAT JERK.
2-A
MORNIN', KUROIWA ♡
TODAY'S THE DAY I FINALLY CATCH YOUR EYE!

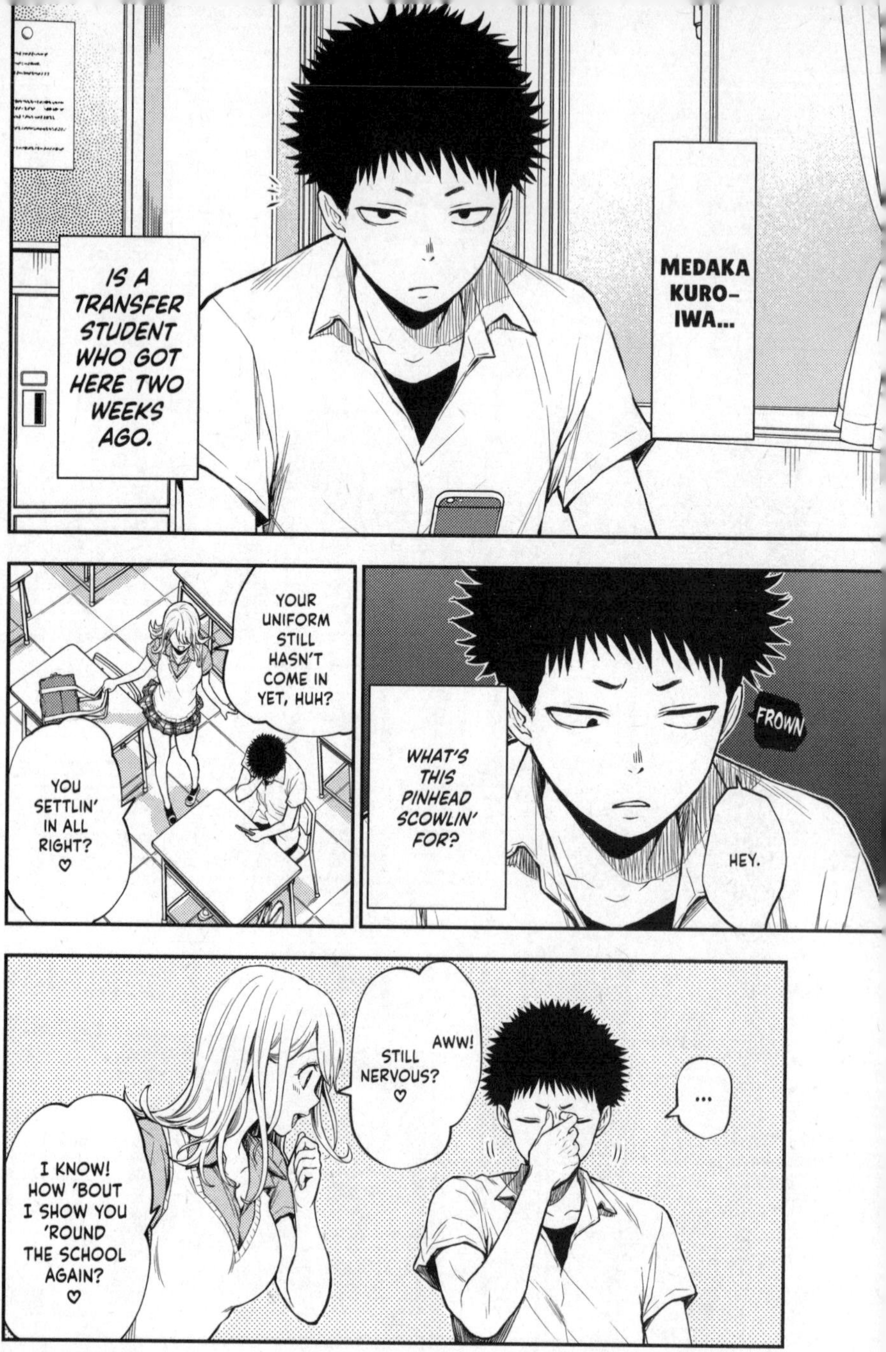
MEDAKA KURO-IWA...
IS A TRANSFER STUDENT WHO GOT HERE TWO WEEKS AGO.
FROWN
WHAT'S THIS PINHEAD SCOWLIN' FOR?
HEY.
YOUR UNIFORM STILL HASN'T COME IN YET, HUH?
YOU SETTLIN' IN ALL RIGHT? ♡
...
AWW! STILL NERVOUS? ♡
I KNOW! HOW 'BOUT I SHOW YOU 'ROUND THE SCHOOL AGAIN? ♡

I'M HERE IF YOU NEED ANY LI'L THING, SO JUST ASK! ♥
M'KAY? ♥
AH!
KUROIWA'S GETTING ALL OF MONA'S ATTENTION AGAIN!
WHISPER
WHISPER
UGH, I'M SO JEALOUS ...!
GRIND
HEY, UMM...
!
YEEES? ♥
COULD YOU, LIKE...
BACK OFF, PLEASE?
H- HE SHOT DOWN MONA'S KIND-NESS...!
MUR
IS HE INSANE?!
MUR
SPURT

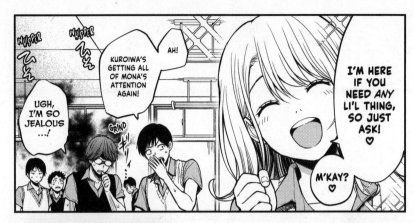

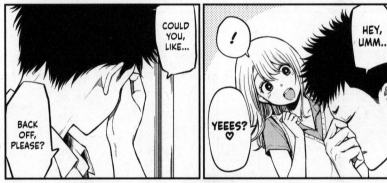

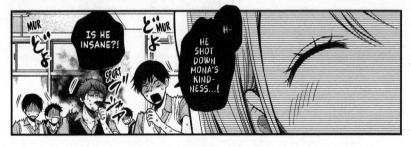

Chapter 1 ★ The Jerk Who Won't Fall for Me

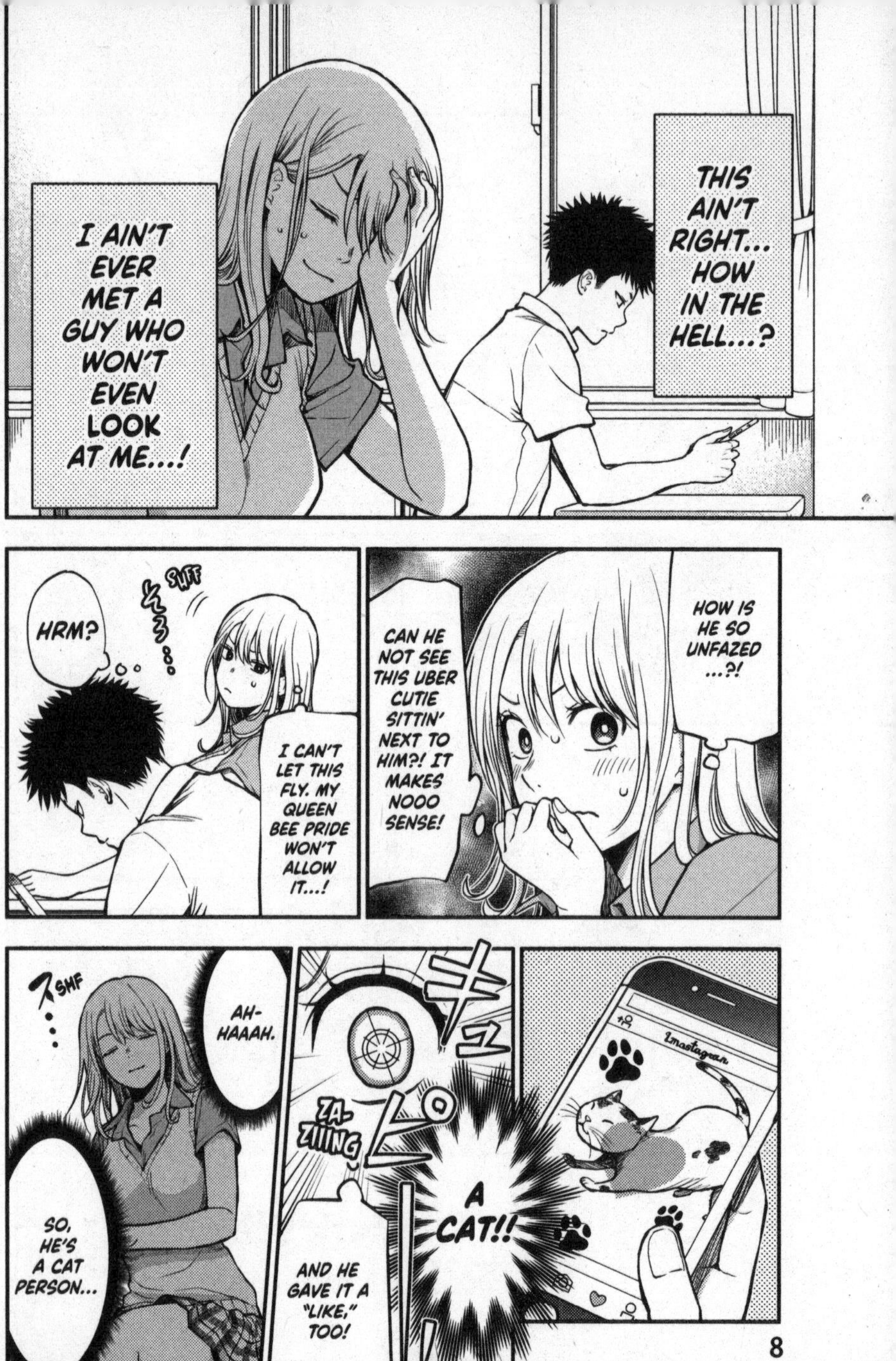
THIS AIN'T RIGHT... HOW IN THE HELL...?
I AIN'T EVER MET A GUY WHO WON'T EVEN LOOK AT ME...!
HOW IS HE SO UNFAZED ...?!
CAN HE NOT SEE THIS UBER CUTIE SITTIN' NEXT TO HIM?! IT MAKES NOOO SENSE!
SWFF
HRM?
I CAN'T LET THIS FLY. MY QUEEN BEE PRIDE WON'T ALLOW IT...!
Imastagram
A CAT!!
AH-HAAAH.
ZA-ZIIING
AND HE GAVE IT A "LIKE," TOO!
SHF
SO, HE'S A CAT PERSON...

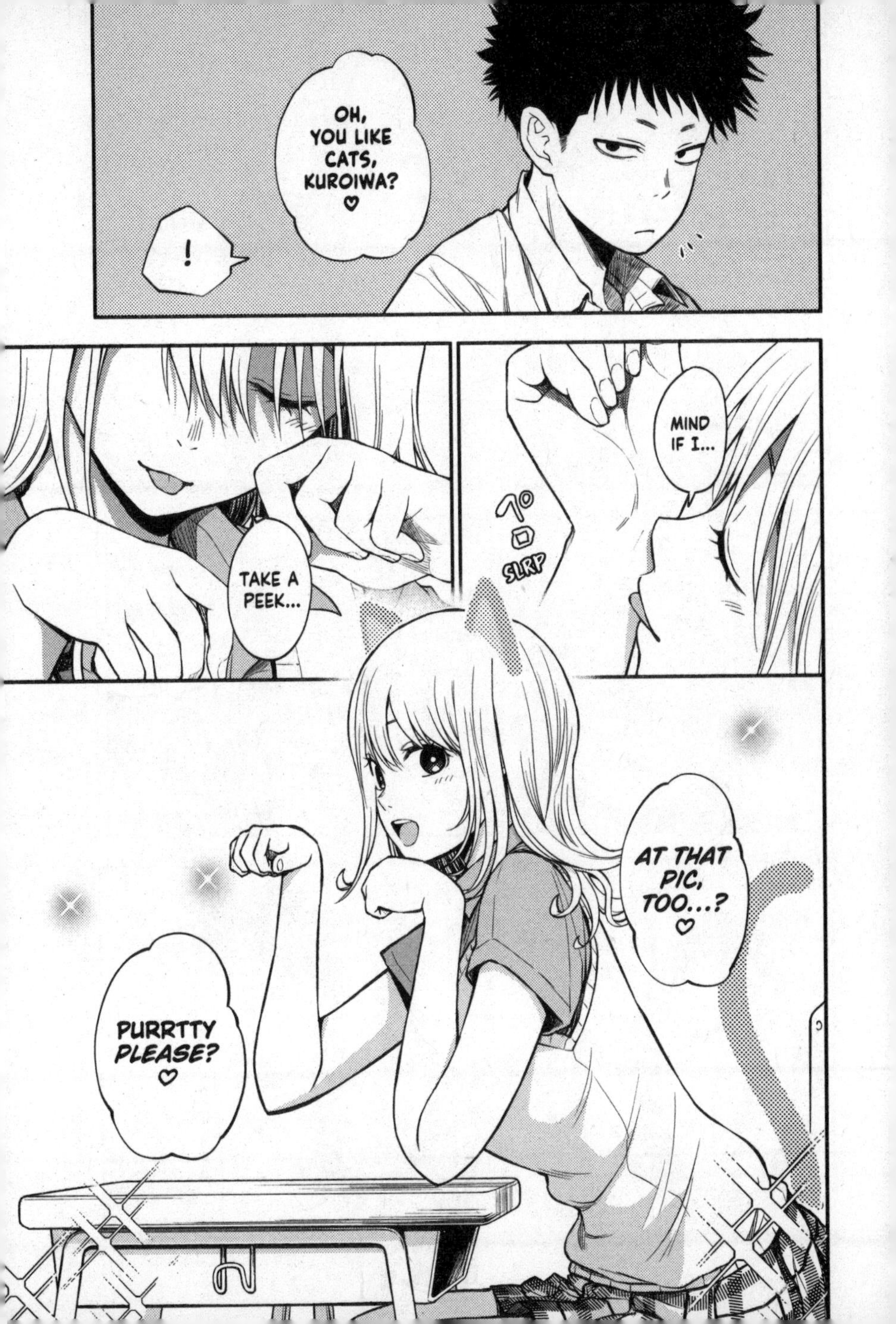
OH, YOU LIKE CATS, KUROIWA? ♡
!
MIND IF I...
SLRP
TAKE A PEEK...
AT THAT PIC, TOO...? ♡
PURRTTY PLEASE? ♡

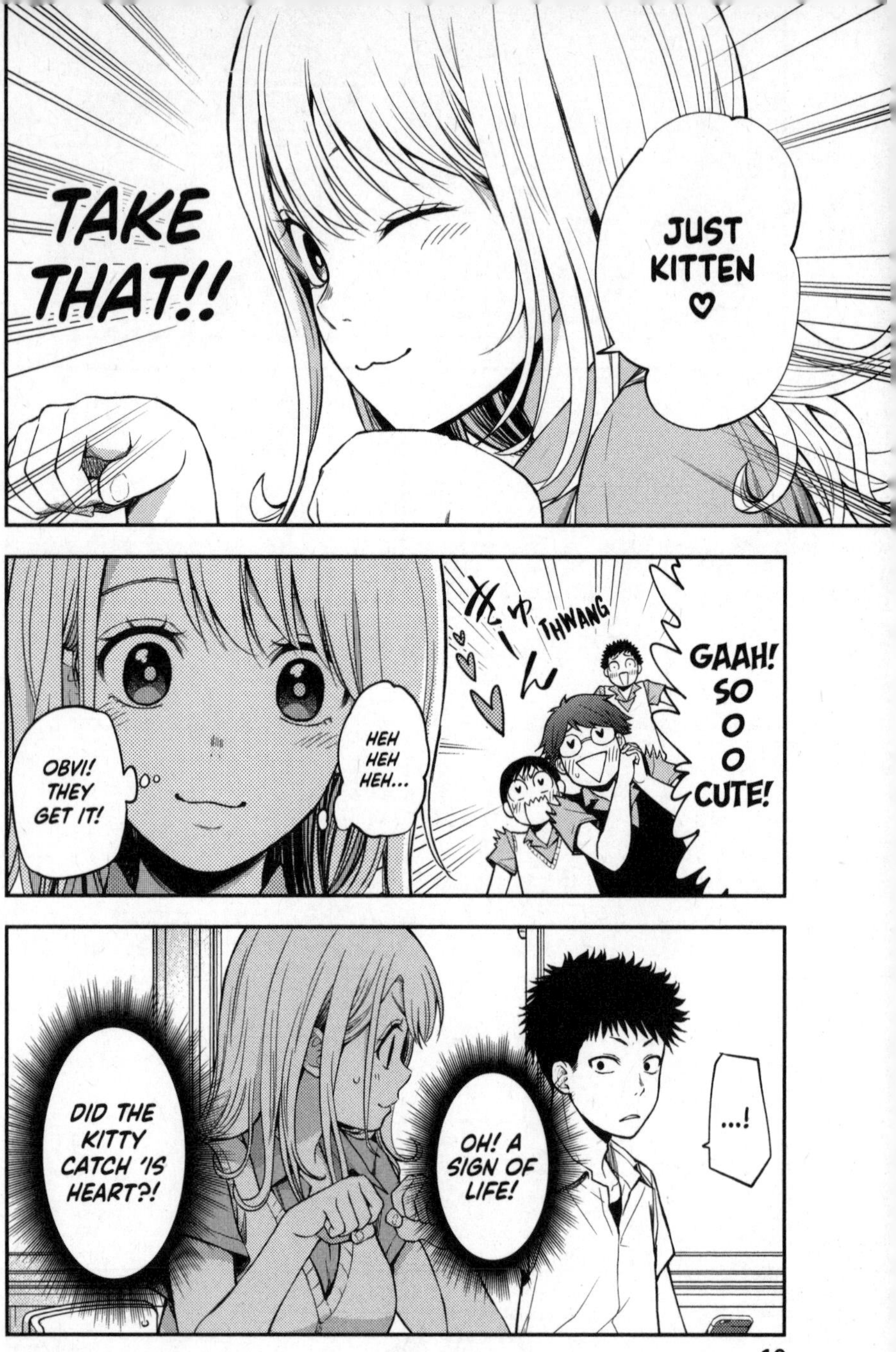
JUST KITTEN ♥
TAKE THAT!!
GAAH! SO OOO CUTE!
THWANG
HEH HEH HEH...
OBVI! THEY GET IT!
...!
OH! A SIGN OF LIFE!
DID THE KITTY CATCH 'IS HEART?!

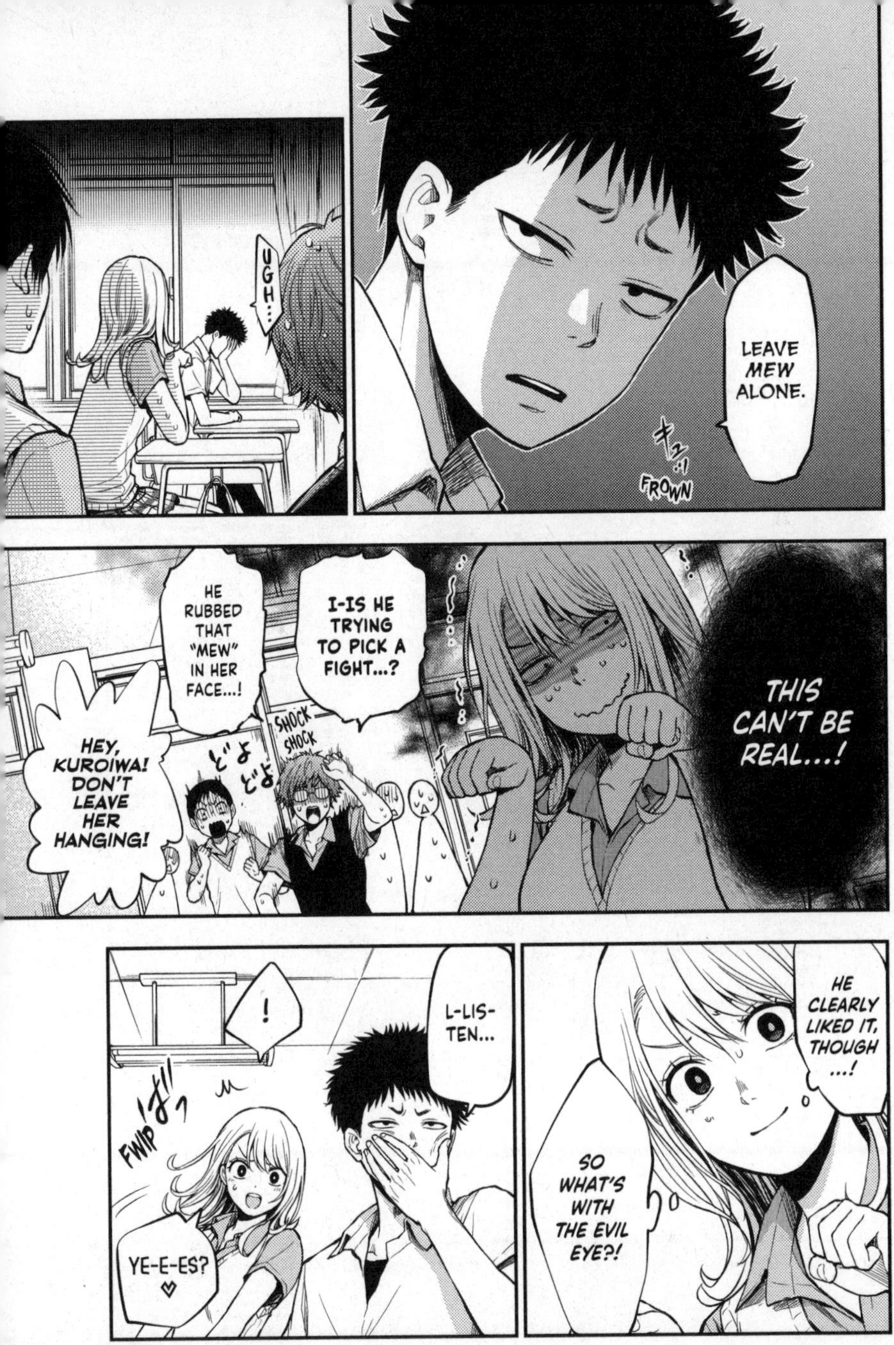
LEAVE MEW ALONE.
FROWN
UGH...
THIS CAN'T BE REAL...!
I-IS HE TRYING TO PICK A FIGHT...?
HE RUBBED THAT "MEW" IN HER FACE...!
SHOCK SHOCK
HEY, KUROIWA! DON'T LEAVE HER HANGING!
HE CLEARLY LIKED IT, THOUGH...!
SO WHAT'S WITH THE EVIL EYE?!
L-LIS-TEN...
!
FWIP
YE-E-ES? ♡

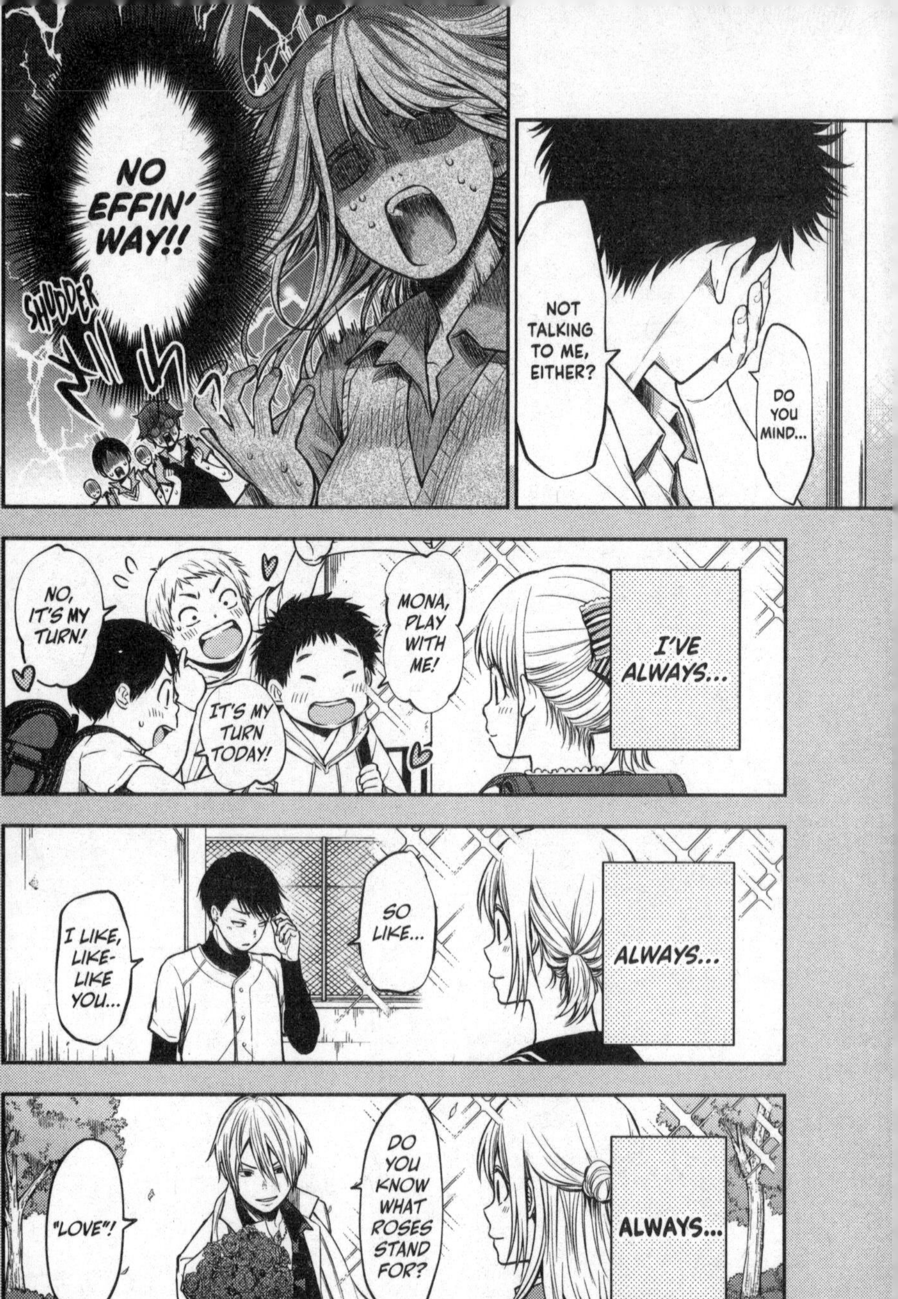
DO YOU MIND...
NOT TALKING TO ME, EITHER?
NO EFFIN' WAY!!
SHUDDER
I'VE ALWAYS...
MONA, PLAY WITH ME!
IT'S MY TURN TODAY!
NO, IT'S MY TURN!
ALWAYS...
SO LIKE...
I LIKE, LIKE-LIKE YOU...
ALWAYS...
DO YOU KNOW WHAT ROSES STAND FOR?
"LOVE"!

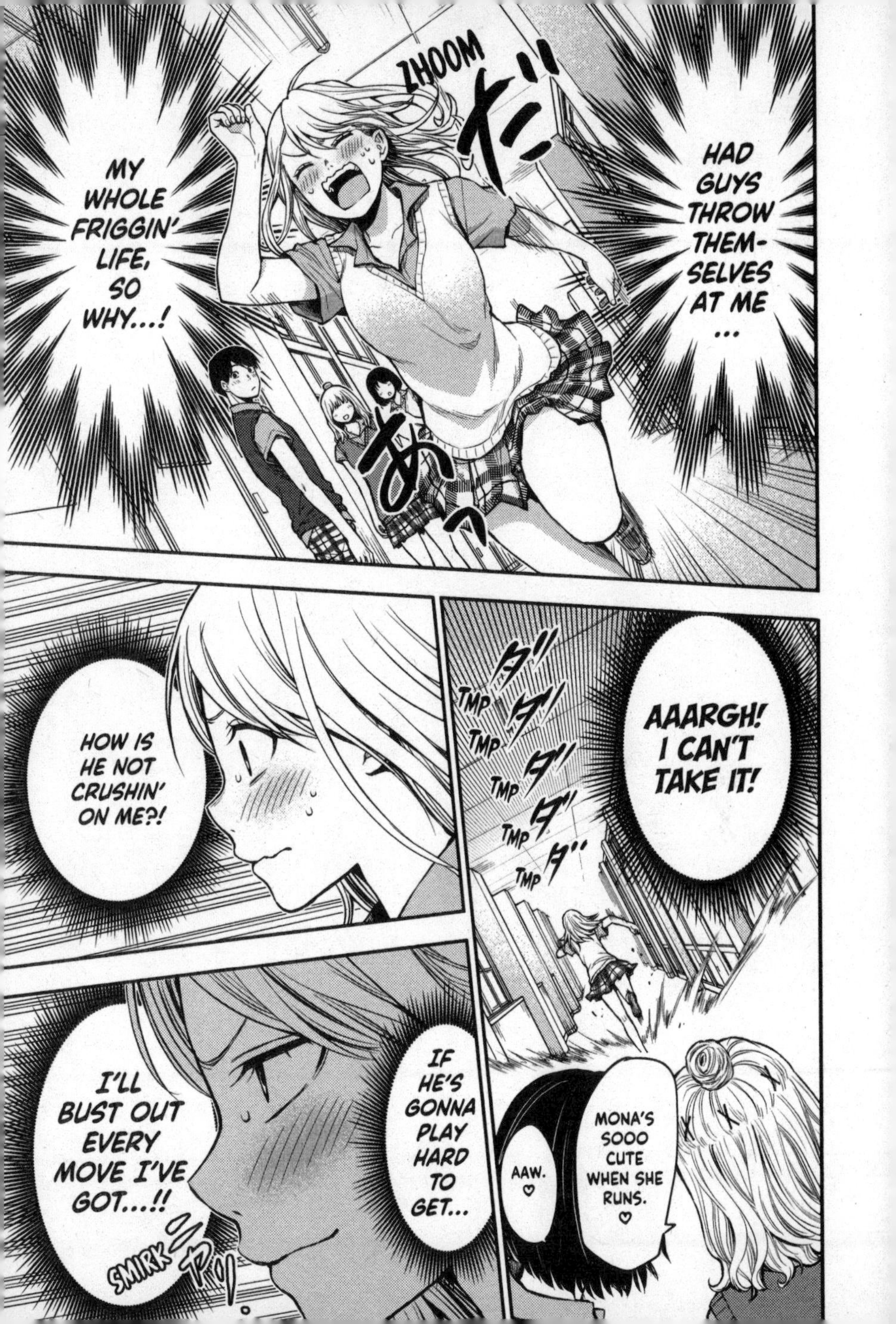
ZHOOM
HAD GUYS THROW THEM-SELVES AT ME ...
MY WHOLE FRIGGIN' LIFE, SO WHY...!
AAARGH! I CAN'T TAKE IT!
TMP TMP TMP TMP TMP
HOW IS HE NOT CRUSHIN' ON ME?!
MONA'S SOOO CUTE WHEN SHE RUNS. ♡
AAW. ♡
IF HE'S GONNA PLAY HARD TO GET...
I'LL BUST OUT EVERY MOVE I'VE GOT...!!
SMIRK

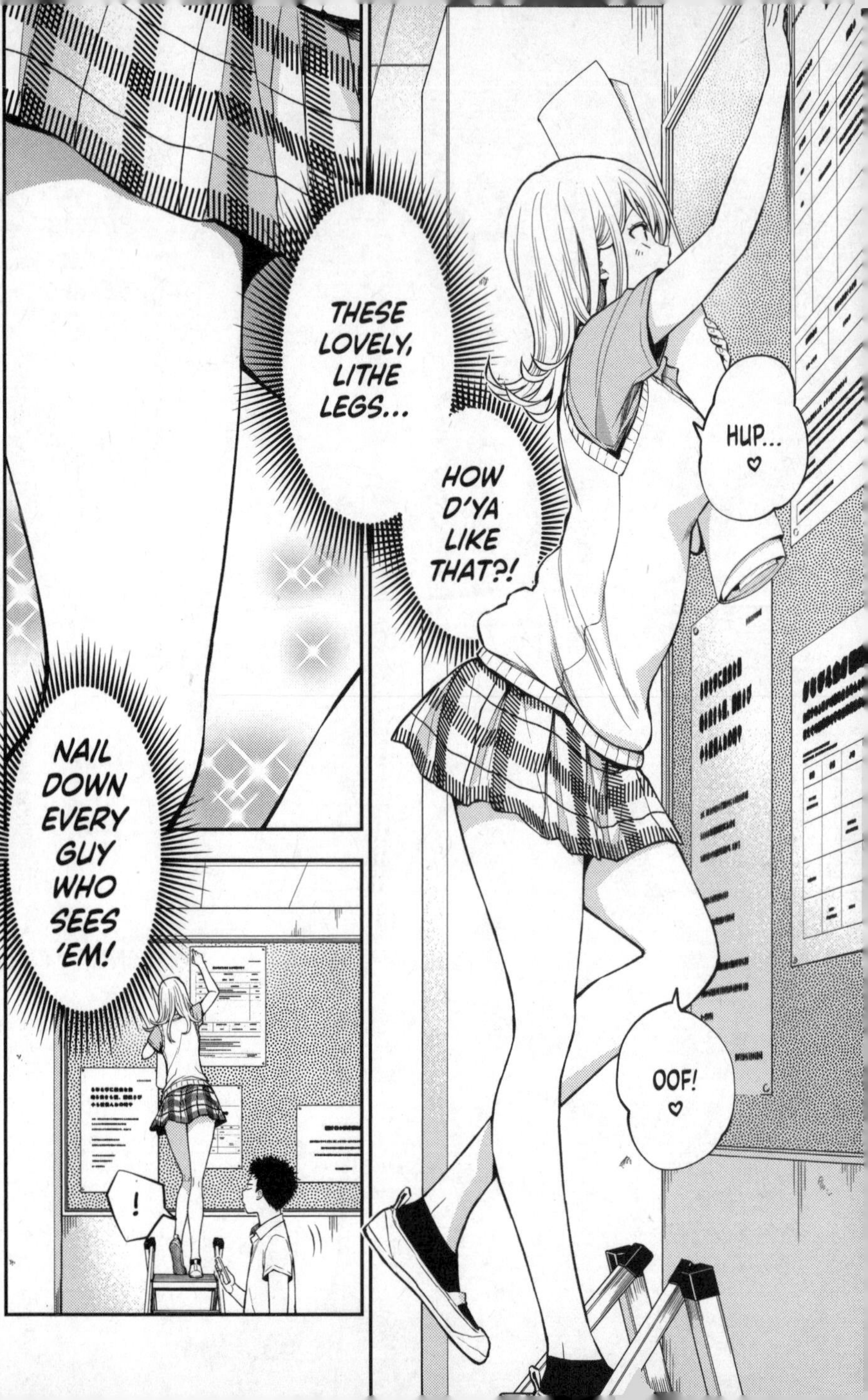
HUP... ♡
THESE LOVELY, LITHE LEGS...
HOW D'YA LIKE THAT?!
NAIL DOWN EVERY GUY WHO SEES 'EM!
OOF! ♡
!

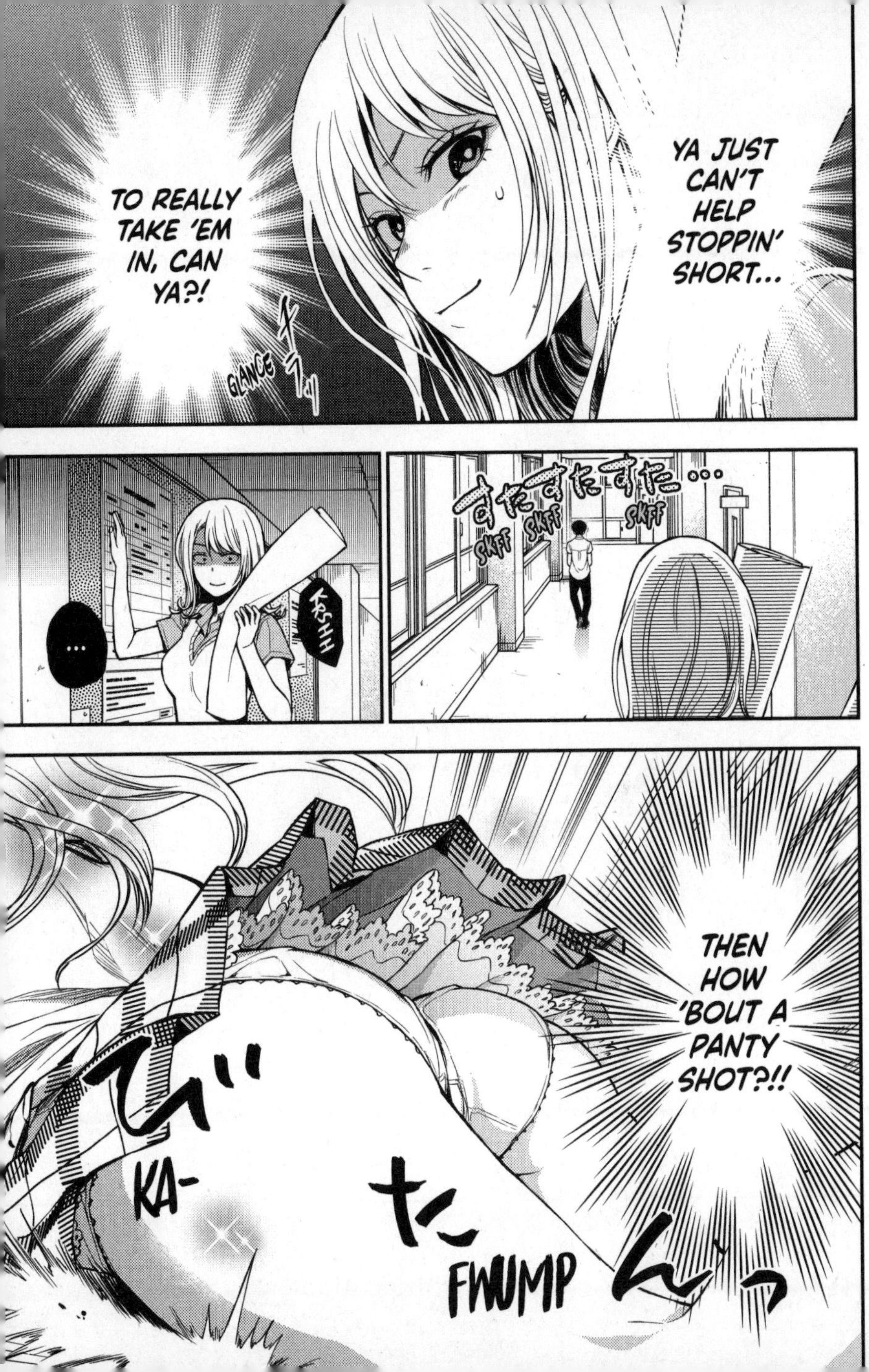
YA JUST CAN'T HELP STOPPIN' SHORT...
TO REALLY TAKE 'EM IN, CAN YA?!
GLANCE
すたすたすた…
SKFF
SKFF
SKFF
...
KRSHH
THEN HOW 'BOUT A PANTY SHOT?!!
KA-
FWUMP

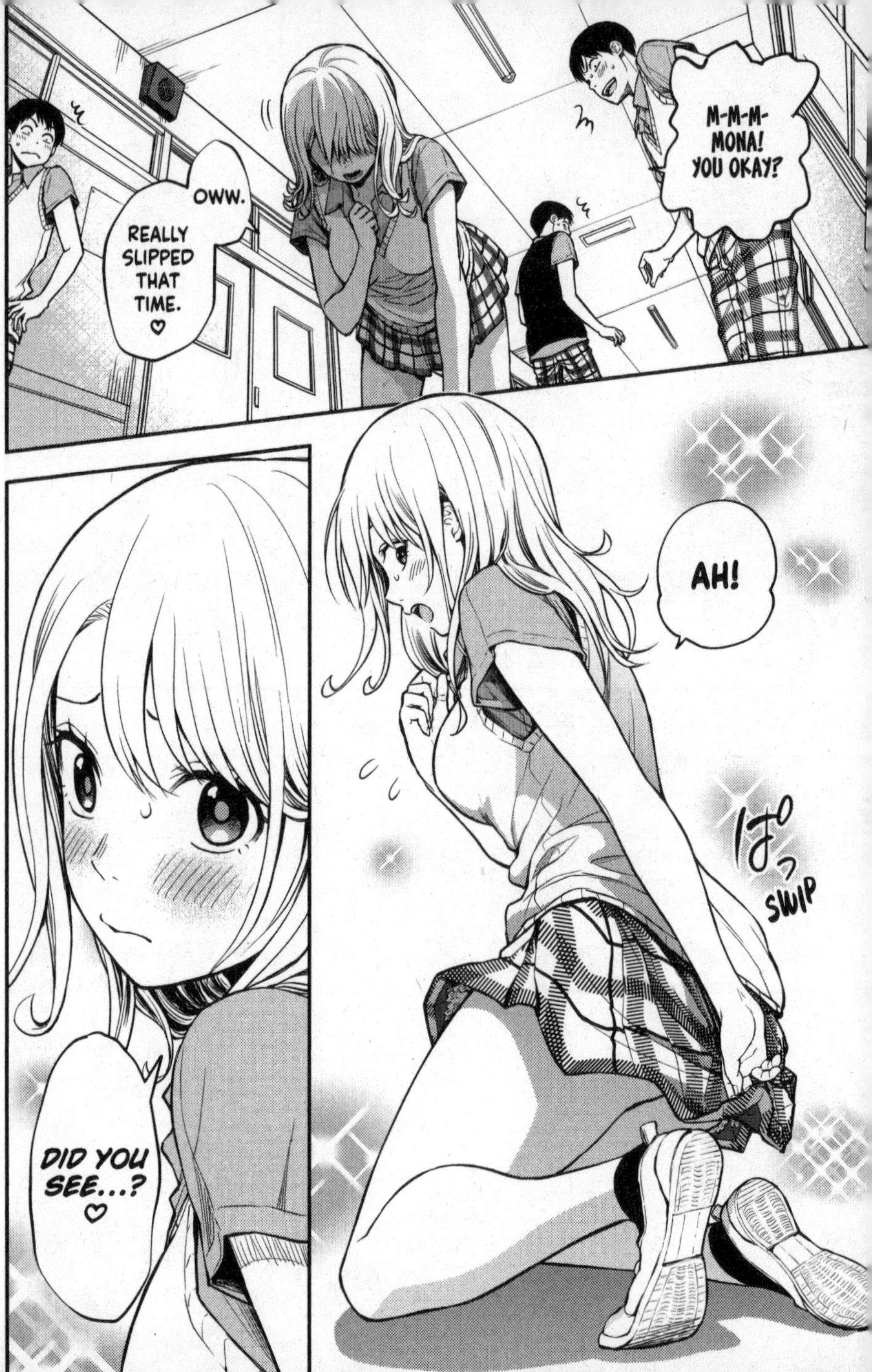
M-M-M-MONA! YOU OKAY?
OWW.
REALLY SLIPPED THAT TIME. ♡
AH!
ぱっ
SWIP
DID YOU SEE...? ♡

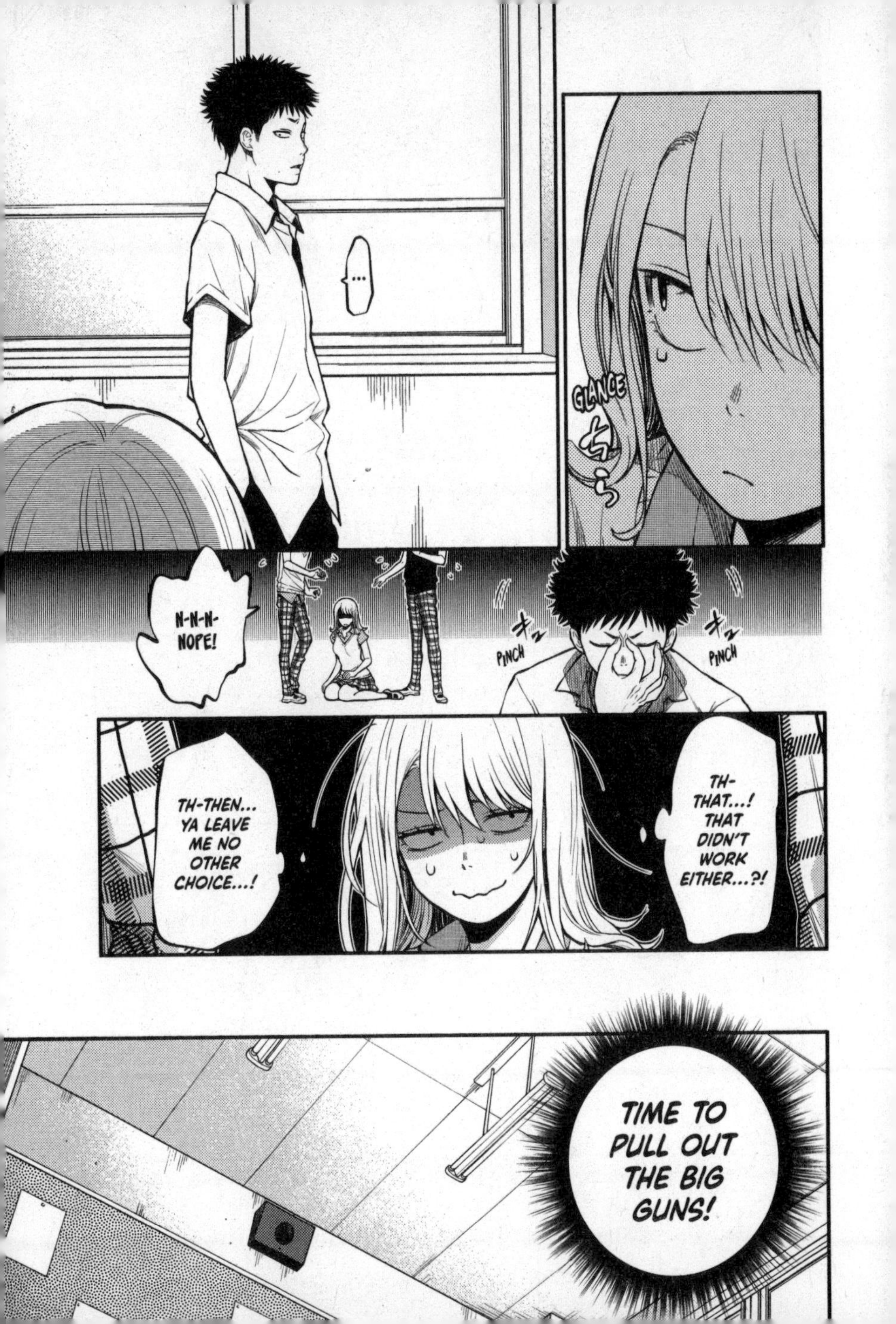
GLANCE
ちら
...
キュ PINCH
キュ PINCH
N-N-N-NOPE!
TH-THAT...! THAT DIDN'T WORK EITHER...?!
TH-THEN... YA LEAVE ME NO OTHER CHOICE...!
TIME TO PULL OUT THE BIG GUNS!

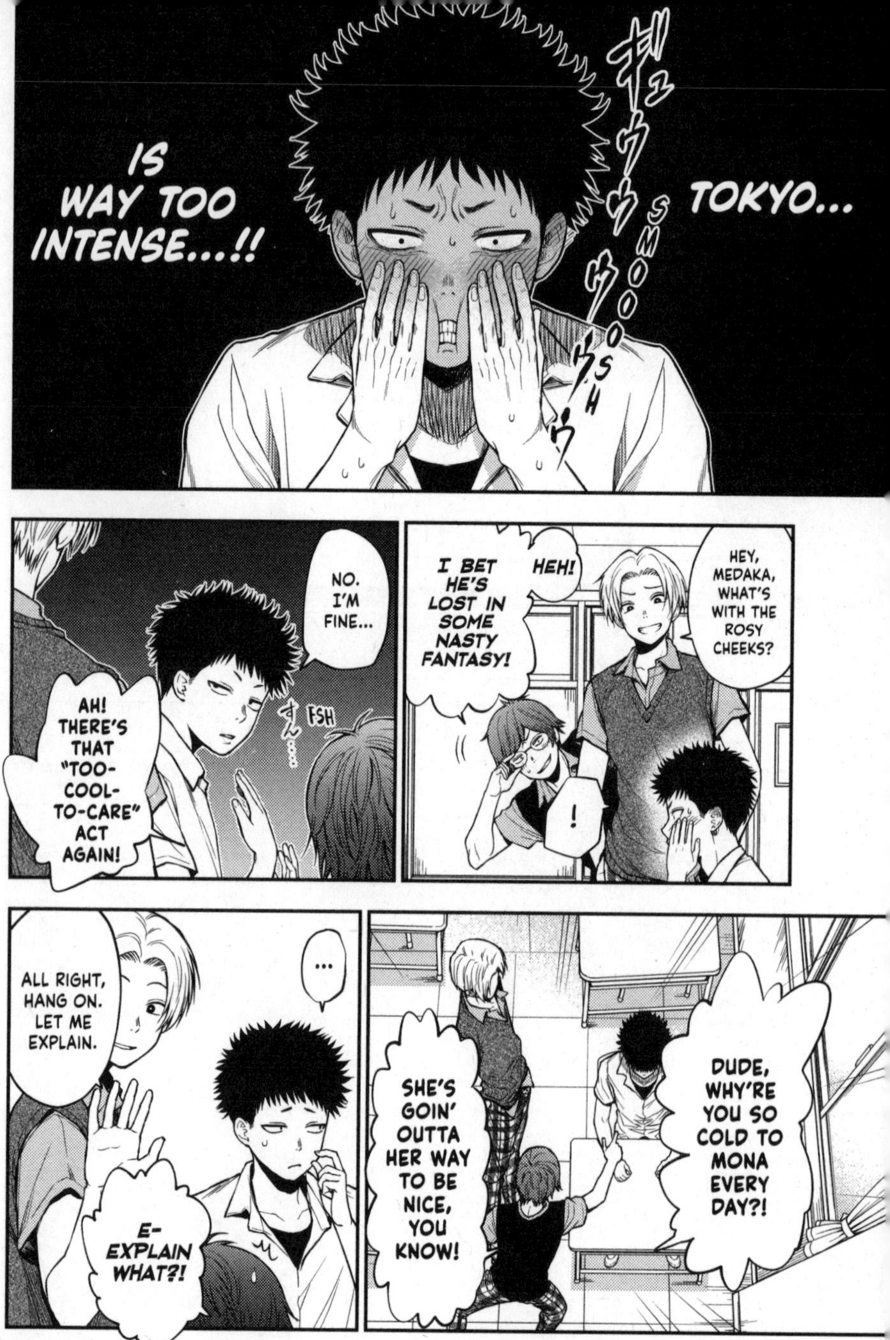
TOKYO...
SMOOOOSH
IS WAY TOO INTENSE...!!
HEY, MEDAKA, WHAT'S WITH THE ROSY CHEEKS?
HEH!
I BET HE'S LOST IN SOME NASTY FANTASY!
!
NO. I'M FINE...
FSH
AH! THERE'S THAT "TOO-COOL-TO-CARE" ACT AGAIN!
DUDE, WHY'RE YOU SO COLD TO MONA EVERY DAY?!
SHE'S GOIN' OUTTA HER WAY TO BE NICE, YOU KNOW!
...
ALL RIGHT, HANG ON. LET ME EXPLAIN.
E-EXPLAIN WHAT?!

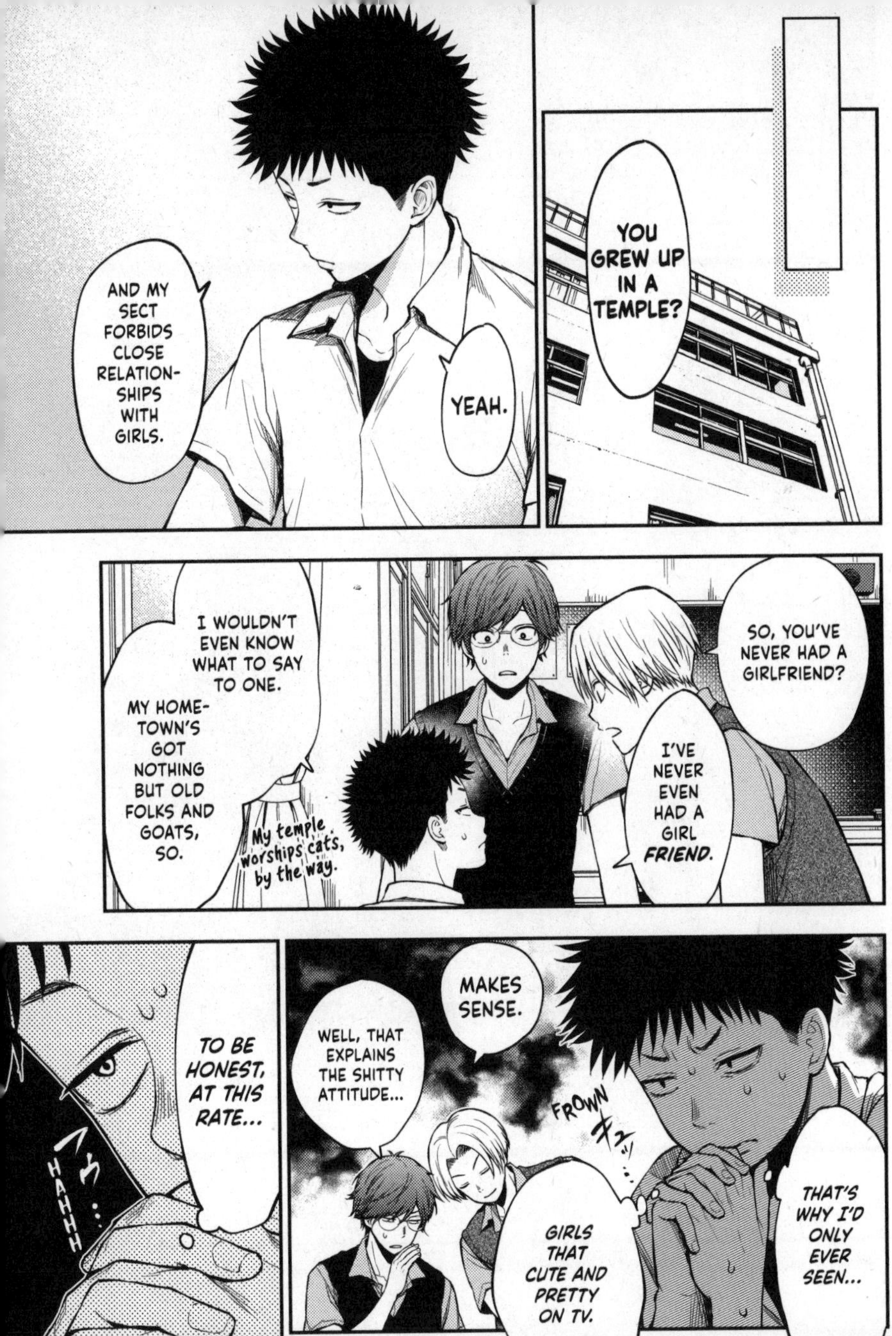
YOU GREW UP IN A TEMPLE?
YEAH.
AND MY SECT FORBIDS CLOSE RELATIONSHIPS WITH GIRLS.
SO, YOU'VE NEVER HAD A GIRLFRIEND?
I'VE NEVER EVEN HAD A GIRL *FRIEND*.
I WOULDN'T EVEN KNOW WHAT TO SAY TO ONE.
MY HOMETOWN'S GOT NOTHING BUT OLD FOLKS AND GOATS, SO.
My temple worships cats, by the way.
THAT'S WHY I'D ONLY EVER SEEN...
GIRLS THAT CUTE AND PRETTY ON TV.
FROWN
MAKES SENSE.
WELL, THAT EXPLAINS THE SHITTY ATTITUDE...
TO BE HONEST, AT THIS RATE...
HAHHH

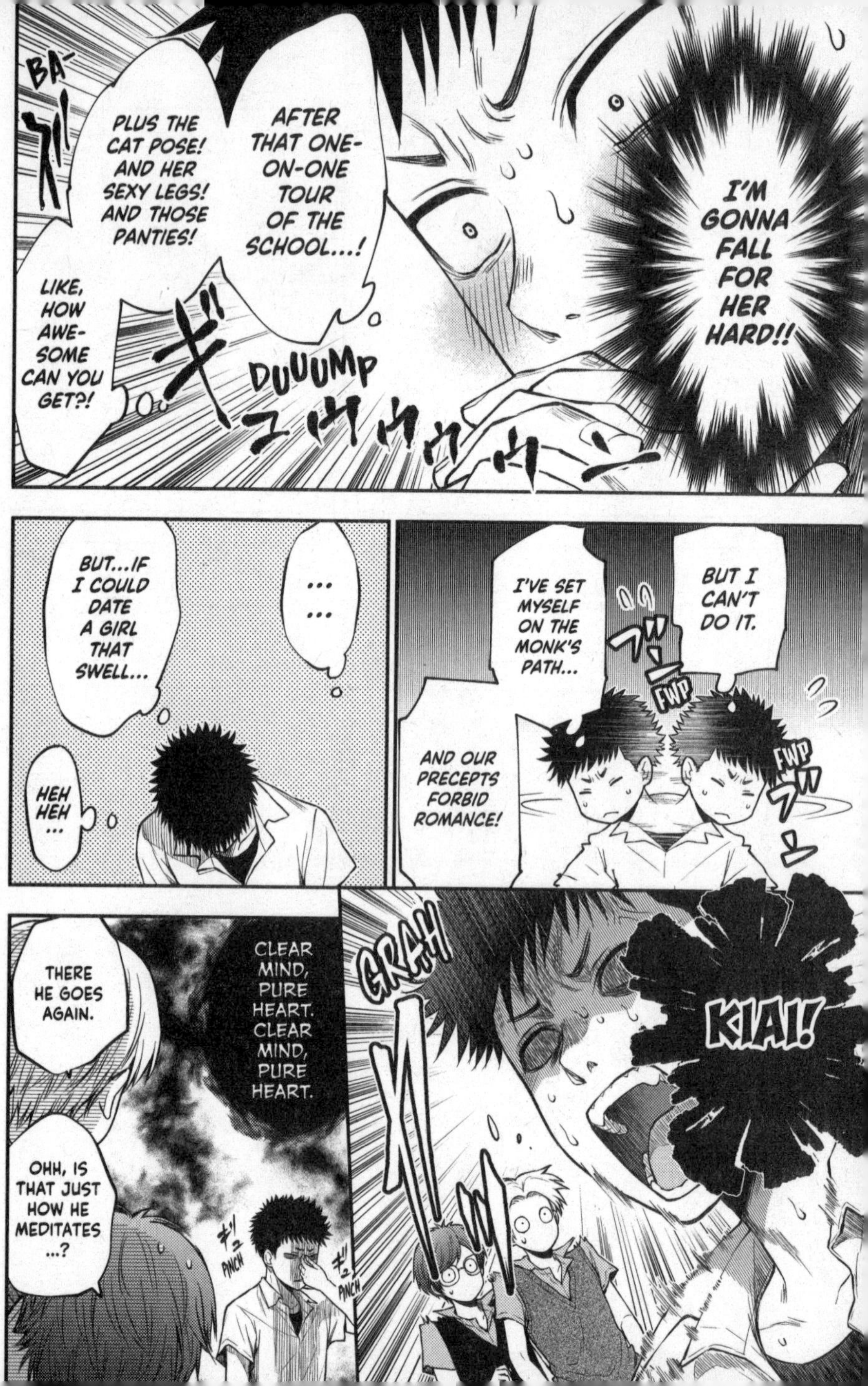
I'M GONNA FALL FOR HER HARD!!
AFTER THAT ONE-ON-ONE TOUR OF THE SCHOOL...!
PLUS THE CAT POSE! AND HER SEXY LEGS! AND THOSE PANTIES!
BA
LIKE, HOW AWE-SOME CAN YOU GET?!
DUUUMp
BUT I CAN'T DO IT.
I'VE SET MYSELF ON THE MONK'S PATH...
FWP
FWP
AND OUR PRECEPTS FORBID ROMANCE!
......
BUT...IF I COULD DATE A GIRL THAT SWELL...
HEH HEH...
KIAI!
GRAH
CLEAR MIND, PURE HEART. CLEAR MIND, PURE HEART.
THERE HE GOES AGAIN.
OHH, IS THAT JUST HOW HE MEDITATES...?
PINCH
PINCH

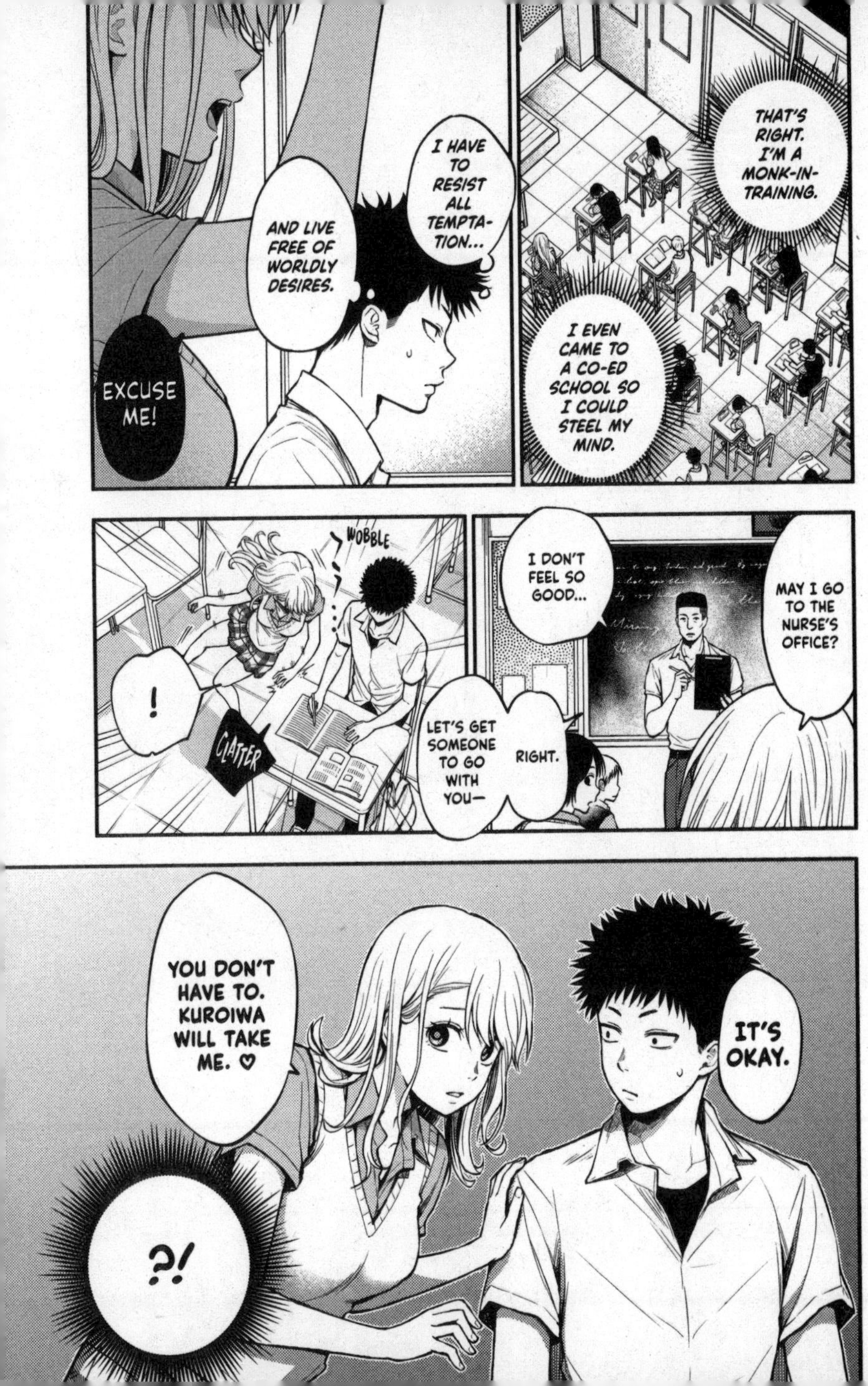
THAT'S RIGHT. I'M A MONK-IN-TRAINING.
I EVEN CAME TO A CO-ED SCHOOL SO I COULD STEEL MY MIND.
I HAVE TO RESIST ALL TEMPTATION...
AND LIVE FREE OF WORLDLY DESIRES.
EXCUSE ME!
MAY I GO TO THE NURSE'S OFFICE?
I DON'T FEEL SO GOOD...
RIGHT.
LET'S GET SOMEONE TO GO WITH YOU—
WOBBLE
!
CLATTER
IT'S OKAY.
YOU DON'T HAVE TO. KUROIWA WILL TAKE ME. ♡
?!

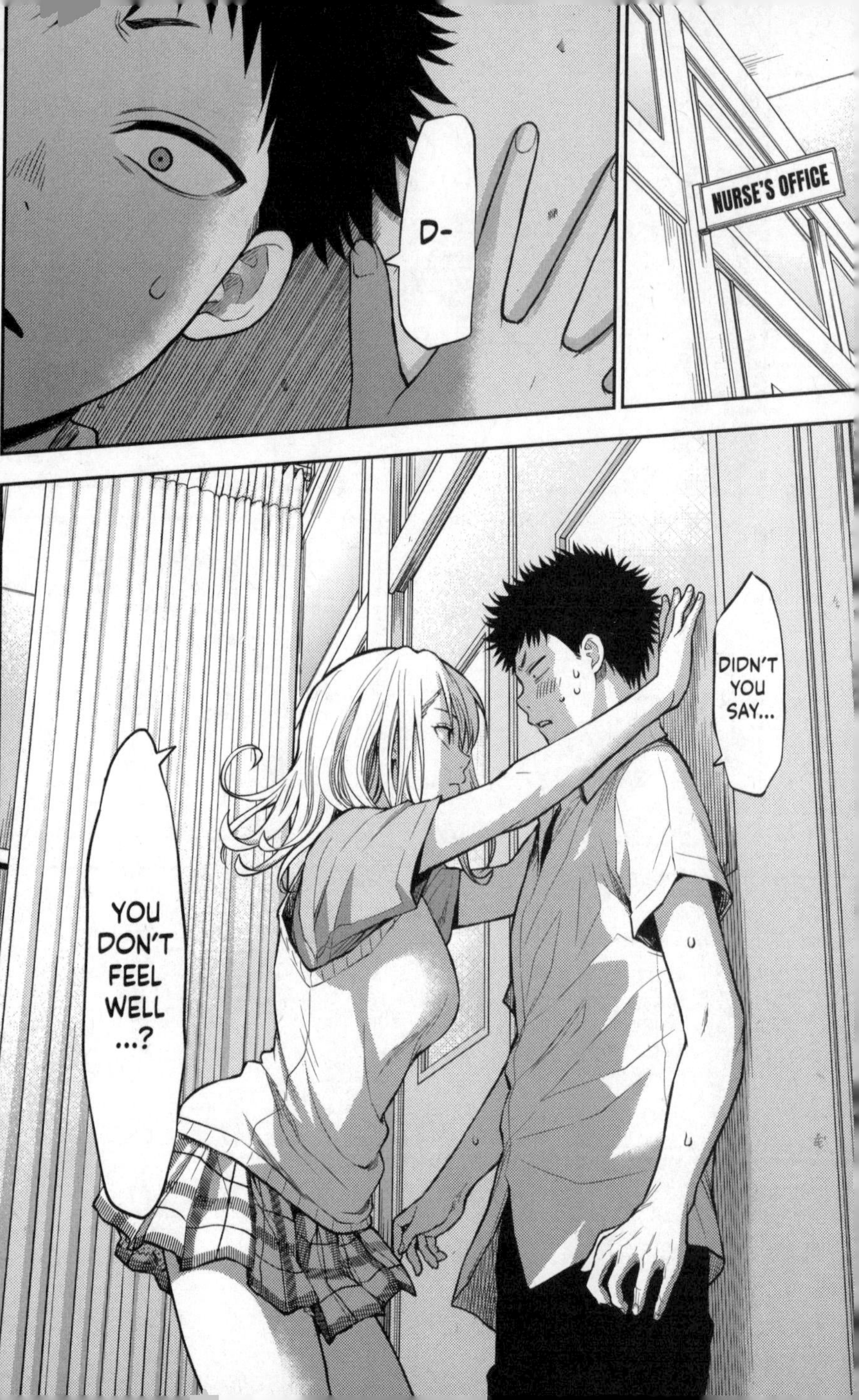
NURSE'S OFFICE
D-
DIDN'T YOU SAY...
YOU DON'T FEEL WELL ...?

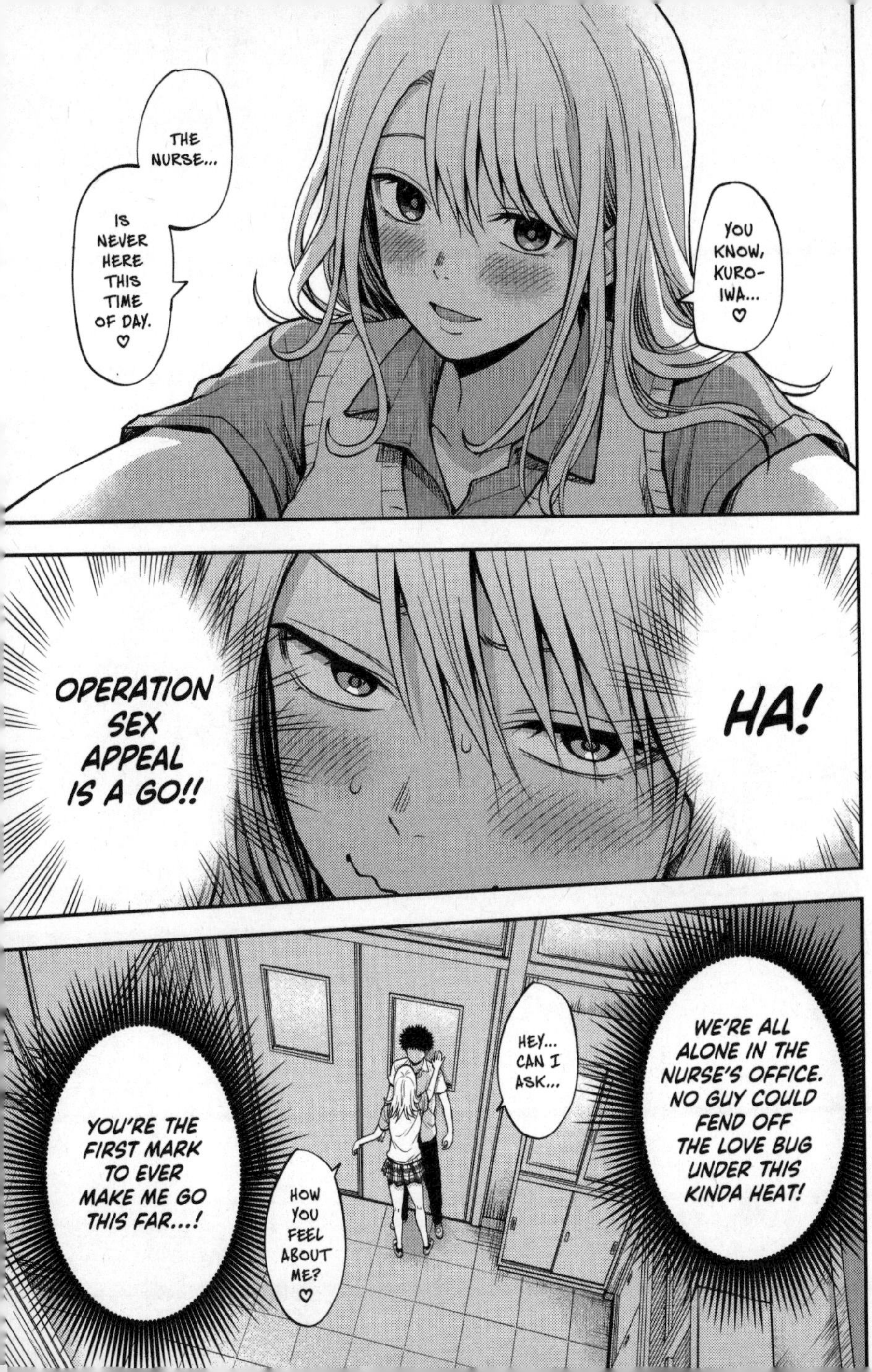
YOU KNOW, KURO-IWA... ♡
THE NURSE...
IS NEVER HERE THIS TIME OF DAY. ♡
HA!
OPERATION SEX APPEAL IS A GO!!
WE'RE ALL ALONE IN THE NURSE'S OFFICE. NO GUY COULD FEND OFF THE LOVE BUG UNDER THIS KINDA HEAT!
HEY... CAN I ASK...
HOW YOU FEEL ABOUT ME? ♡
YOU'RE THE FIRST MARK TO EVER MAKE ME GO THIS FAR...!

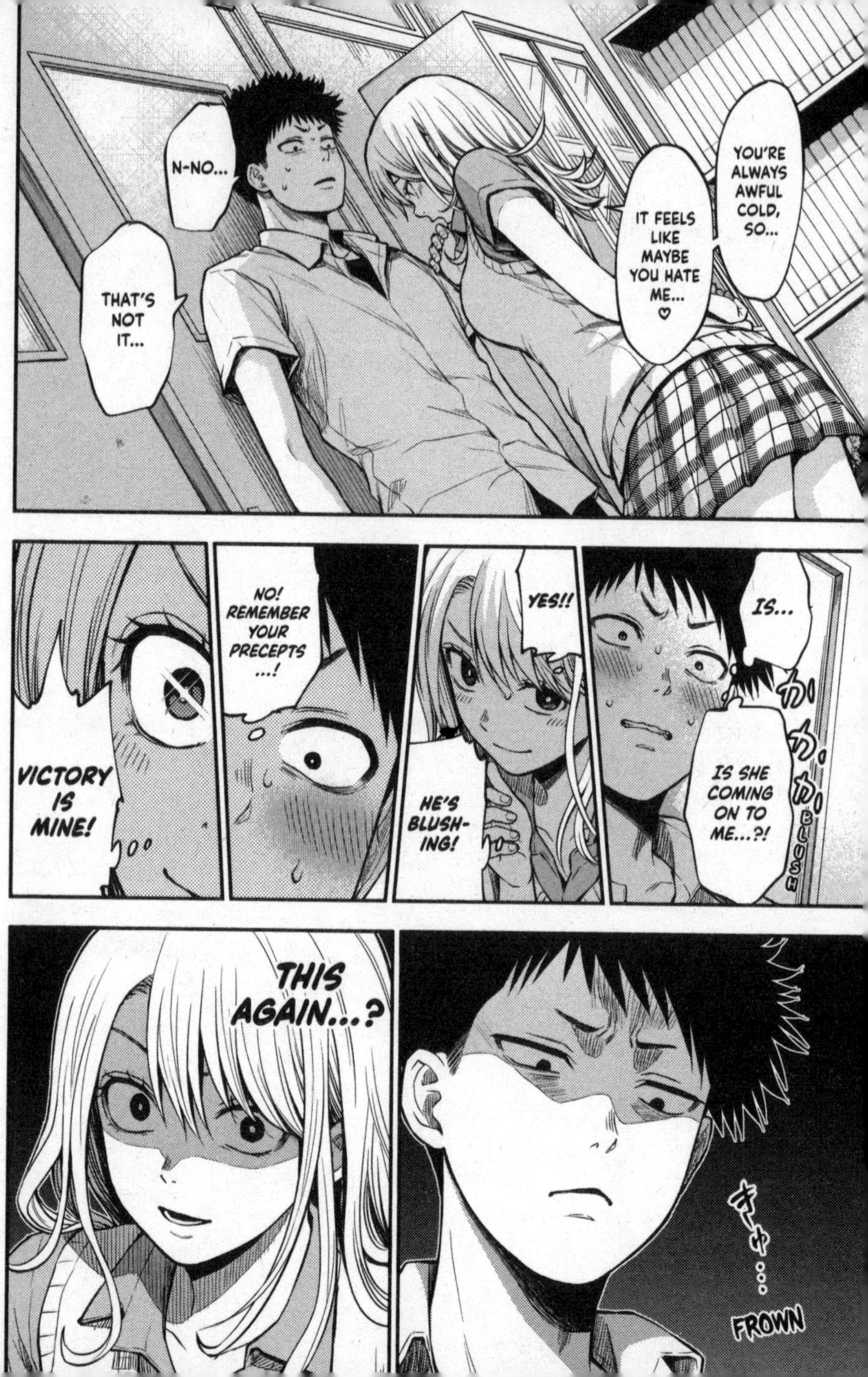
YOU'RE ALWAYS AWFUL COLD, SO...
IT FEELS LIKE MAYBE YOU HATE ME... ♡
N-NO...
THAT'S NOT IT...
IS...
IS SHE COMING ON TO ME...?!
BLUSH
YES!!
HE'S BLUSH-ING!
NO! REMEMBER YOUR PRECEPTS ...!
VICTORY IS MINE!
FROWN
THIS AGAIN...?

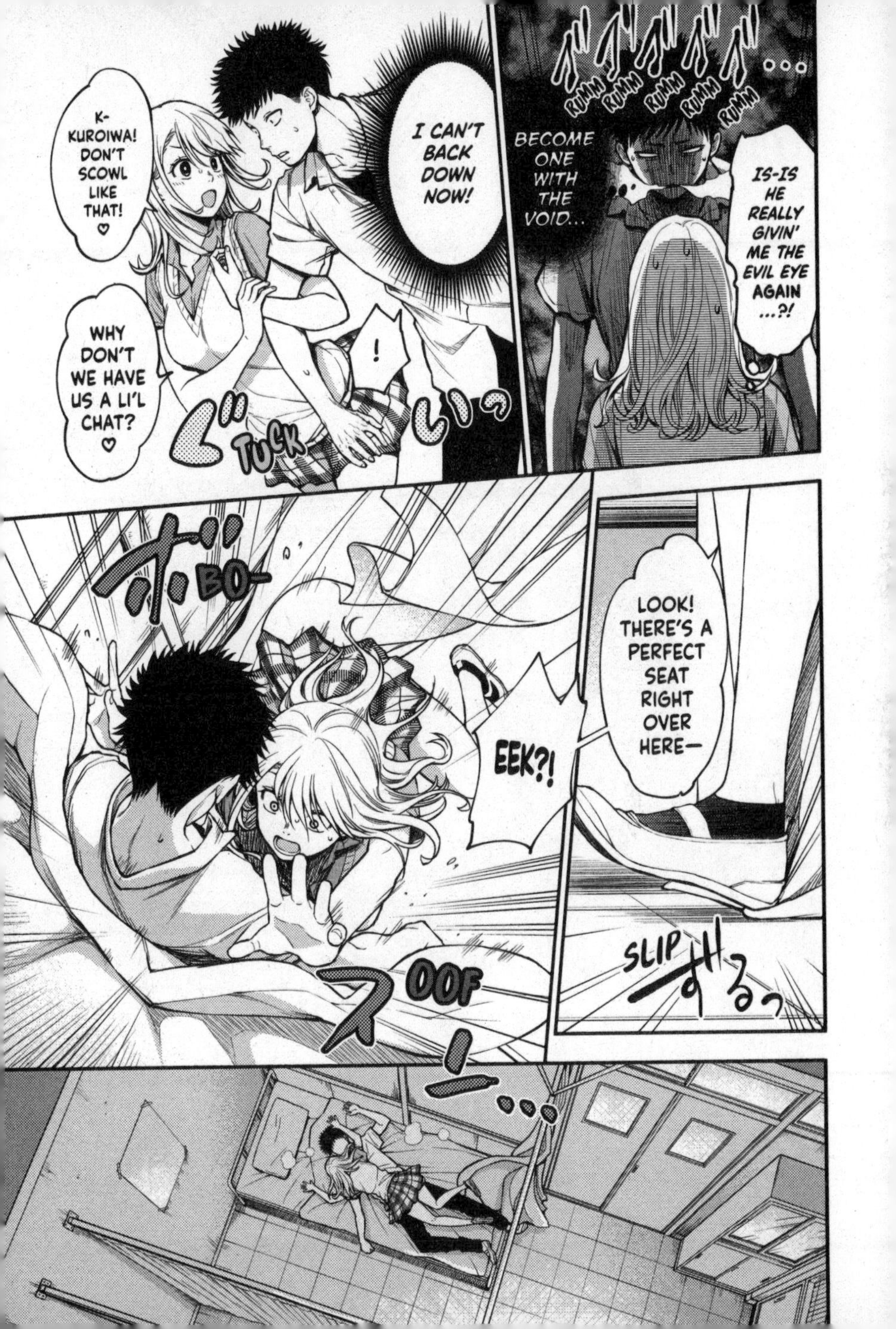
RUMM RUMM RUMM RUMM RUMM
...
IS-IS HE REALLY GIVIN' ME THE EVIL EYE AGAIN ...?!
BECOME ONE WITH THE VOID...
I CAN'T BACK DOWN NOW!
K-KUROIWA! DON'T SCOWL LIKE THAT! ♡
!
WHY DON'T WE HAVE US A LI'L CHAT? ♡
TUCK
LOOK! THERE'S A PERFECT SEAT RIGHT OVER HERE—
SLIP
BO—
EEK?!
OOF
...

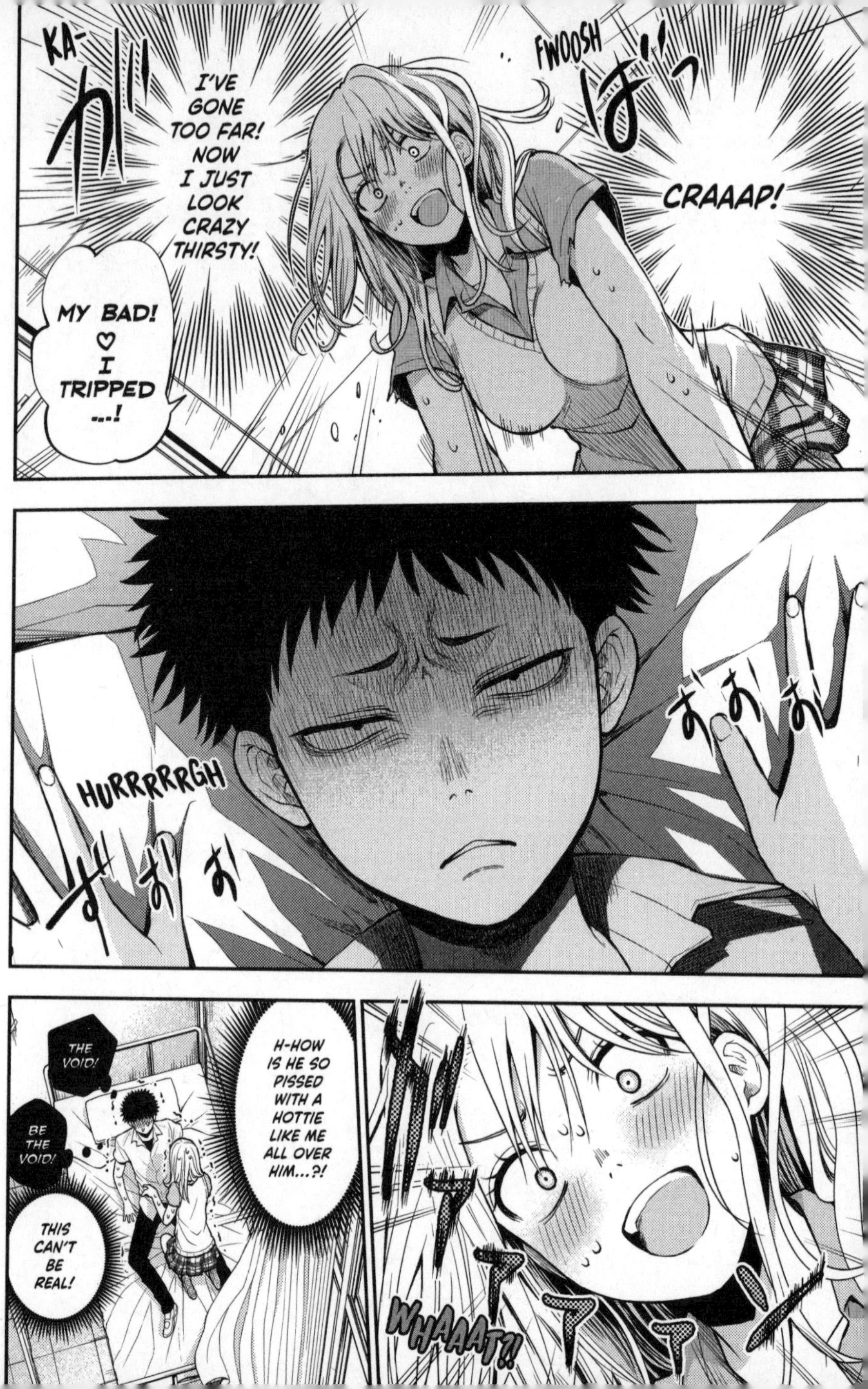
FWOOSH
ばっ
CRAAAP!
I'VE GONE TOO FAR! NOW I JUST LOOK CRAZY THIRSTY!
KA-
MY BAD! ♡ I TRIPPED ...!
HURRRRRGH
WHAAAT?!
H-HOW IS HE SO PISSED WITH A HOTTIE LIKE ME ALL OVER HIM...?!
THE VOID!
BE THE VOID!
THIS CAN'T BE REAL!

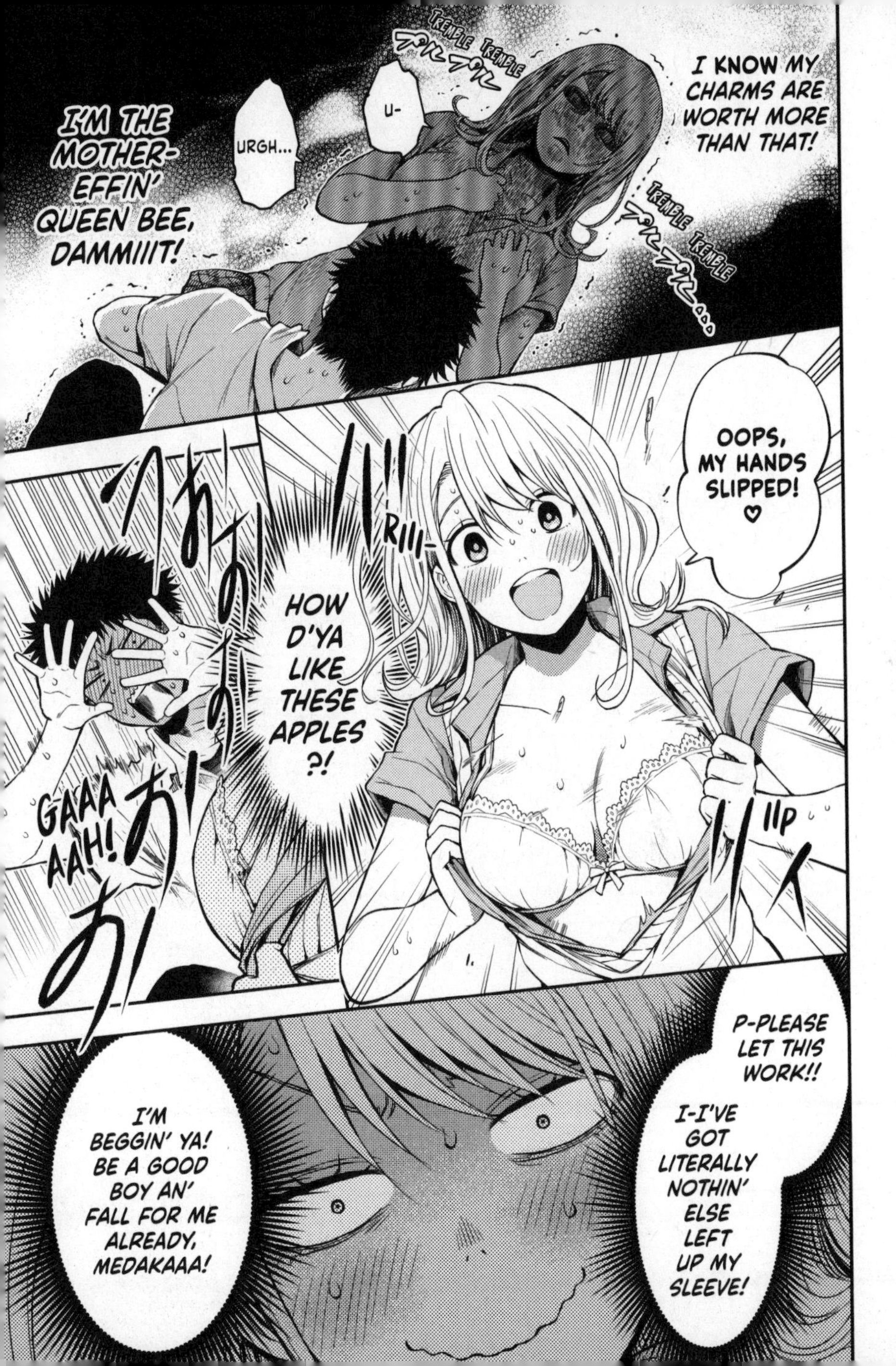
I KNOW MY CHARMS ARE WORTH MORE THAN THAT!
TREMBLE TREMBLE
U-
URGH...
TREMBLE TREMBLE
I'M THE MOTHER-EFFIN' QUEEN BEE, DAMMIIIT!
OOPS, MY HANDS SLIPPED! ♥
RIII-
IIP
HOW D'YA LIKE THESE APPLES?!
GAAAAAH!
P-PLEASE LET THIS WORK!!
I-I'VE GOT LITERALLY NOTHIN' ELSE LEFT UP MY SLEEVE!
I'M BEGGIN' YA! BE A GOOD BOY AN' FALL FOR ME ALREADY, MEDAKAAA!

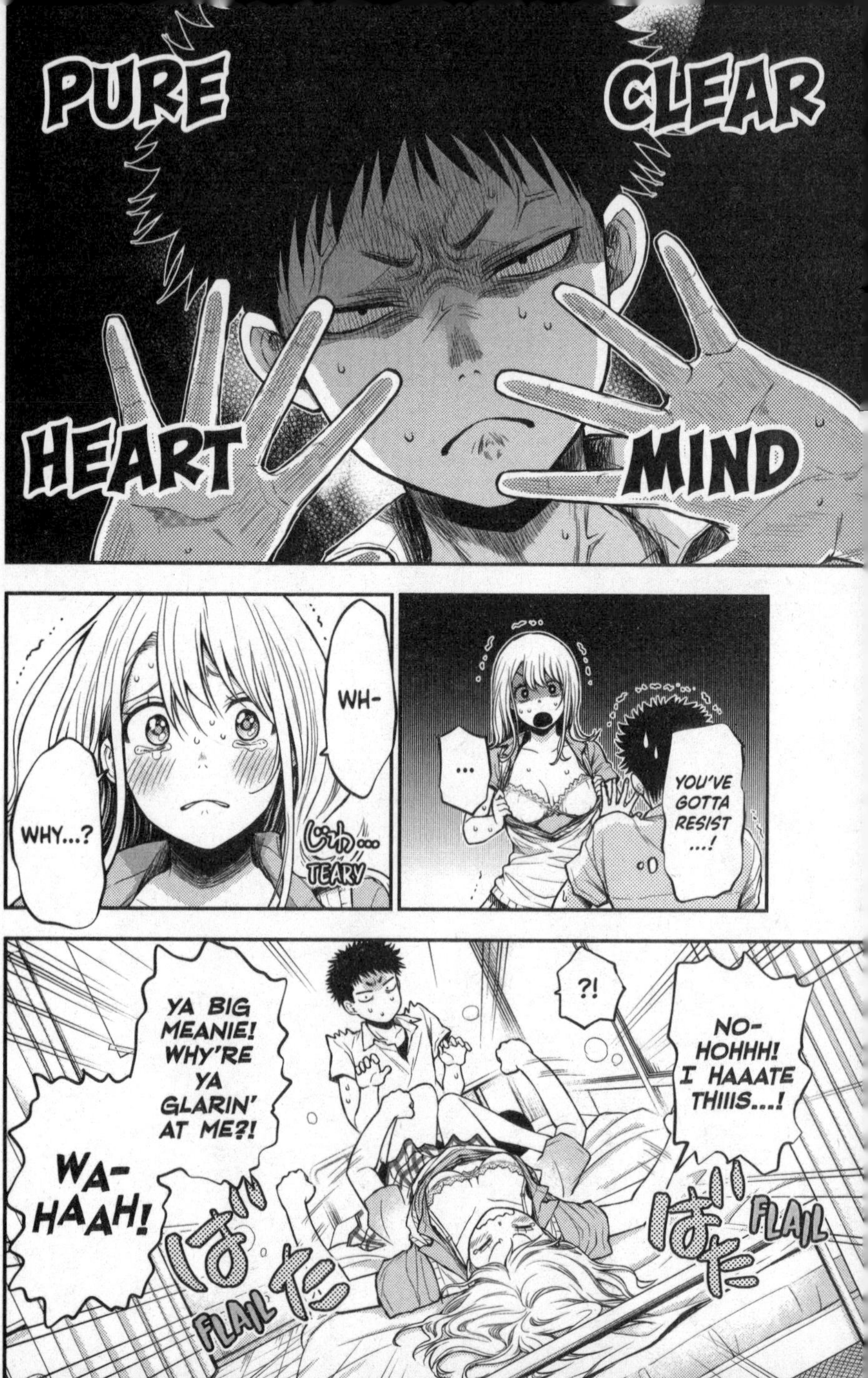
CLEAR
PURE
MIND
HEART
YOU'VE GOTTA RESIST ...!
...
WH-
WHY...?
じわ…
TEARY
?!
NO-HOHHH! I HAAATE THIIIS...!
YA BIG MEANIE! WHY'RE YA GLARIN' AT ME?!
WA-HAAAH!
ばた
FLAIL
ばた
FLAIL

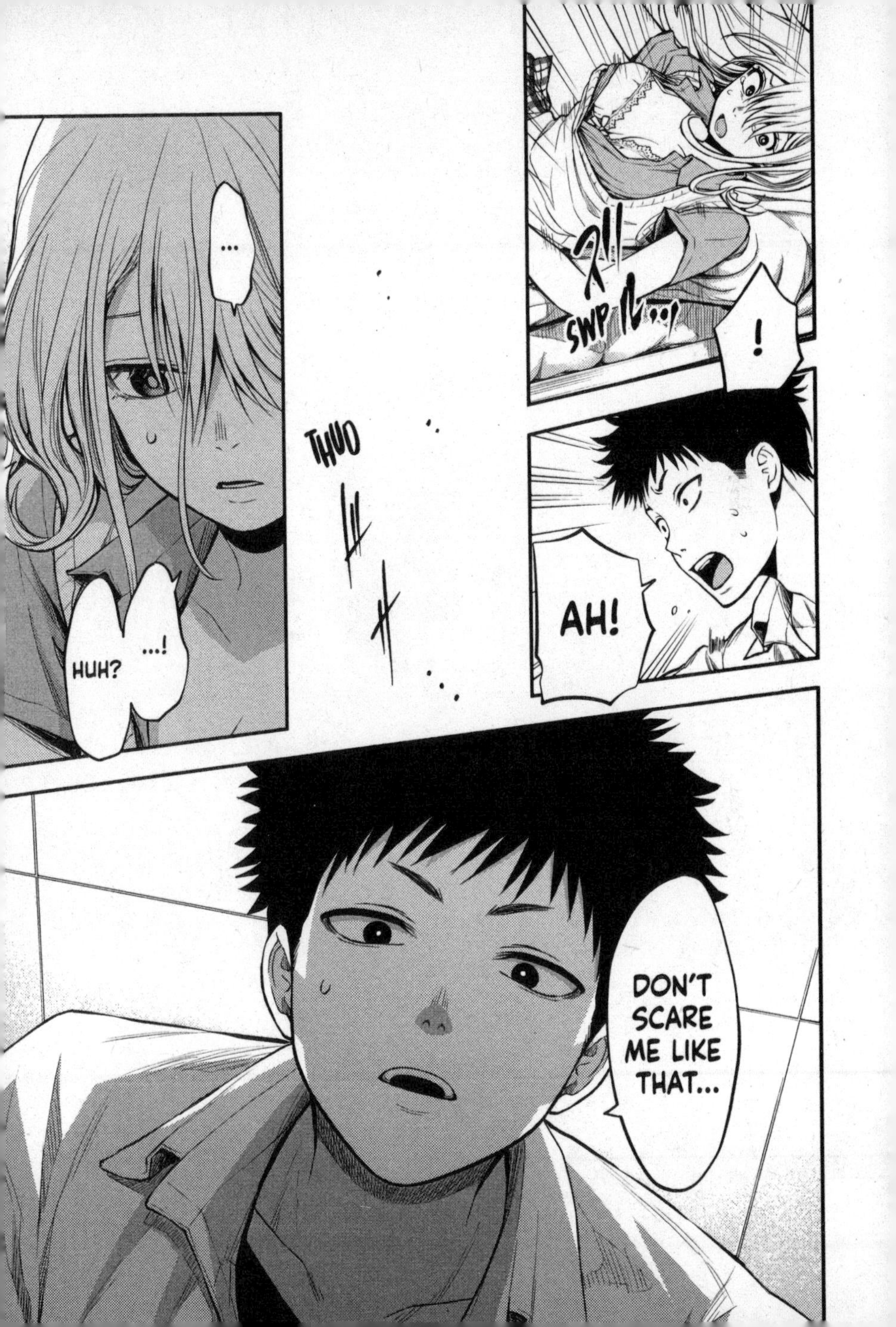
SWP
!
AH!
THUD
...
...!
HUH?
DON'T SCARE ME LIKE THAT...

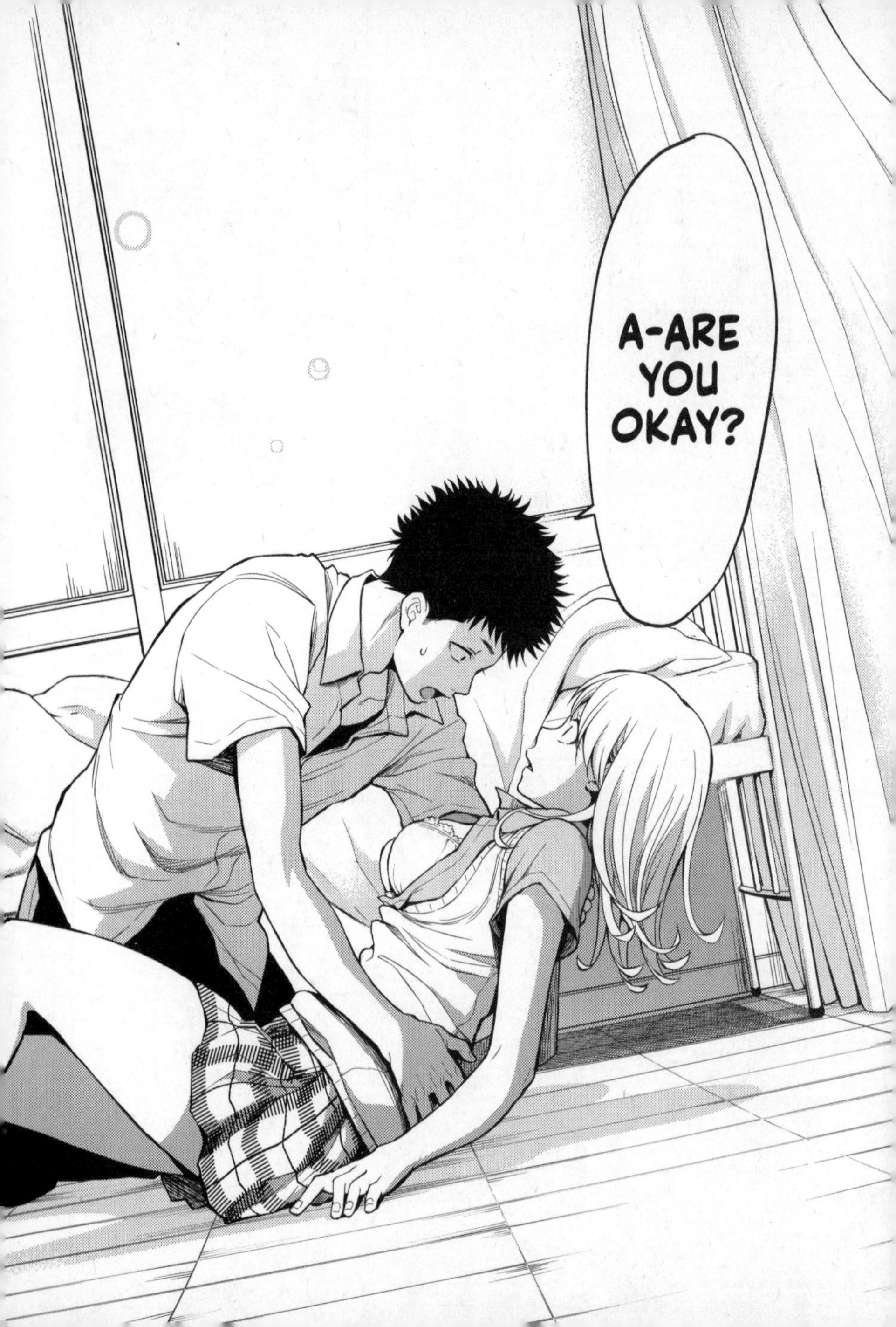
A-ARE YOU OKAY?

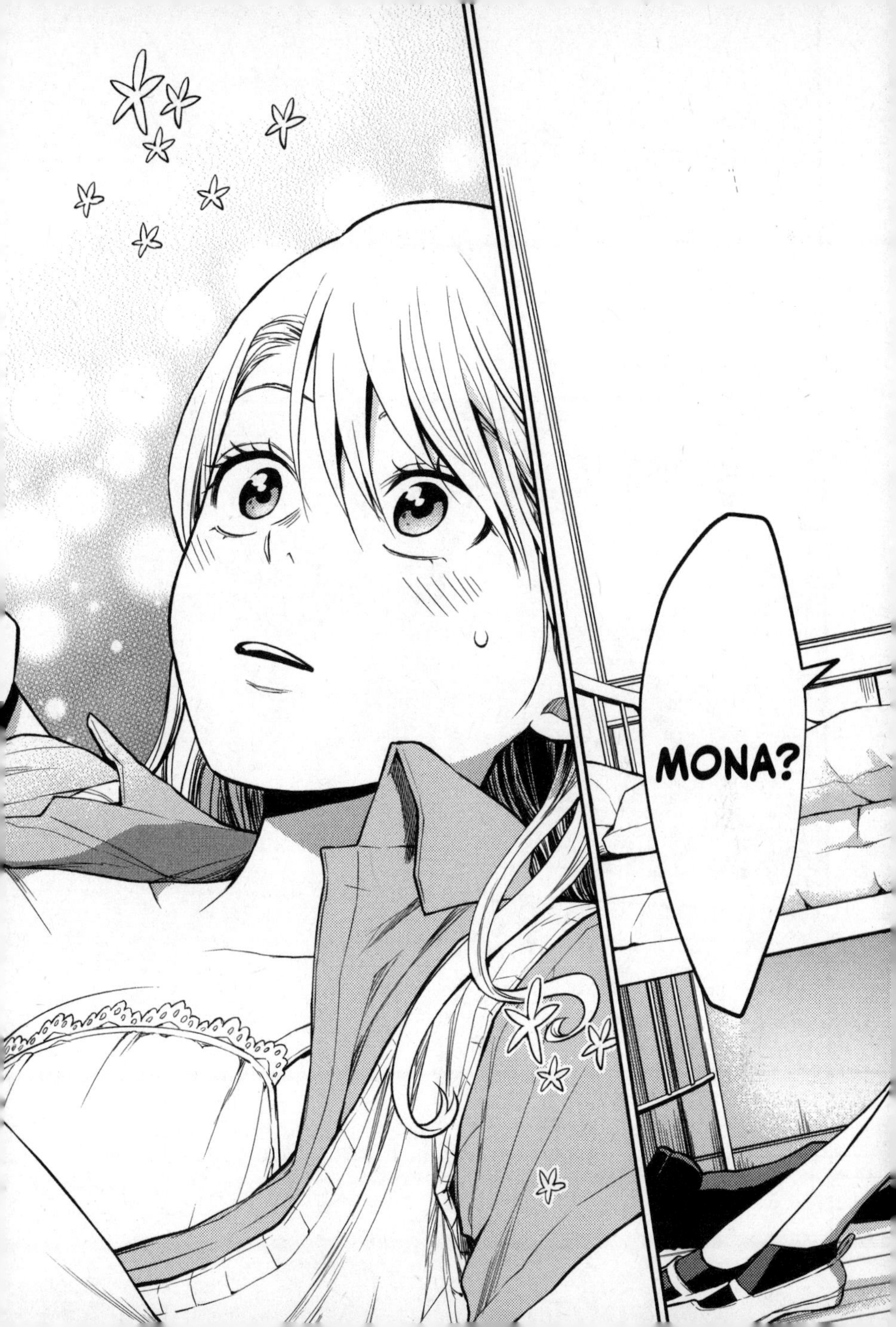
MONA?

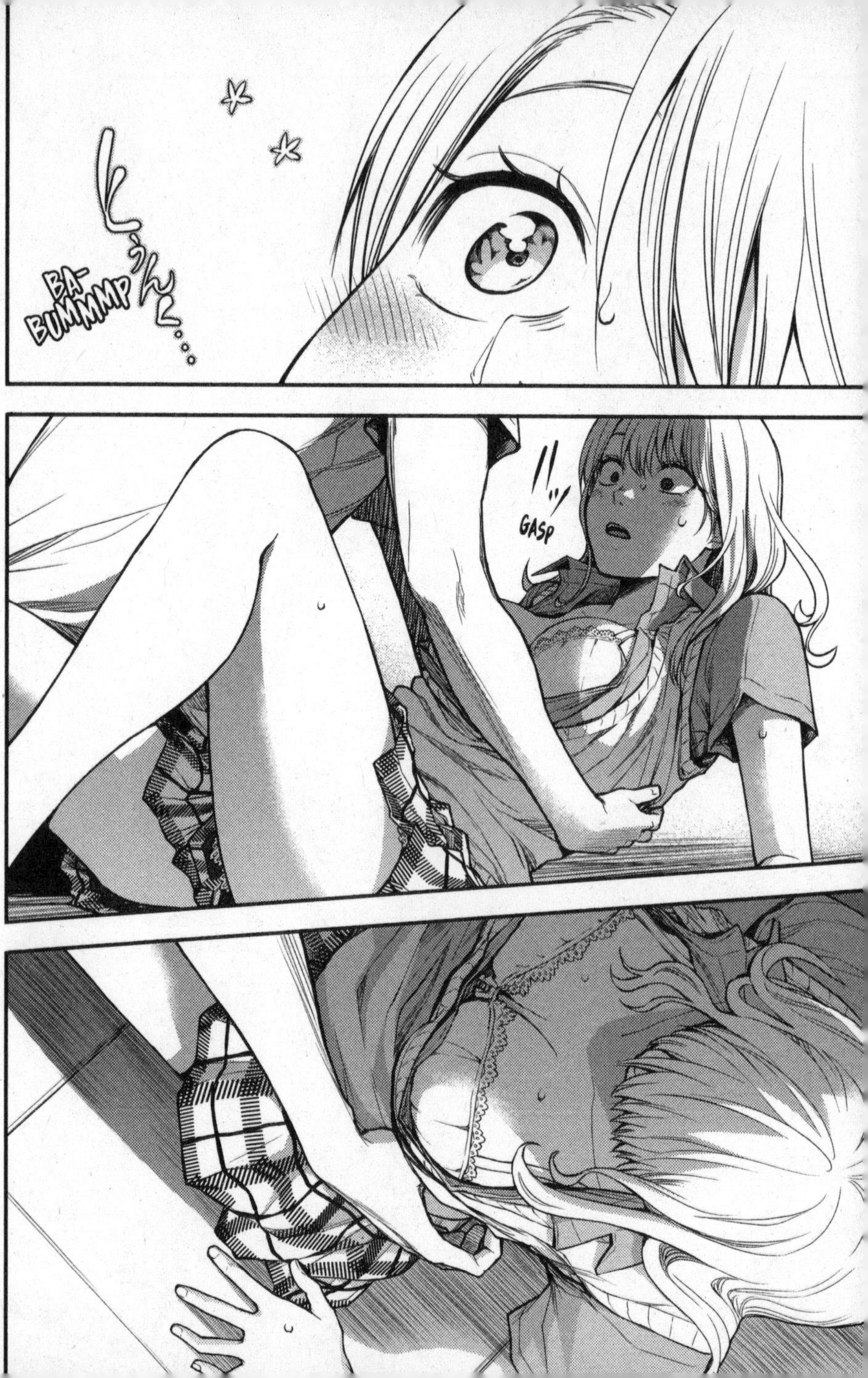
とぅんく…
BA-BUMMMP
!!
GASP

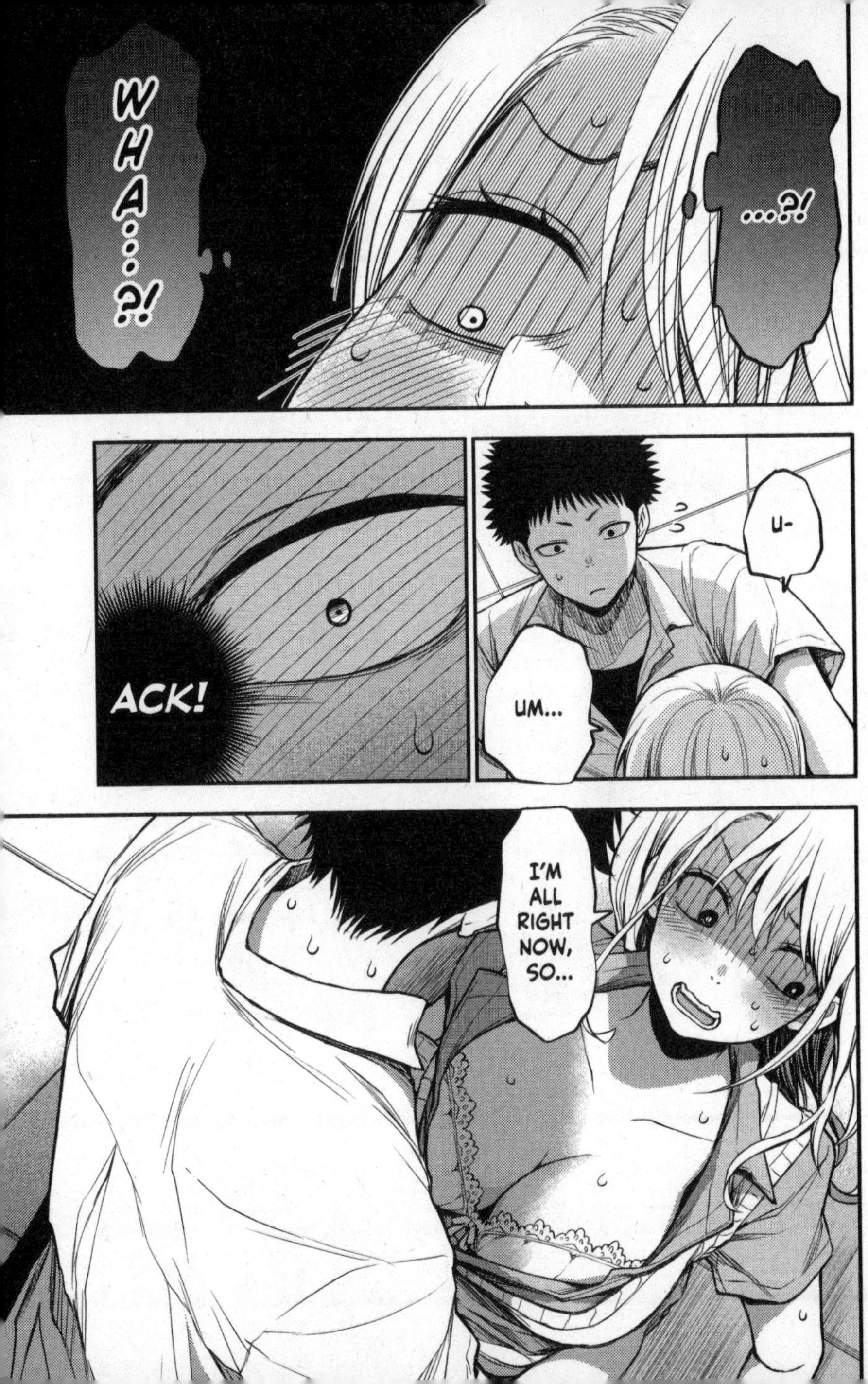
...?!
WHA...?!
U-
UM...
ACK!
I'M ALL RIGHT NOW, SO...

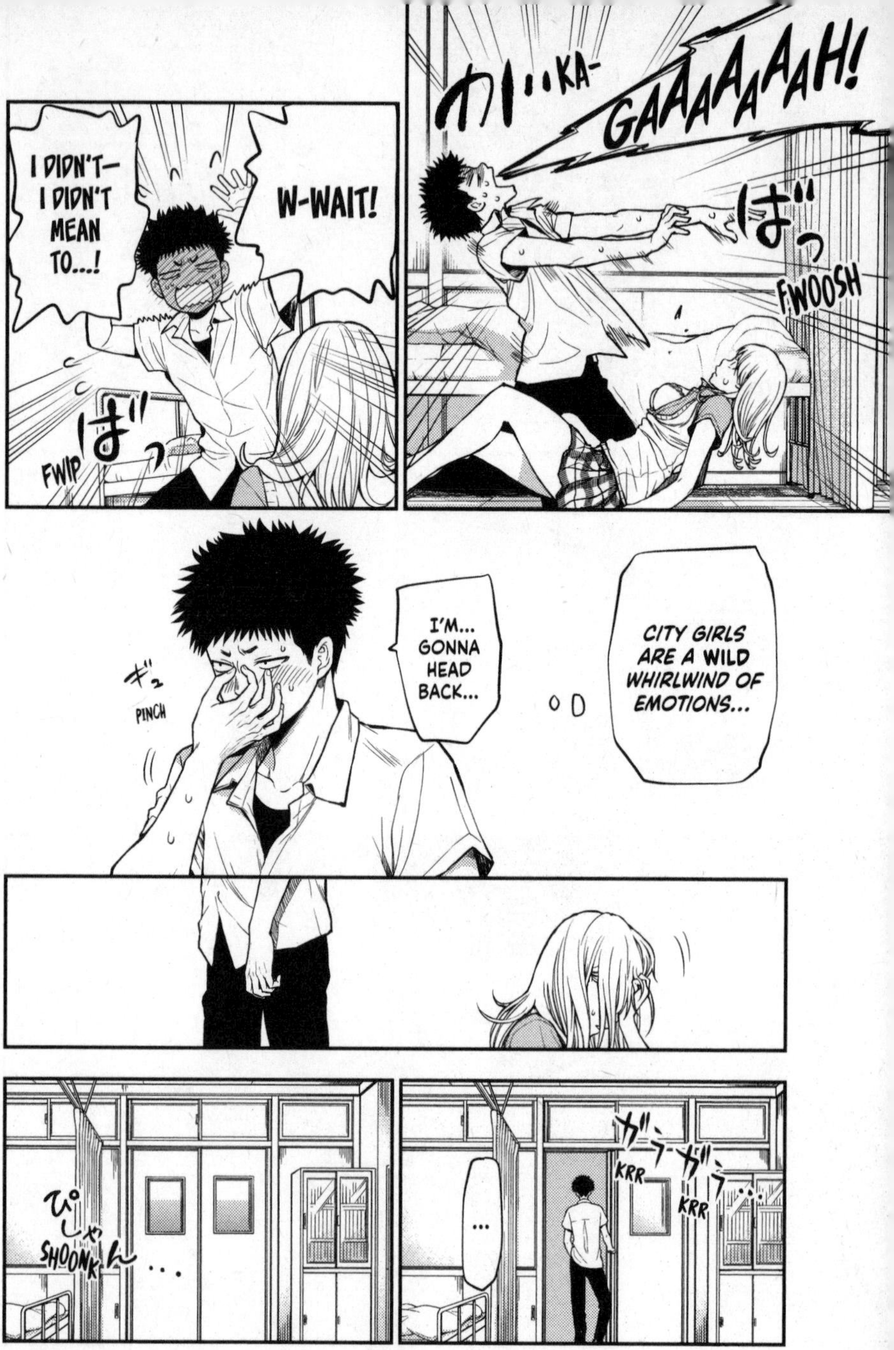
わ!! KA-
GAAAAAAAH!
ばっ
FWOOSH
W-WAIT!
I DIDN'T— I DIDN'T MEAN TO...!
ばっ
FWIP
CITY GIRLS ARE A WILD WHIRLWIND OF EMOTIONS...
I'M... GONNA HEAD BACK...
ギュ
PINCH
...
ガラ
KRR
ガラ
KRR
ぴしゃん
SHOONK
...

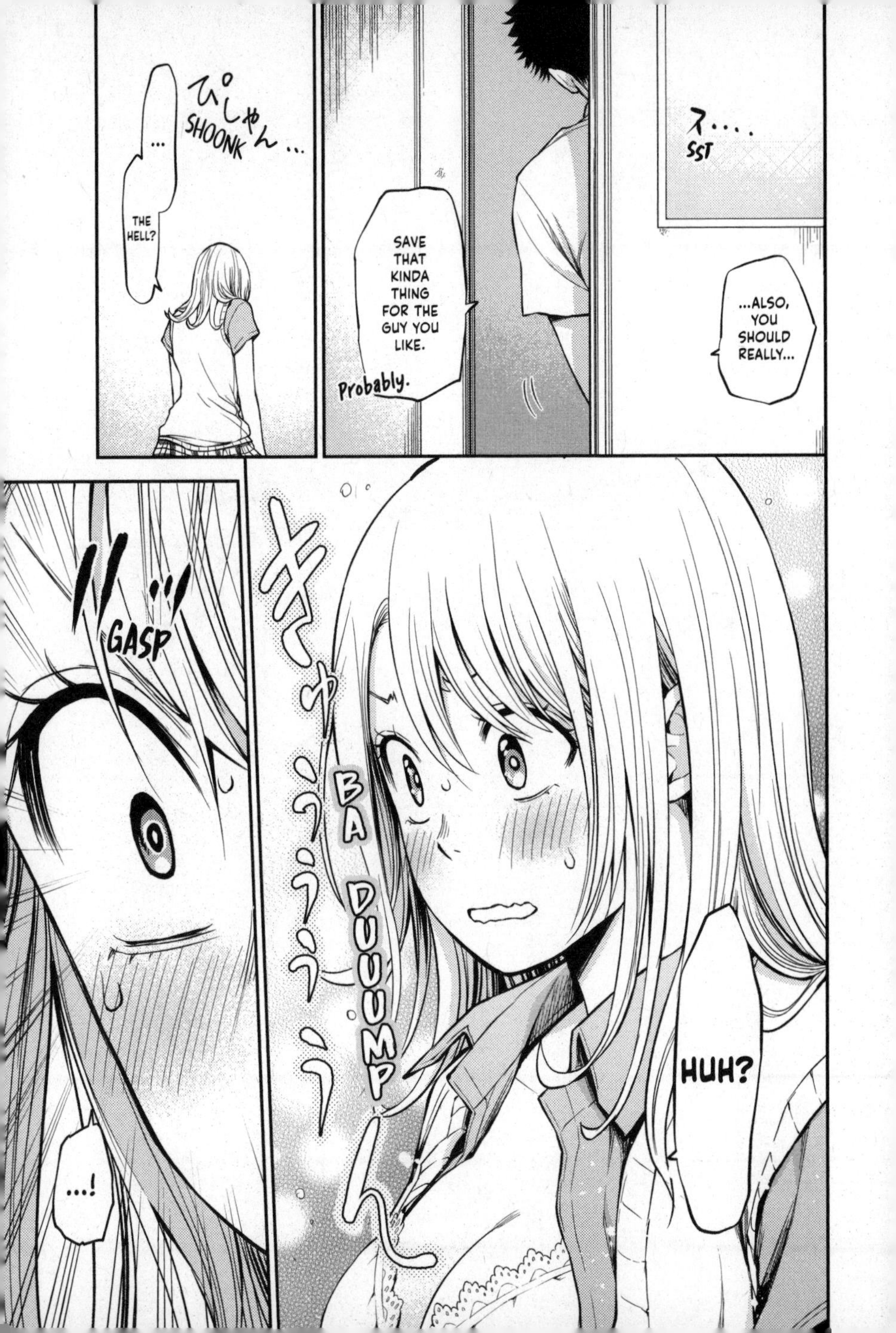
ス….
SST
...ALSO, YOU SHOULD REALLY...
SAVE THAT KINDA THING FOR THE GUY YOU LIKE.
Probably.
ぴしゃん…
SHOONK...
...
THE HELL?
きゅううううん
BA DUUUMP
HUH?
GASP
...!

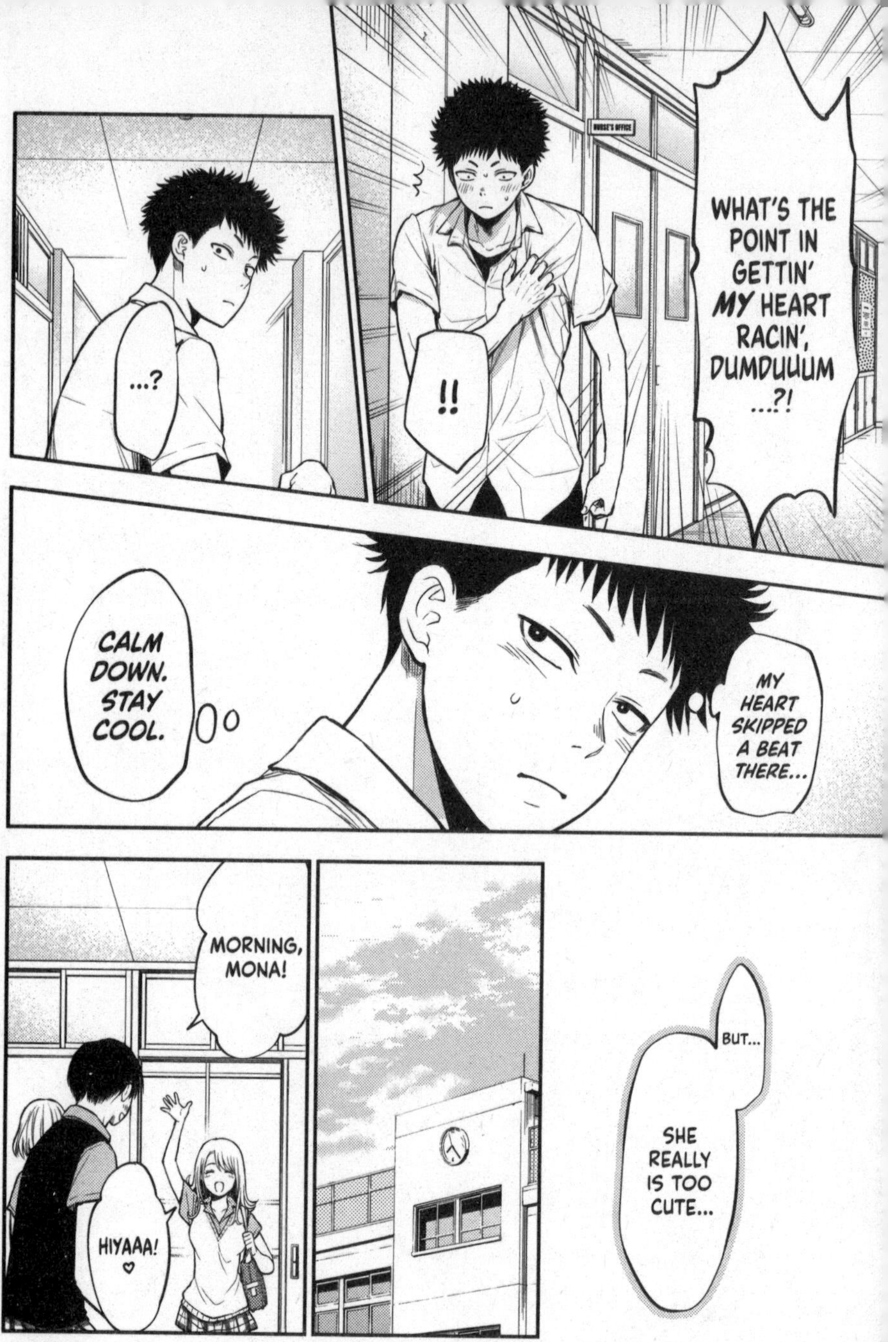
WHAT'S THE POINT IN GETTIN' MY HEART RACIN', DUMDUUUM ...?!
!!
...?
MY HEART SKIPPED A BEAT THERE...
CALM DOWN. STAY COOL.
BUT...
SHE REALLY IS TOO CUTE...
MORNING, MONA!
HIYAAA! ♡

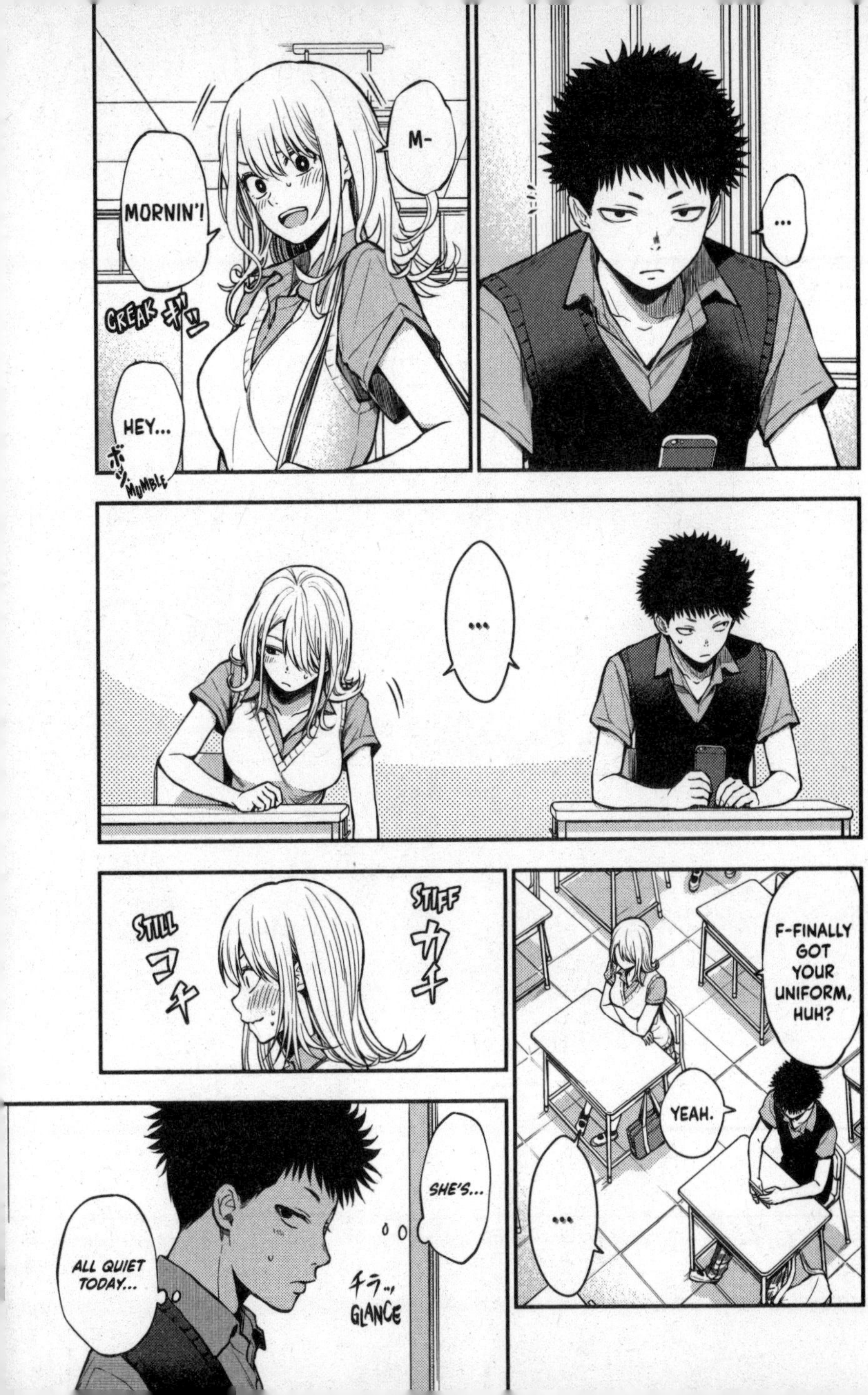
...
M-
MORNIN'!
CREAK ギュ
HEY...
ボソッ MUMBLE
...
F-FINALLY GOT YOUR UNIFORM, HUH?
YEAH.
...
STIFF カチ
STILL コチ
SHE'S...
チラッ GLANCE
ALL QUIET TODAY...

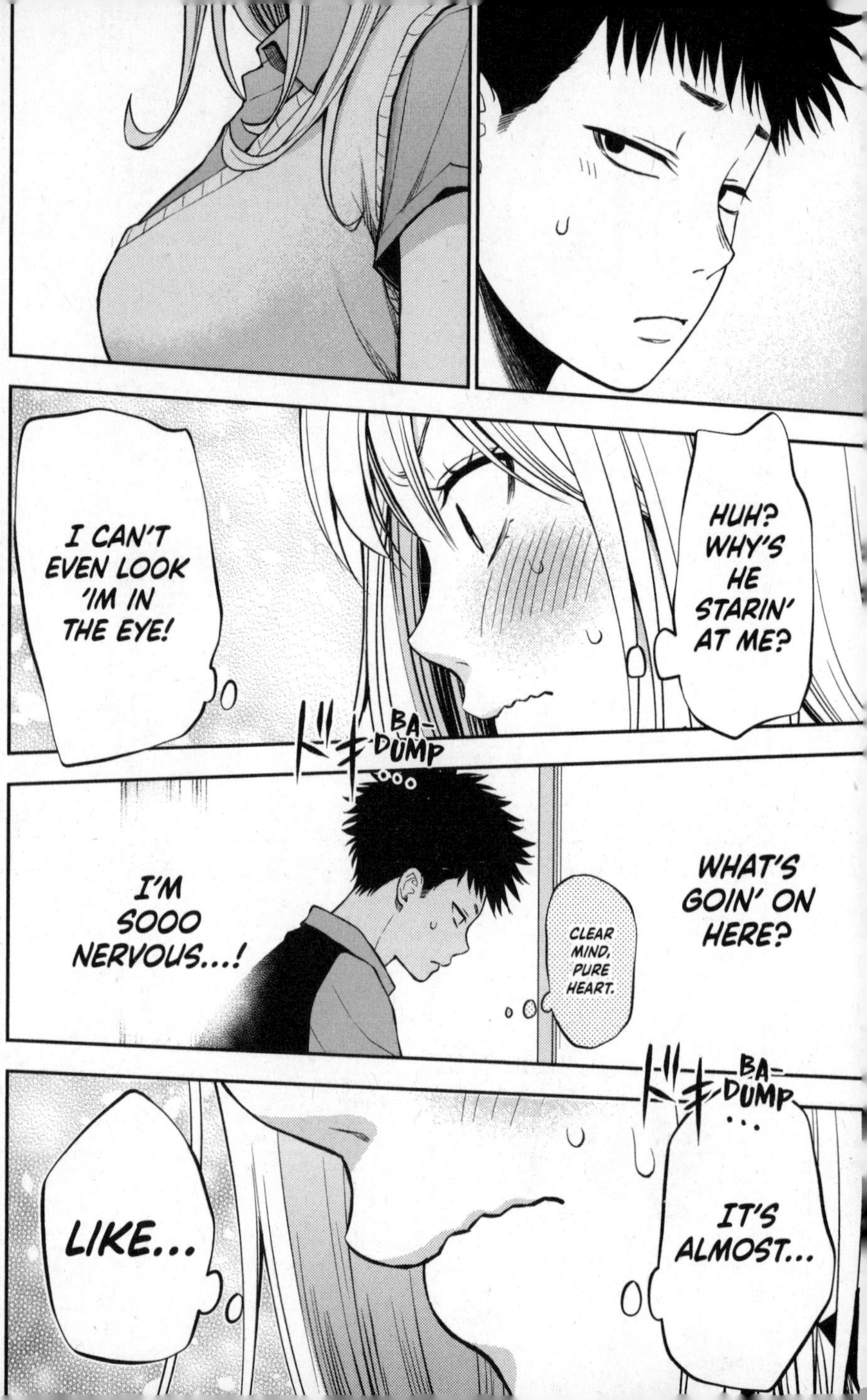

HUH? WHY'S HE STARIN' AT ME?
I CAN'T EVEN LOOK 'IM IN THE EYE!
BA-DUMP
WHAT'S GOIN' ON HERE?
CLEAR MIND, PURE HEART.
I'M SOOO NERVOUS...!
BA-DUMP...
IT'S ALMOST...
LIKE...

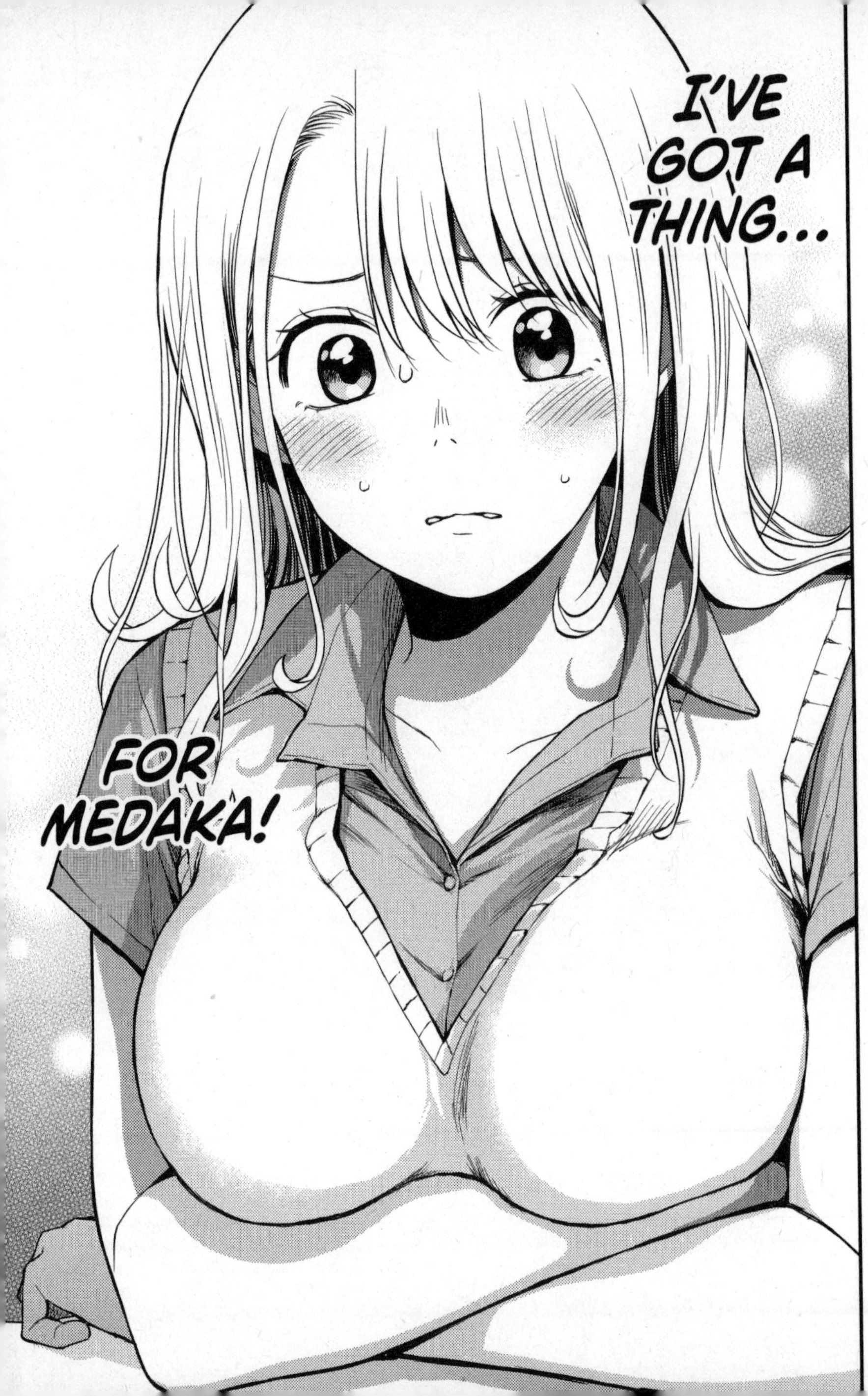
I'VE GOT A THING...
FOR MEDAKA!

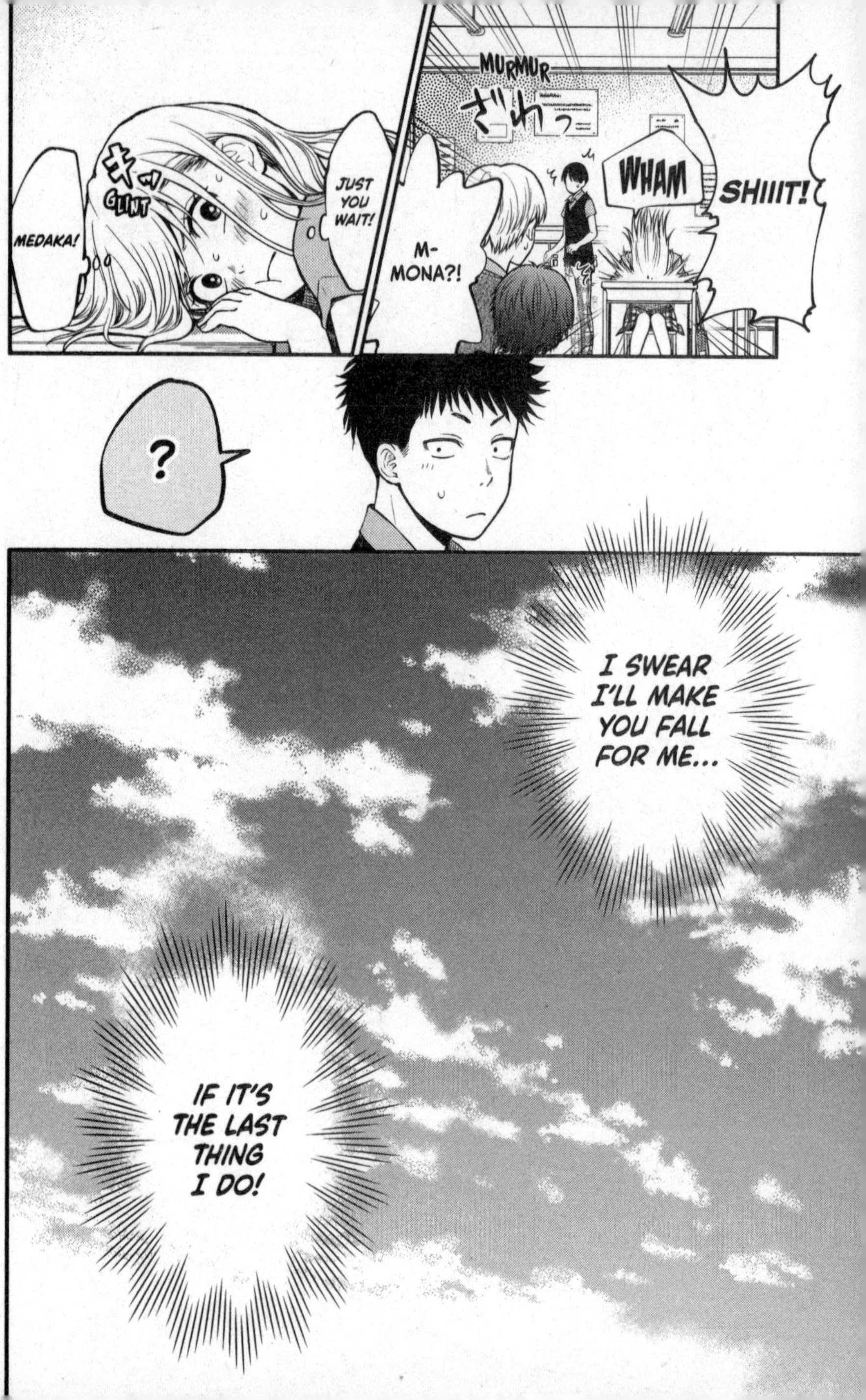
SHIIIT!
WHAM
MURMUR
ざわっ
M-MONA?!
JUST YOU WAIT!
キッ
GLINT
MEDAKA!
?
I SWEAR I'LL MAKE YOU FALL FOR ME...
IF IT'S THE LAST THING I DO!

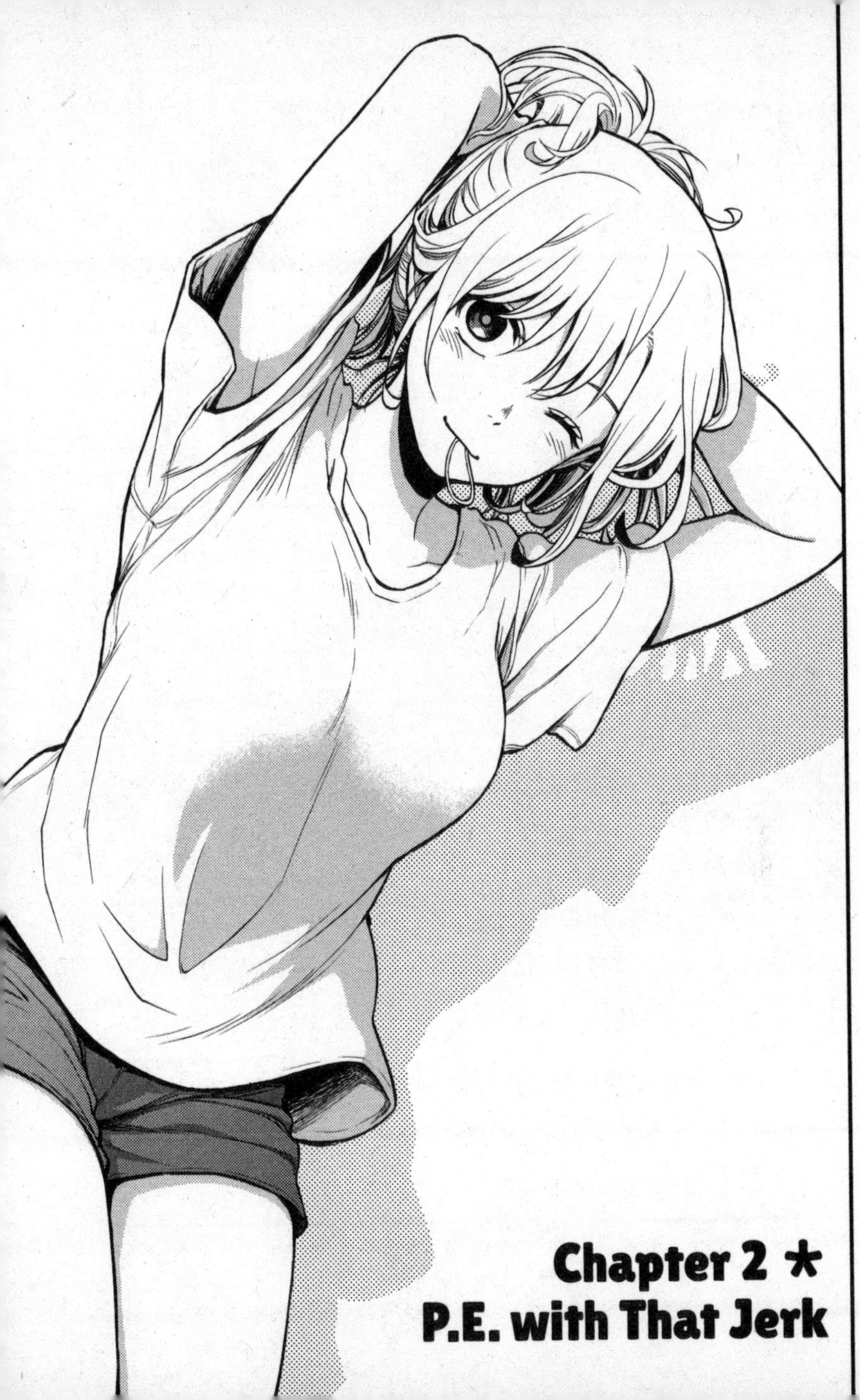

Chapter 2 ★ P.E. with That Jerk

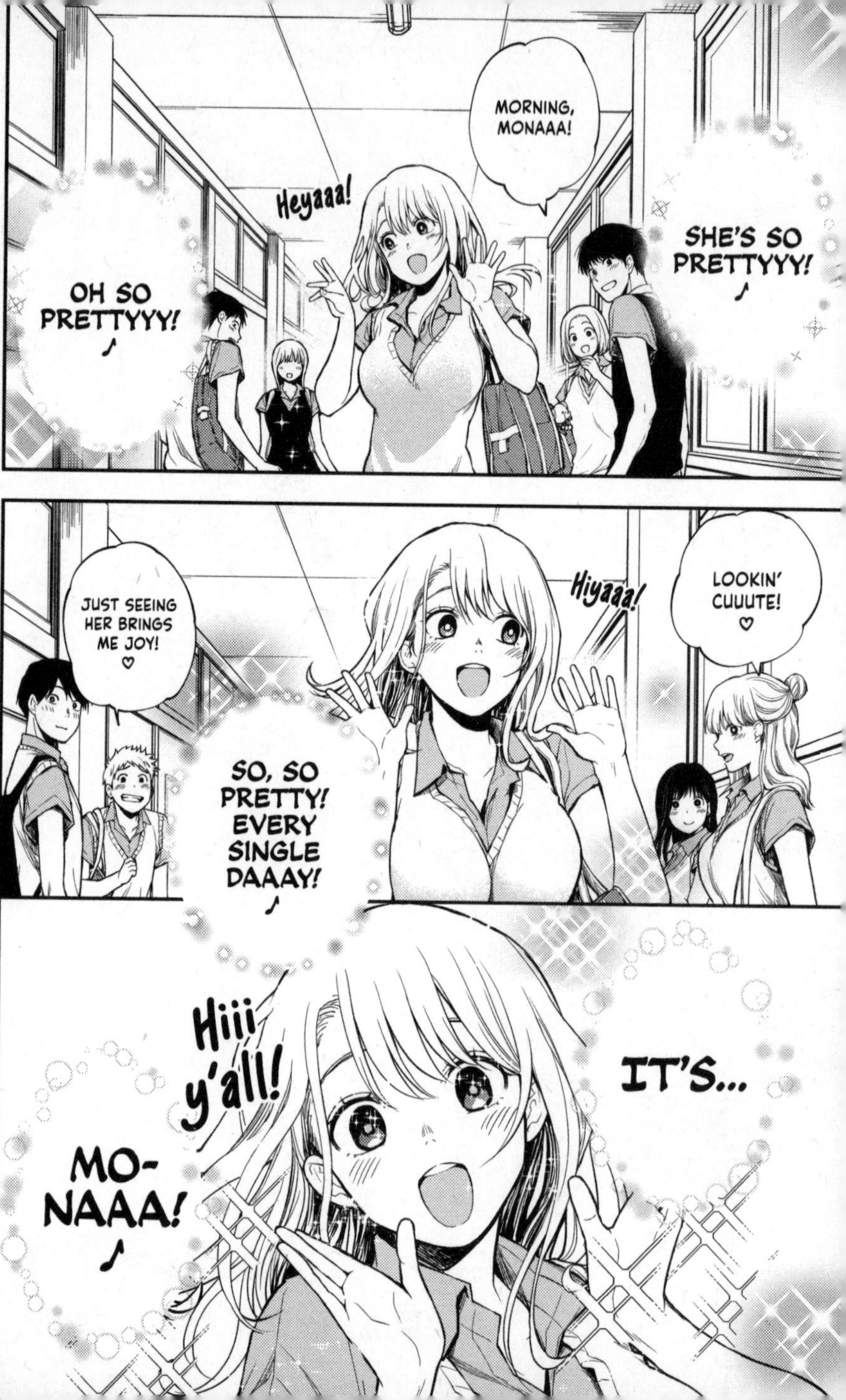
MORNING, MONAAA!
SHE'S SO PRETTYYY! ♪
Heyaaa!
OH SO PRETTYYY! ♪
LOOKIN' CUUUTE! ♡
Hiyaaa!
JUST SEEING HER BRINGS ME JOY! ♡
SO, SO PRETTY! EVERY SINGLE DAAAY! ♪
IT'S...
Hiii y'all!
MO-NAAA! ♪

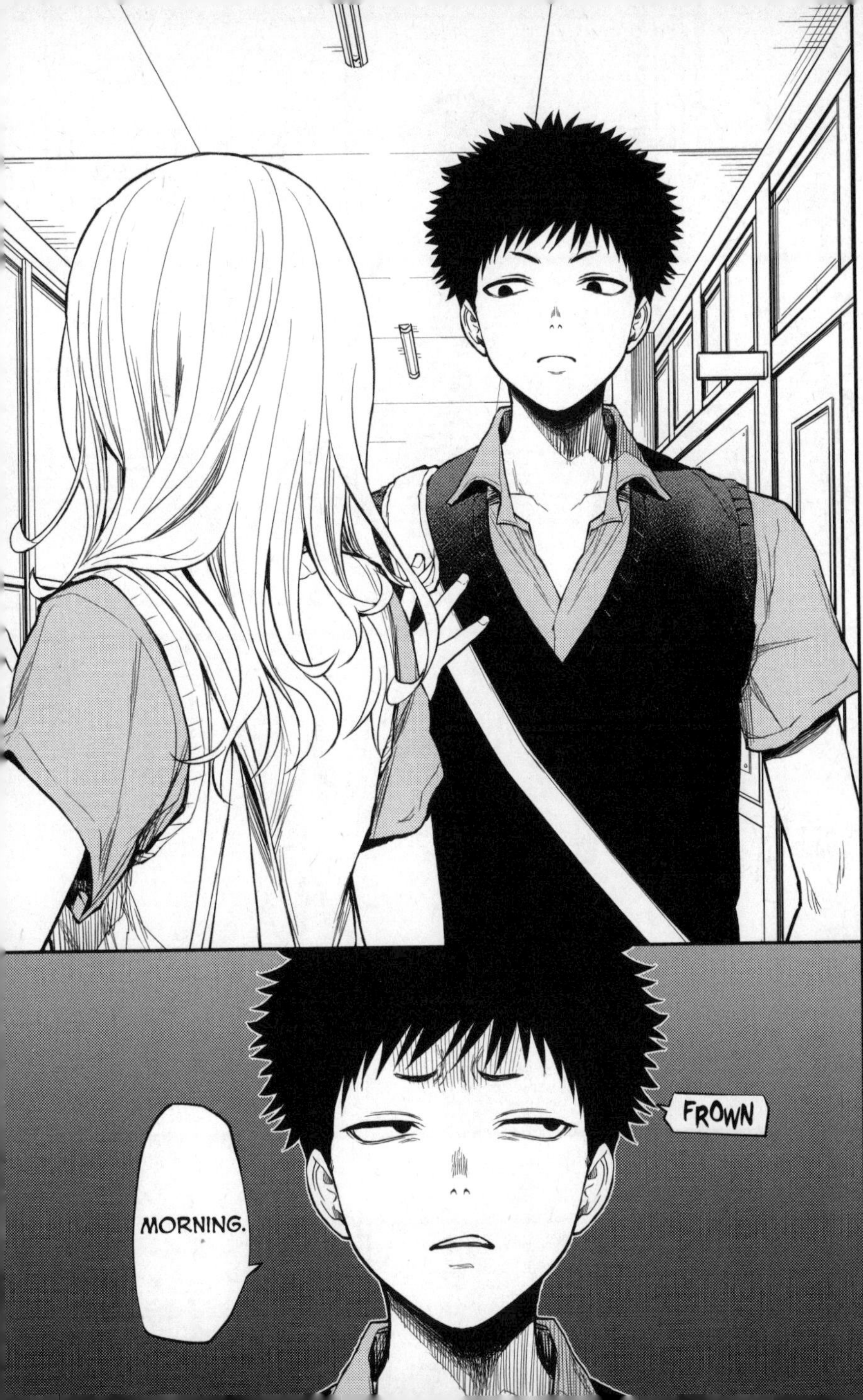
FROWN
MORNING.

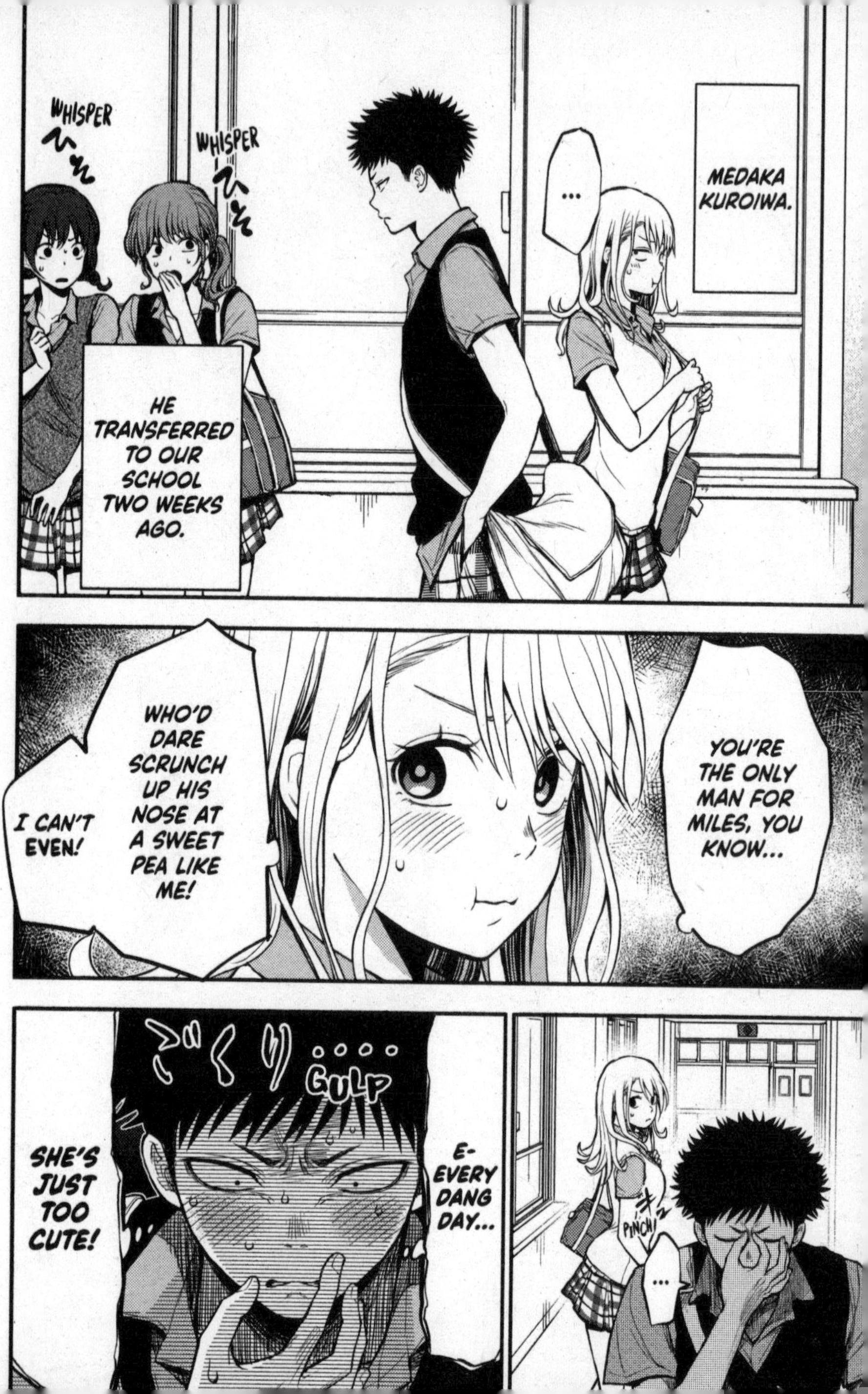
MEDAKA KUROIWA.
...
WHISPER
WHISPER
HE TRANSFERRED TO OUR SCHOOL TWO WEEKS AGO.
YOU'RE THE ONLY MAN FOR MILES, YOU KNOW...
WHO'D DARE SCRUNCH UP HIS NOSE AT A SWEET PEA LIKE ME!
I CAN'T EVEN!
PINCH!
...
E-EVERY DANG DAY...
GULP
SHE'S JUST TOO CUTE!

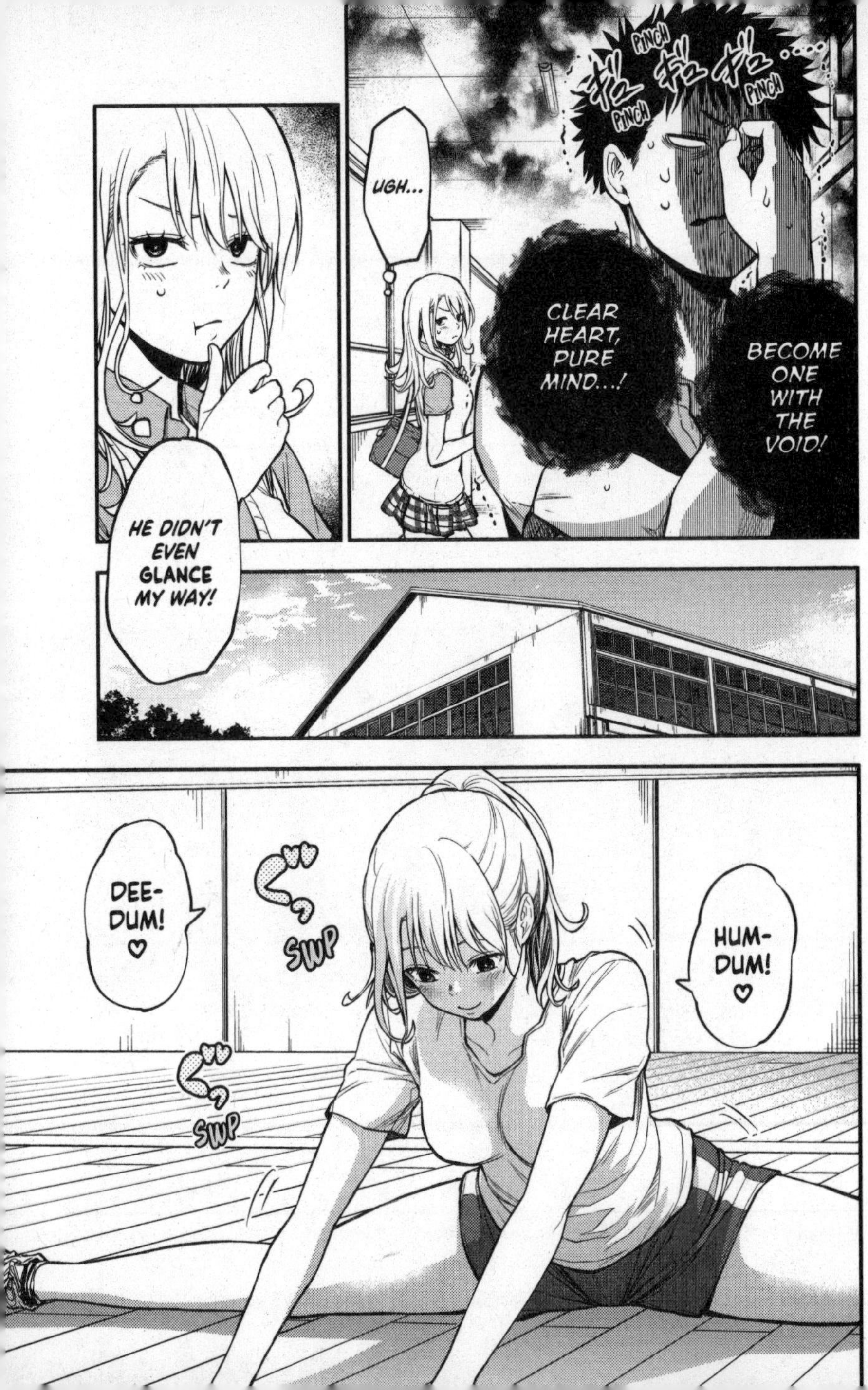
PINCH PINCH PINCH PINCH
UGH...
CLEAR HEART, PURE MIND...!
BECOME ONE WITH THE VOID!
HE DIDN'T EVEN GLANCE MY WAY!
HUM-DUM! ♡
SWP
DEE-DUM! ♡
SWP

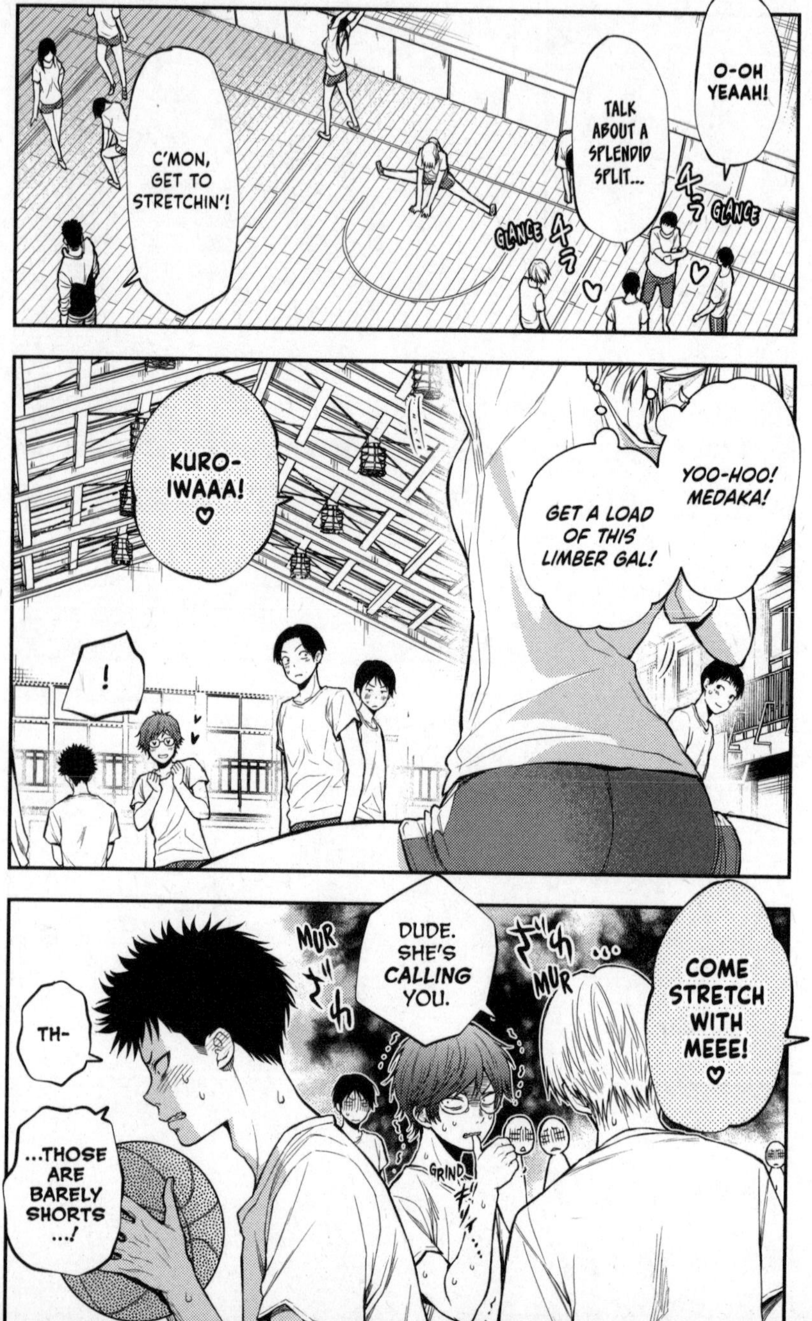
O-OH YEAAH!
TALK ABOUT A SPLENDID SPLIT...
GLANCE
GLANCE
C'MON, GET TO STRETCHIN'!
YOO-HOO! MEDAKA!
GET A LOAD OF THIS LIMBER GAL!
KURO-IWAAA! ♡
!
COME STRETCH WITH MEEE! ♡
MUR
DUDE. SHE'S CALLING YOU.
MUR
GRIND
TH-
...THOSE ARE BARELY SHORTS ...!

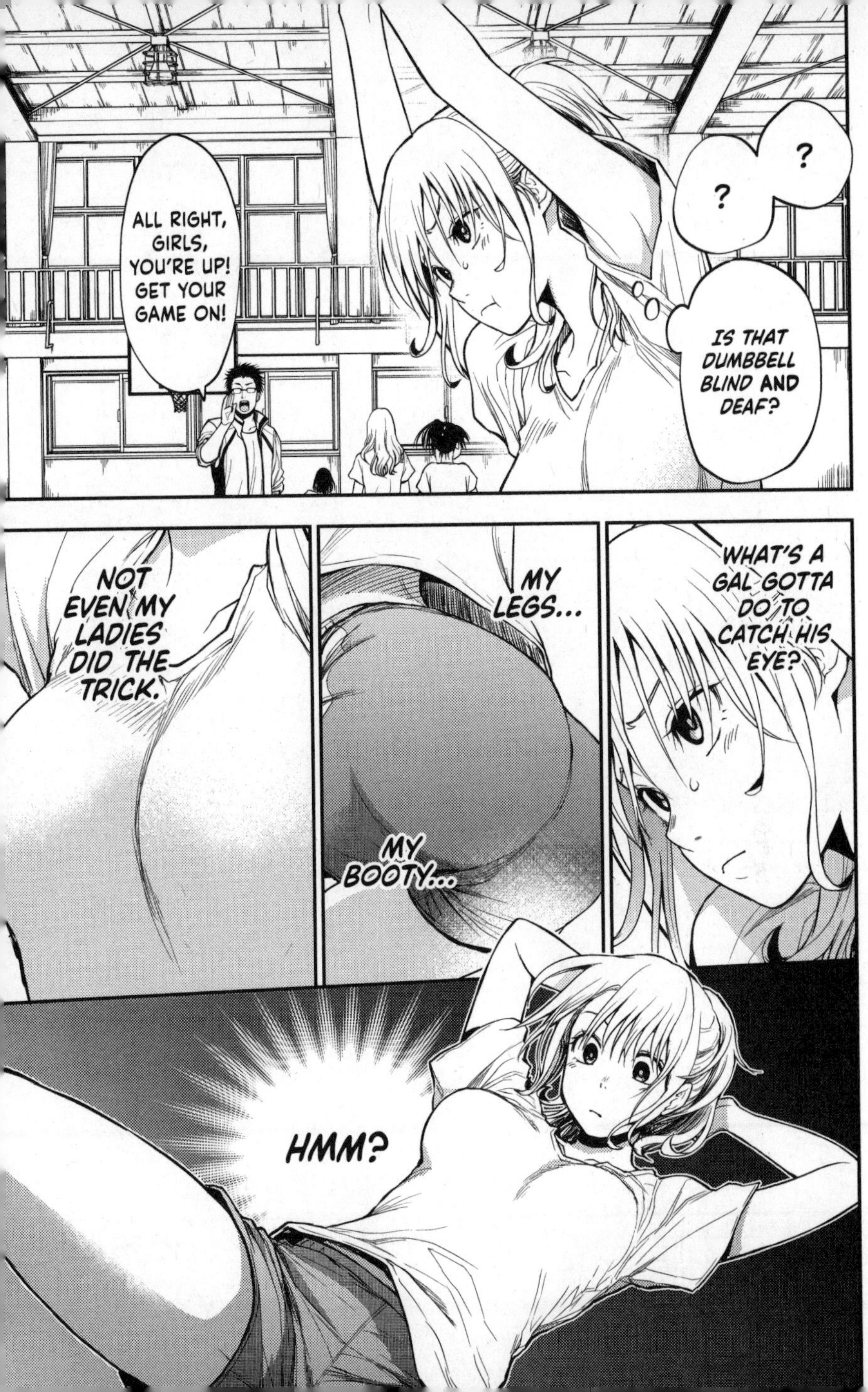
? ?
IS THAT DUMBBELL BLIND AND DEAF?
ALL RIGHT, GIRLS, YOU'RE UP! GET YOUR GAME ON!
WHAT'S A GAL GOTTA DO TO CATCH HIS EYE?
MY LEGS...
MY BOOTY...
NOT EVEN MY LADIES DID THE TRICK.
HMM?

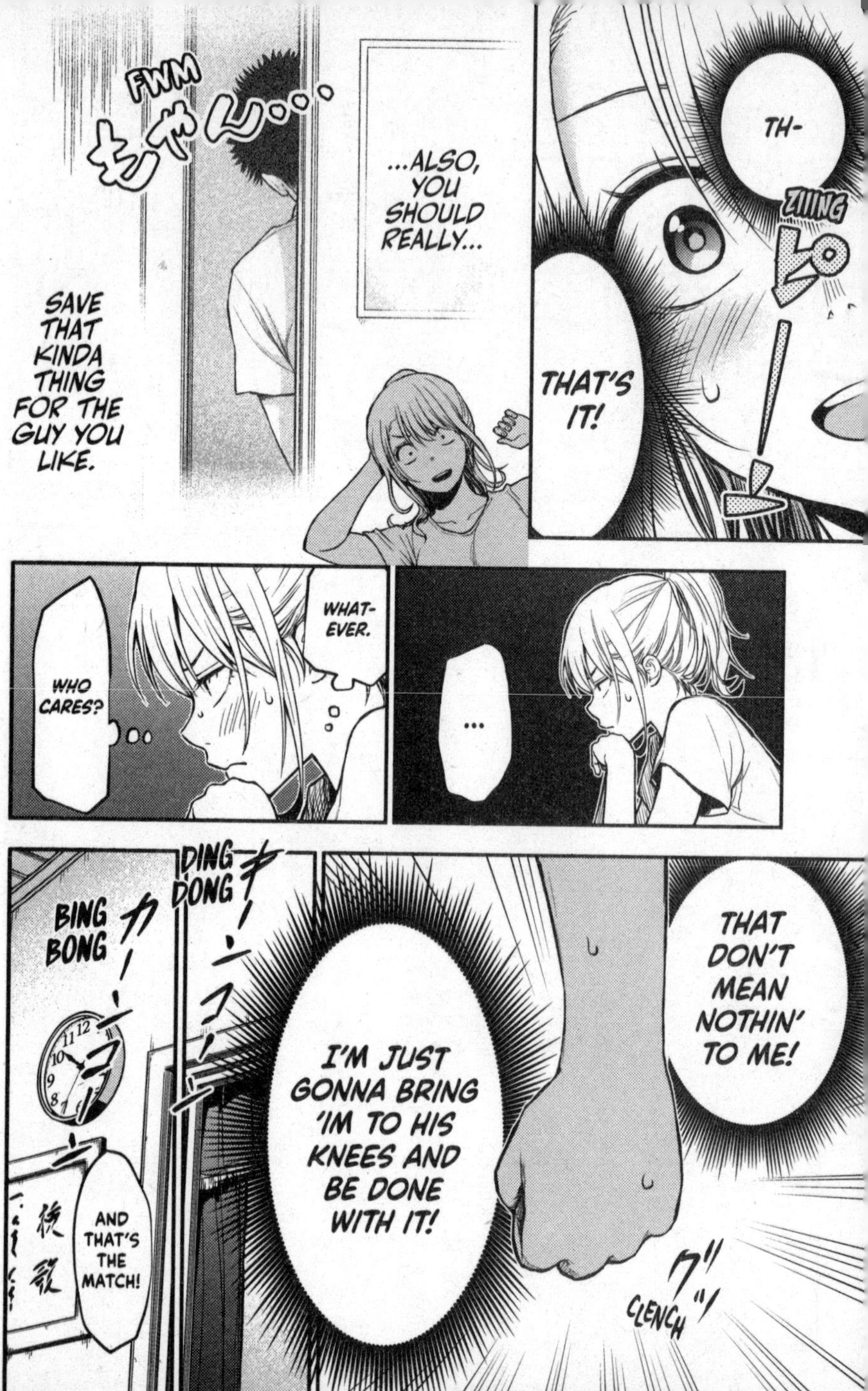
TH-
ZIIING
THAT'S IT!
...ALSO, YOU SHOULD REALLY...
FWM
もやん…
SAVE THAT KINDA THING FOR THE GUY YOU LIKE.
...
WHAT-EVER.
WHO CARES?
THAT DON'T MEAN NOTHIN' TO ME!
CLENCH
I'M JUST GONNA BRING 'IM TO HIS KNEES AND BE DONE WITH IT!
DING-DONG
BING BONG
AND THAT'S THE MATCH!

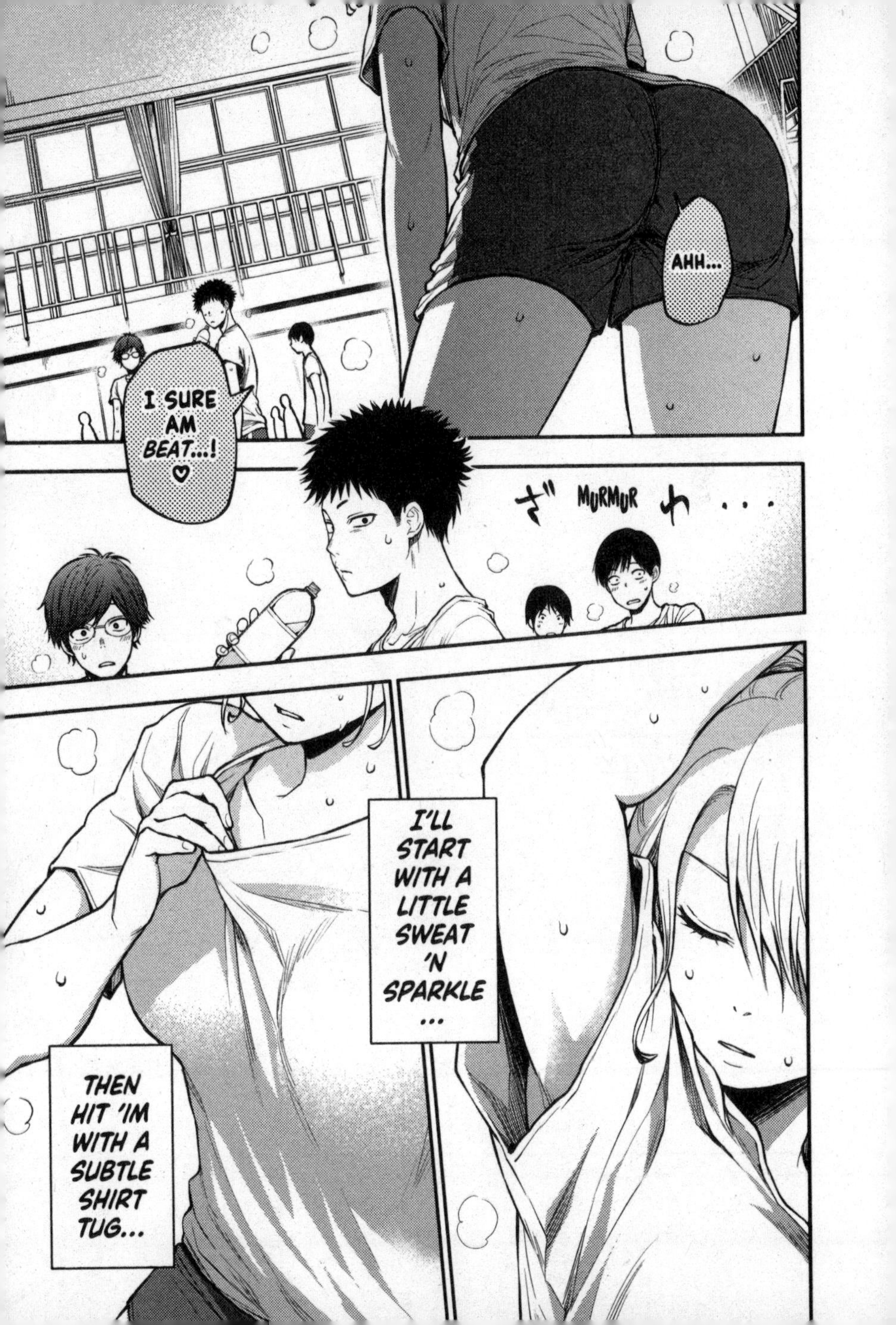
AHH...
I SURE AM BEAT...! ♡
ざ MURMUR わ...
I'LL START WITH A LITTLE SWEAT 'N SPARKLE...
THEN HIT 'IM WITH A SUBTLE SHIRT TUG...

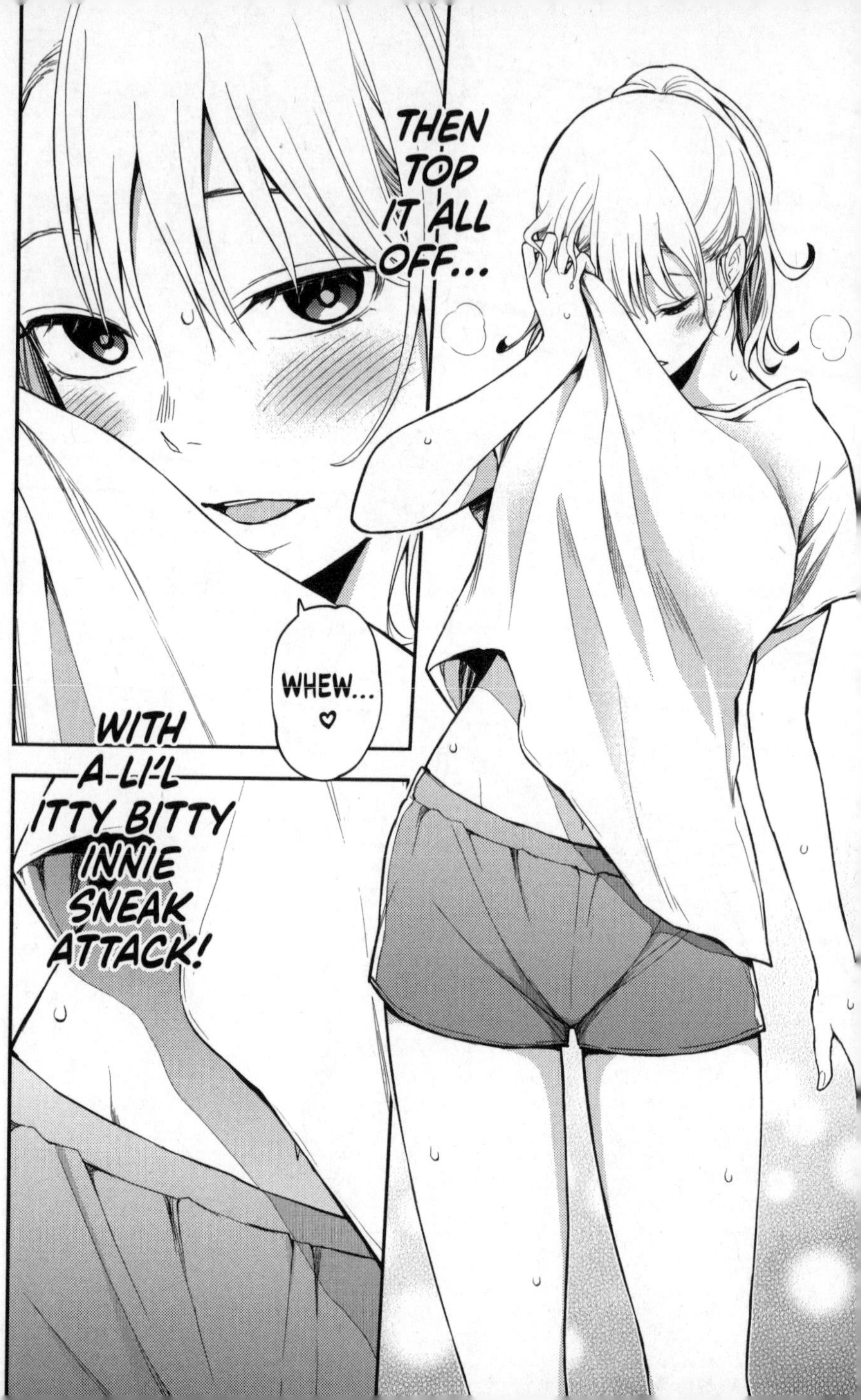
THEN TOP IT ALL OFF...
WHEW... ♡
WITH A-LI'L ITTY BITTY INNIE SNEAK ATTACK!

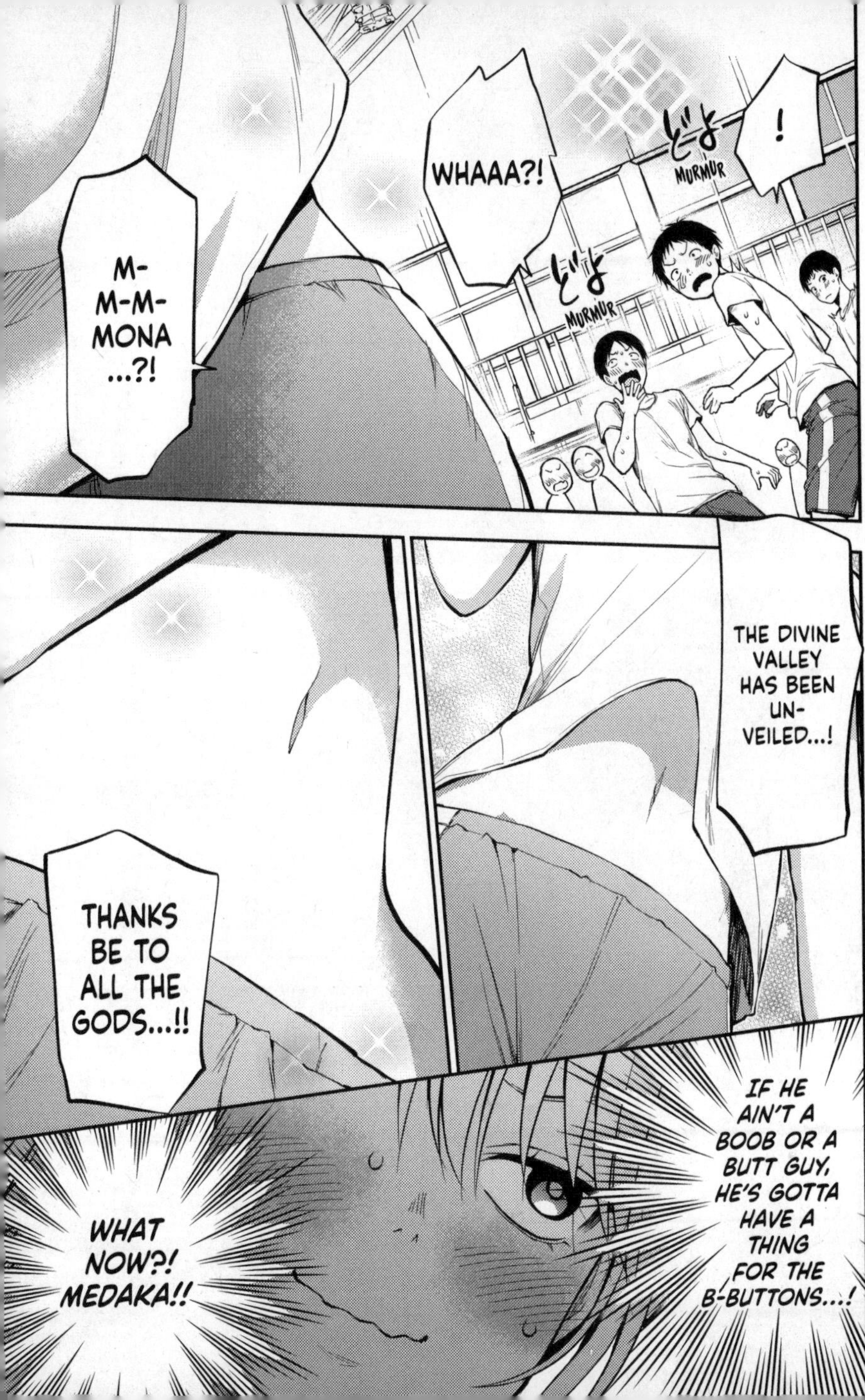
!
どよ
MURMUR
WHAAA?!
どよ
MURMUR
M-M-M-MONA...?!
THE DIVINE VALLEY HAS BEEN UN-VEILED...!
THANKS BE TO ALL THE GODS...!!
IF HE AIN'T A BOOB OR A BUTT GUY, HE'S GOTTA HAVE A THING FOR THE B-BUTTONS...!
WHAT NOW?! MEDAKA!!

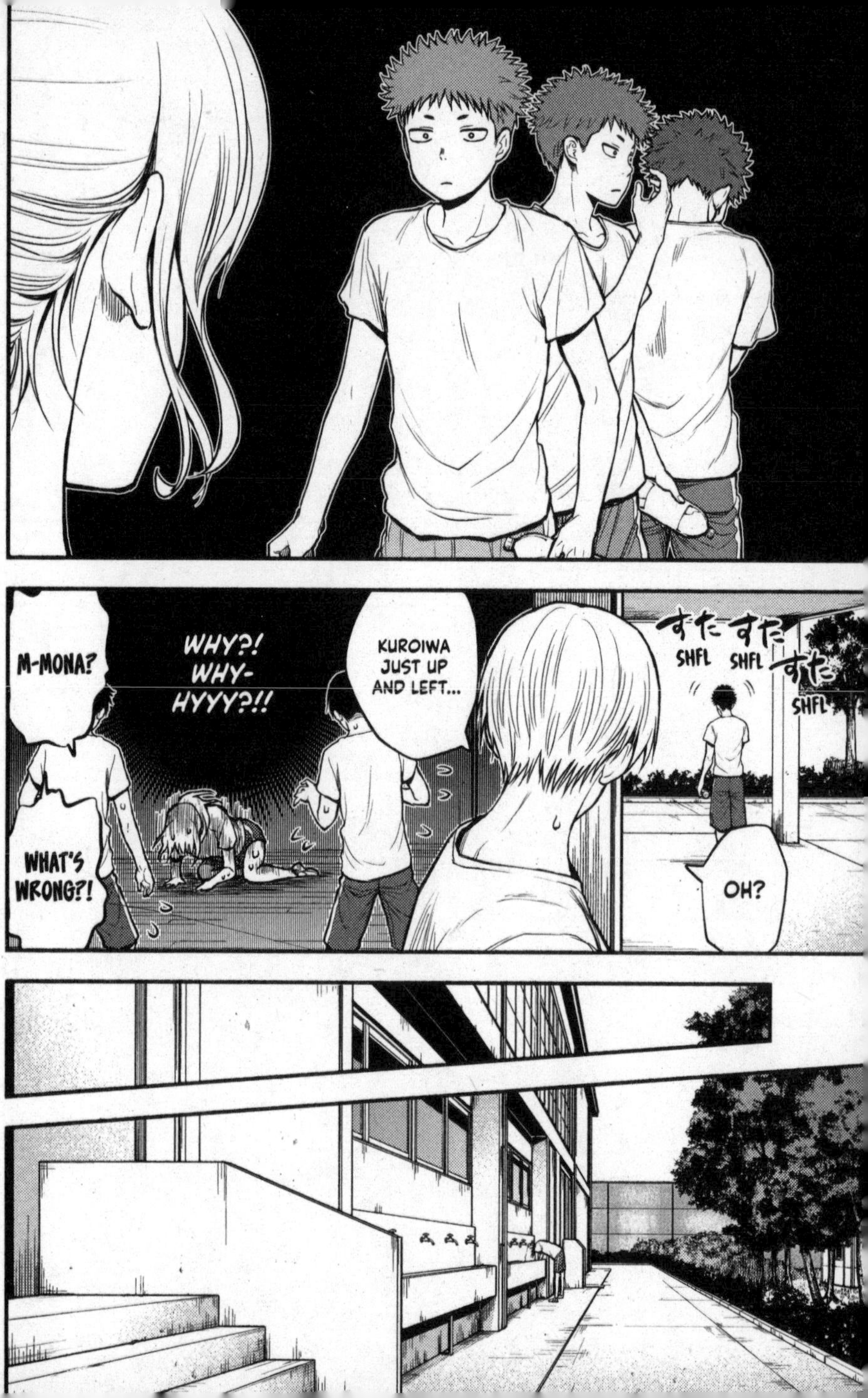
すたすた
SHFL SHFL
すた
SHFL
OH?
KUROIWA JUST UP AND LEFT...
WHY?! WHY-HYYY?!!
M-MONA?
WHAT'S WRONG?!

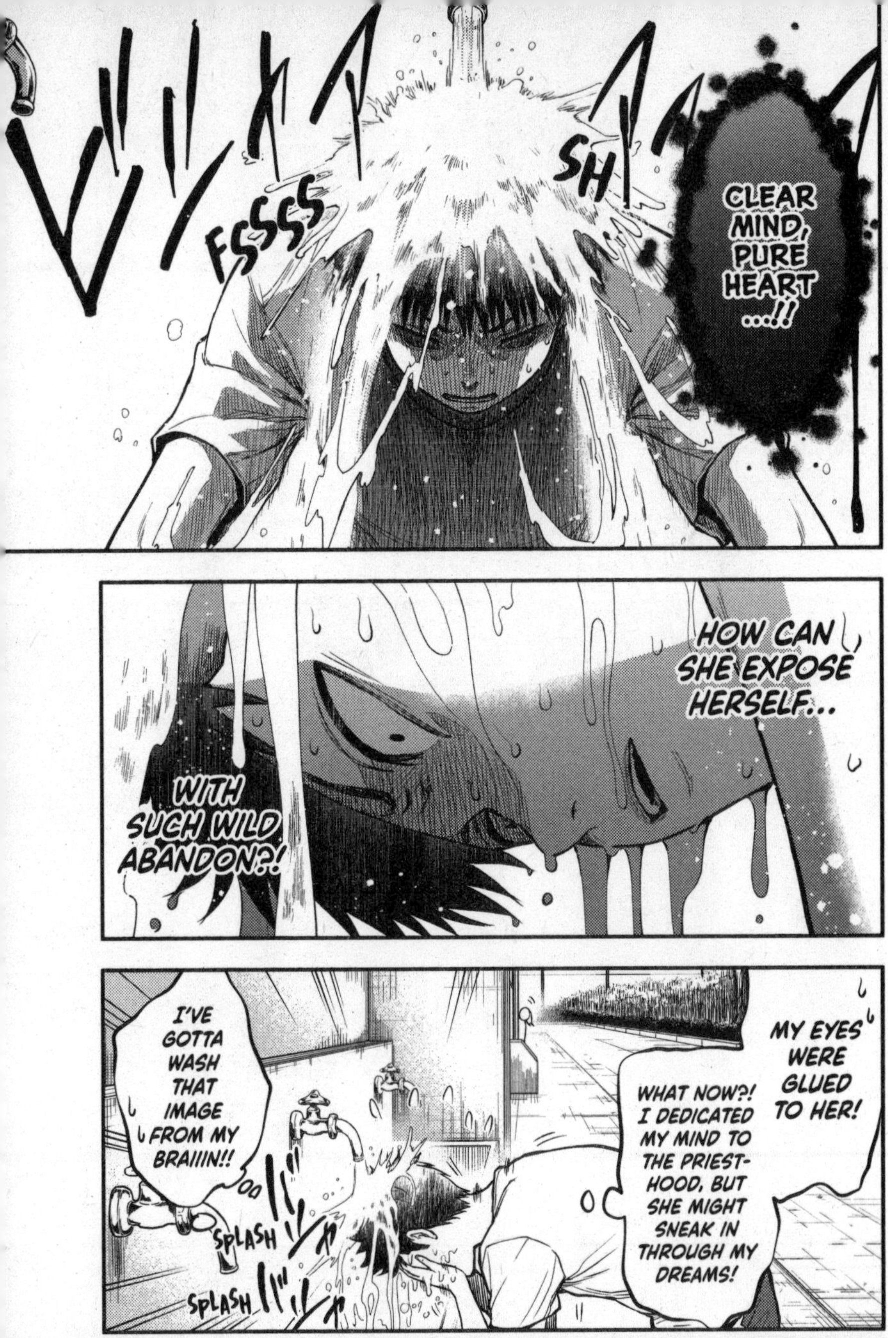
CLEAR MIND, PURE HEART ...!!
SH
FSSSS
HOW CAN SHE EXPOSE HERSELF...
WITH SUCH WILD ABANDON?!
MY EYES WERE GLUED TO HER!
WHAT NOW?! I DEDICATED MY MIND TO THE PRIEST-HOOD, BUT SHE MIGHT SNEAK IN THROUGH MY DREAMS!
I'VE GOTTA WASH THAT IMAGE FROM MY BRAIIIN!!
SPLASH
SPLASH

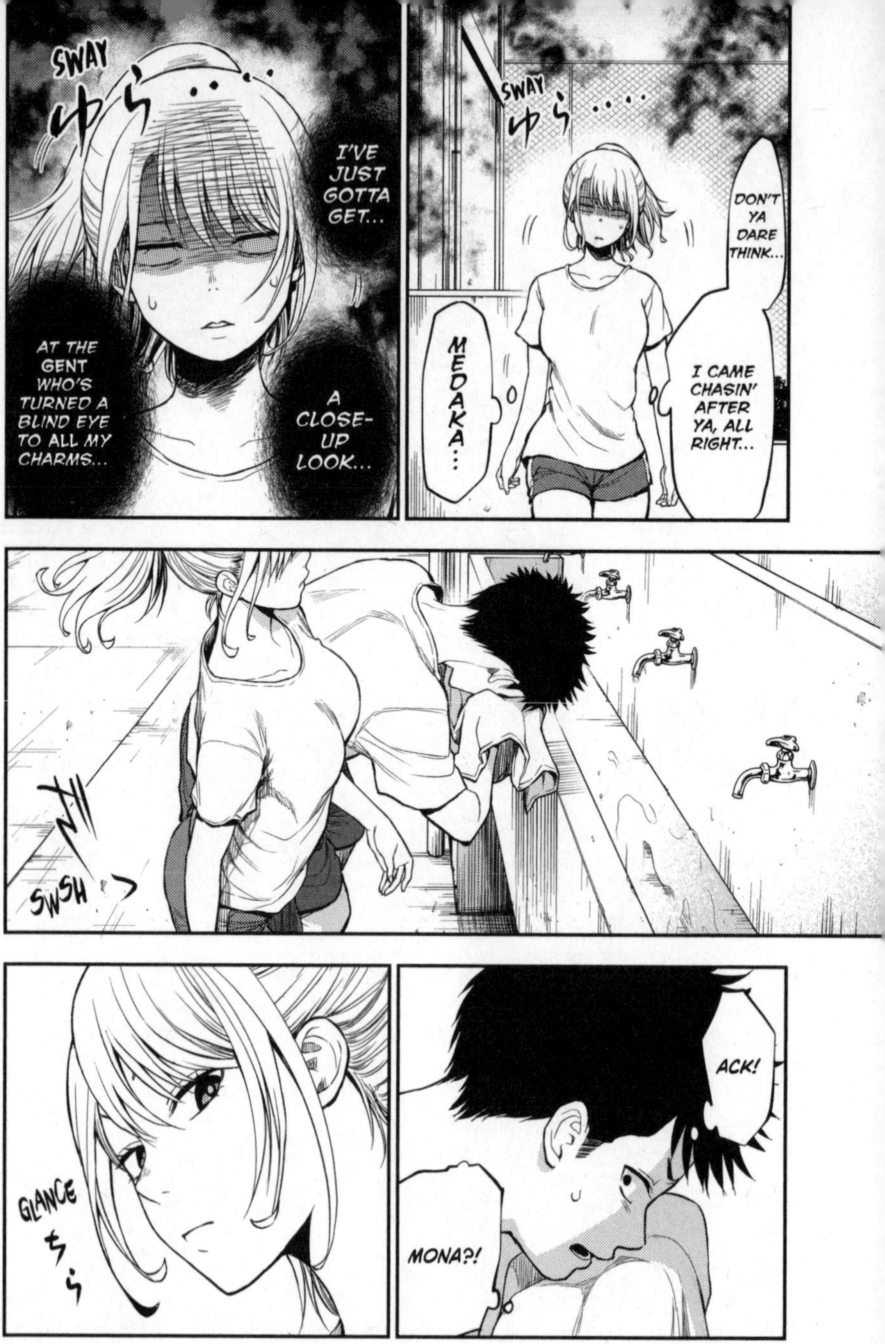
SWAY
ゆら…
DON'T YA DARE THINK...
I CAME CHASIN' AFTER YA, ALL RIGHT...
MEDAKA...
SWAY
ゆら…
I'VE JUST GOTTA GET...
A CLOSE-UP LOOK...
AT THE GENT WHO'S TURNED A BLIND EYE TO ALL MY CHARMS...
SWSH
ACK!
MONA?!
GLANCE
ちら

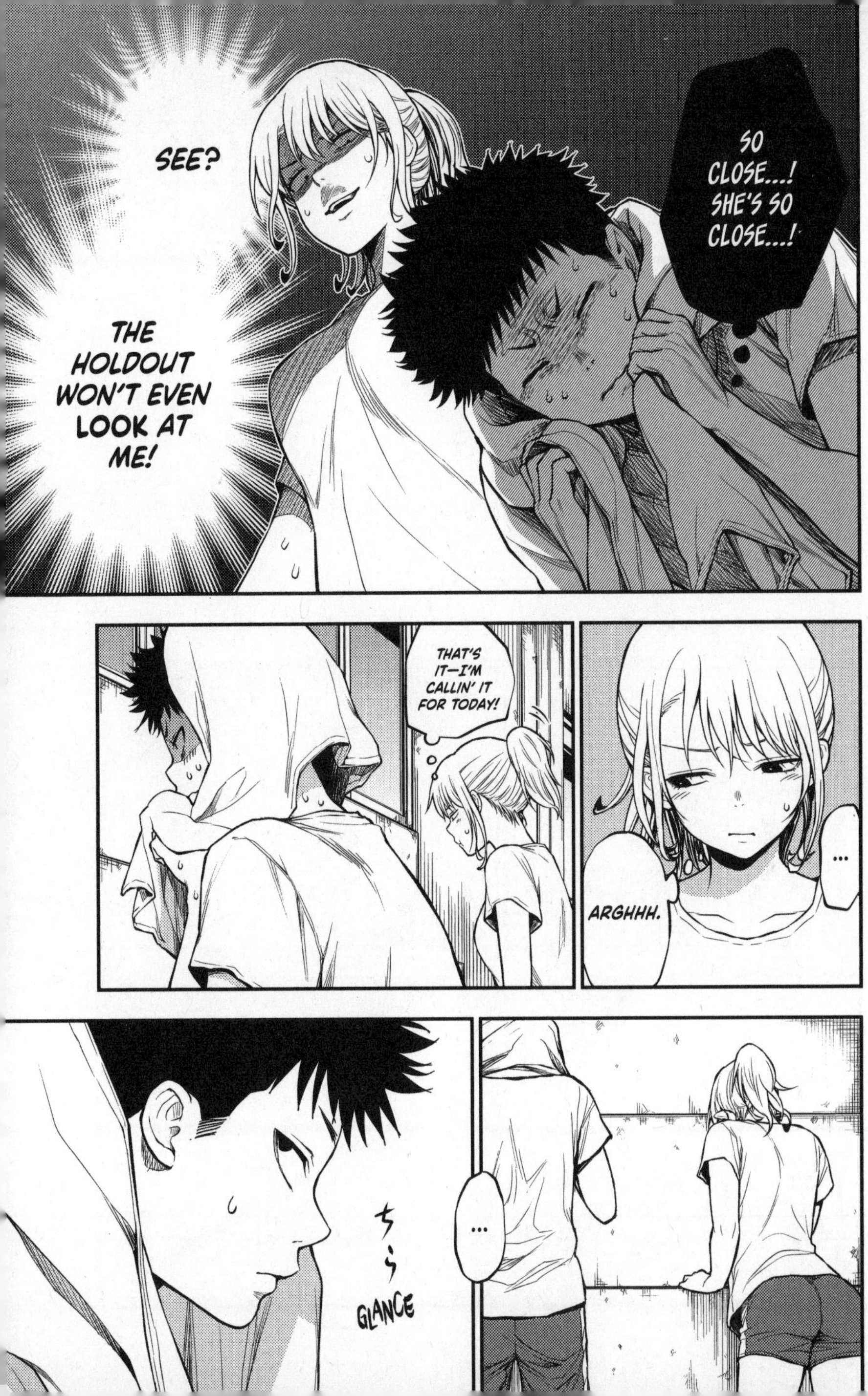
SO CLOSE...! SHE'S SO CLOSE...!
SEE?
THE HOLDOUT WON'T EVEN LOOK AT ME!
...
ARGHHH.
THAT'S IT—I'M CALLIN' IT FOR TODAY!
...
ちら
GLANCE

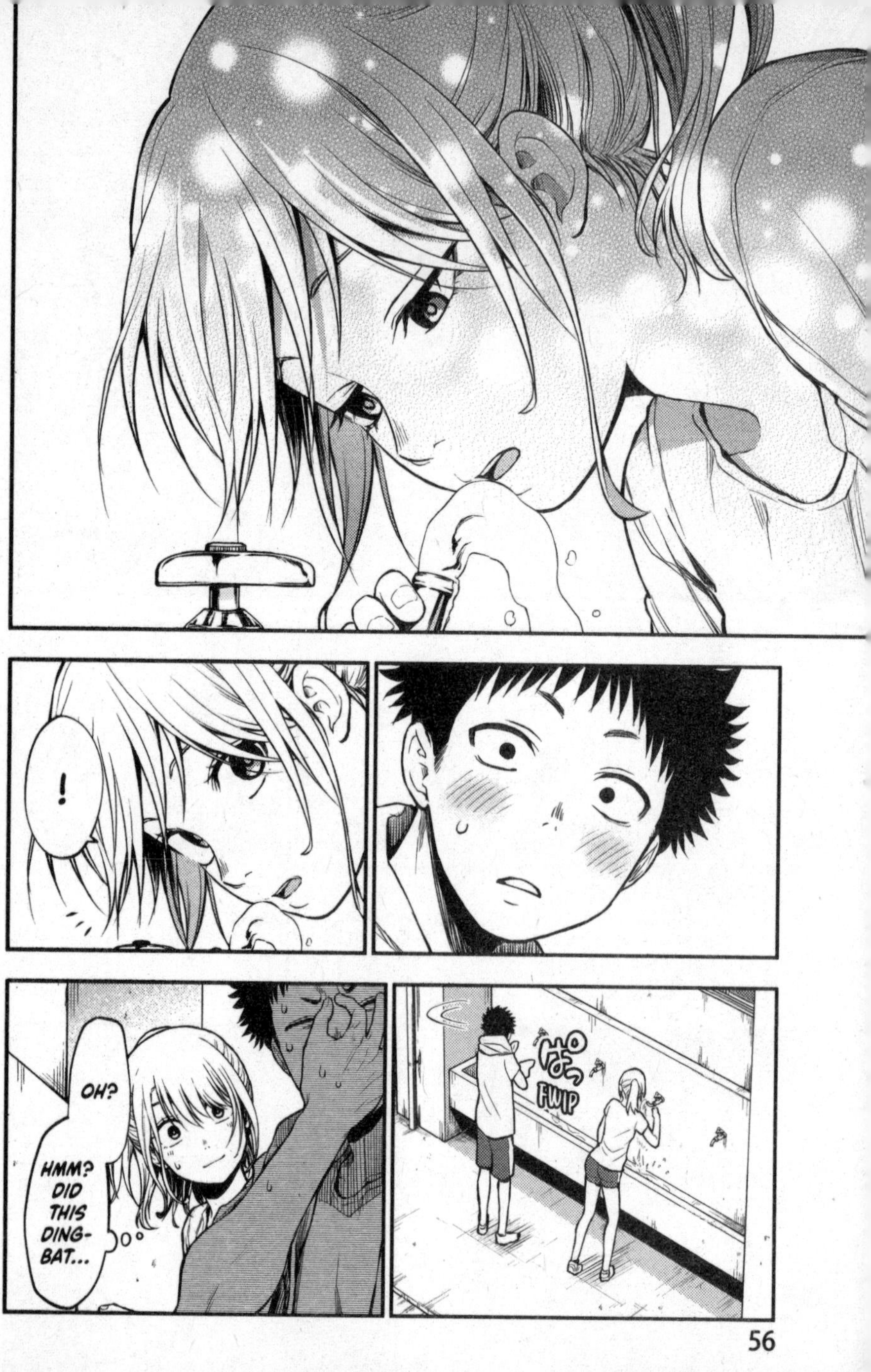
!
ぱっ
FWIP
OH?
HMM? DID THIS DING-BAT...

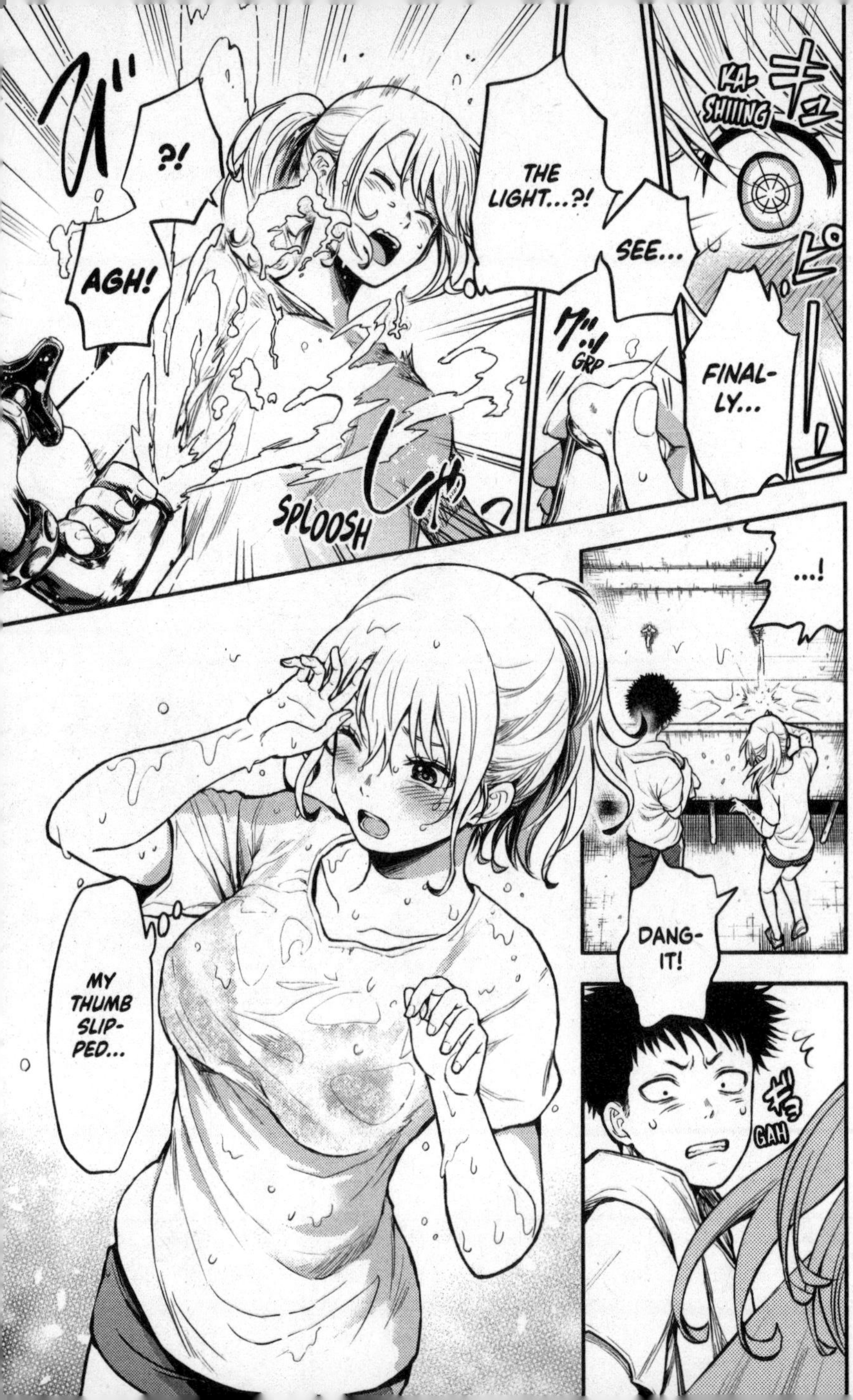
KA-SHIIING
FINAL-LY...
SEE...
GRP
THE LIGHT...?!
?!
AGH!
SPLOOSH
...!
DANG-IT!
GAH
MY THUMB SLIP-PED...

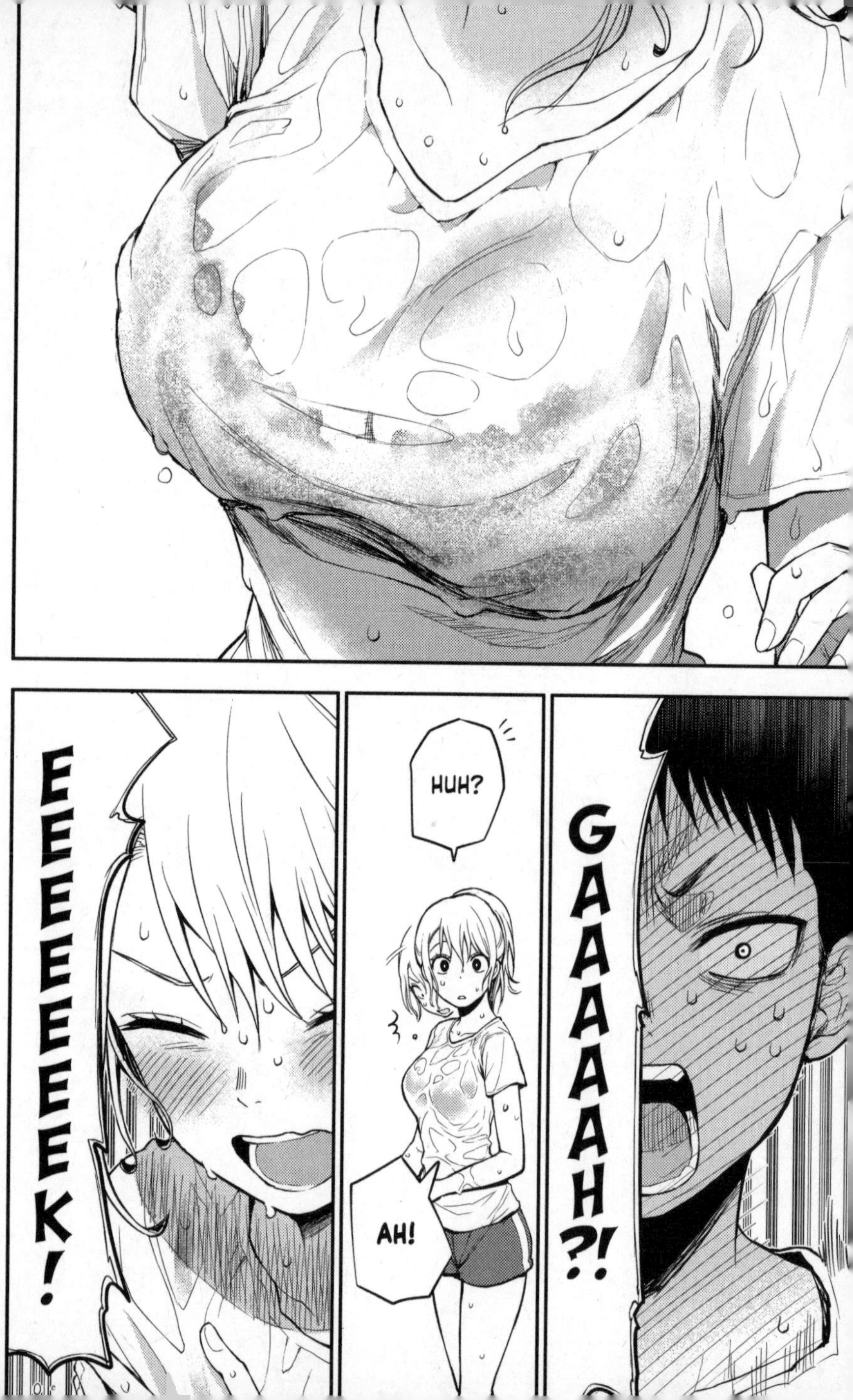
GAAAAAH?!
HUH?
AH!
EEEEEEEK!

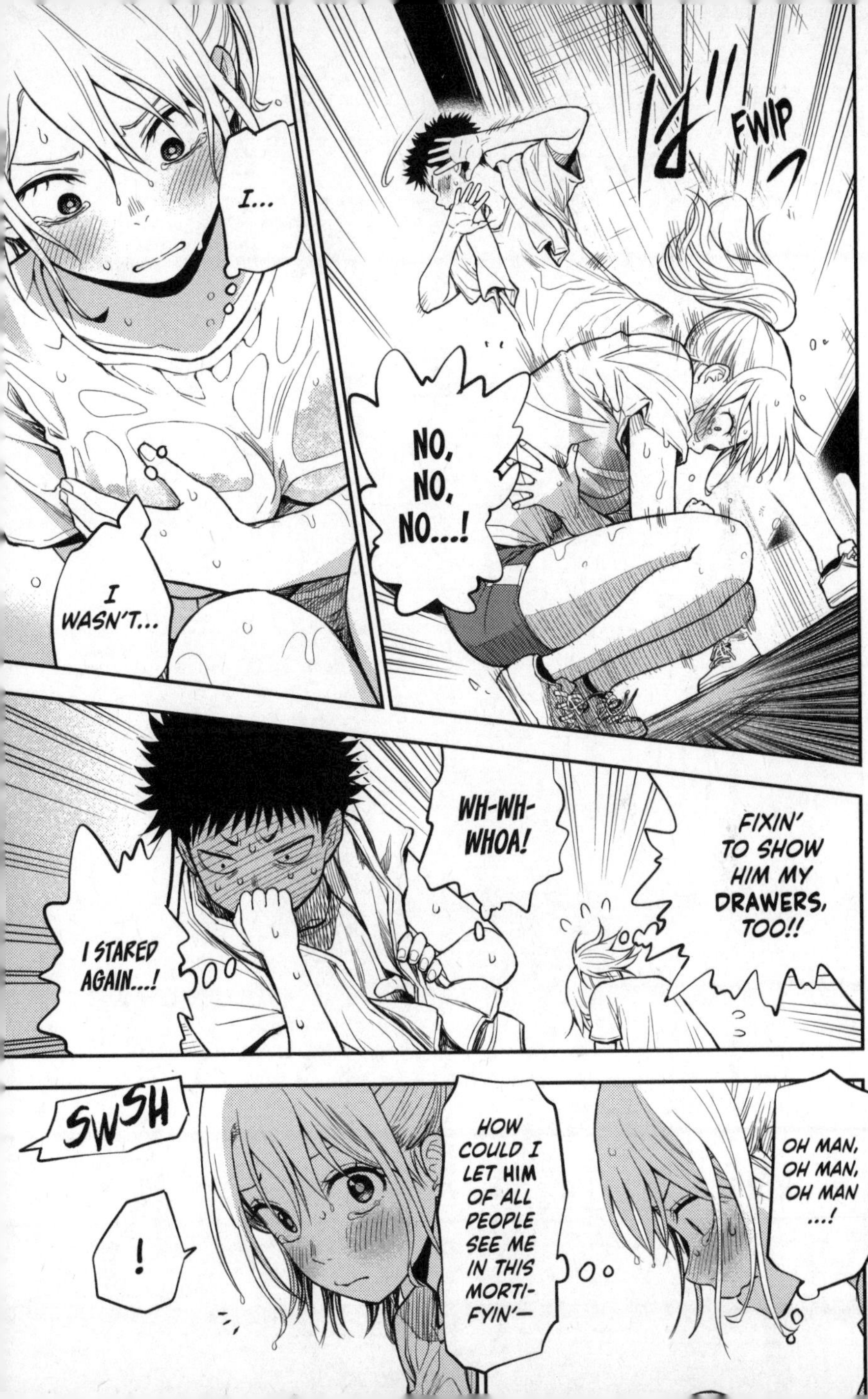
ばっ
FWIP
NO, NO, NO...!
I...
I WASN'T...
FIXIN' TO SHOW HIM MY DRAWERS, TOO!!
WH-WH-WHOA!
I STARED AGAIN...!
OH MAN, OH MAN, OH MAN ...!
HOW COULD I LET HIM OF ALL PEOPLE SEE ME IN THIS MORTI-FYIN'—
SWSH
!

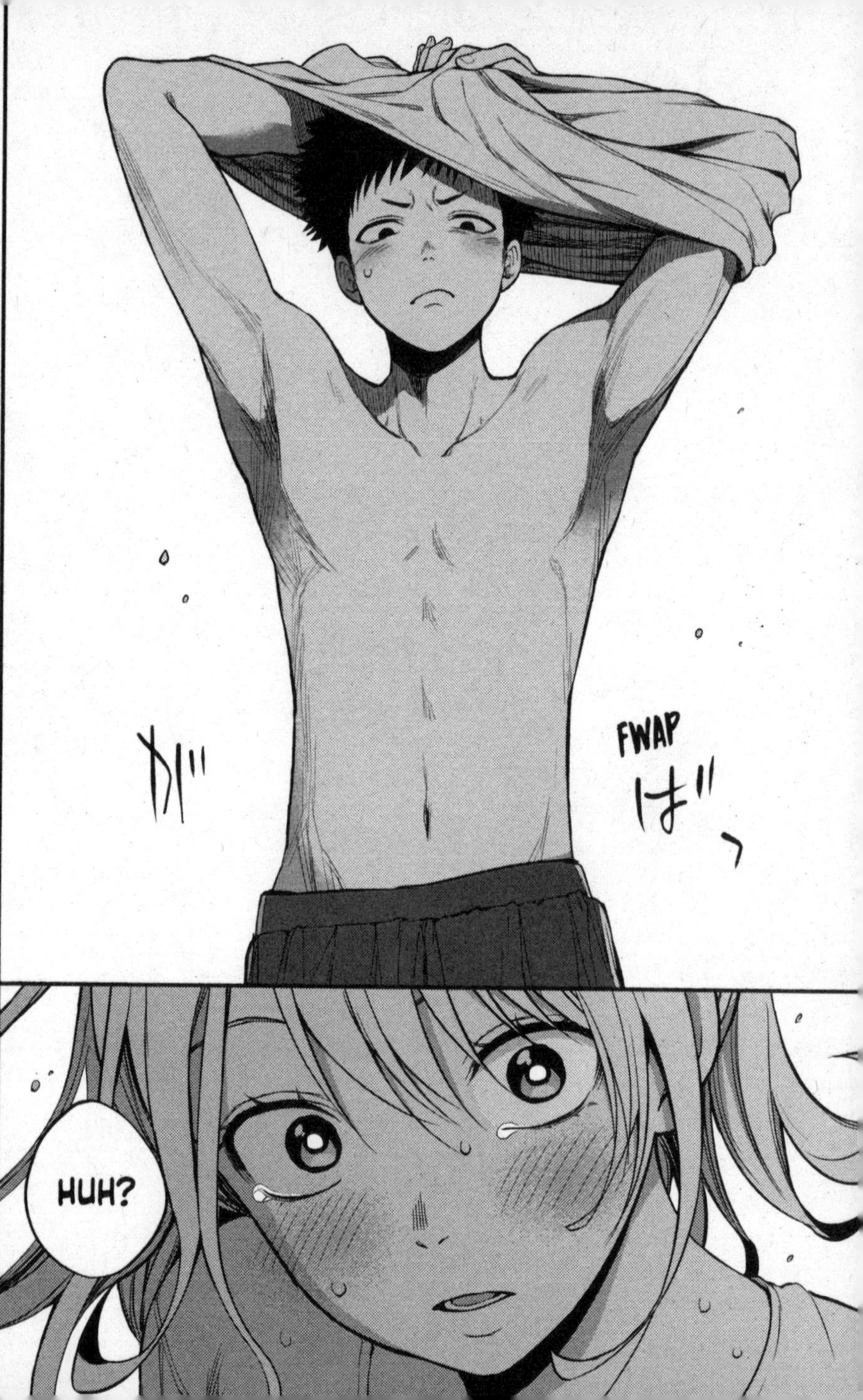
FWAP
HUH?

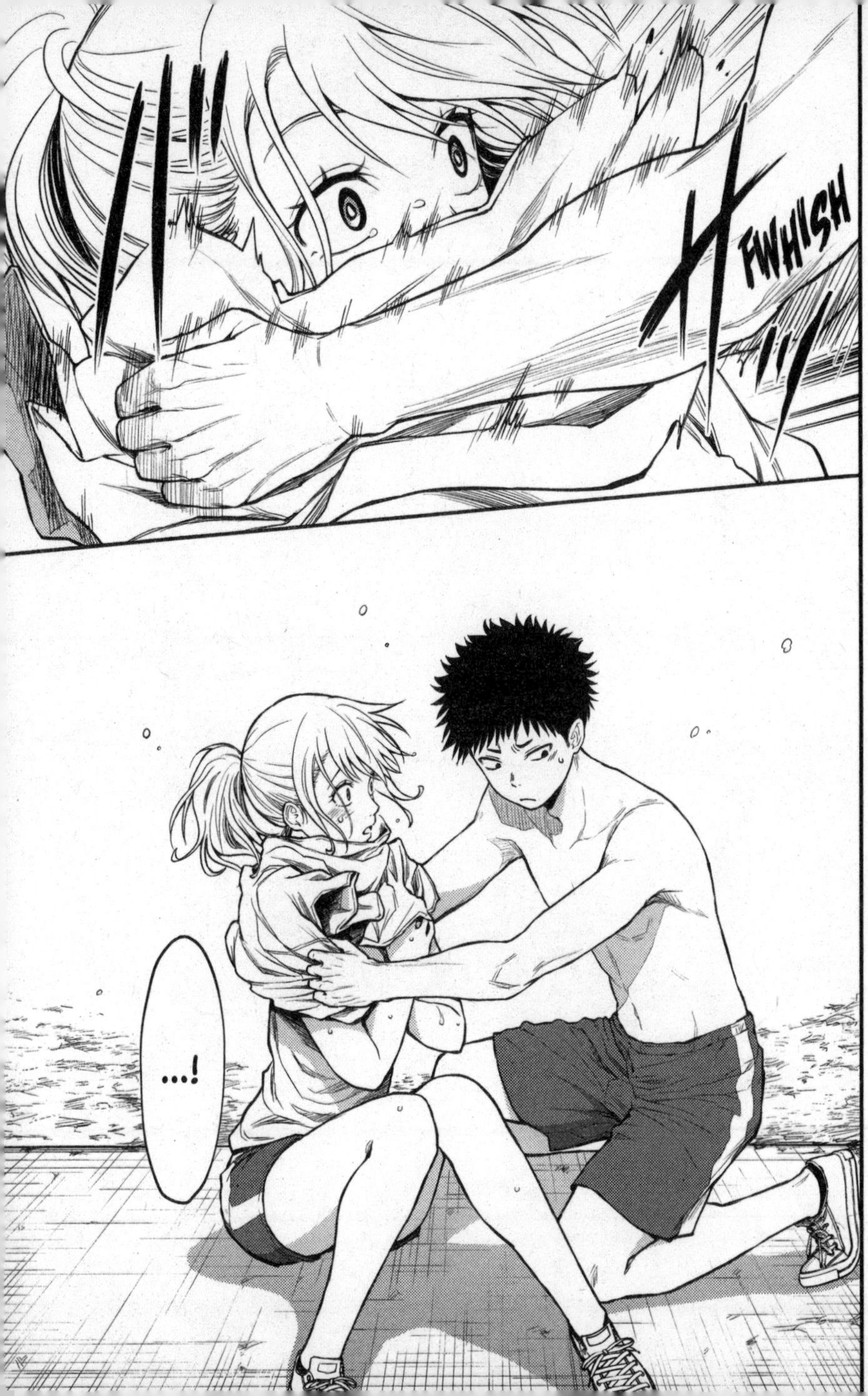
FWHISH
...!

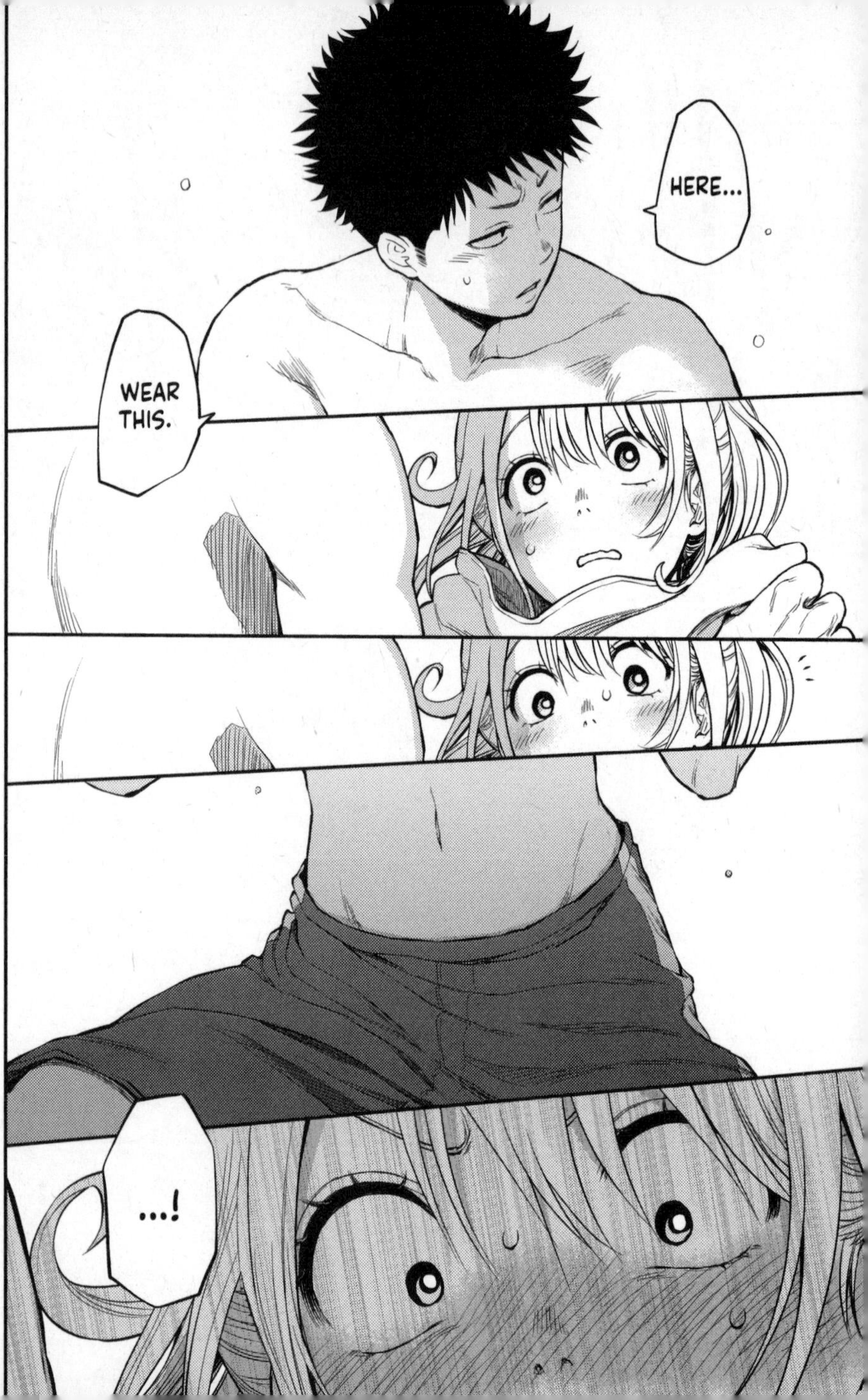
HERE...
WEAR THIS.
...!

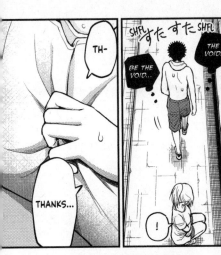

TH-

THANKS...

SHFL すたすた SHFL

BE THE VOID...

THE VOID.

!

I'M GOING BACK...

FWP ぱっ

IT'S NOTH-ING...

63

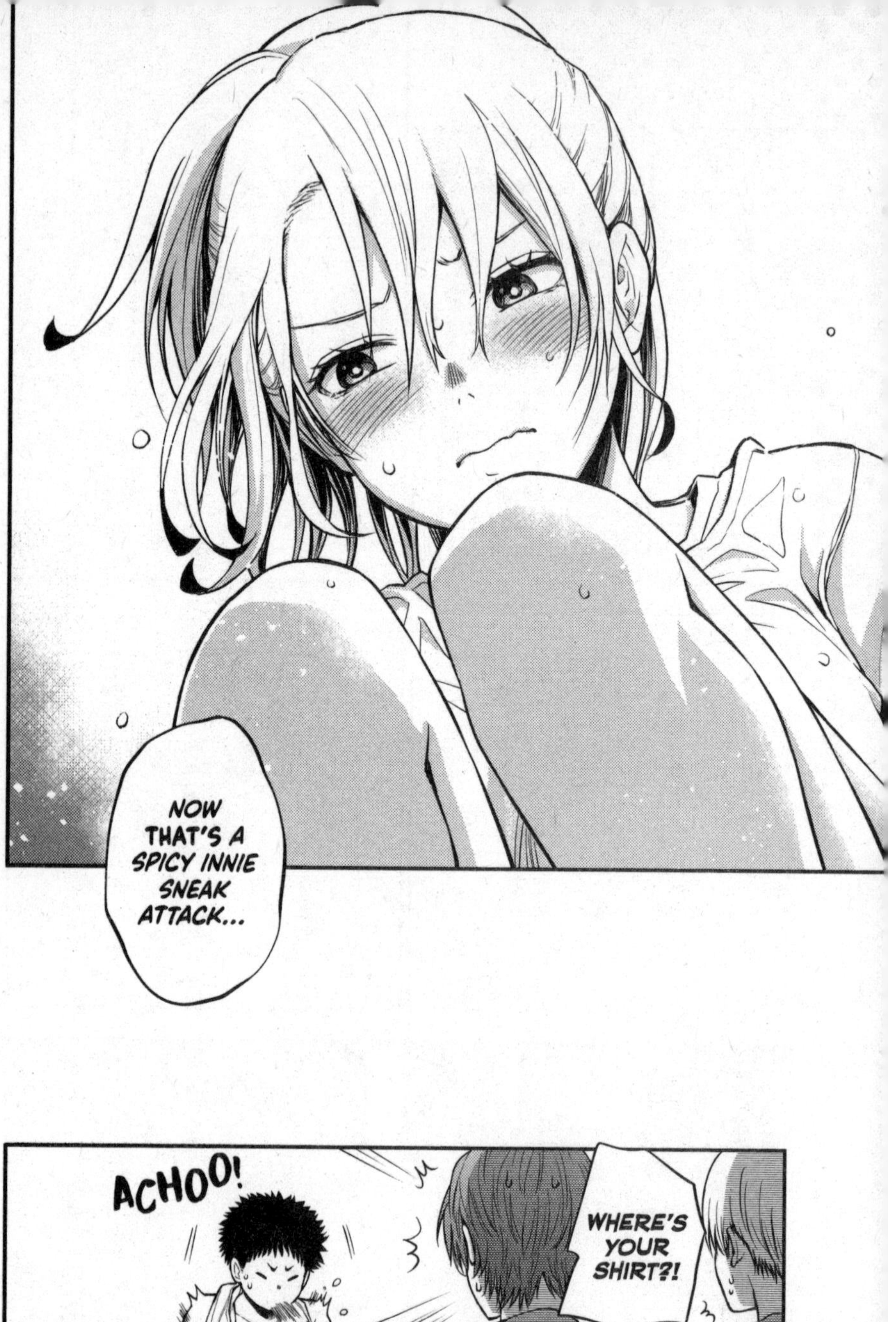
NOW THAT'S A SPICY INNIE SNEAK ATTACK...
WHERE'S YOUR SHIRT?!
ACHOO!

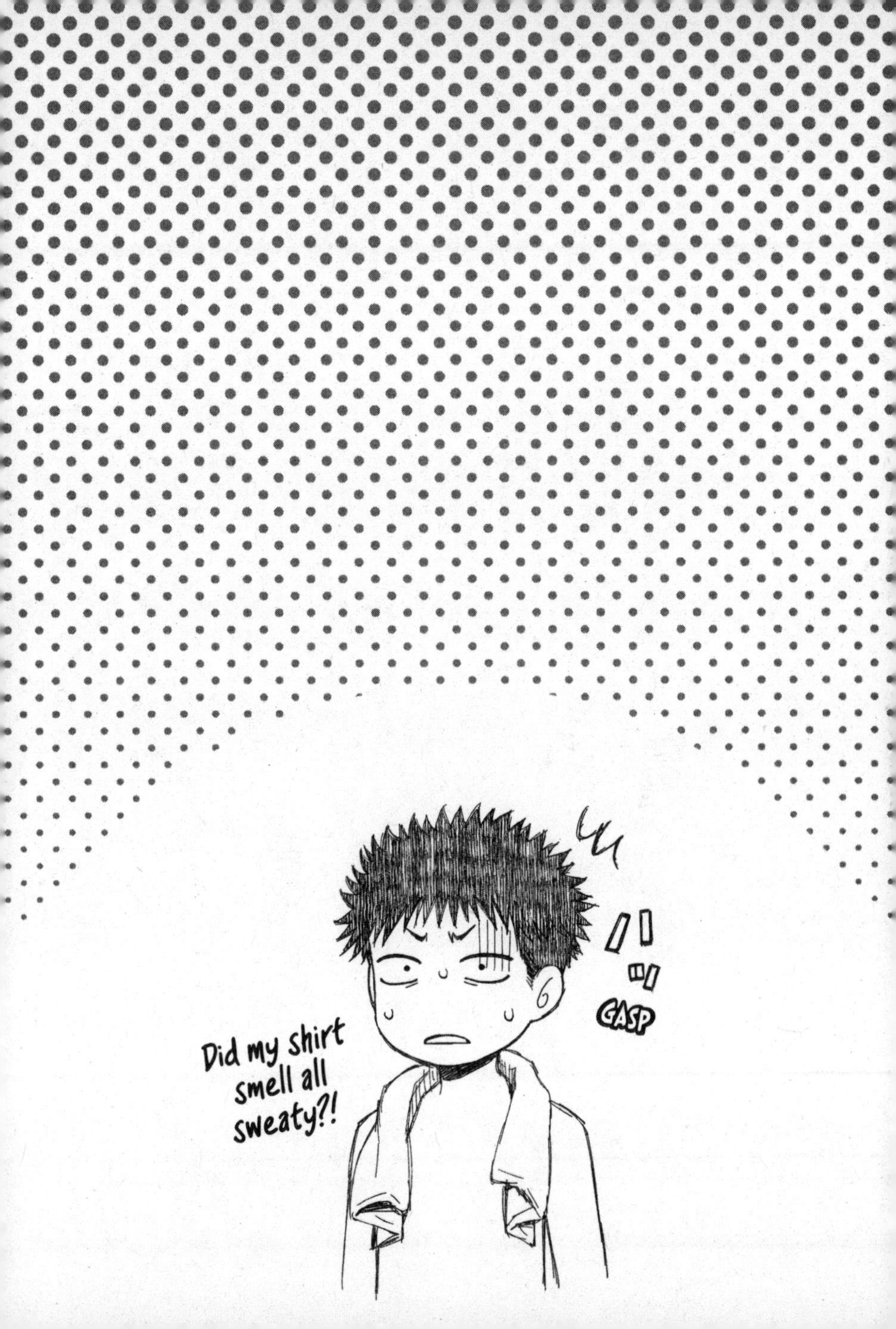
GASP
Did my shirt smell all sweaty?!

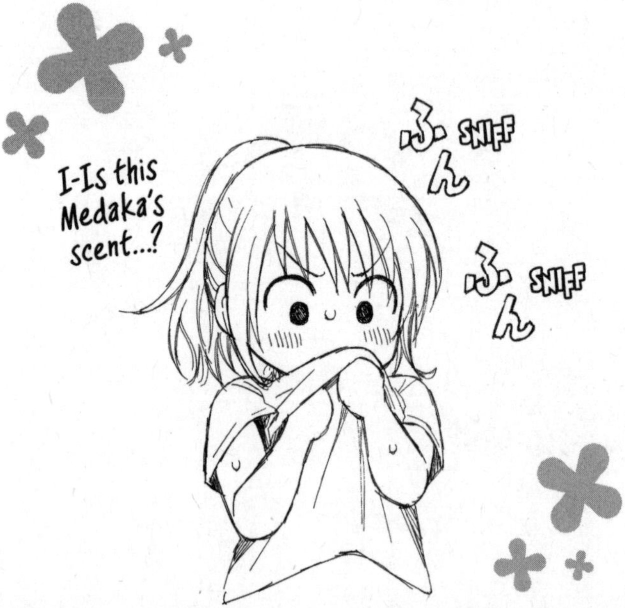
ふん SNIFF
ふん SNIFF
I-Is this Medaka's scent...?

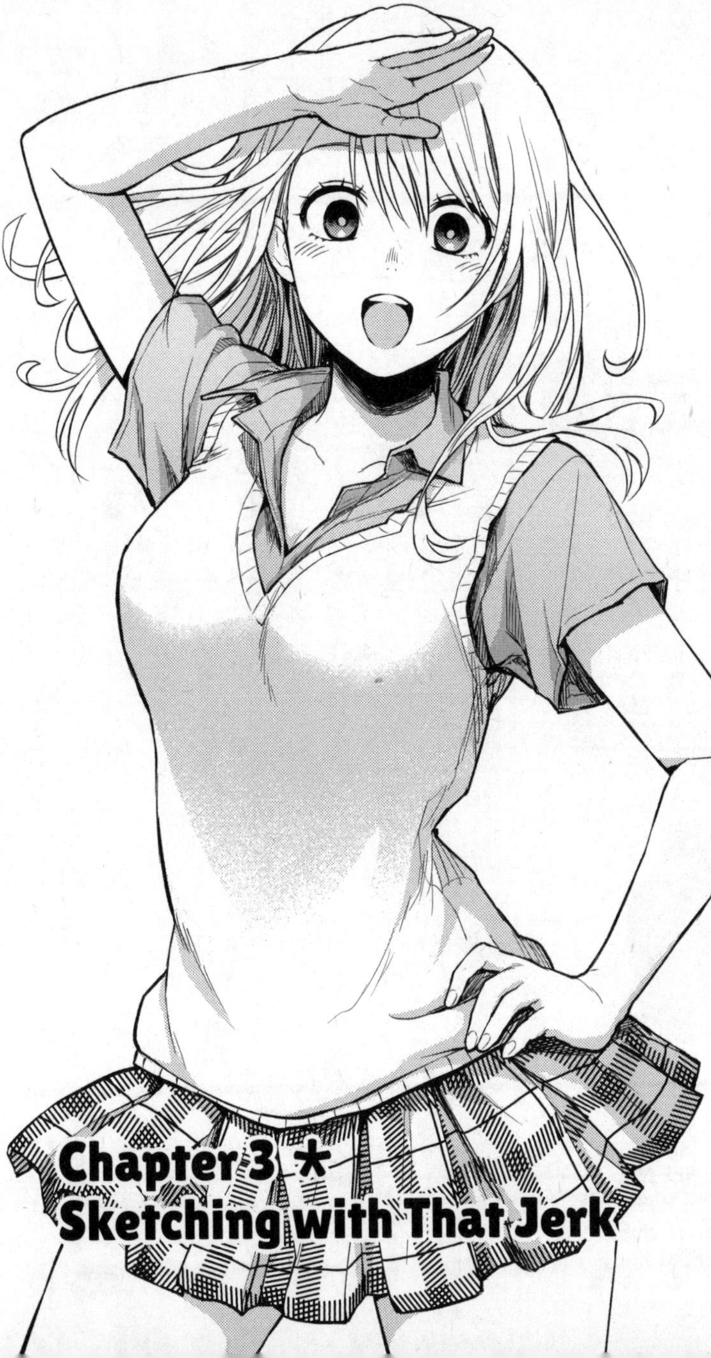

Chapter 3 ★ Sketching with That Jerk

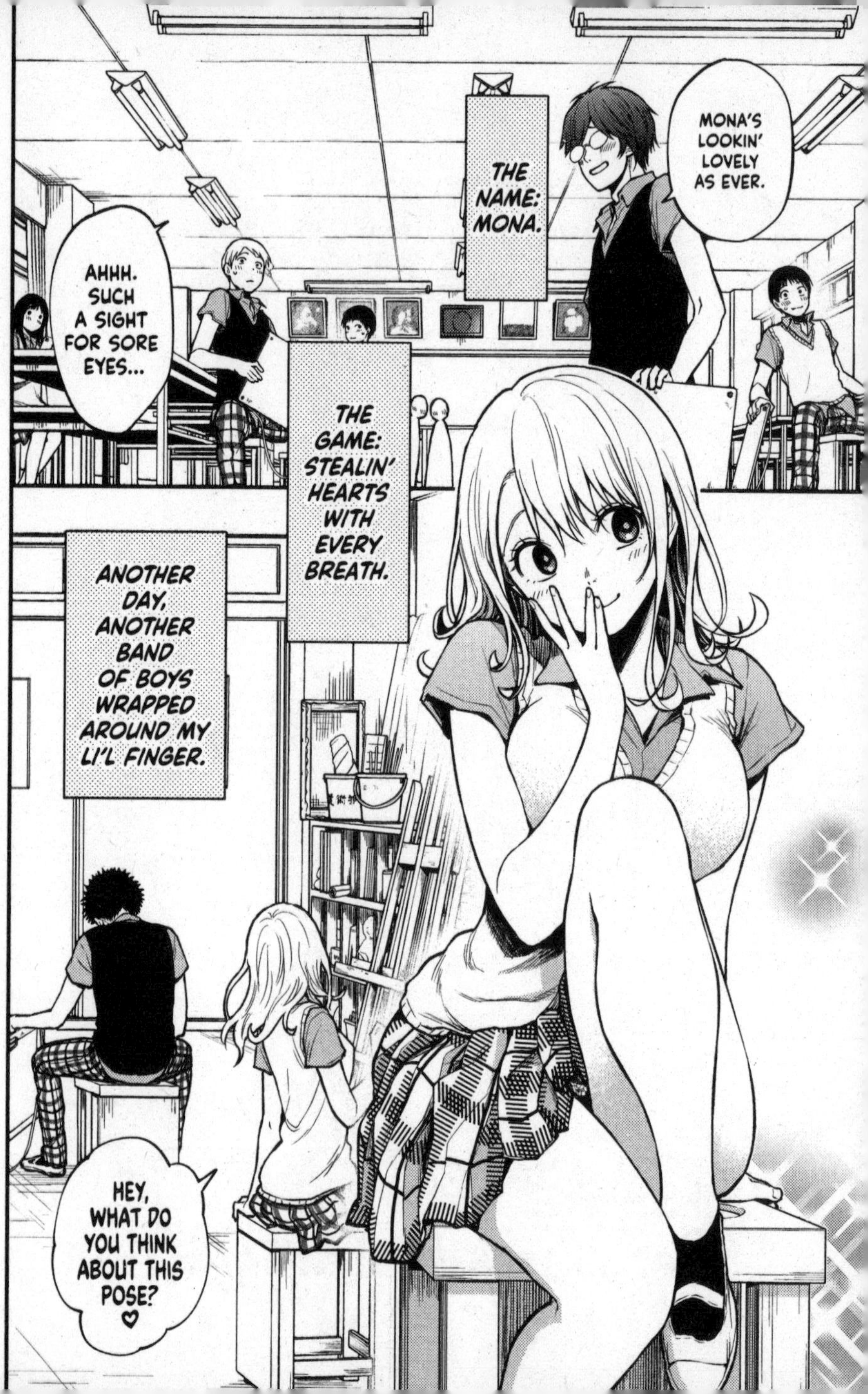
MONA'S LOOKIN' LOVELY AS EVER.
THE NAME: MONA.
AHHH. SUCH A SIGHT FOR SORE EYES...
THE GAME: STEALIN' HEARTS WITH EVERY BREATH.
ANOTHER DAY, ANOTHER BAND OF BOYS WRAPPED AROUND MY LI'L FINGER.
HEY, WHAT DO YOU THINK ABOUT THIS POSE? ♡

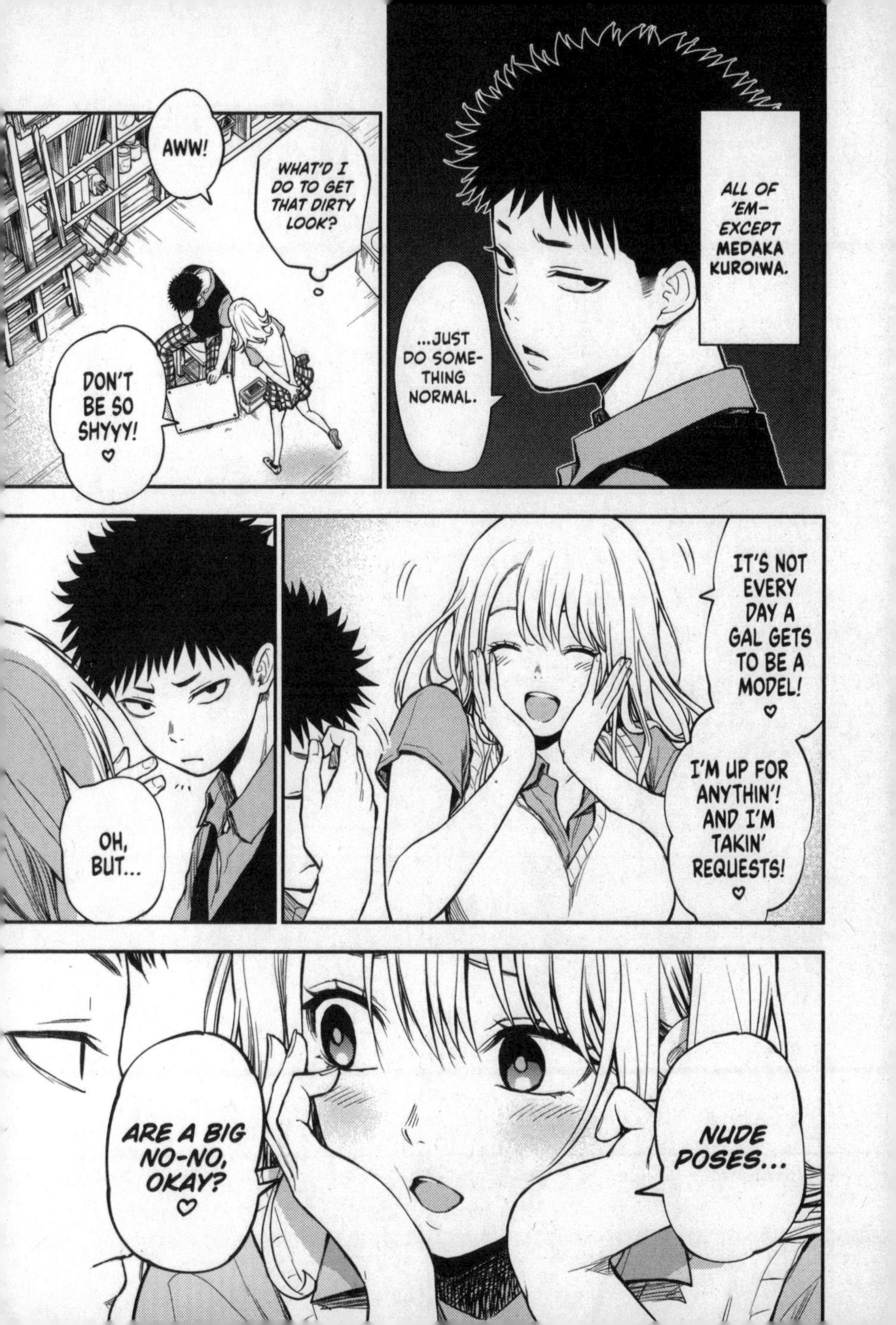
ALL OF 'EM— EXCEPT MEDAKA KUROIWA.
...JUST DO SOME-THING NORMAL.
AWW!
WHAT'D I DO TO GET THAT DIRTY LOOK?
DON'T BE SO SHYYY! ♡
IT'S NOT EVERY DAY A GAL GETS TO BE A MODEL! ♡
I'M UP FOR ANYTHIN'! AND I'M TAKIN' REQUESTS! ♡
OH, BUT...
NUDE POSES...
ARE A BIG NO-NO, OKAY? ♡

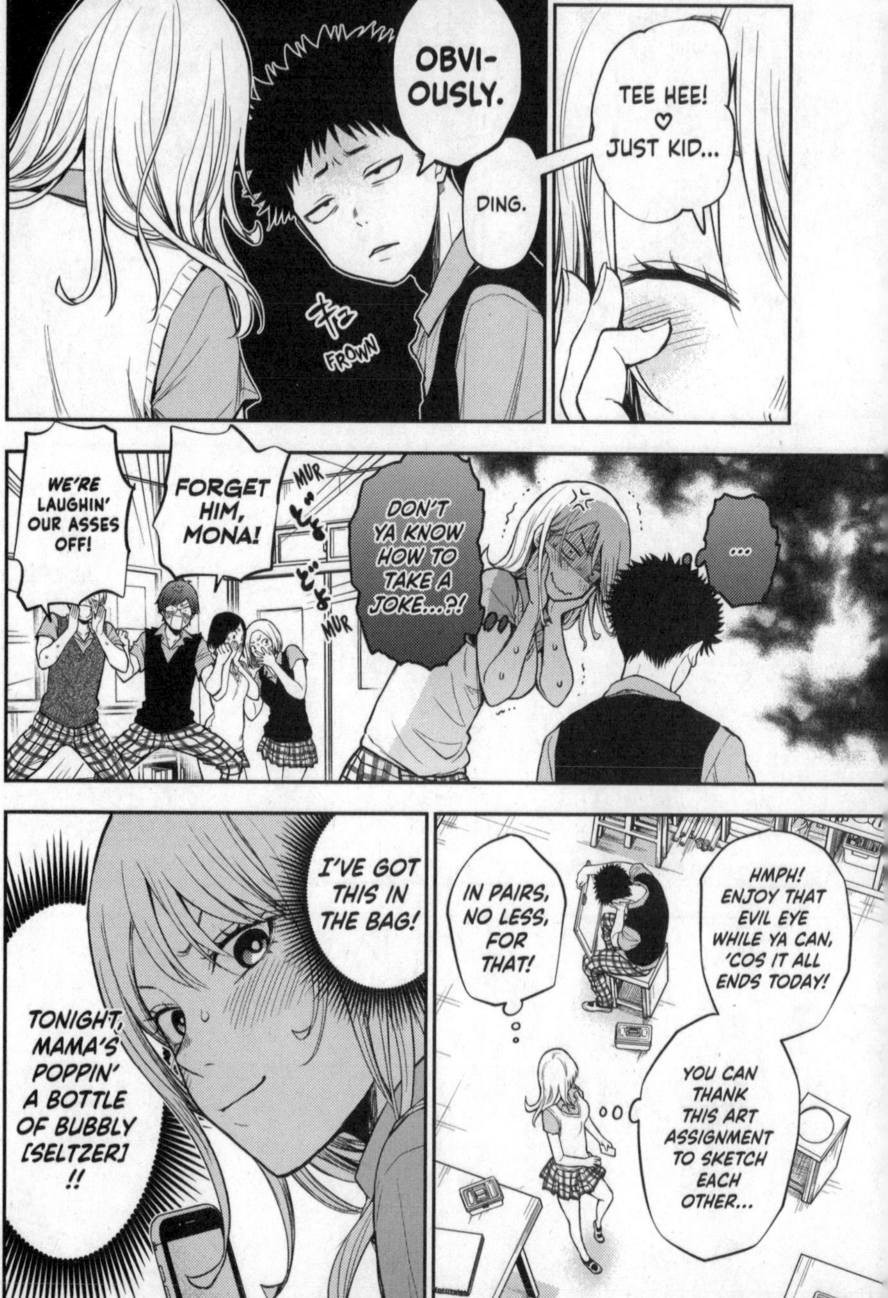
TEE HEE! ♡ JUST KID...
DING.
OBVI-OUSLY.
FROWN
...
DON'T YA KNOW HOW TO TAKE A JOKE...?!
MUR MUR
FORGET HIM, MONA!
WE'RE LAUGHIN' OUR ASSES OFF!
HMPH! ENJOY THAT EVIL EYE WHILE YA CAN, 'COS IT ALL ENDS TODAY!
IN PAIRS, NO LESS, FOR THAT!
YOU CAN THANK THIS ART ASSIGNMENT TO SKETCH EACH OTHER...
I'VE GOT THIS IN THE BAG!
TONIGHT, MAMA'S POPPIN' A BOTTLE OF BUBBLY [SELTZER] !!

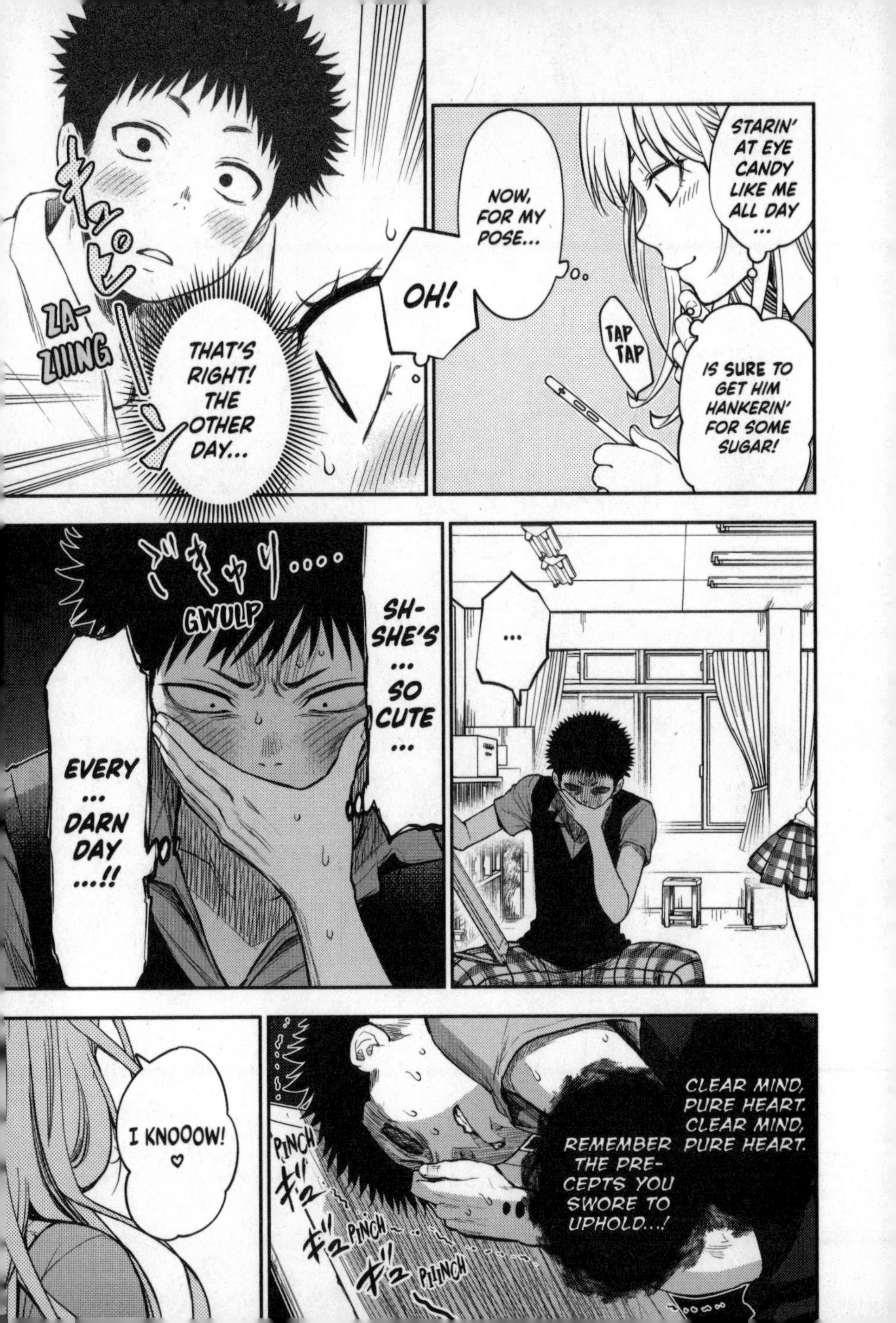
STARIN' AT EYE CANDY LIKE ME ALL DAY ...
IS SURE TO GET HIM HANKERIN' FOR SOME SUGAR!
TAP TAP
NOW, FOR MY POSE...
OH!
THAT'S RIGHT! THE OTHER DAY...
ZA-ZIIING
...
ごきゅり。。。。
GWULP
SH-SHE'S ... SO CUTE ...
EVERY ... DARN DAY ...!!
CLEAR MIND, PURE HEART. CLEAR MIND, PURE HEART.
REMEMBER THE PRE-CEPTS YOU SWORE TO UPHOLD...!
PINCH
PINCH
PIIINCH
I KNOOOW! ♥

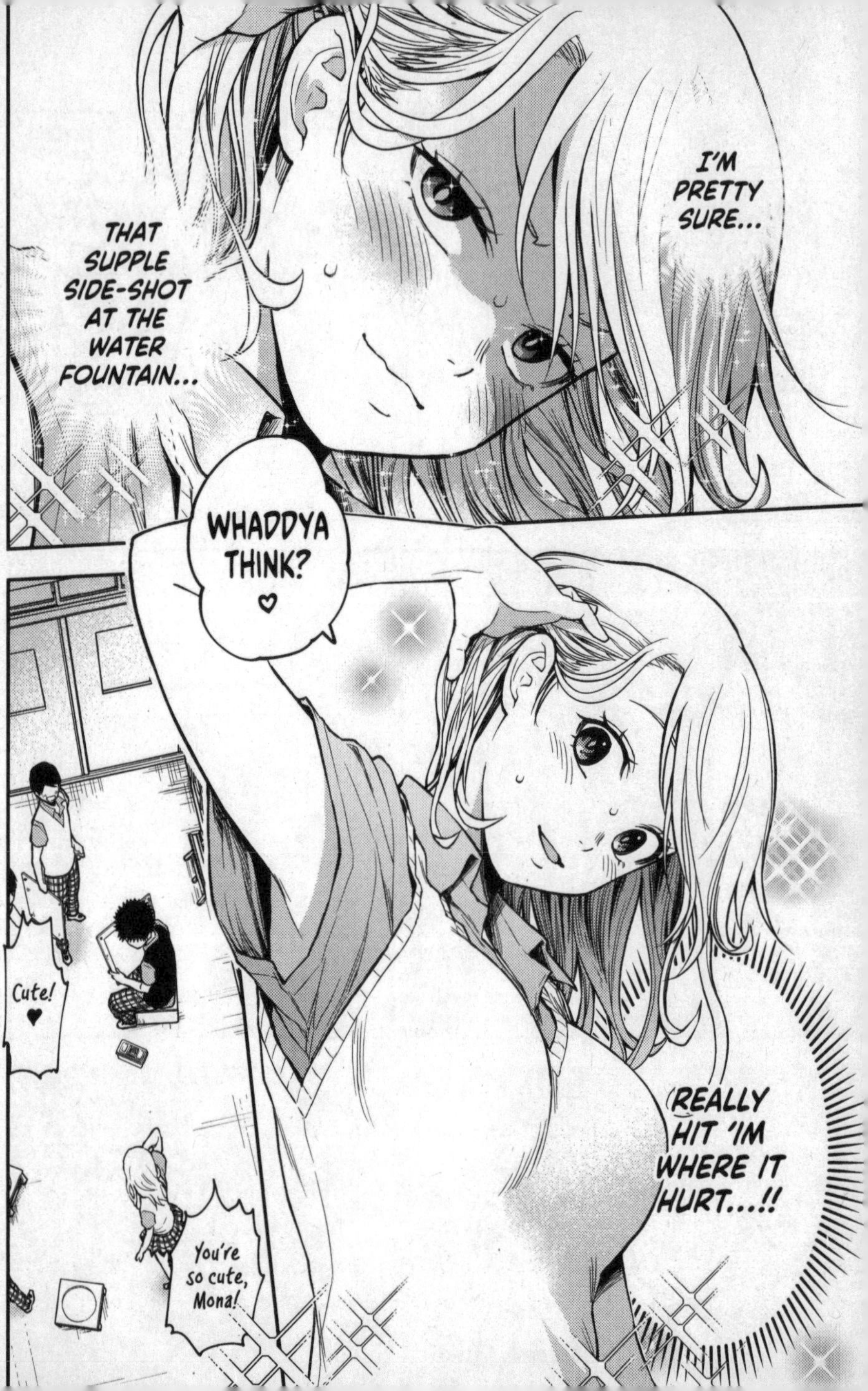
I'M PRETTY SURE...
THAT SUPPLE SIDE-SHOT AT THE WATER FOUNTAIN...
WHADDYA THINK? ♡
REALLY HIT 'IM WHERE IT HURT...!!
Cute! ♥
You're so cute, Mona!

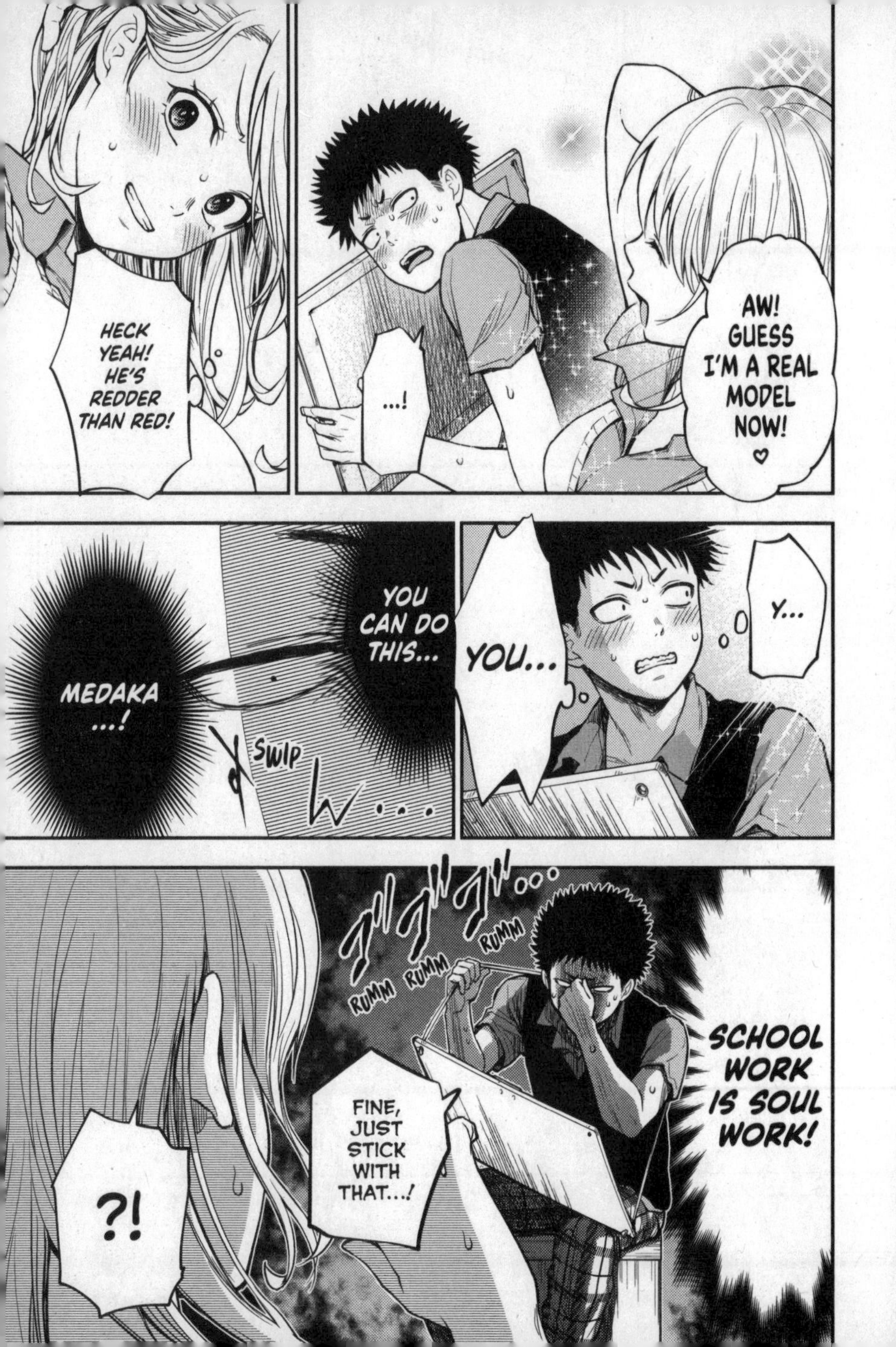
AW! GUESS I'M A REAL MODEL NOW! ♡
...!
HECK YEAH! HE'S REDDER THAN RED!
Y...
YOU...
YOU CAN DO THIS...
MEDAKA ...!
SWIP
W...
SCHOOL WORK IS SOUL WORK!
RUMM RUMM RUMM
FINE, JUST STICK WITH THAT...!
?!

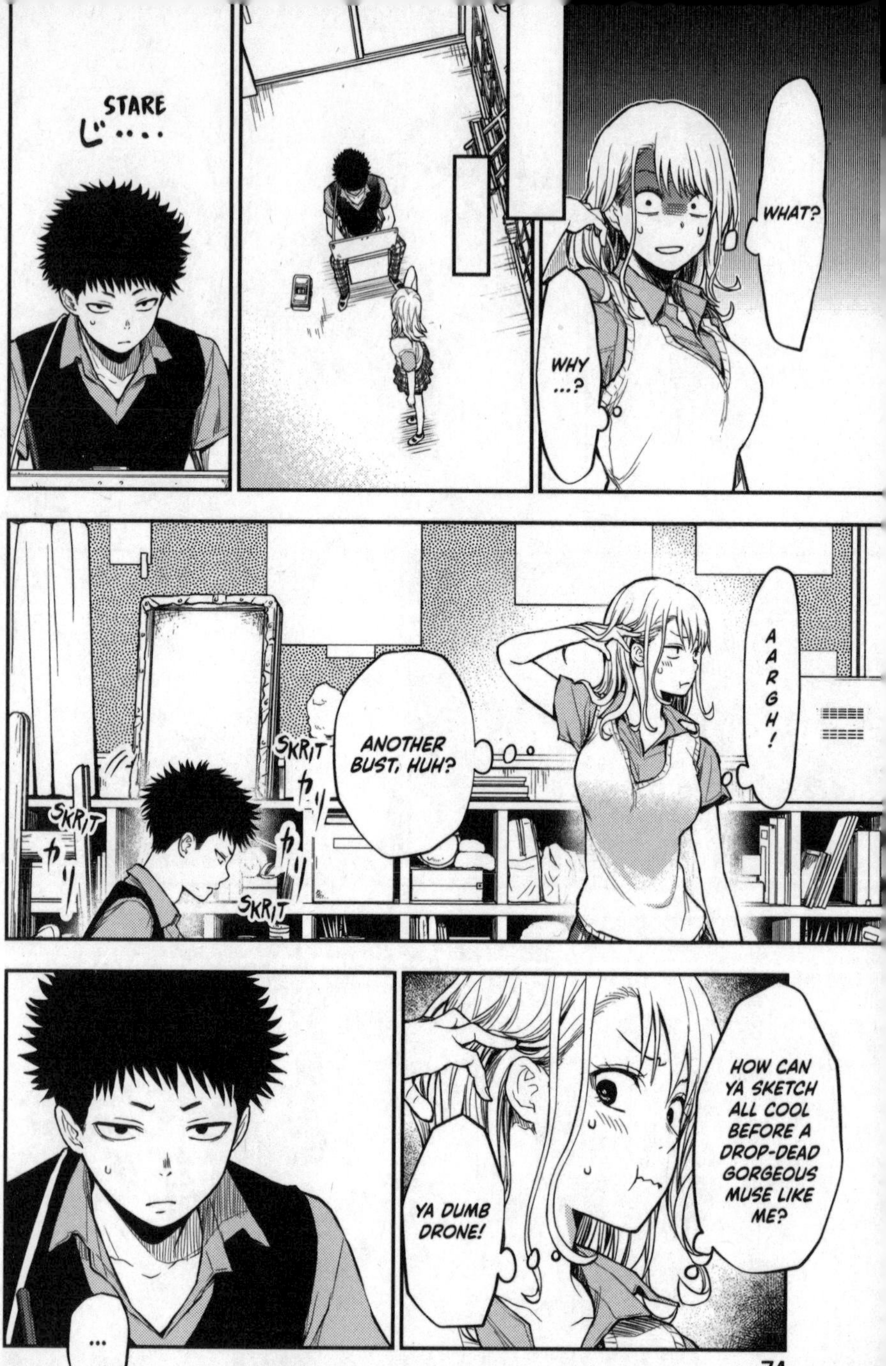
WHAT?
WHY ...?
STARE じ....
AARGH!
ANOTHER BUST, HUH?
SKRIT カリ
SKRIT カリ
SKRIT カリ
HOW CAN YA SKETCH ALL COOL BEFORE A DROP-DEAD GORGEOUS MUSE LIKE ME?
YA DUMB DRONE!
...

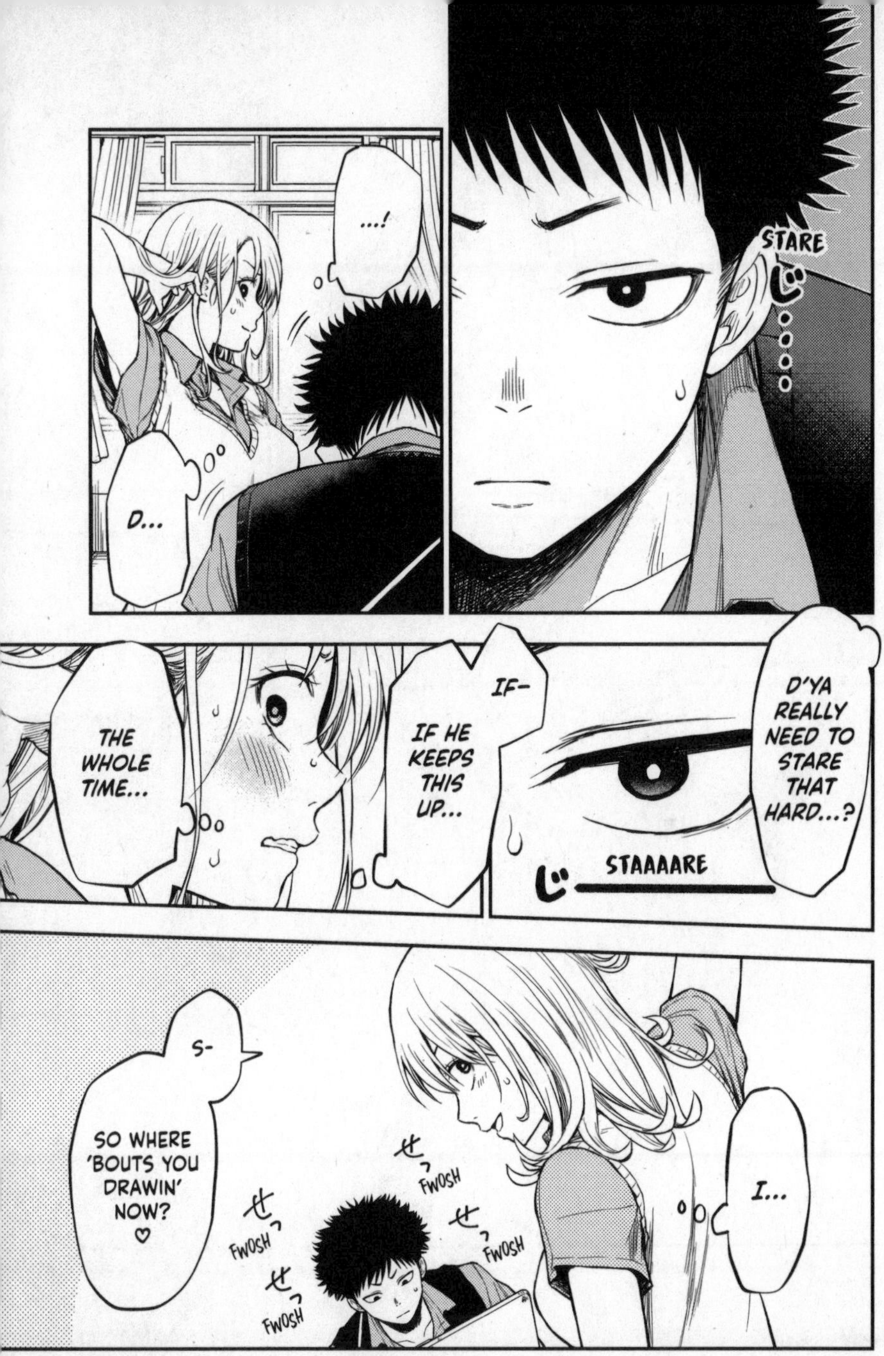
STARE
じ
...!
D...
D'YA REALLY NEED TO STARE THAT HARD...?
じ STAAAARE
IF-
IF HE KEEPS THIS UP...
THE WHOLE TIME...
I...
S-
SO WHERE 'BOUTS YOU DRAWIN' NOW? ♡
せっ FWOSH
せっ FWOSH
せっ FWOSH
せっ FWOSH

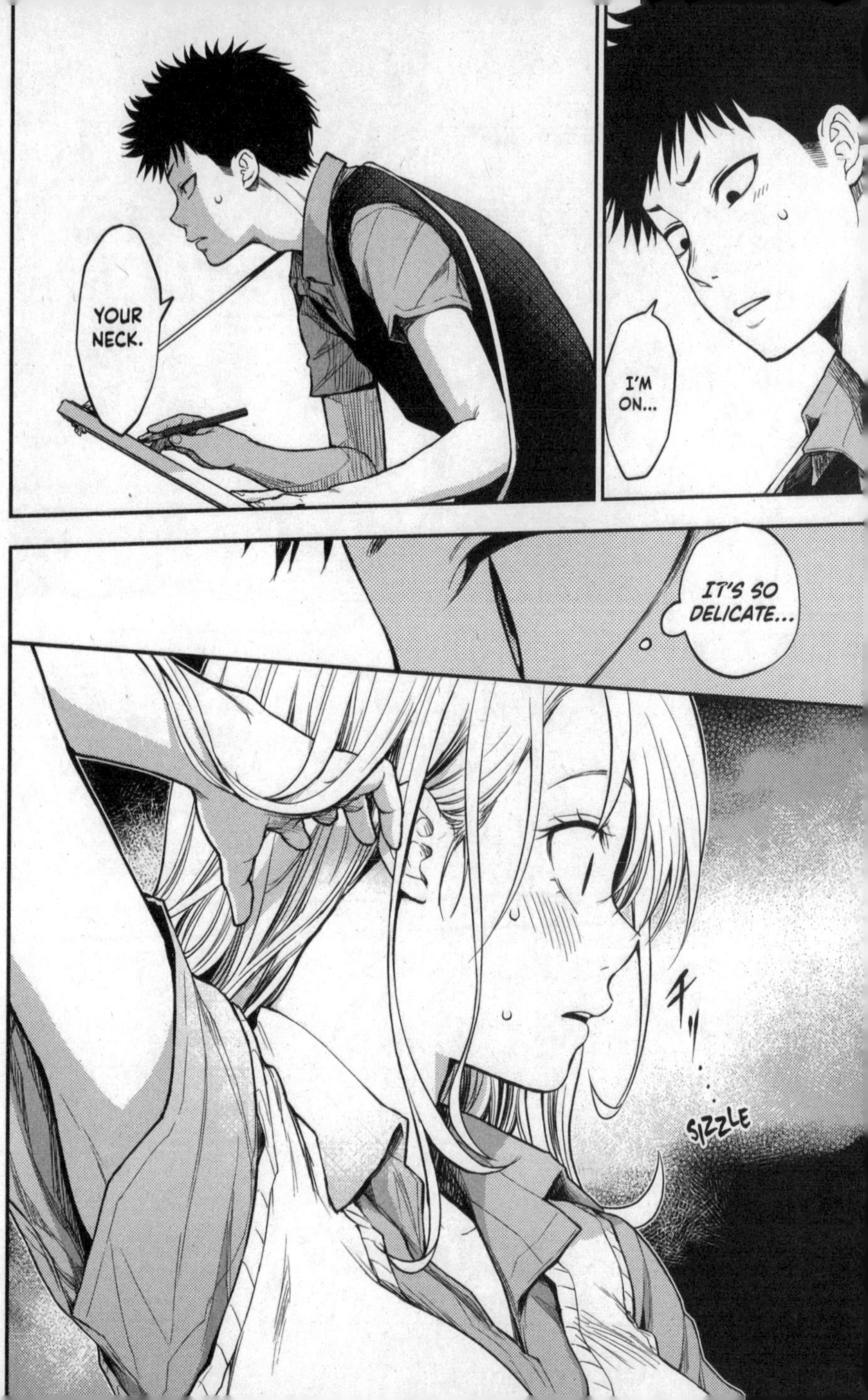
I'M ON...
YOUR NECK.
IT'S SO DELICATE...
SIZZLE

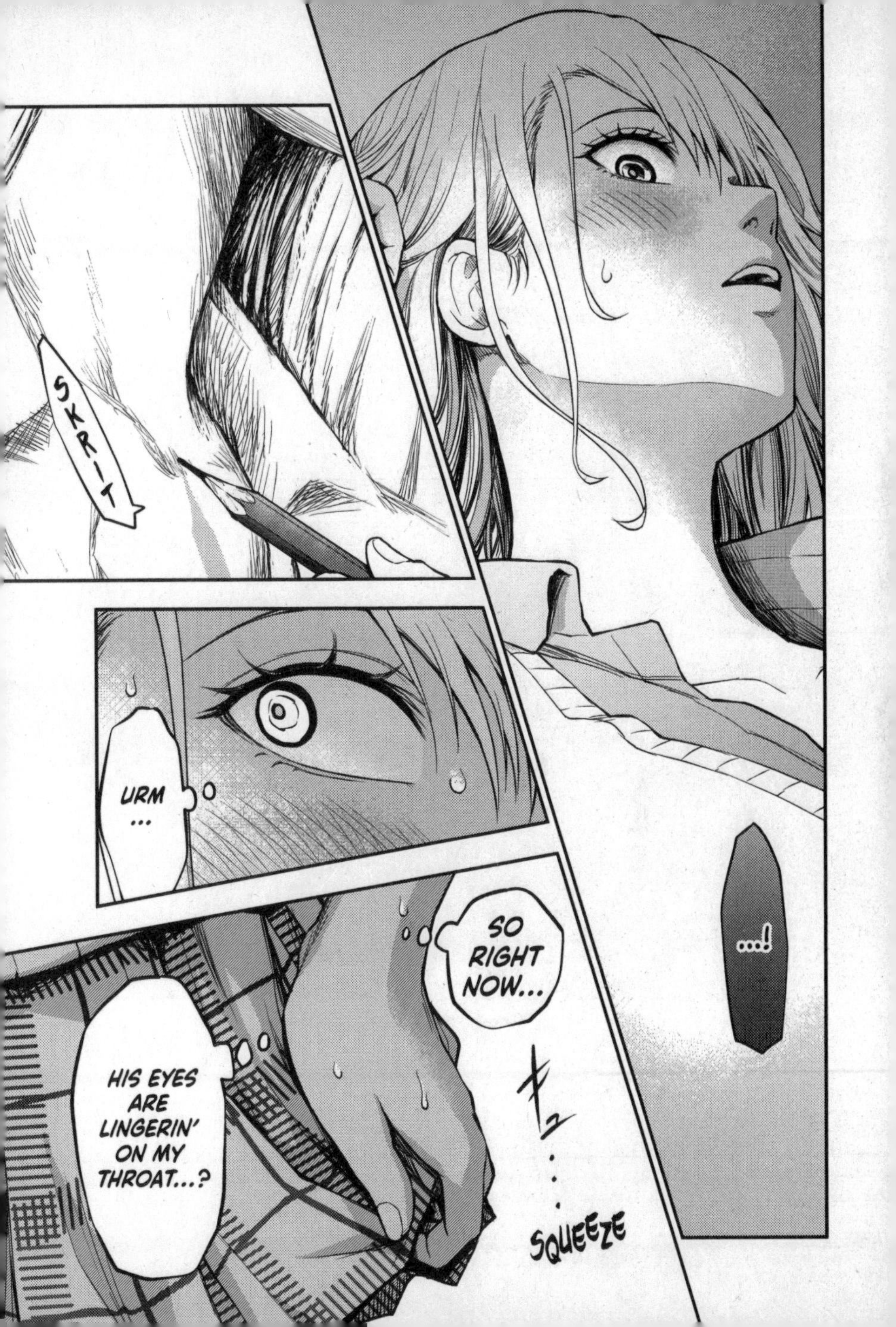
...!
SKRIT
URM ...
SO RIGHT NOW...
HIS EYES ARE LINGERIN' ON MY THROAT...?
SQUEEZE

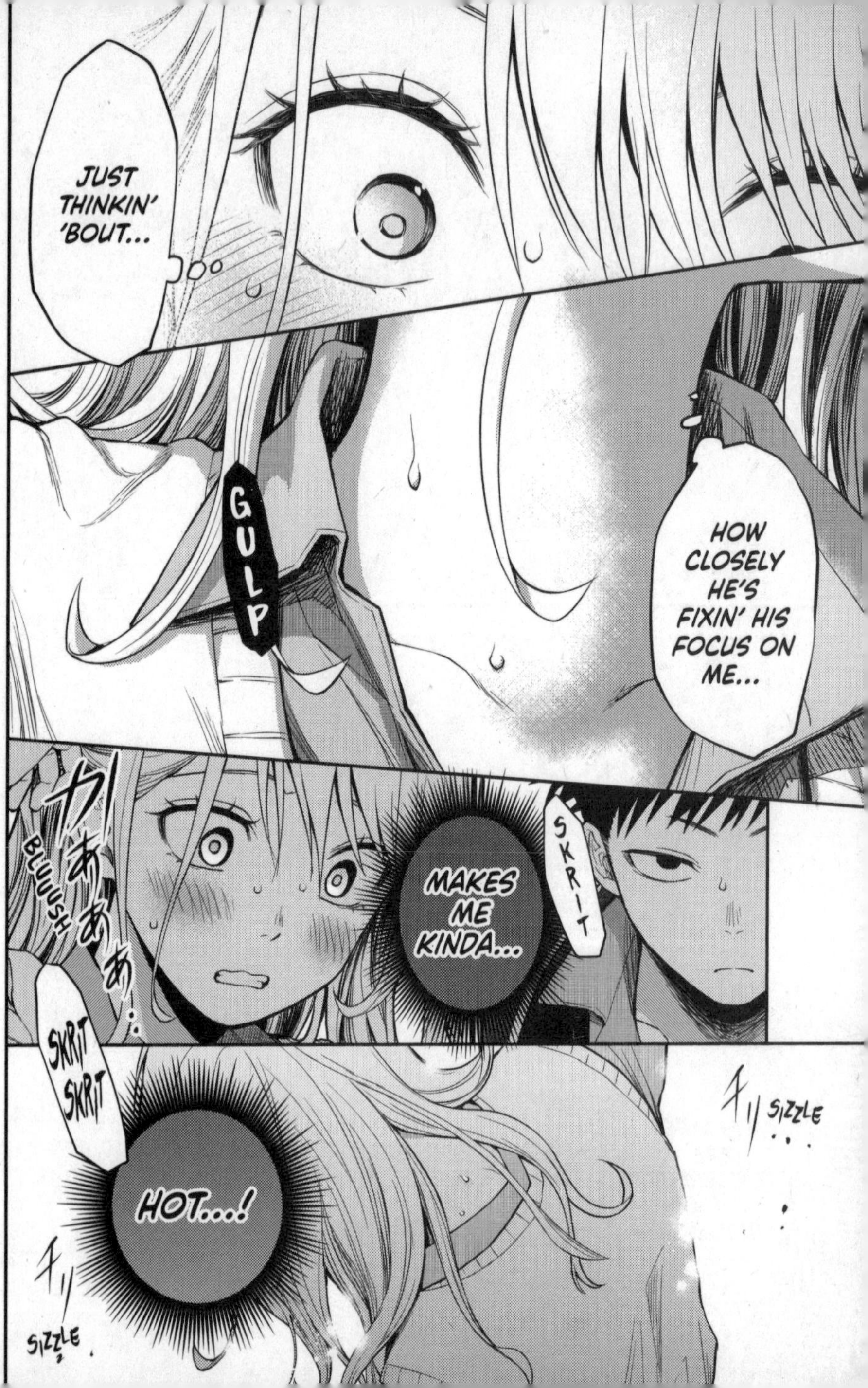
JUST THINKIN' 'BOUT...
GULP
HOW CLOSELY HE'S FIXIN' HIS FOCUS ON ME...
SKRIT
MAKES ME KINDA...
かぁぁぁ
BLUUUSH
SIZZLE
SKRIT SKRIT
HOT...!
SIZZLE

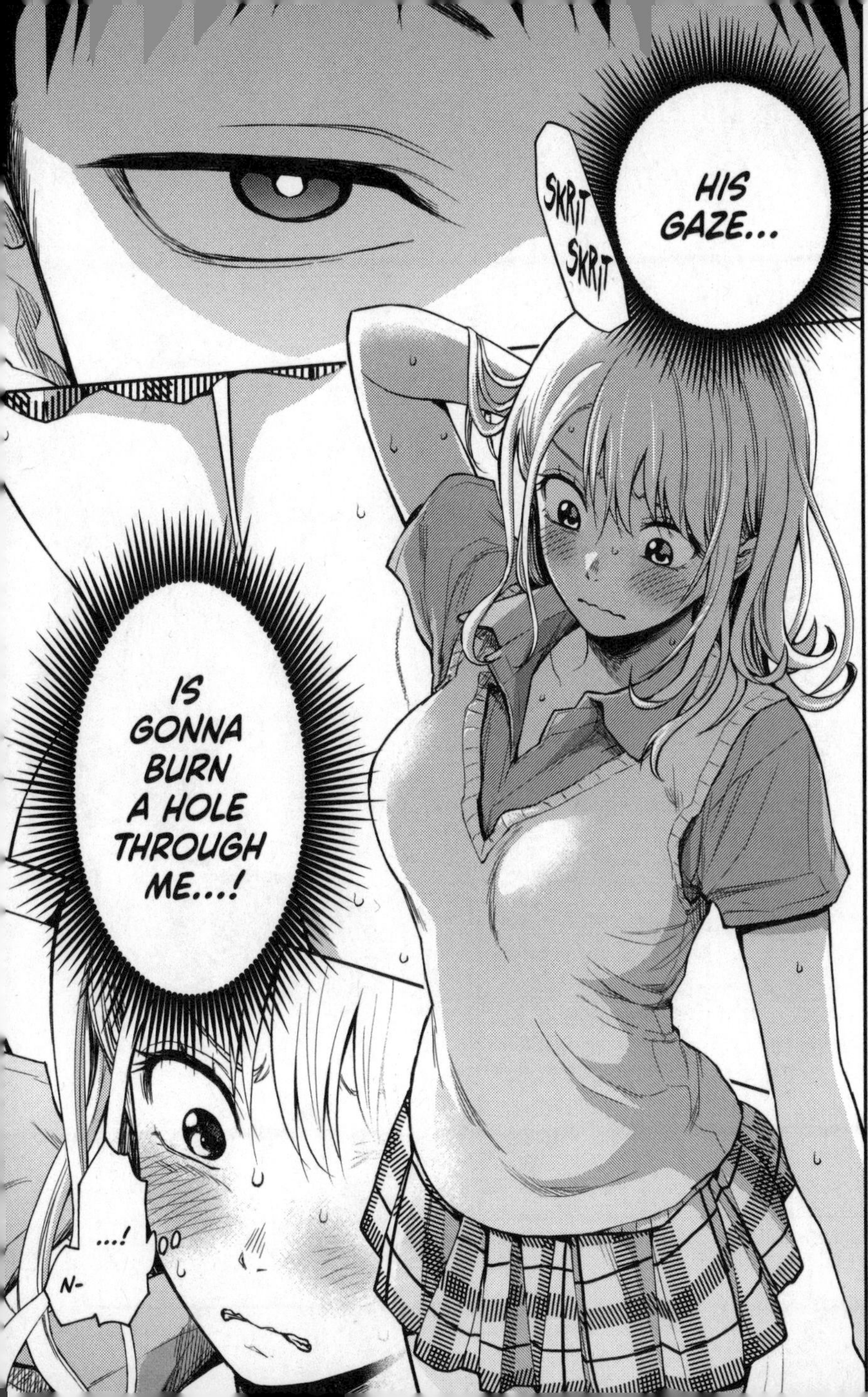
HIS GAZE...
SKRIT SKRIT
IS GONNA BURN A HOLE THROUGH ME...!
...!
N-

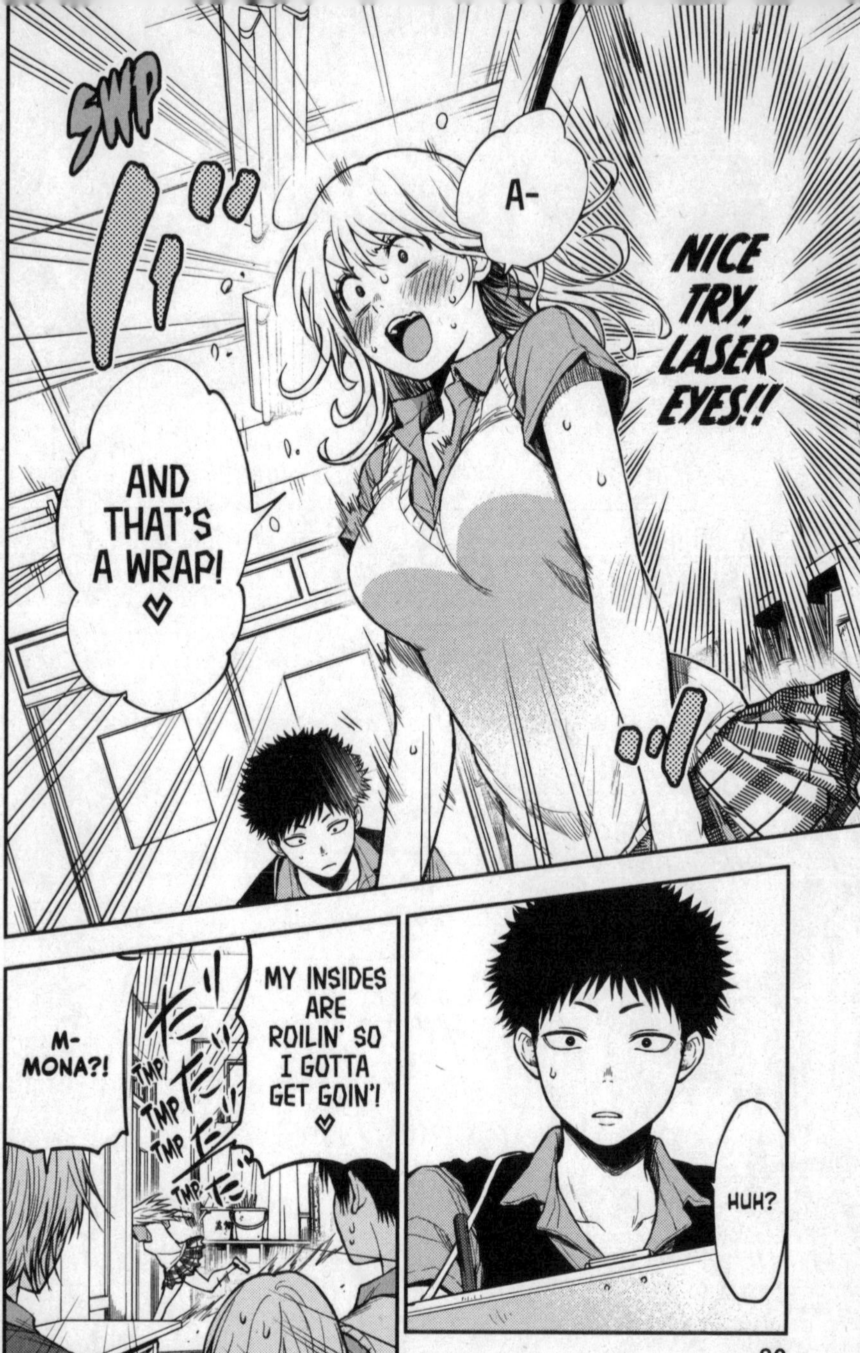
NICE TRY, LASER EYES!!
A-
SWP
AND THAT'S A WRAP! ♡
HUH?
MY INSIDES ARE ROILIN' SO I GOTTA GET GOIN'! ♡
TMP TMP TMP TMP
M-MONA?!

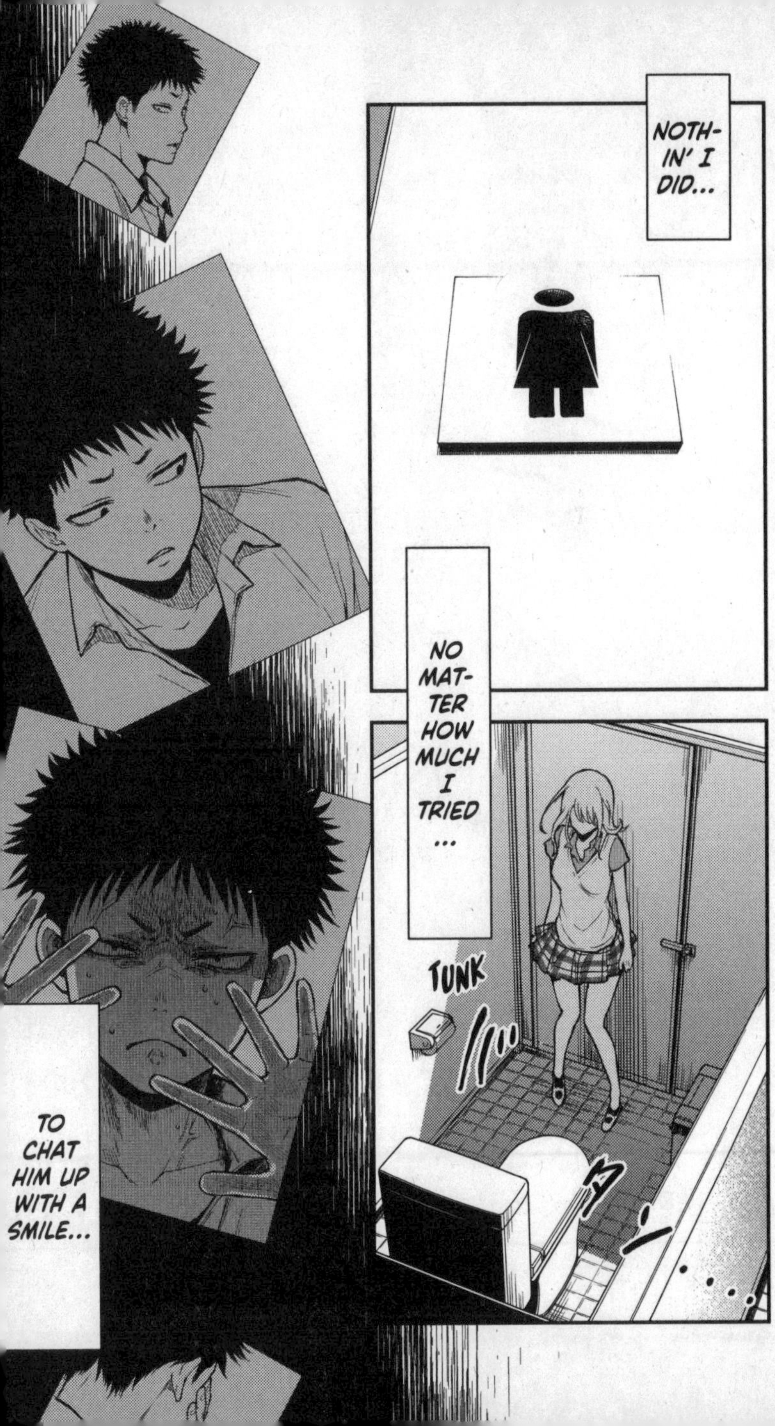
NOTH-IN' I DID...
NO MAT-TER HOW MUCH I TRIED...
TUNK
TO CHAT HIM UP WITH A SMILE...

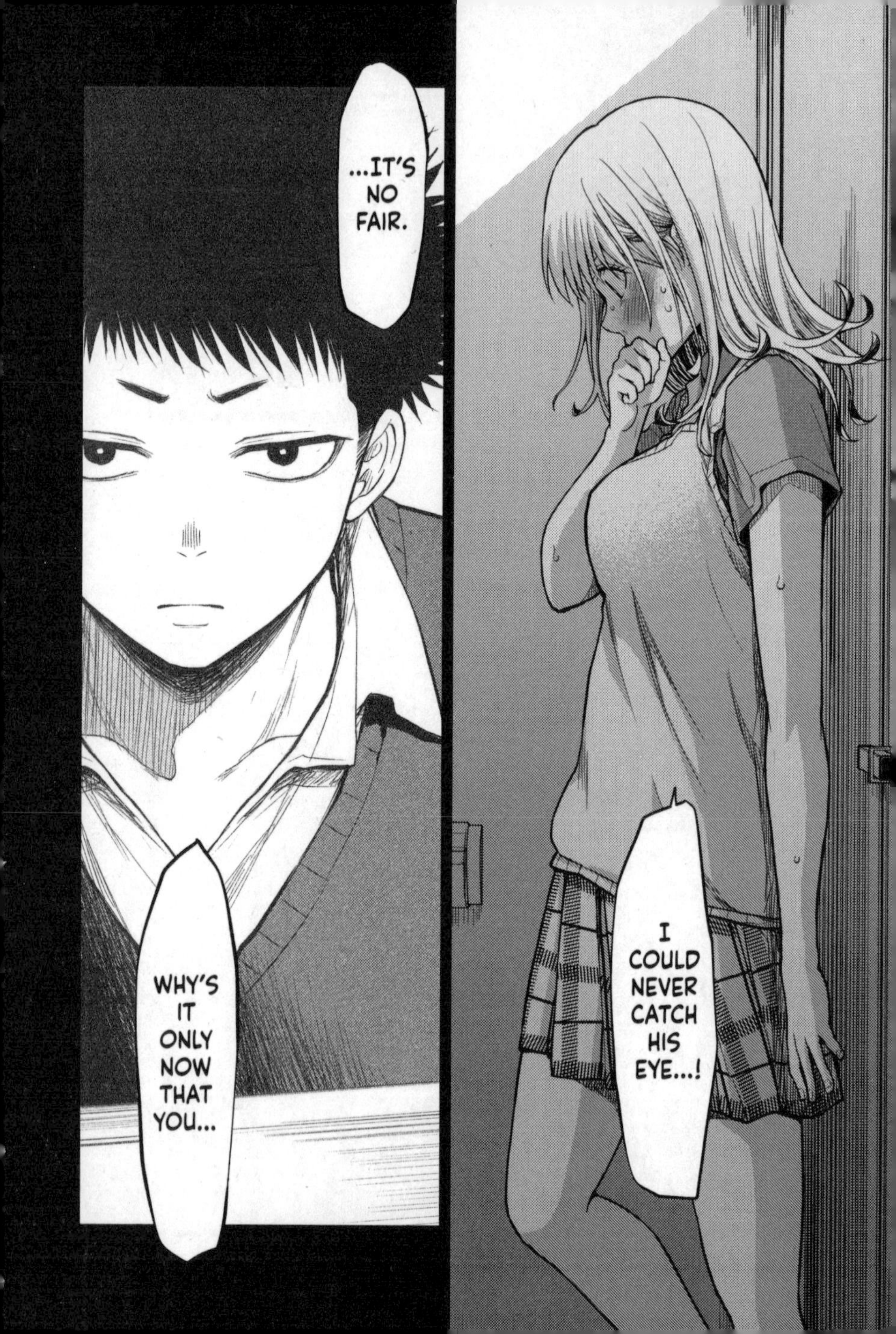
I COULD NEVER CATCH HIS EYE...!
...IT'S NO FAIR.
WHY'S IT ONLY NOW THAT YOU...

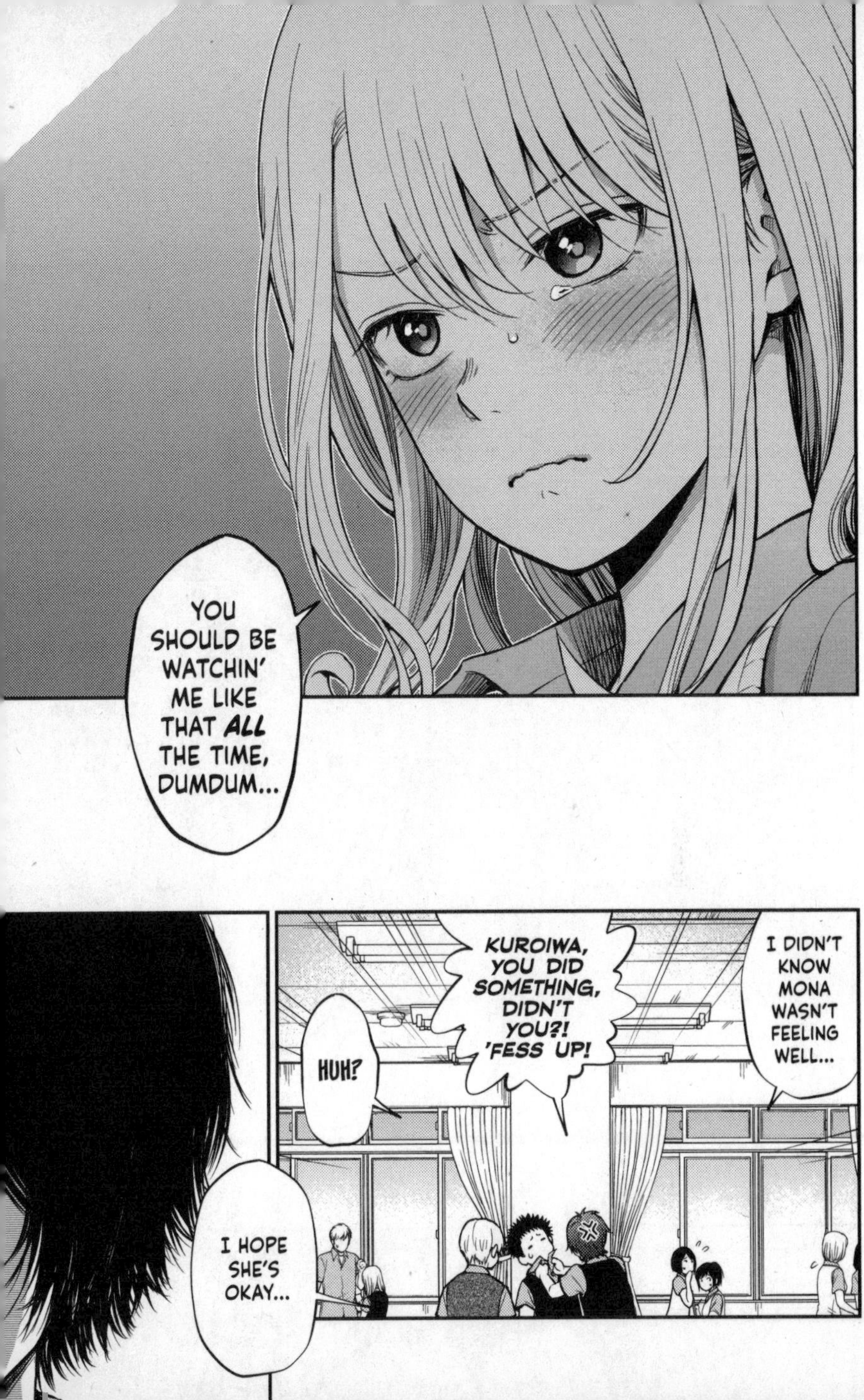
YOU SHOULD BE WATCHIN' ME LIKE THAT ALL THE TIME, DUMDUM...
I DIDN'T KNOW MONA WASN'T FEELING WELL...
KUROIWA, YOU DID SOMETHING, DIDN'T YOU?! 'FESS UP!
HUH?
I HOPE SHE'S OKAY...

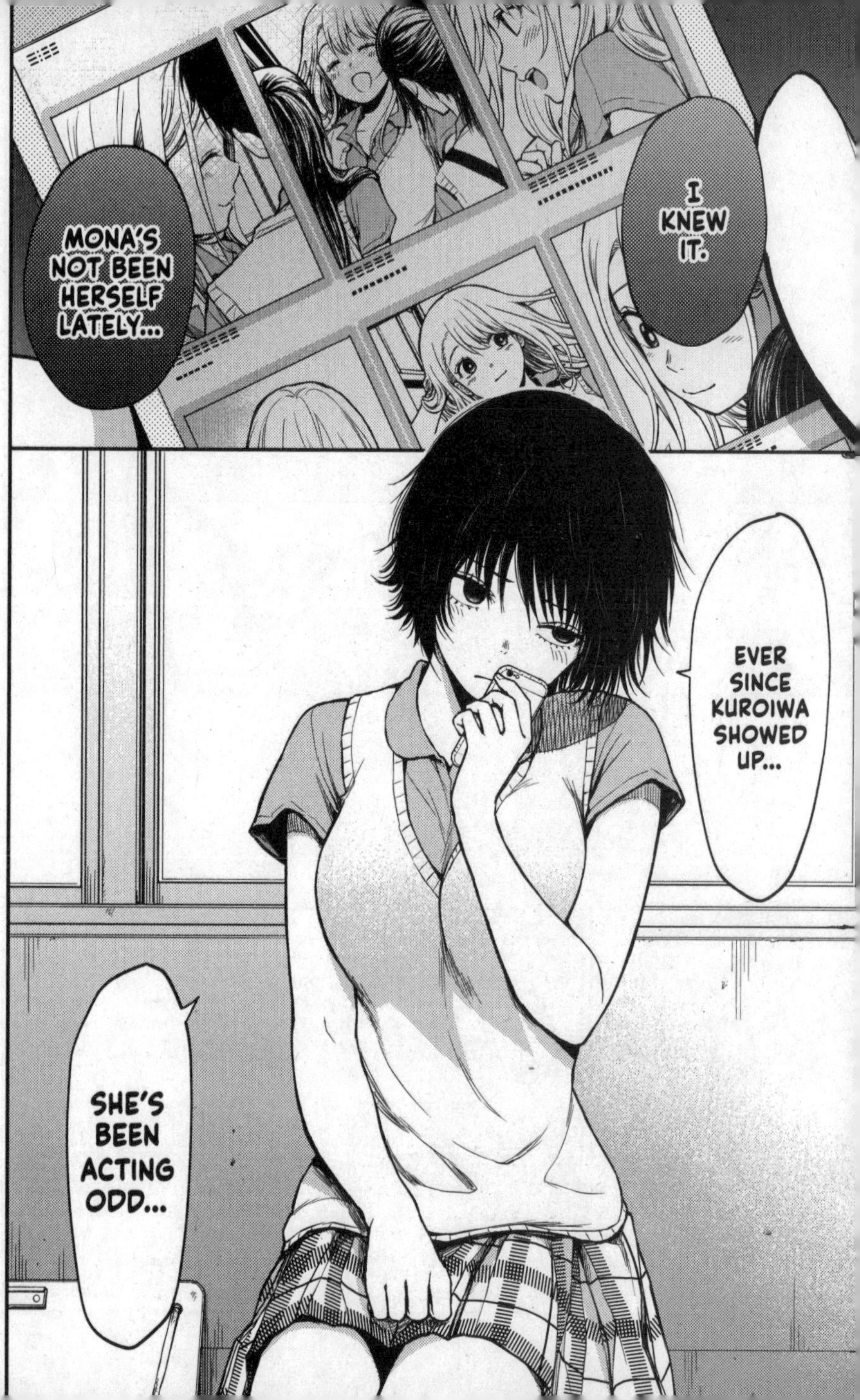
I KNEW IT.
MONA'S NOT BEEN HERSELF LATELY...
EVER SINCE KUROIWA SHOWED UP...
SHE'S BEEN ACTING ODD...

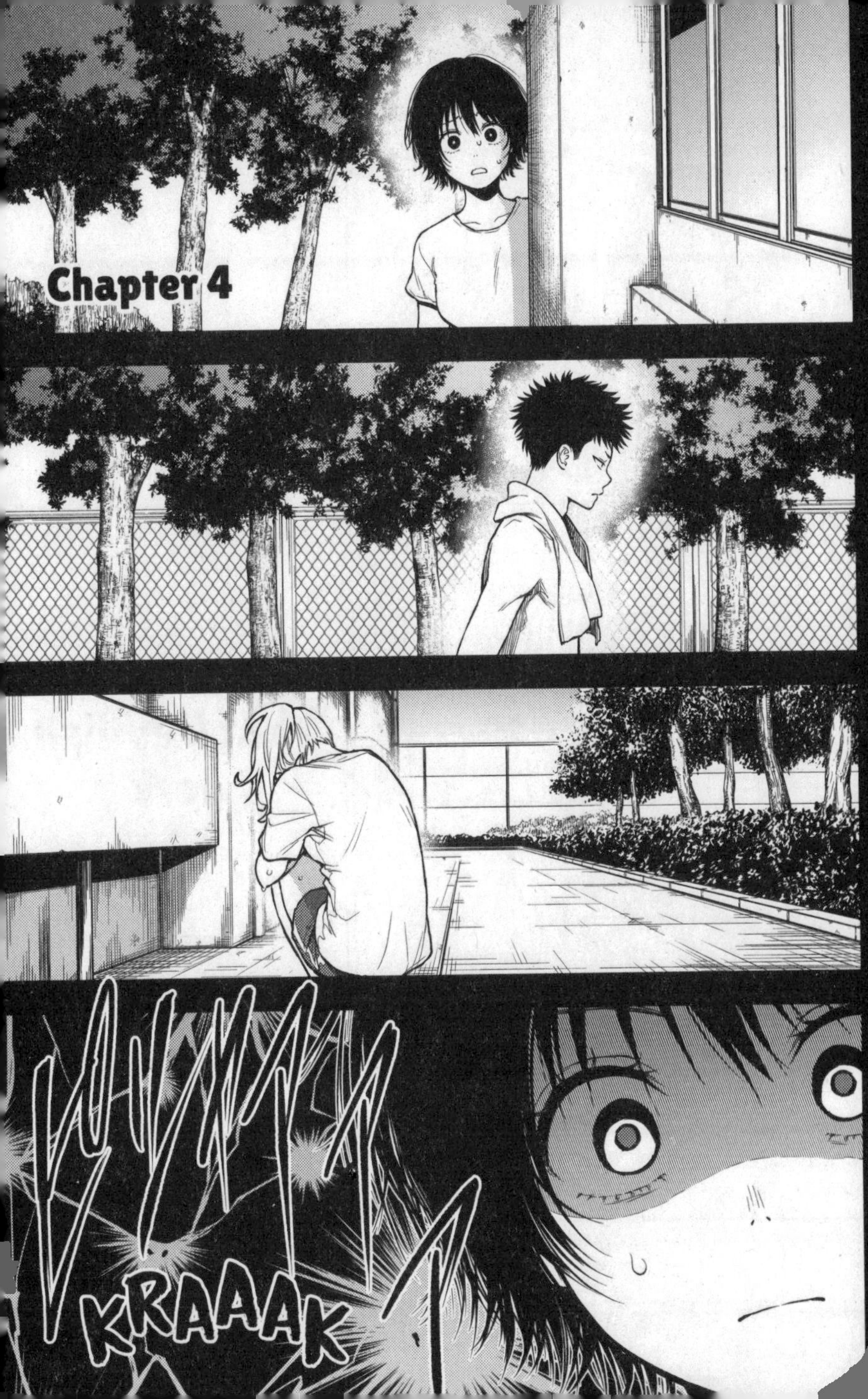
Chapter 4
KRAAAK

Chapter 4 ★ That Devilish Jerk

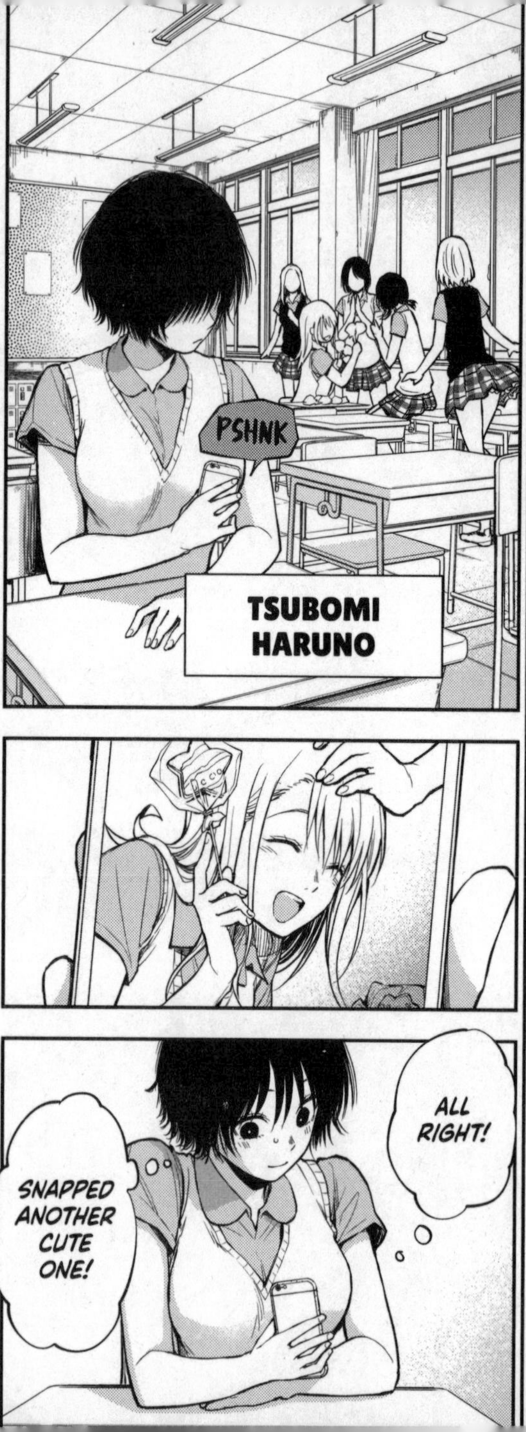
PSHNK
TSUBOMI HARUNO
ALL RIGHT!
SNAPPED ANOTHER CUTE ONE!

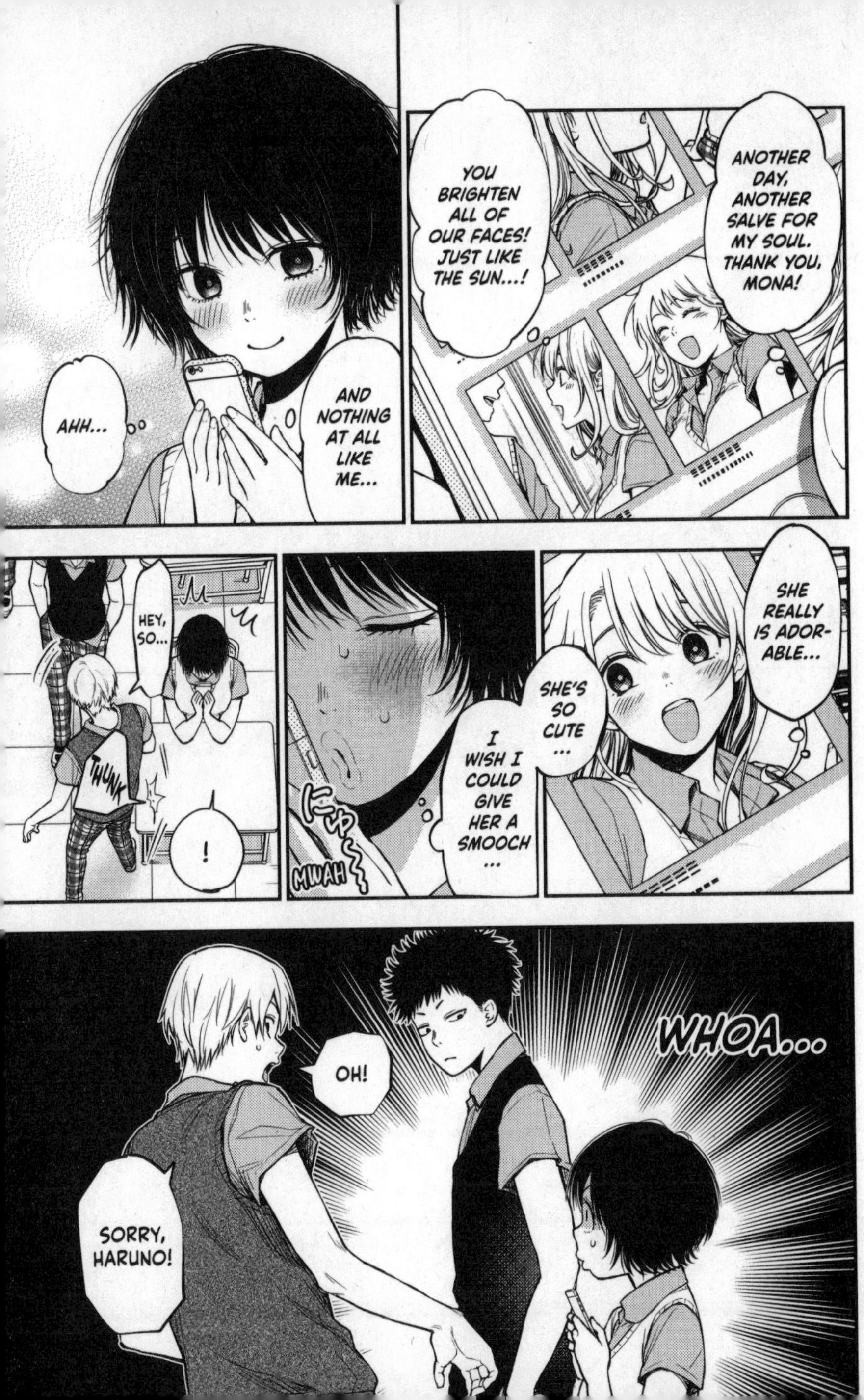
ANOTHER DAY, ANOTHER SALVE FOR MY SOUL. THANK YOU, MONA!
YOU BRIGHTEN ALL OF OUR FACES! JUST LIKE THE SUN...!
AND NOTHING AT ALL LIKE ME...
AHH...
SHE REALLY IS ADORABLE...
SHE'S SO CUTE...
I WISH I COULD GIVE HER A SMOOCH...
にゅ
MWAH
HEY, SO...
THUNK
!
WHOA...
OH!
SORRY, HARUNO!

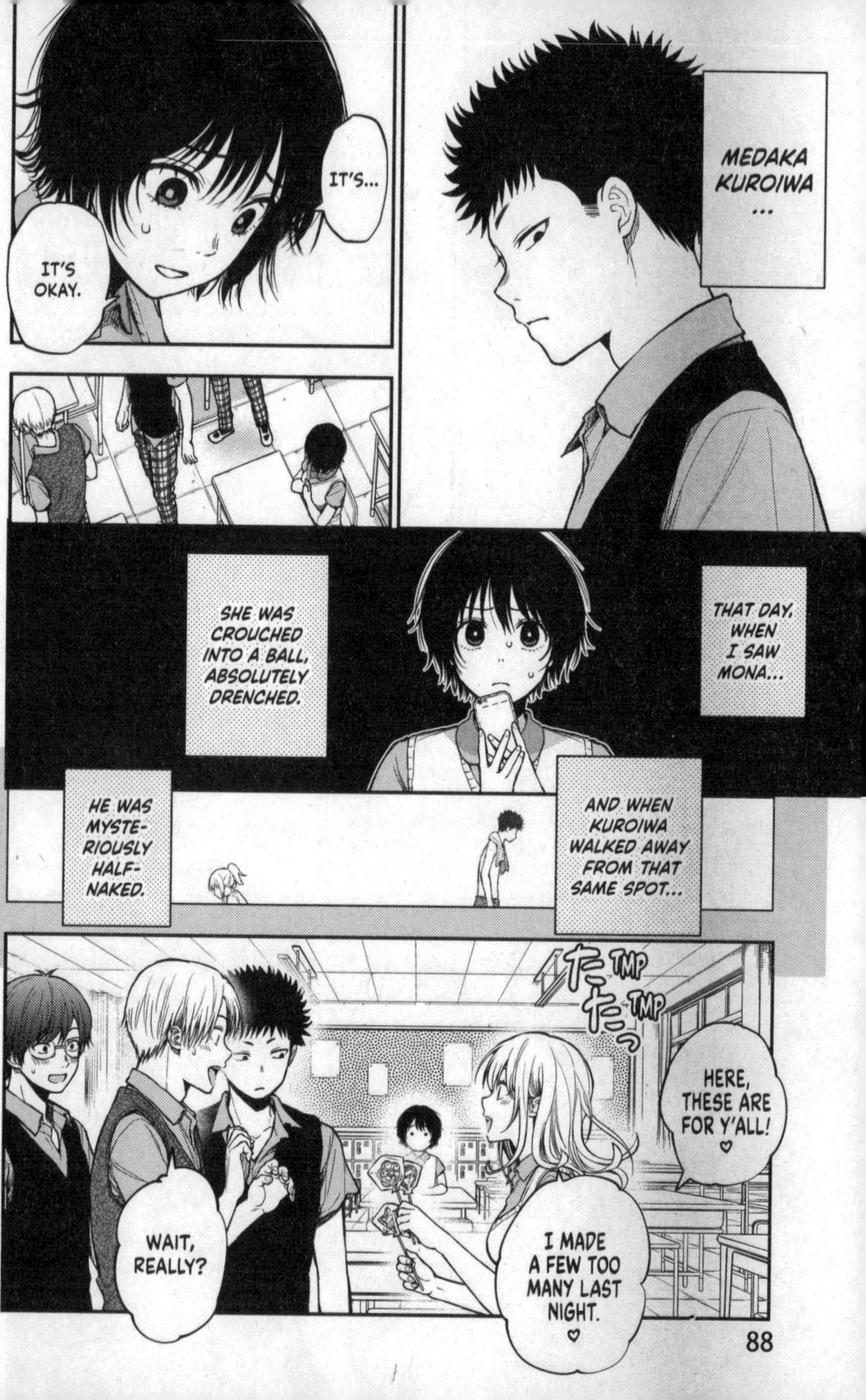
MEDAKA KUROIWA ...
IT'S...
IT'S OKAY.
THAT DAY, WHEN I SAW MONA...
SHE WAS CROUCHED INTO A BALL, ABSOLUTELY DRENCHED.
AND WHEN KUROIWA WALKED AWAY FROM THAT SAME SPOT...
HE WAS MYSTERIOUSLY HALF-NAKED.
TMP
TMP
HERE, THESE ARE FOR Y'ALL! ♡
I MADE A FEW TOO MANY LAST NIGHT. ♡
WAIT, REALLY?

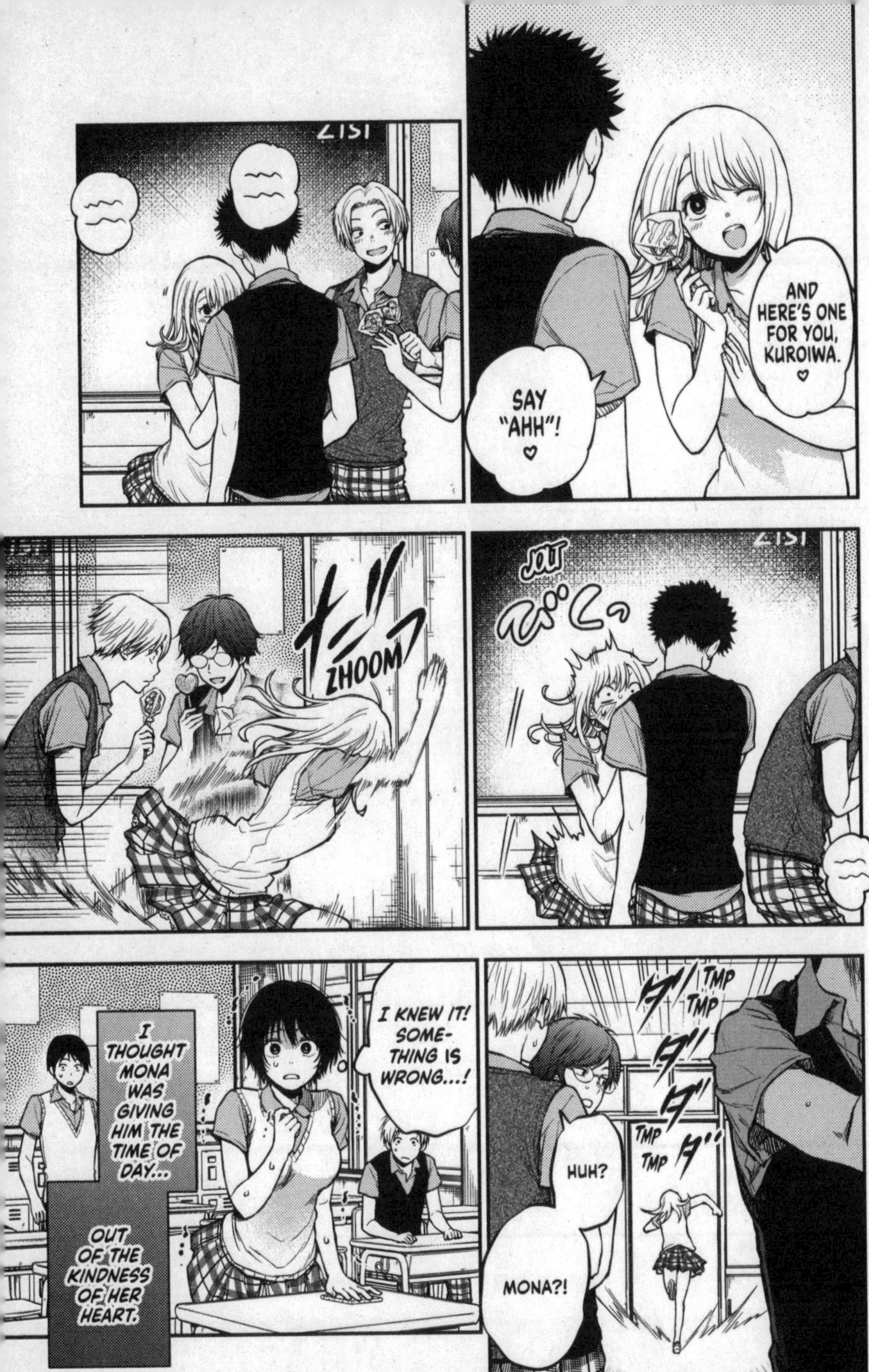
AND HERE'S ONE FOR YOU, KUROIWA. ♡
SAY "AHH"! ♡
JOLT
ZHOOM
TMP TMP
TMP TMP
HUH?
MONA?!
I KNEW IT! SOMETHING IS WRONG...!
I THOUGHT MONA WAS GIVING HIM THE TIME OF DAY...
OUT OF THE KINDNESS OF HER HEART.

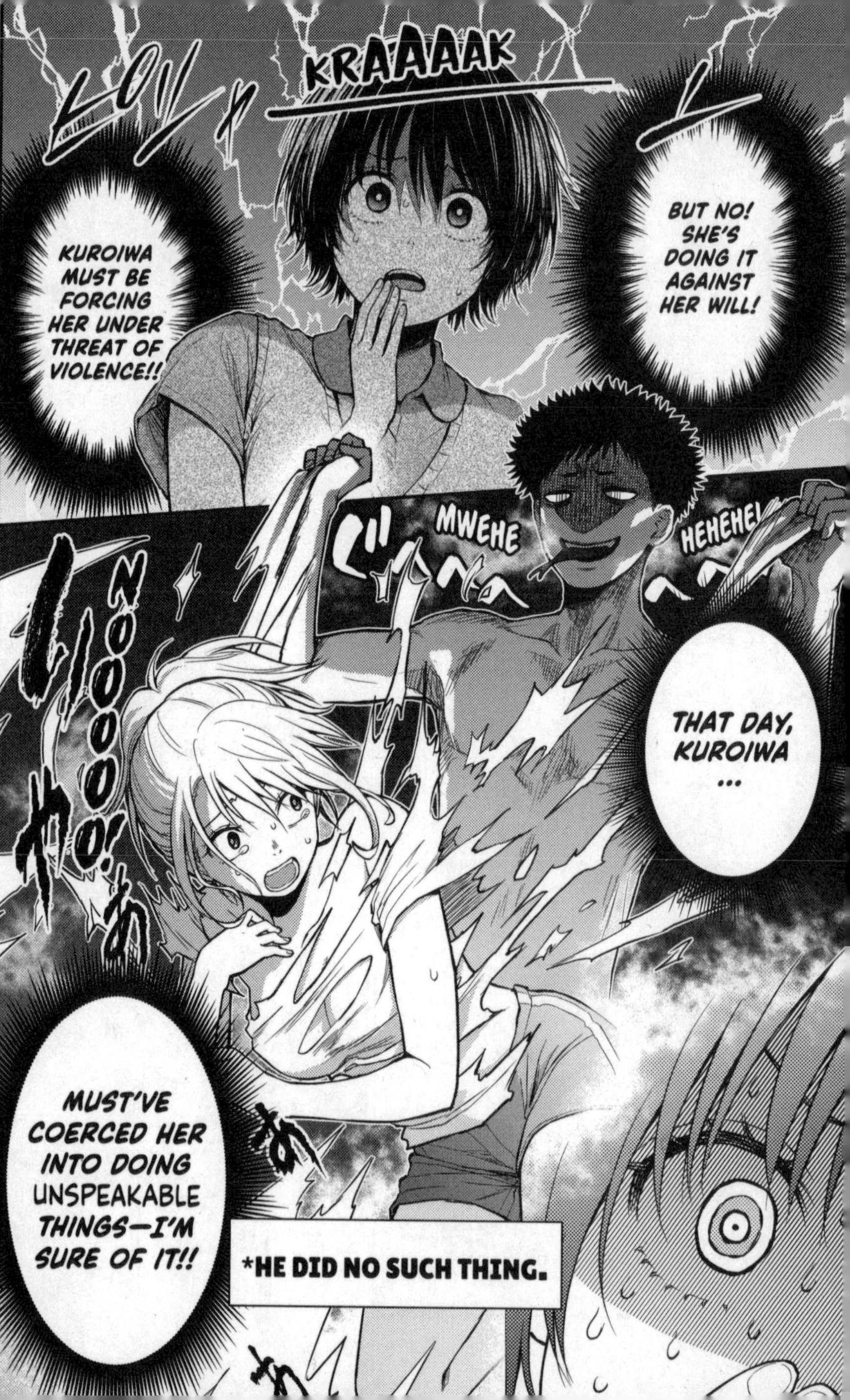
KRAAAAK
BUT NO! SHE'S DOING IT AGAINST HER WILL!
KUROIWA MUST BE FORCING HER UNDER THREAT OF VIOLENCE!!
HEHEHE!
MWEHE
THAT DAY, KUROIWA ...
NOOOOOOO!
MUST'VE COERCED HER INTO DOING UNSPEAKABLE THINGS—I'M SURE OF IT!!
*HE DID NO SUCH THING.

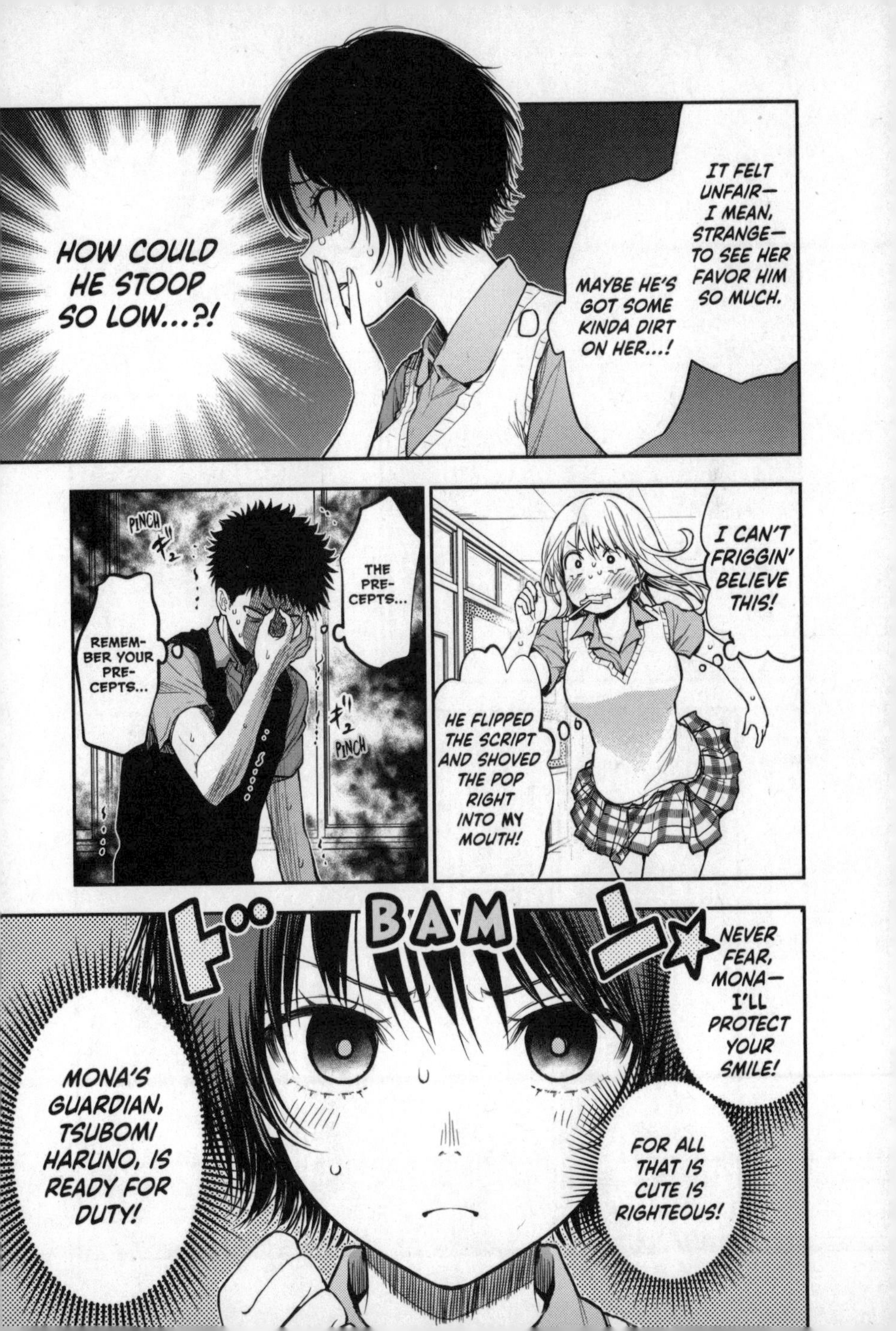
IT FELT UNFAIR— I MEAN, STRANGE— TO SEE HER FAVOR HIM SO MUCH.
MAYBE HE'S GOT SOME KINDA DIRT ON HER...!
HOW COULD HE STOOP SO LOW...?!
I CAN'T FRIGGIN' BELIEVE THIS!
HE FLIPPED THE SCRIPT AND SHOVED THE POP RIGHT INTO MY MOUTH!
PINCH
THE PRE-CEPTS...
REMEM-BER YOUR PRE-CEPTS...
PINCH
BAM
NEVER FEAR, MONA— I'LL PROTECT YOUR SMILE!
FOR ALL THAT IS CUTE IS RIGHTEOUS!
MONA'S GUARDIAN, TSUBOMI HARUNO, IS READY FOR DUTY!

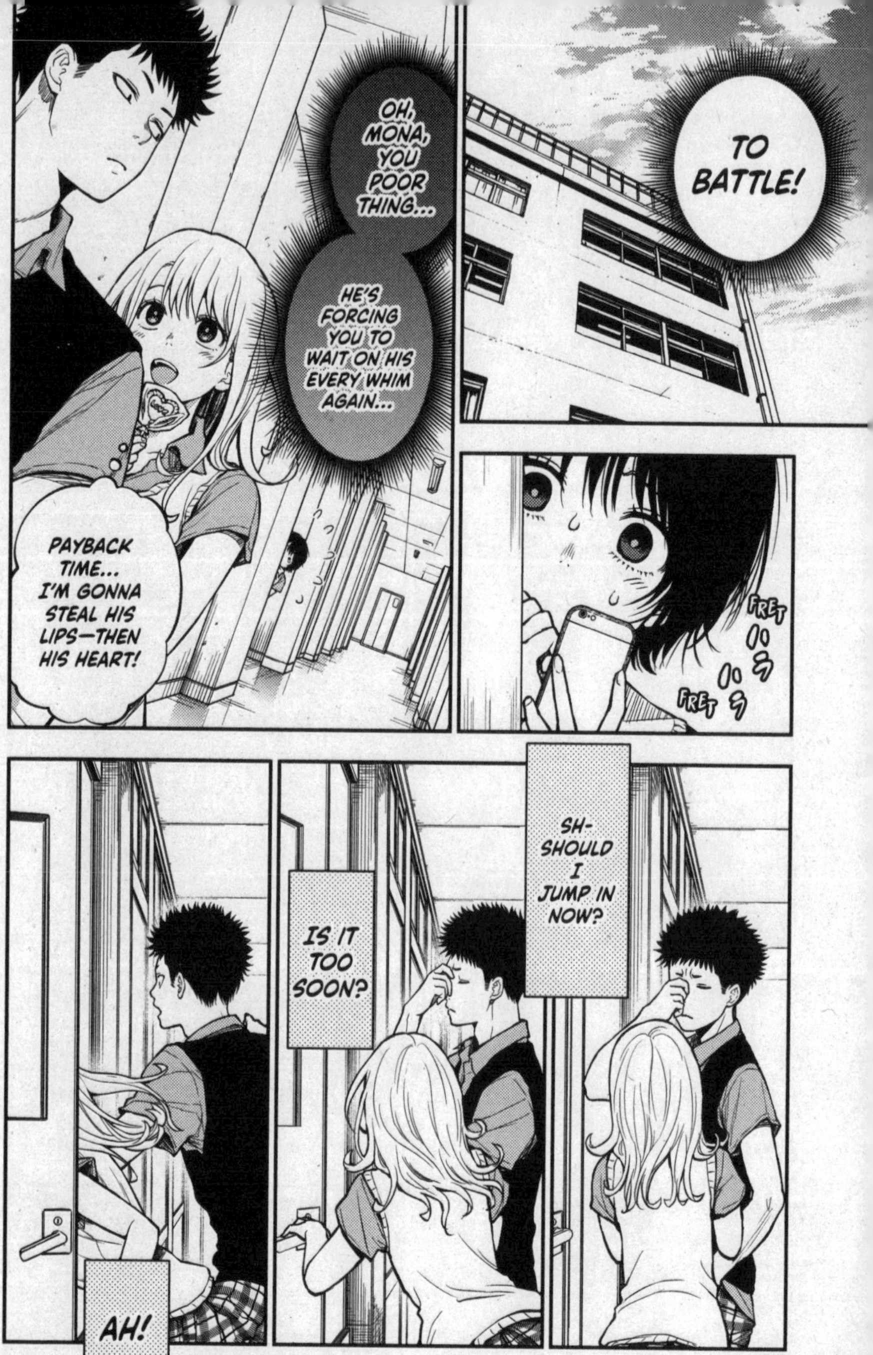
TO BATTLE!
FRET FRET
OH, MONA, YOU POOR THING...
HE'S FORCING YOU TO WAIT ON HIS EVERY WHIM AGAIN...
PAYBACK TIME... I'M GONNA STEAL HIS LIPS—THEN HIS HEART!
SH-SHOULD I JUMP IN NOW?
IS IT TOO SOON?
AH!

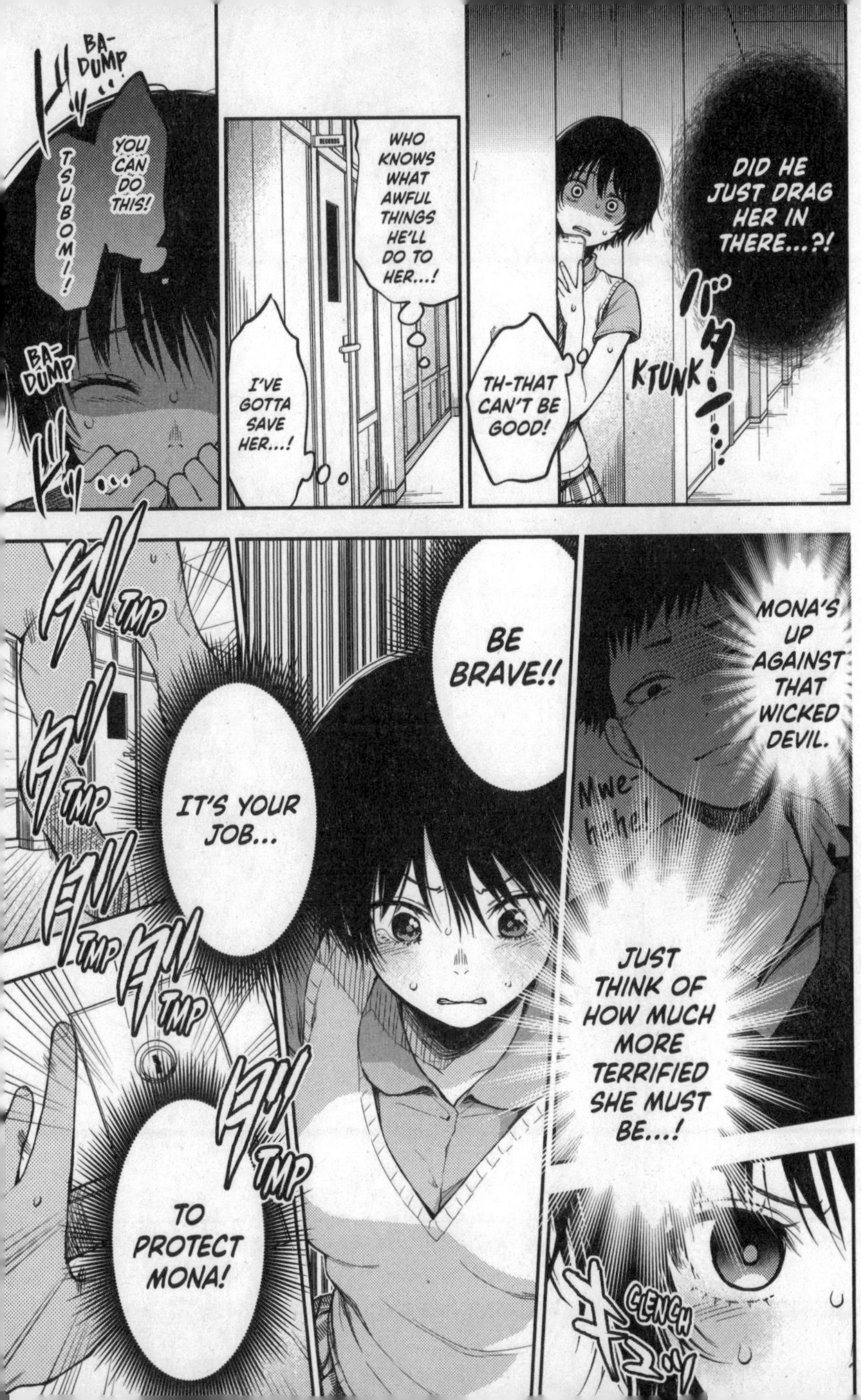
DID HE JUST DRAG HER IN THERE...?!
KTUNK
TH-THAT CAN'T BE GOOD!
WHO KNOWS WHAT AWFUL THINGS HE'LL DO TO HER...!
I'VE GOTTA SAVE HER...!
BA-DUMP
YOU CAN DO THIS!
TSUBOMI!
BA-DUMP
MONA'S UP AGAINST THAT WICKED DEVIL.
Mwe-hehe!
JUST THINK OF HOW MUCH MORE TERRIFIED SHE MUST BE...!
CLENCH
BE BRAVE!!
IT'S YOUR JOB...
TO PROTECT MONA!
TMP
TMP
TMP
TMP
TMP

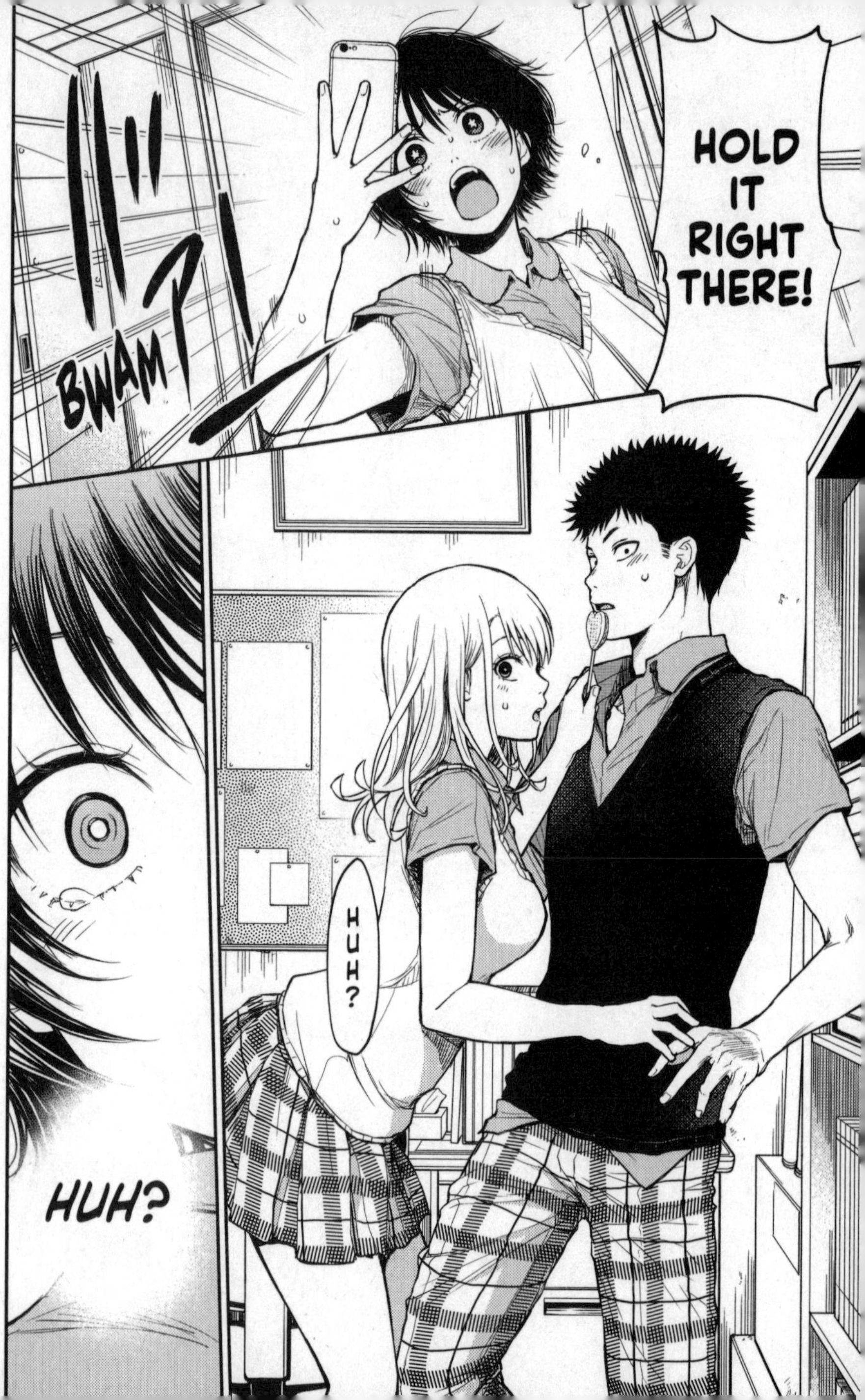
HOLD IT RIGHT THERE!
BWAM
HUH?
HUH?

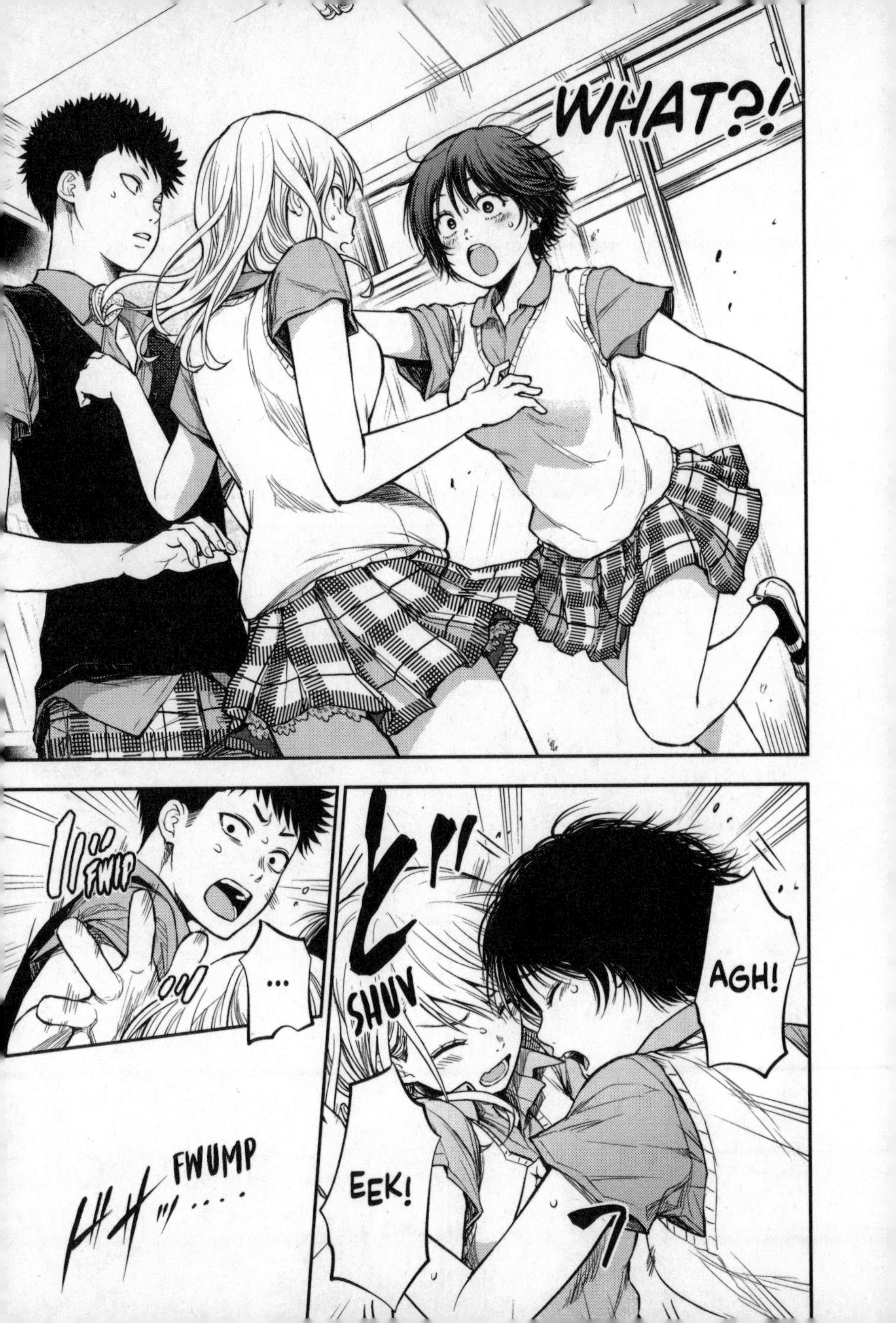
WHAT?!
AGH!
SHUV
EEK!
FWIP
...
FWUMP

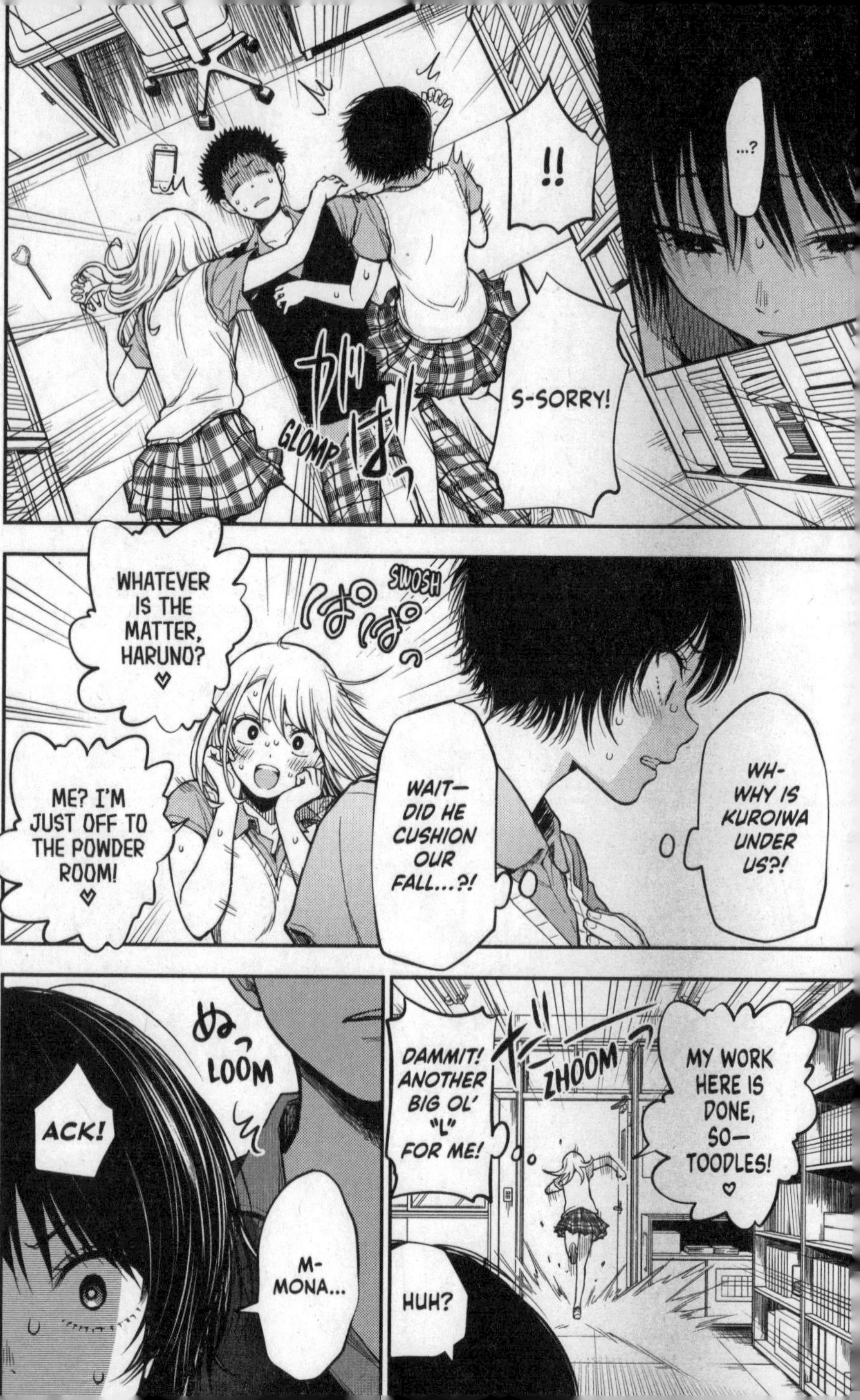
...?
!!
S-SORRY!
GLOMP
WH-WHY IS KUROIWA UNDER US?!
WAIT—DID HE CUSHION OUR FALL...?!
SWOSH
WHATEVER IS THE MATTER, HARUNO? ♡
ME? I'M JUST OFF TO THE POWDER ROOM! ♡
MY WORK HERE IS DONE, SO—TOODLES! ♡
ZHOOM
DAMMIT! ANOTHER BIG OL' "L" FOR ME!
HUH?
LOOM
ACK!
M-MONA...

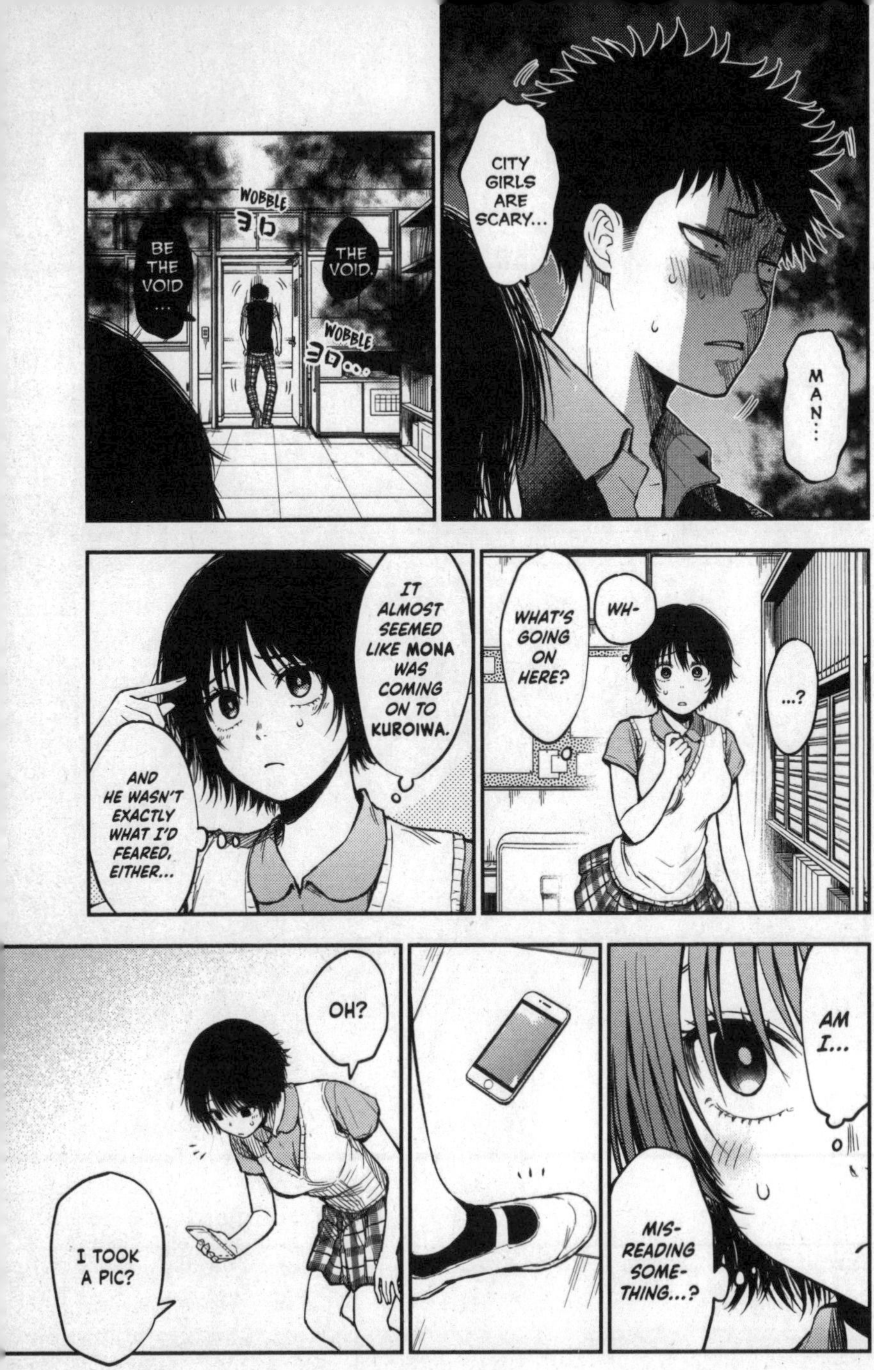
CITY GIRLS ARE SCARY...
MAN...
WOBBLE
THE VOID.
BE THE VOID ...
WOBBLE
ヨロ...
WH-
WHAT'S GOING ON HERE?
...?
IT ALMOST SEEMED LIKE MONA WAS COMING ON TO KUROIWA.
AND HE WASN'T EXACTLY WHAT I'D FEARED, EITHER...
AM I...
MIS-READING SOME-THING...?
OH?
I TOOK A PIC?

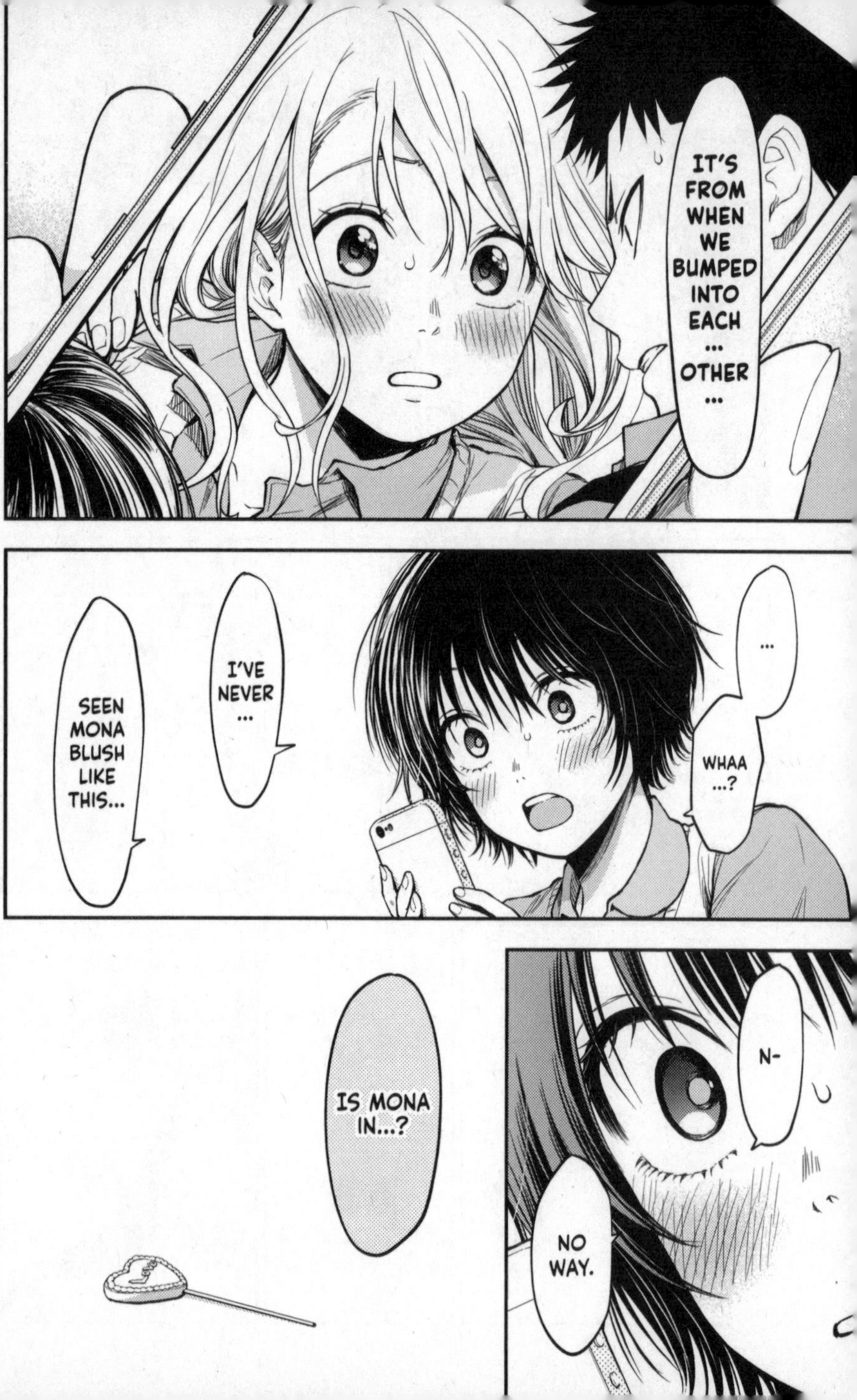
IT'S FROM WHEN WE BUMPED INTO EACH ... OTHER ...
...
WHAA ...?
I'VE NEVER ...
SEEN MONA BLUSH LIKE THIS...
N-
NO WAY.
IS MONA IN...?

Chapter 5 ★ In the Library with That Jerk

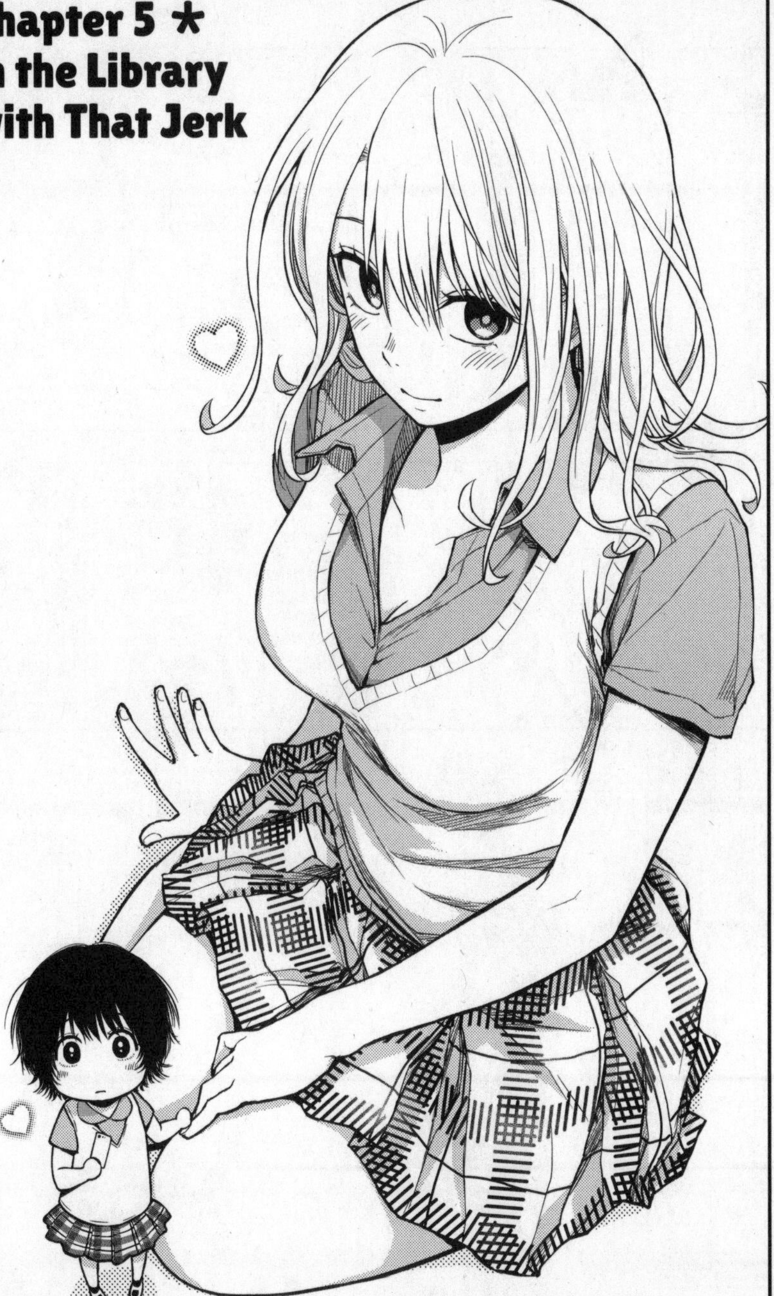

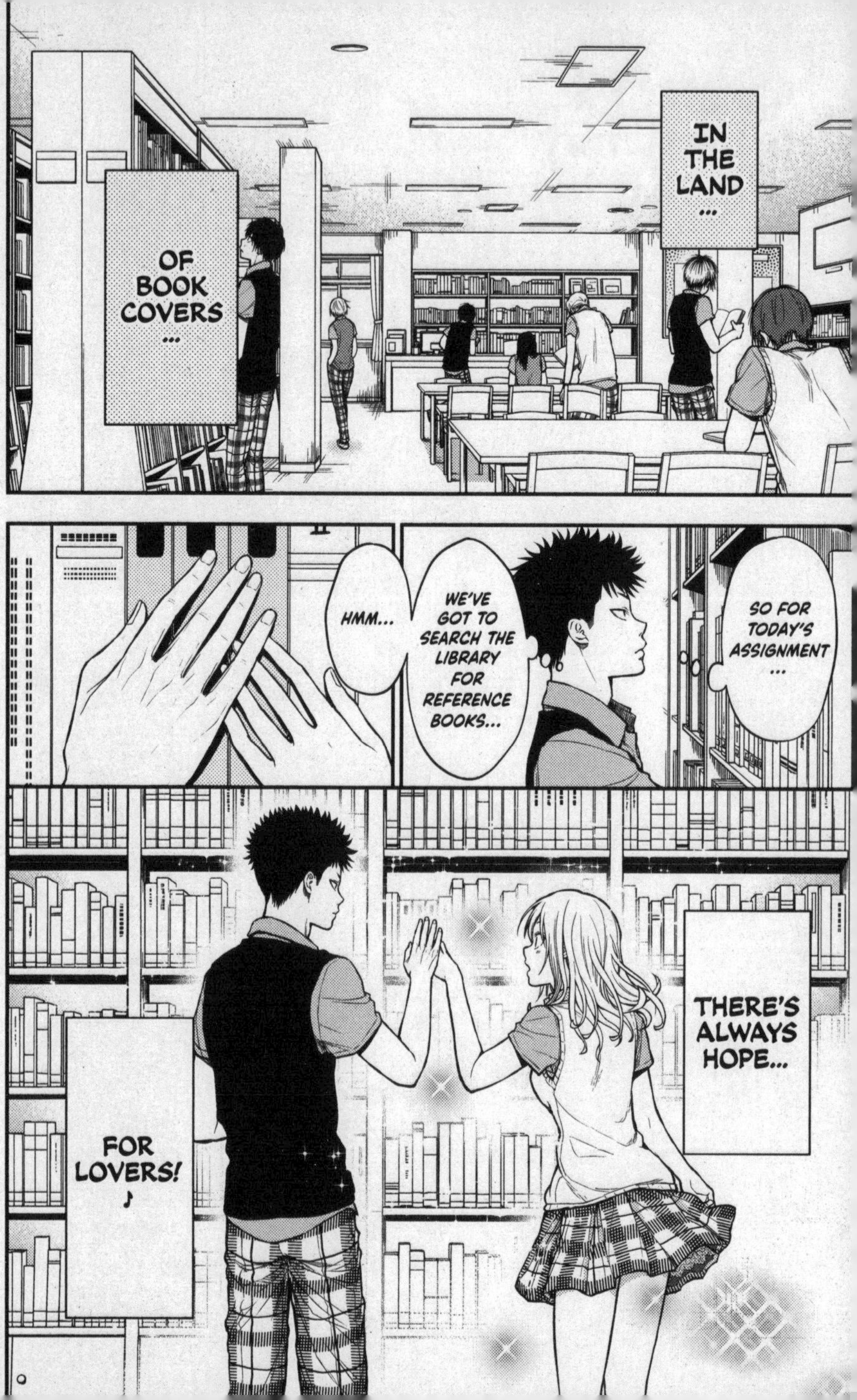
IN THE LAND...
OF BOOK COVERS...
SO FOR TODAY'S ASSIGNMENT...
WE'VE GOT TO SEARCH THE LIBRARY FOR REFERENCE BOOKS...
HMM...
THERE'S ALWAYS HOPE...
FOR LOVERS! ♪

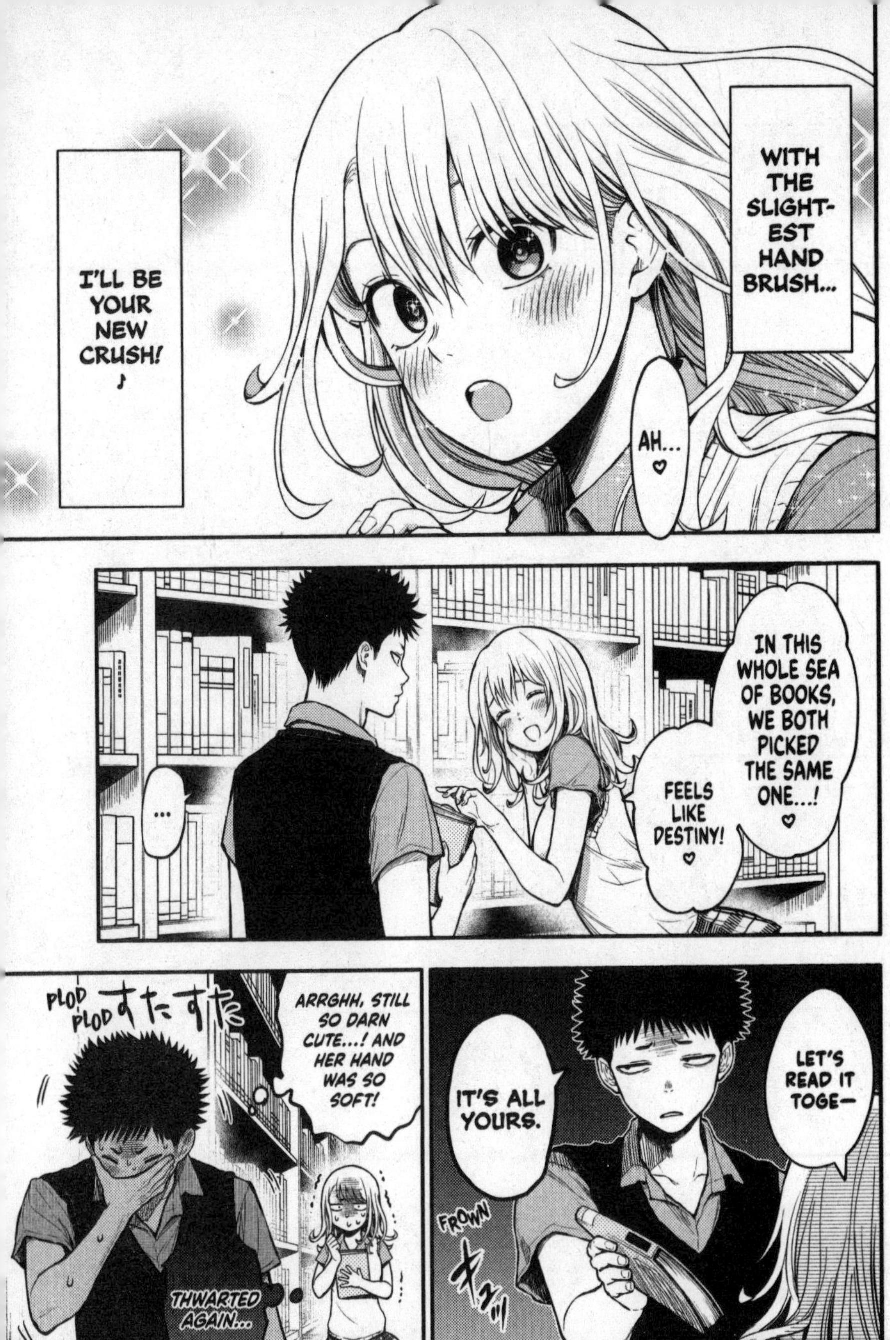
WITH THE SLIGHTEST HAND BRUSH...
AH... ♡
I'LL BE YOUR NEW CRUSH! ♪
IN THIS WHOLE SEA OF BOOKS, WE BOTH PICKED THE SAME ONE...! ♡
FEELS LIKE DESTINY! ♡
...
LET'S READ IT TOGE—
IT'S ALL YOURS.
FROWN
PLOD PLOD
すたすた
ARRGHH, STILL SO DARN CUTE...! AND HER HAND WAS SO SOFT!
THWARTED AGAIN...

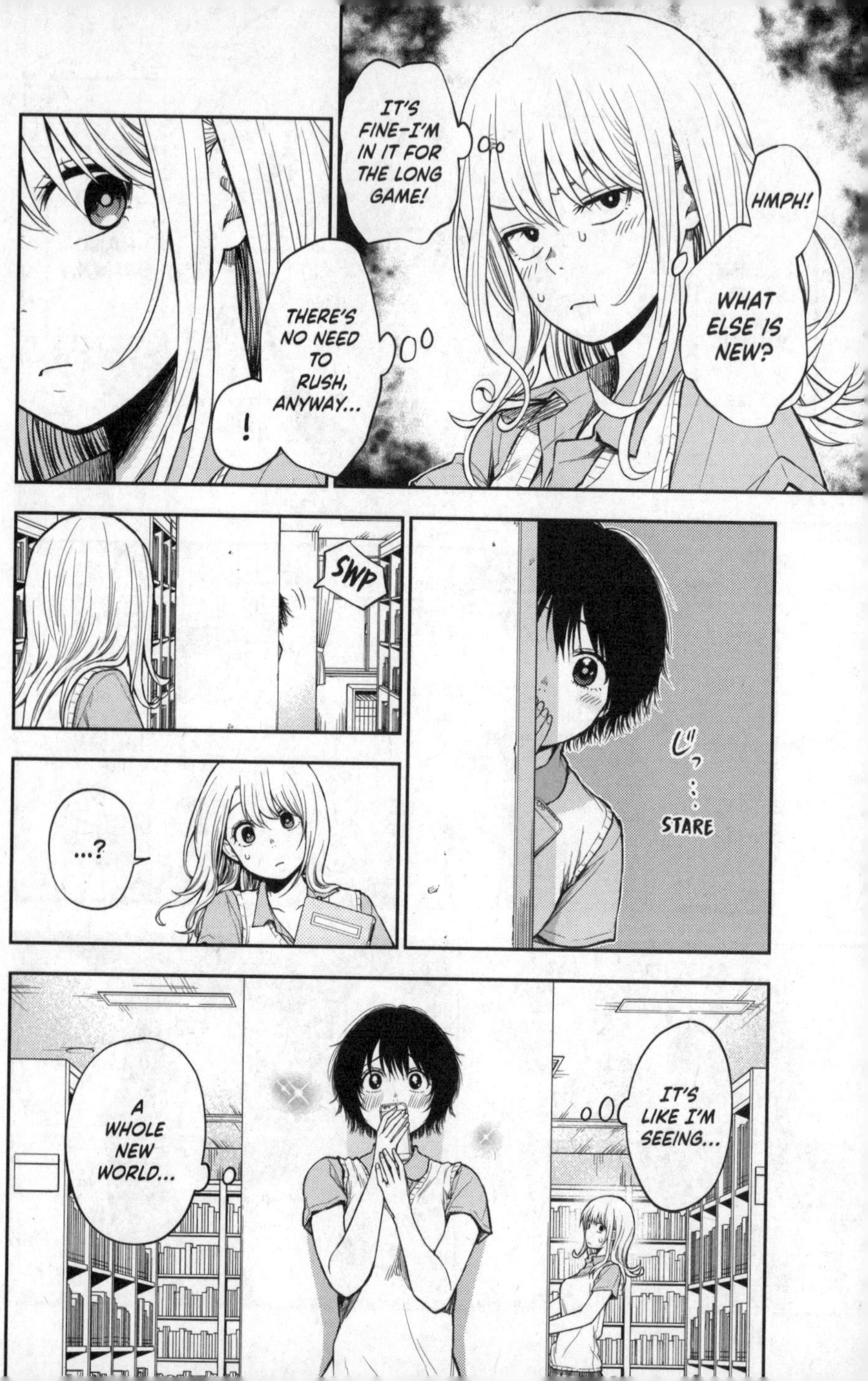
HMPH!
WHAT ELSE IS NEW?
IT'S FINE—I'M IN IT FOR THE LONG GAME!
THERE'S NO NEED TO RUSH, ANYWAY...
!
じっ…
STARE
SWP
...?
IT'S LIKE I'M SEEING...
A WHOLE NEW WORLD...

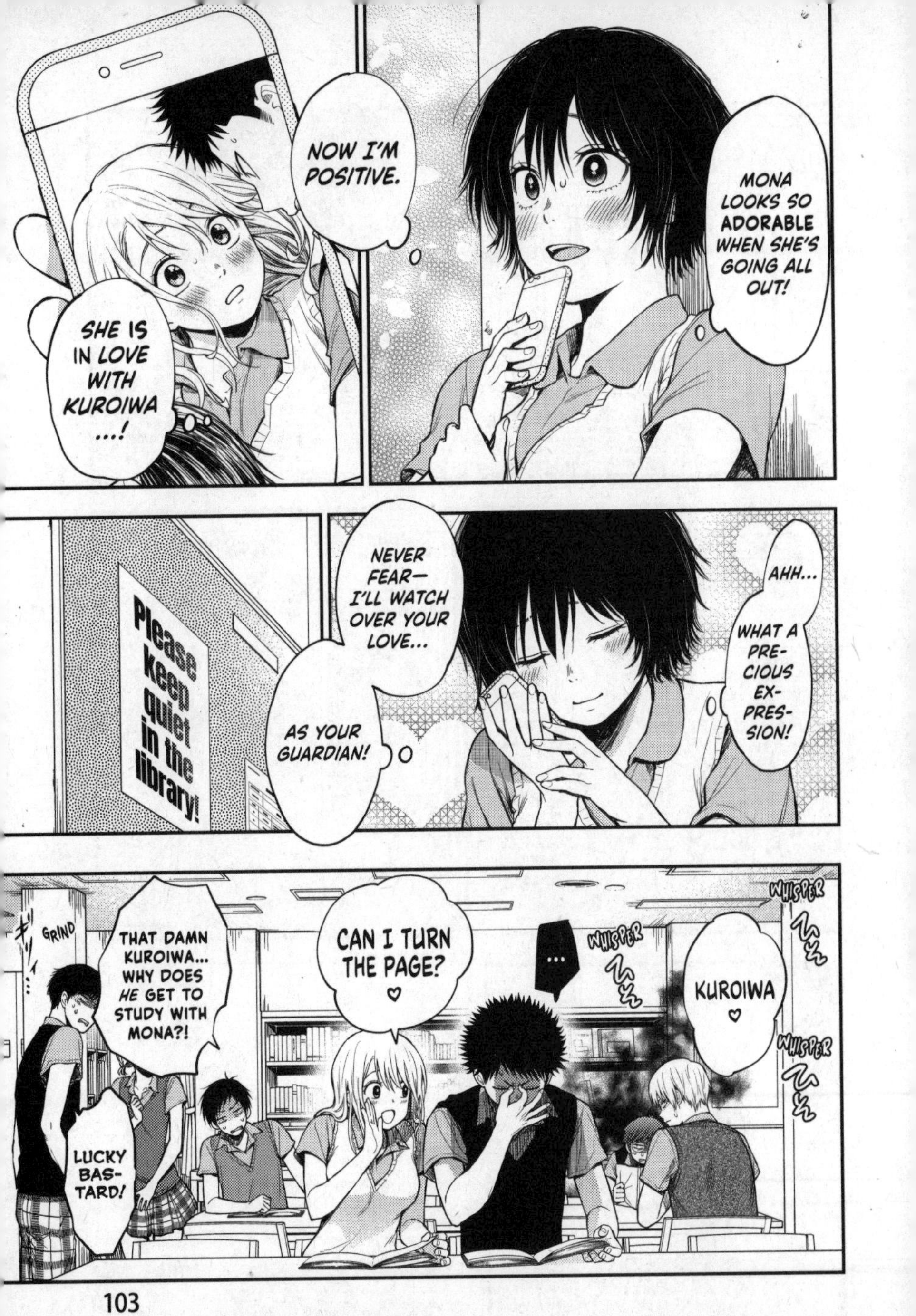
MONA LOOKS SO ADORABLE WHEN SHE'S GOING ALL OUT!
NOW I'M POSITIVE.
SHE IS IN LOVE WITH KUROIWA ...!
AHH... WHAT A PRE-CIOUS EX-PRES-SION!
NEVER FEAR— I'LL WATCH OVER YOUR LOVE...
AS YOUR GUARDIAN!
Please keep quiet in the library!
WHISPER
KUROIWA ♡
WHISPER
WHISPER
...
CAN I TURN THE PAGE? ♡
THAT DAMN KUROIWA... WHY DOES HE GET TO STUDY WITH MONA?!
GRIND
LUCKY BAS-TARD!

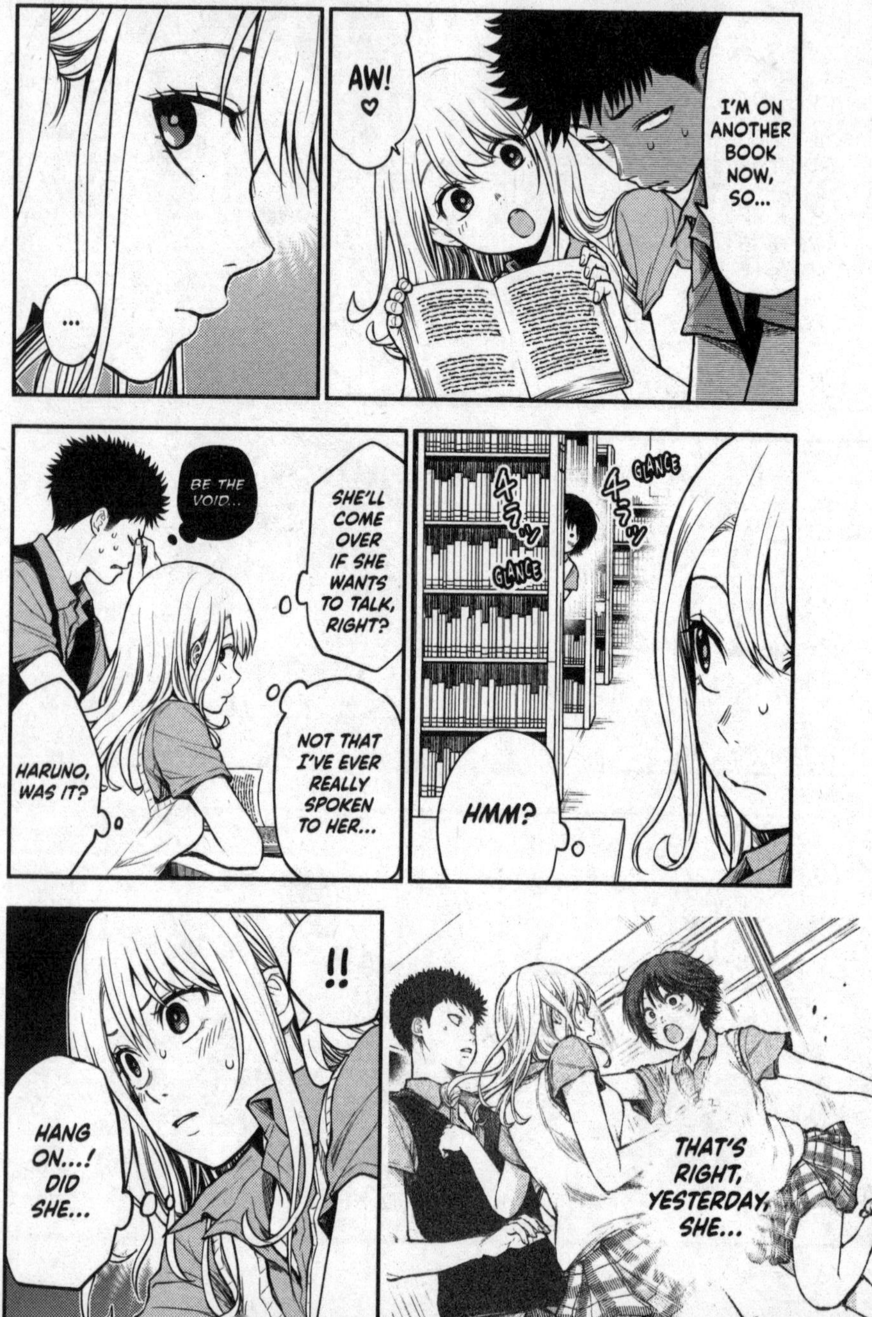

I'M ON ANOTHER BOOK NOW, SO...
AW! ♡
...
GLANCE
GLANCE
HMM?
SHE'LL COME OVER IF SHE WANTS TO TALK, RIGHT?
BE THE VOID...
NOT THAT I'VE EVER REALLY SPOKEN TO HER...
HARUNO, WAS IT?
THAT'S RIGHT, YESTERDAY, SHE...
!!
HANG ON...! DID SHE...

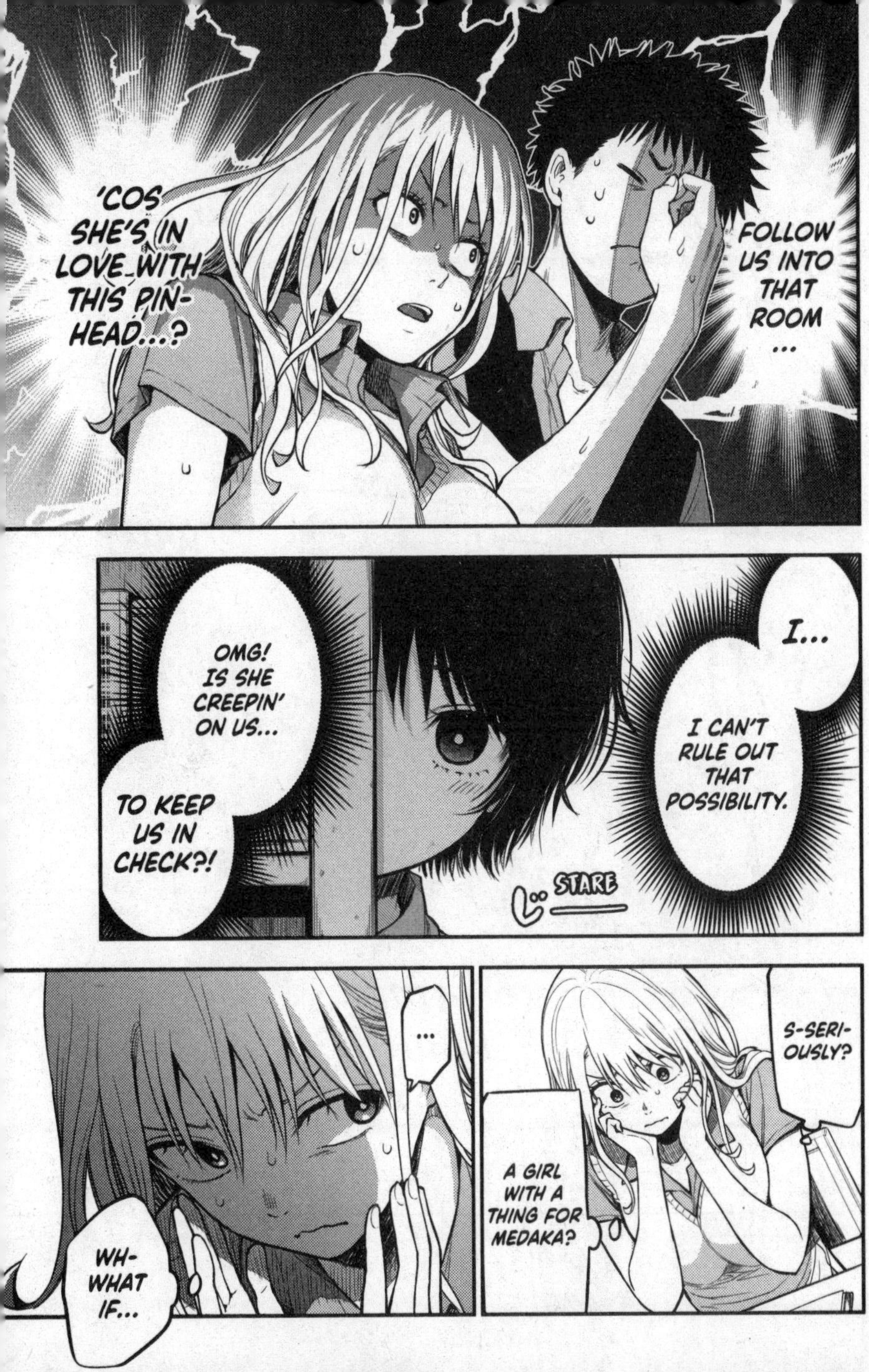
FOLLOW US INTO THAT ROOM ...
'COS SHE'S IN LOVE WITH THIS PIN-HEAD...?
I...
I CAN'T RULE OUT THAT POSSIBILITY.
STARE
OMG! IS SHE CREEPIN' ON US...
TO KEEP US IN CHECK?!
S-SERI-OUSLY?
A GIRL WITH A THING FOR MEDAKA?
...
WH-WHAT IF...

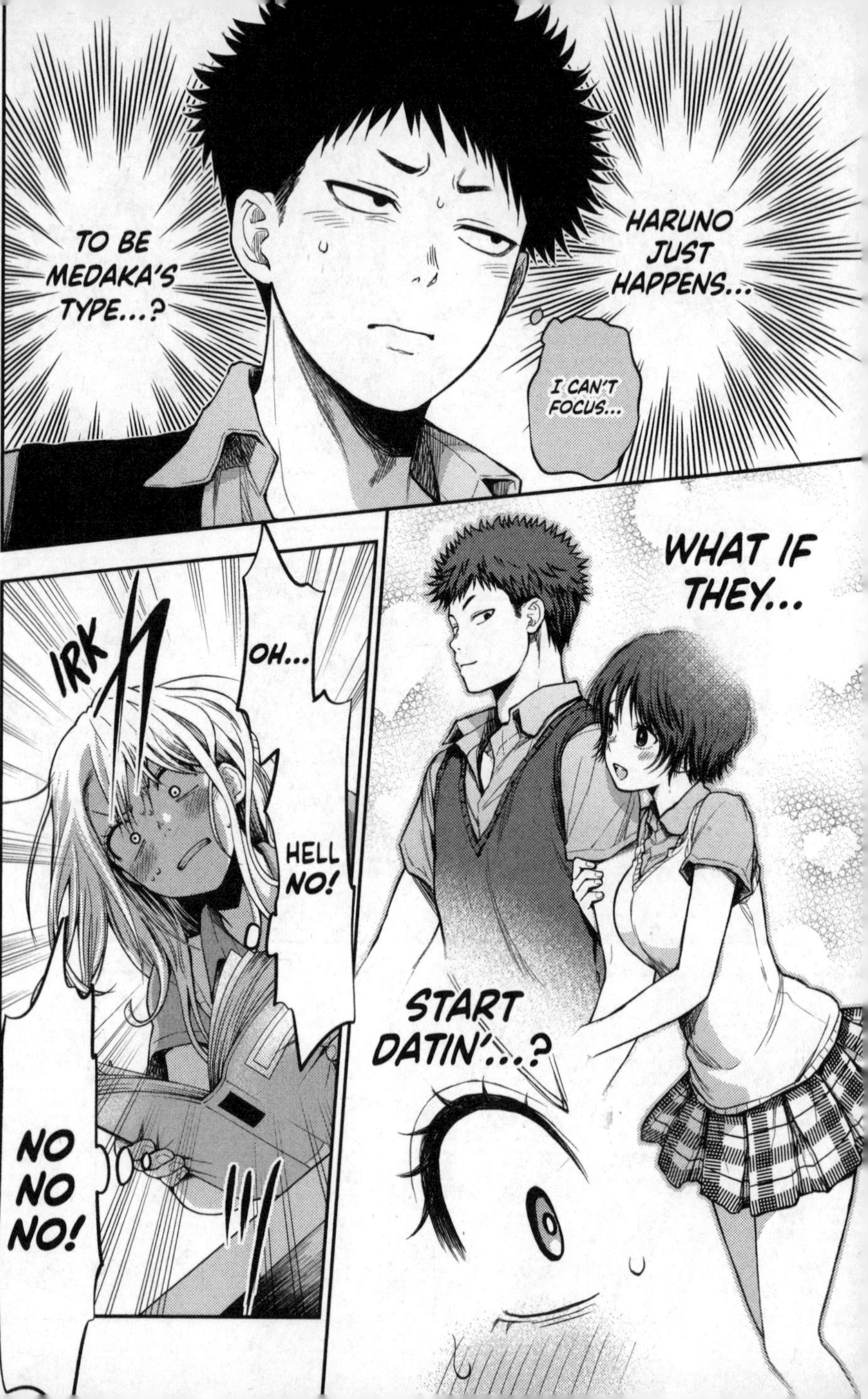
HARUNO JUST HAPPENS...
TO BE MEDAKA'S TYPE...?
I CAN'T FOCUS...
WHAT IF THEY...
START DATIN'...?
OH...
IRK
HELL NO!
NO NO NO!

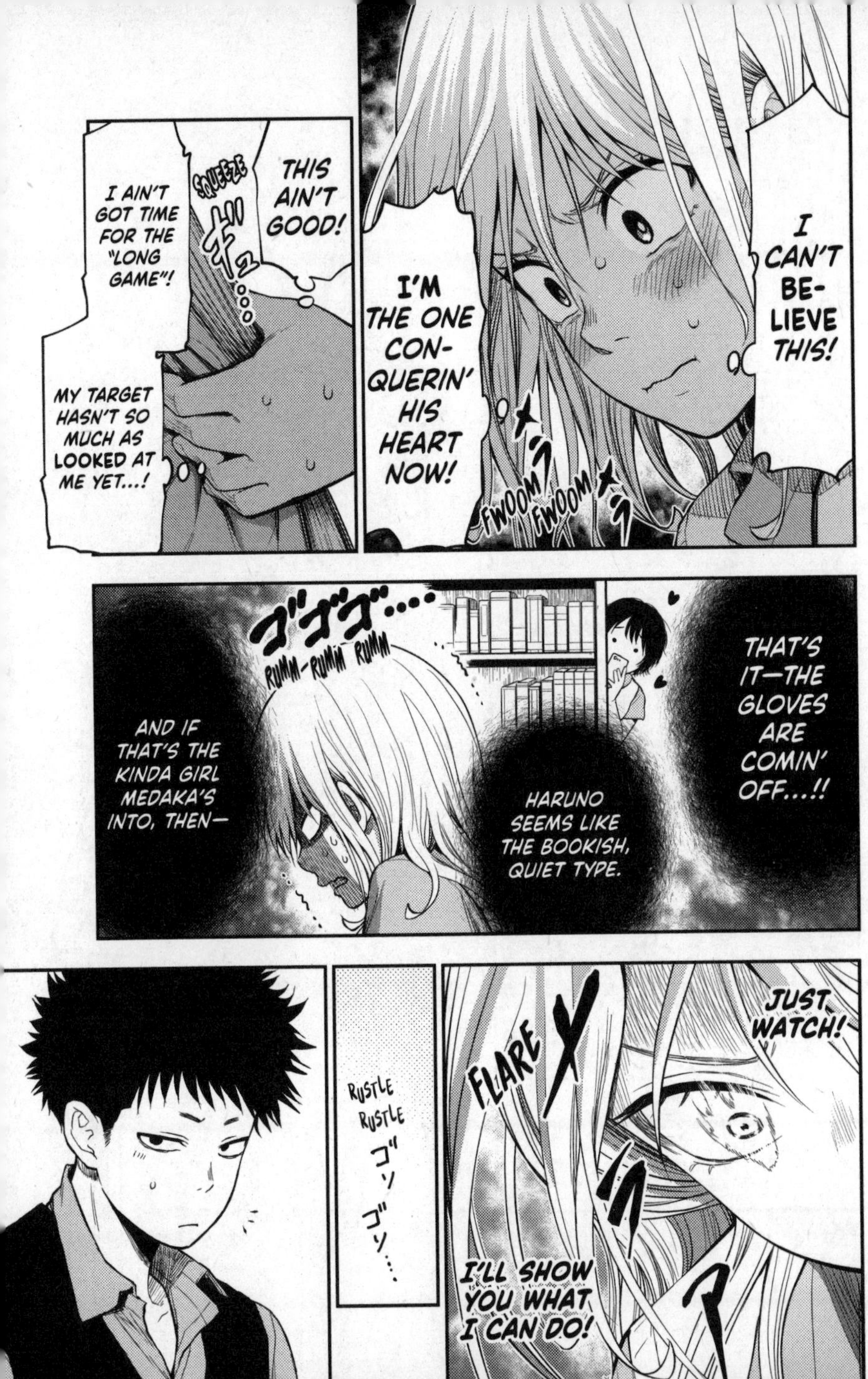
I CAN'T BE-LIEVE THIS!
I'M THE ONE CON-QUERIN' HIS HEART NOW!
FWOOM FWOOM
THIS AIN'T GOOD!
SQUEEZE
I AIN'T GOT TIME FOR THE "LONG GAME"!
MY TARGET HASN'T SO MUCH AS LOOKED AT ME YET...!
RUMM-RUMM RUMM
HARUNO SEEMS LIKE THE BOOKISH, QUIET TYPE.
AND IF THAT'S THE KINDA GIRL MEDAKA'S INTO, THEN—
THAT'S IT—THE GLOVES ARE COMIN' OFF...!!
JUST WATCH!
FLARE
I'LL SHOW YOU WHAT I CAN DO!
RUSTLE RUSTLE

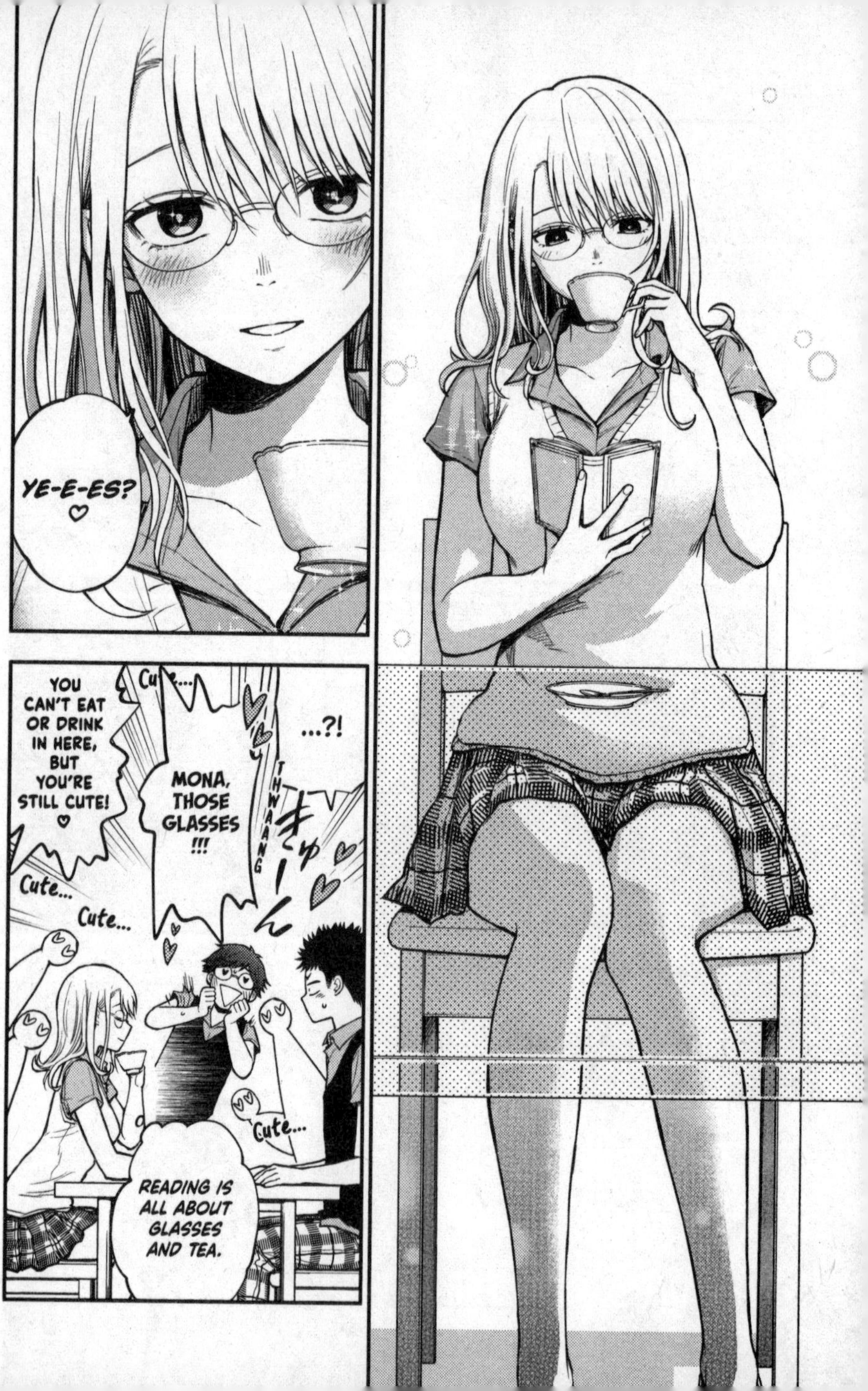
YE-E-ES? ♡
...?!
THWAANG
きゅーん
MONA, THOSE GLASSES!!!
Cute...
YOU CAN'T EAT OR DRINK IN HERE, BUT YOU'RE STILL CUTE! ♡
Cute...
Cute...
Cute...
READING IS ALL ABOUT GLASSES AND TEA.

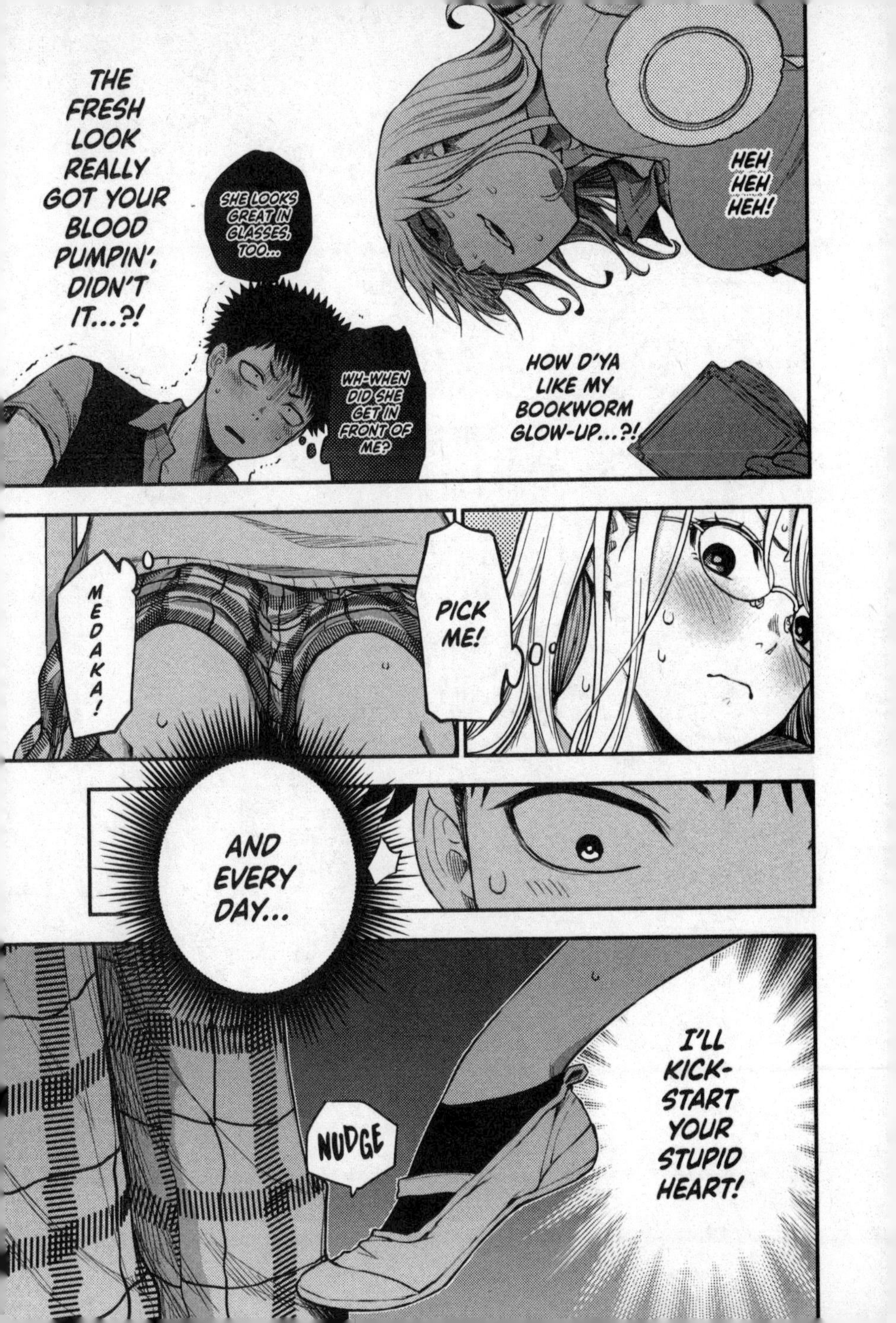
HEH HEH HEH!
HOW D'YA LIKE MY BOOKWORM GLOW-UP...?!
THE FRESH LOOK REALLY GOT YOUR BLOOD PUMPIN', DIDN'T IT...?!
SHE LOOKS GREAT IN GLASSES, TOO...
WH-WHEN DID SHE GET IN FRONT OF ME?
PICK ME!
MEDAKA!
AND EVERY DAY...
I'LL KICK-START YOUR STUPID HEART!
NUDGE

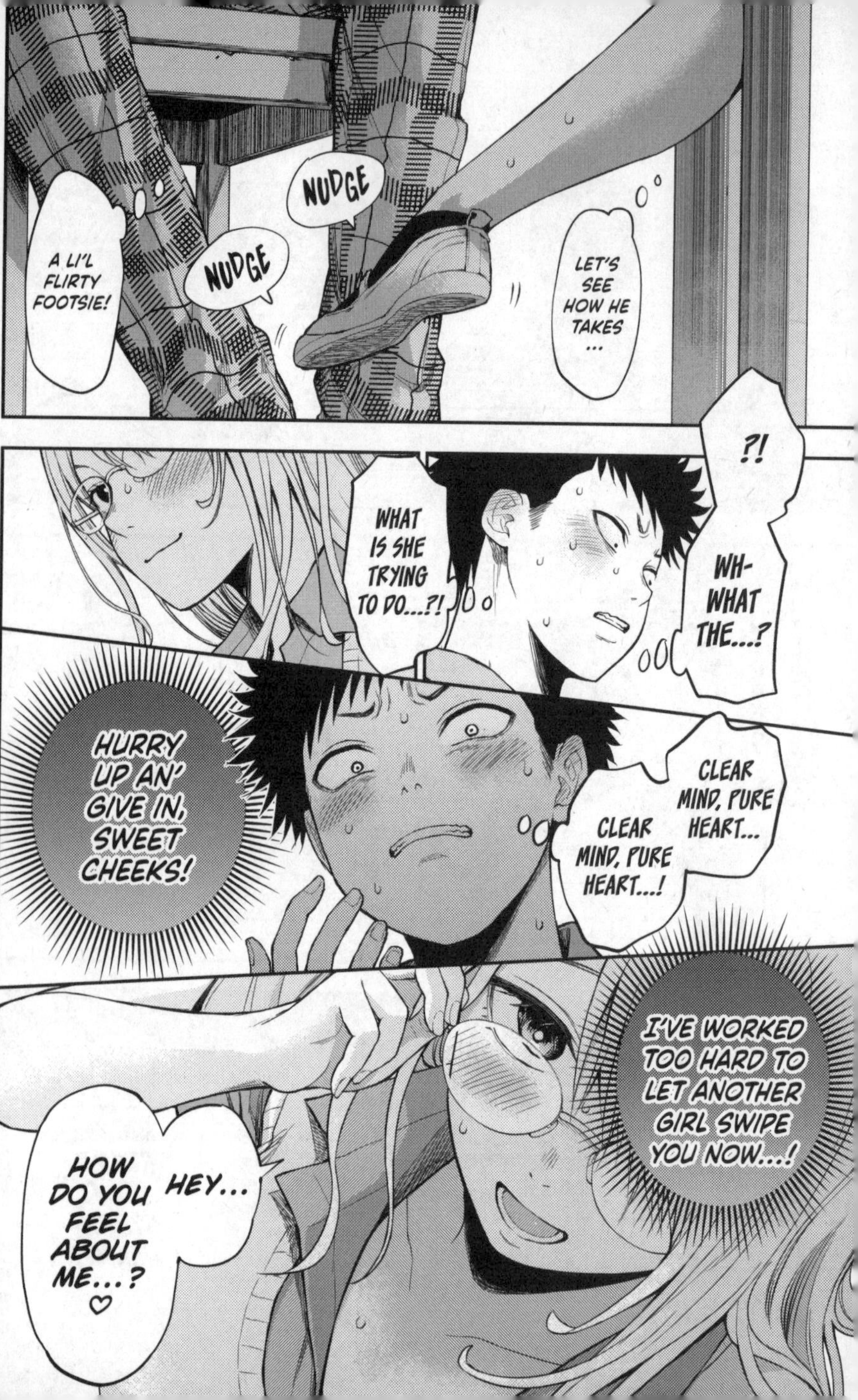
LET'S SEE HOW HE TAKES ...
NUDGE
NUDGE
A LI'L FLIRTY FOOTSIE!
?!
WH- WHAT THE...?
WHAT IS SHE TRYING TO DO...?!
CLEAR MIND, PURE HEART...
CLEAR MIND, PURE HEART...!
HURRY UP AN' GIVE IN, SWEET CHEEKS!
I'VE WORKED TOO HARD TO LET ANOTHER GIRL SWIPE YOU NOW...!
HEY...
HOW DO YOU FEEL ABOUT ME...? ♡

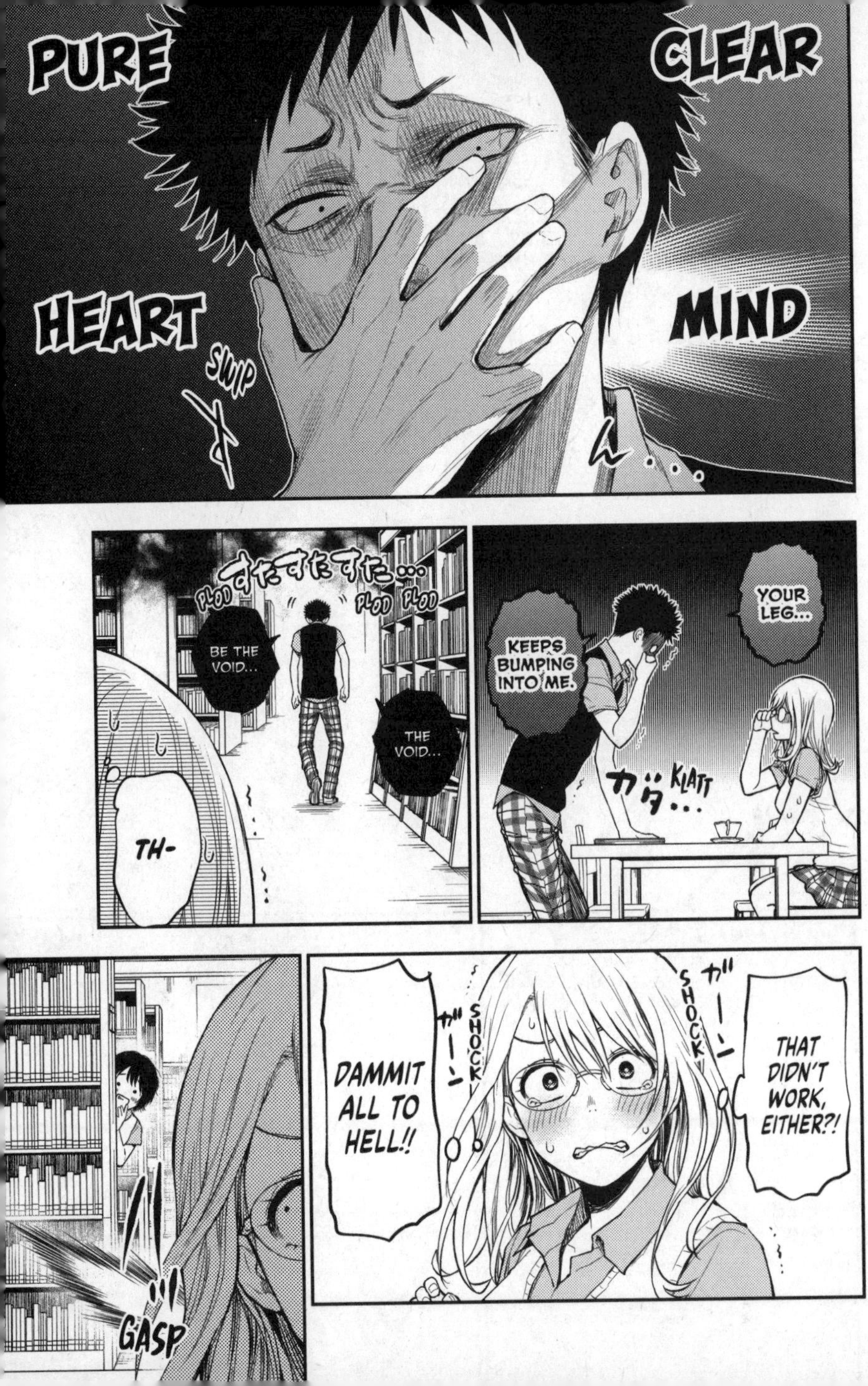
CLEAR
PURE
MIND
HEART
SWIP
YOUR LEG...
KEEPS BUMPING INTO ME.
KLATT
PLOD PLOD PLOD
BE THE VOID...
THE VOID...
TH-
THAT DIDN'T WORK, EITHER?!
SHOCK
SHOCK
DAMMIT ALL TO HELL!!
GASP

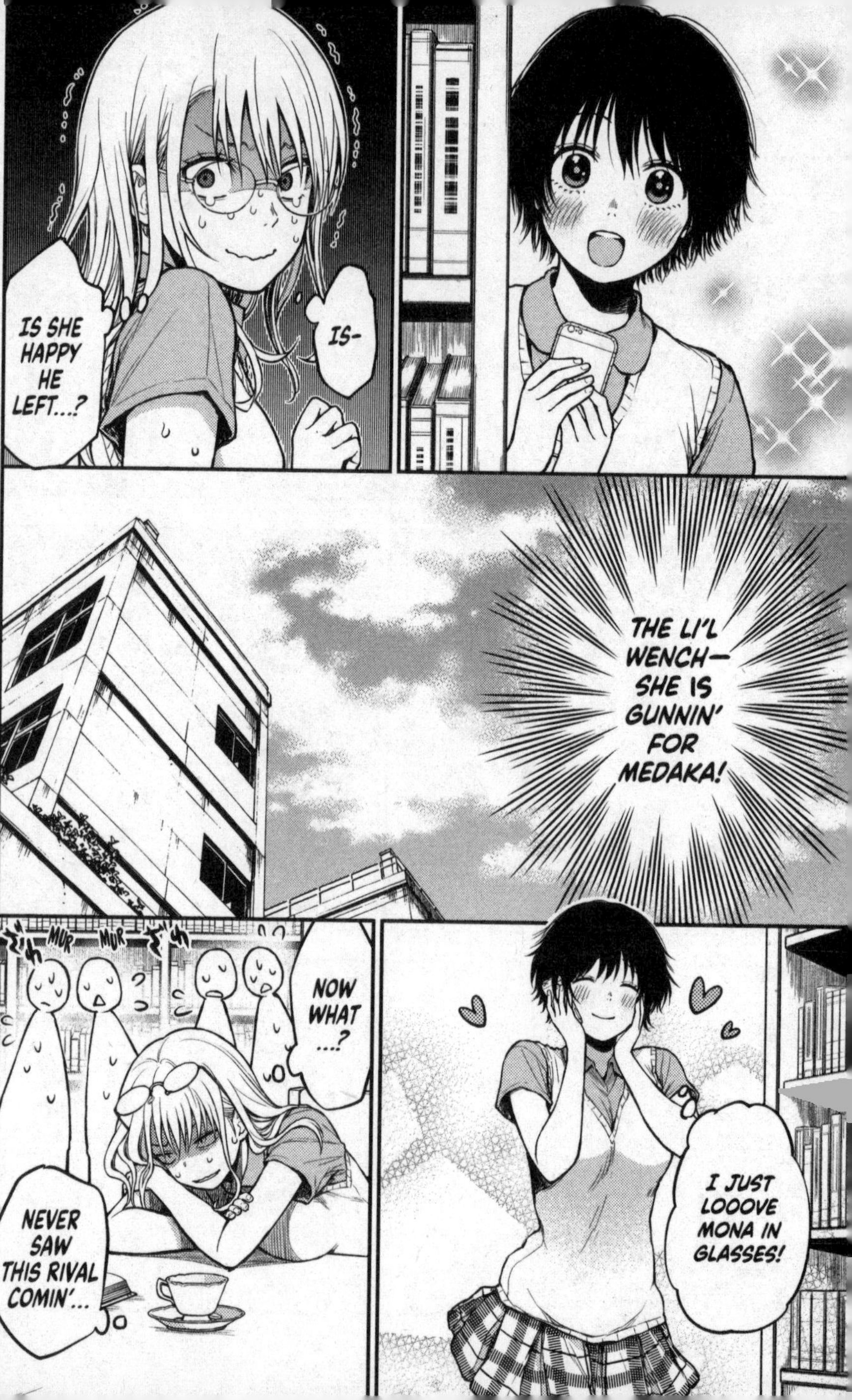
IS-
IS SHE HAPPY HE LEFT...?
THE LI'L WENCH— SHE IS GUNNIN' FOR MEDAKA!
I JUST LOOOVE MONA IN GLASSES!
MUR MUR
NOW WHAT ...?
NEVER SAW THIS RIVAL COMIN'...

Chapter 6

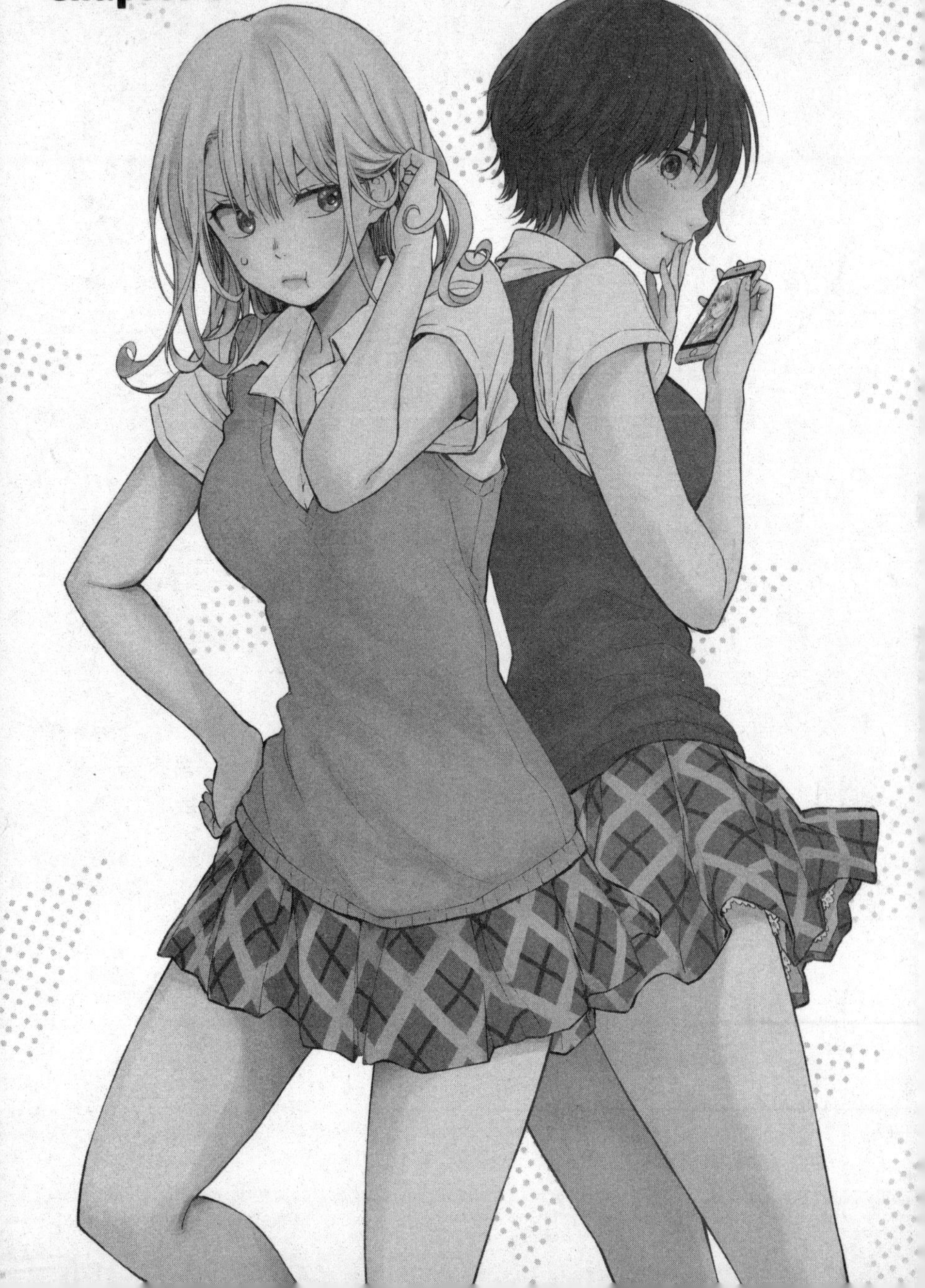

INITIAL DESIGNS FOR MONA KAWAI

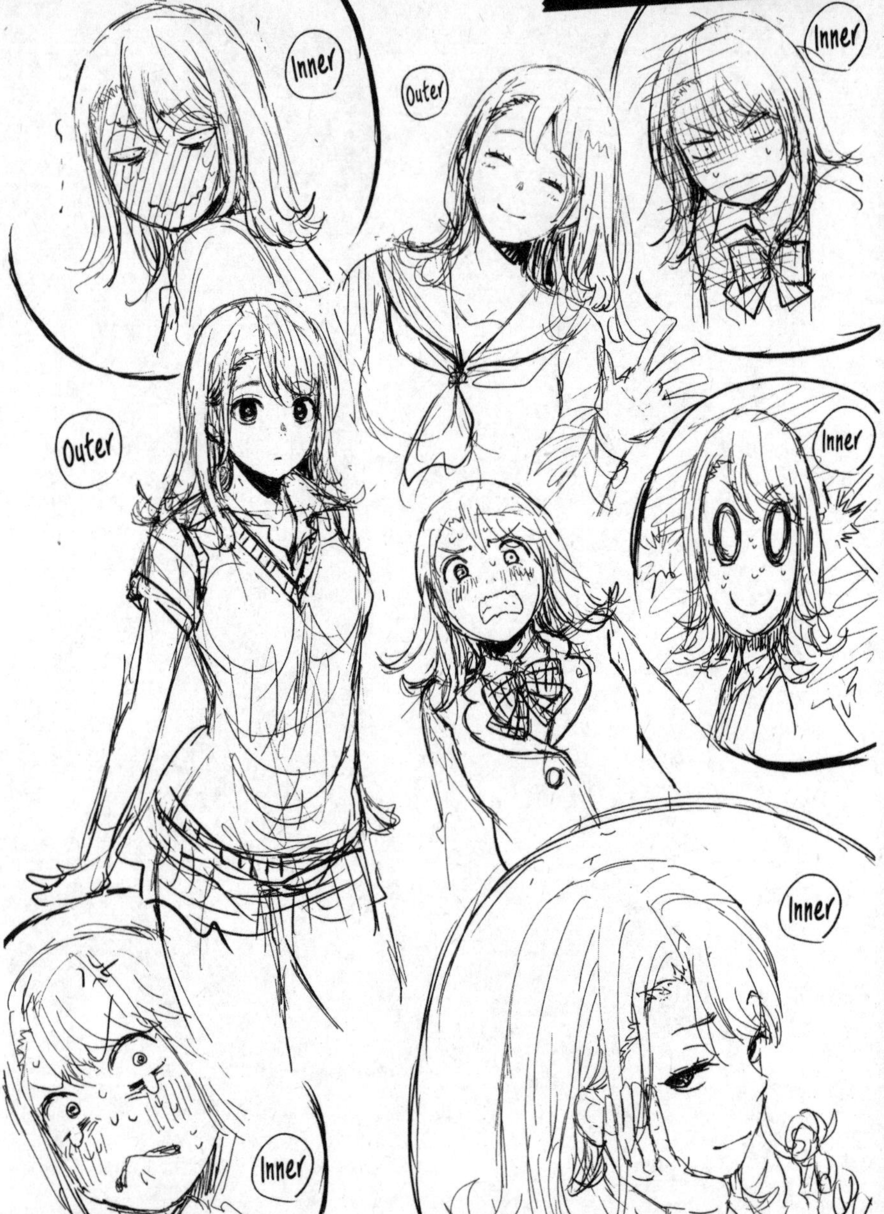
Inner
Outer
Inner
Inner
Outer
Inner
Inner

Chapter 6 ★ "Love" and That Jerk

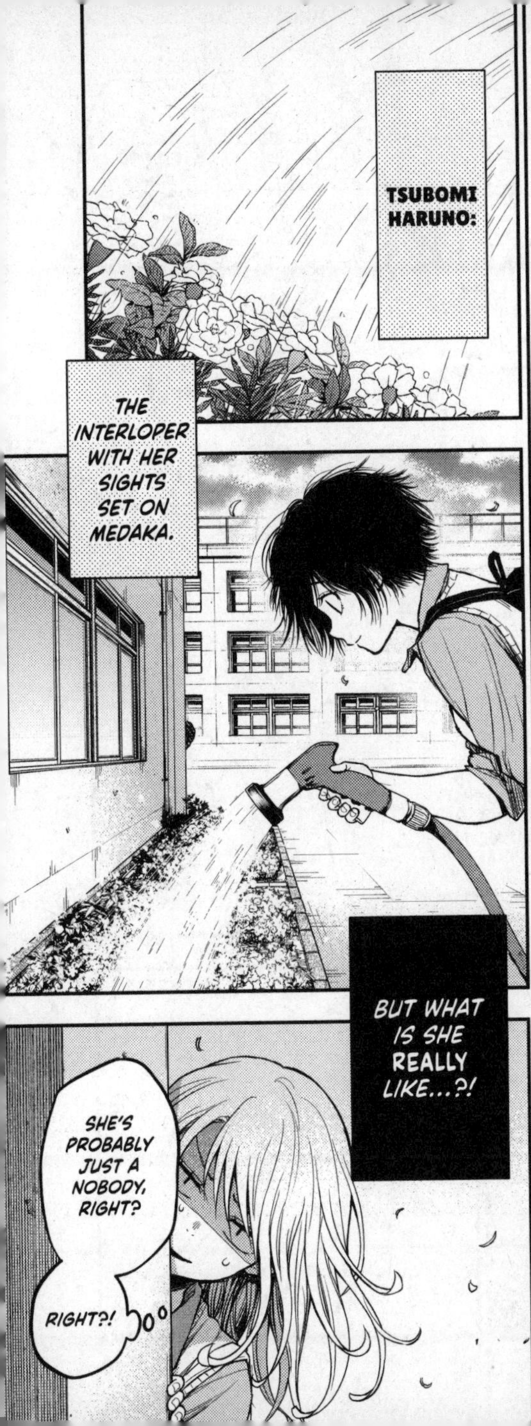
TSUBOMI HARUNO:
THE INTERLOPER WITH HER SIGHTS SET ON MEDAKA.
BUT WHAT IS SHE REALLY LIKE...?!
SHE'S PROBABLY JUST A NOBODY, RIGHT?
RIGHT?!

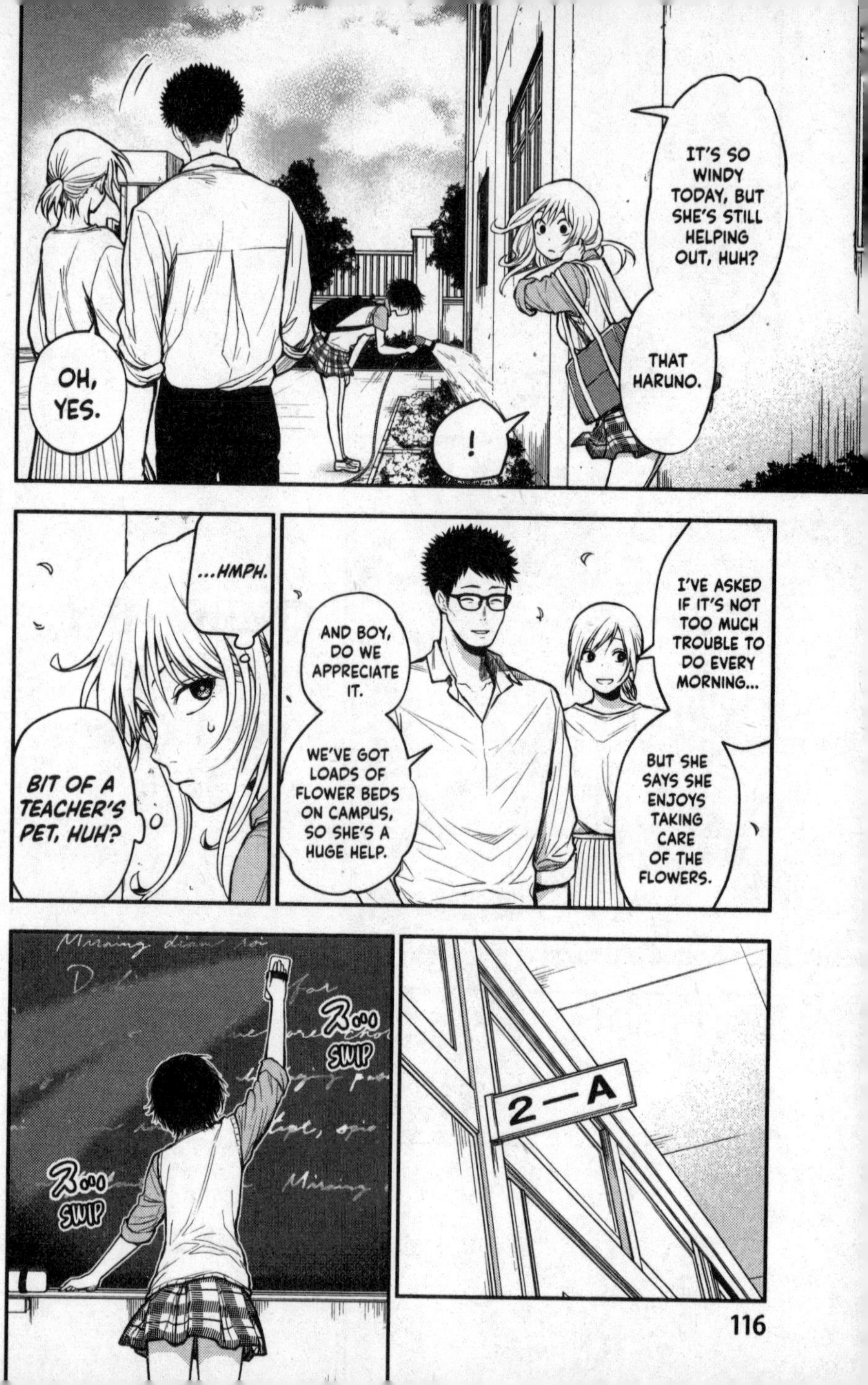
IT'S SO WINDY TODAY, BUT SHE'S STILL HELPING OUT, HUH?
THAT HARUNO.
!
OH, YES.
I'VE ASKED IF IT'S NOT TOO MUCH TROUBLE TO DO EVERY MORNING...
BUT SHE SAYS SHE ENJOYS TAKING CARE OF THE FLOWERS.
AND BOY, DO WE APPRECIATE IT.
WE'VE GOT LOADS OF FLOWER BEDS ON CAMPUS, SO SHE'S A HUGE HELP.
...HMPH.
BIT OF A TEACHER'S PET, HUH?
2—A
SWIP
SWIP

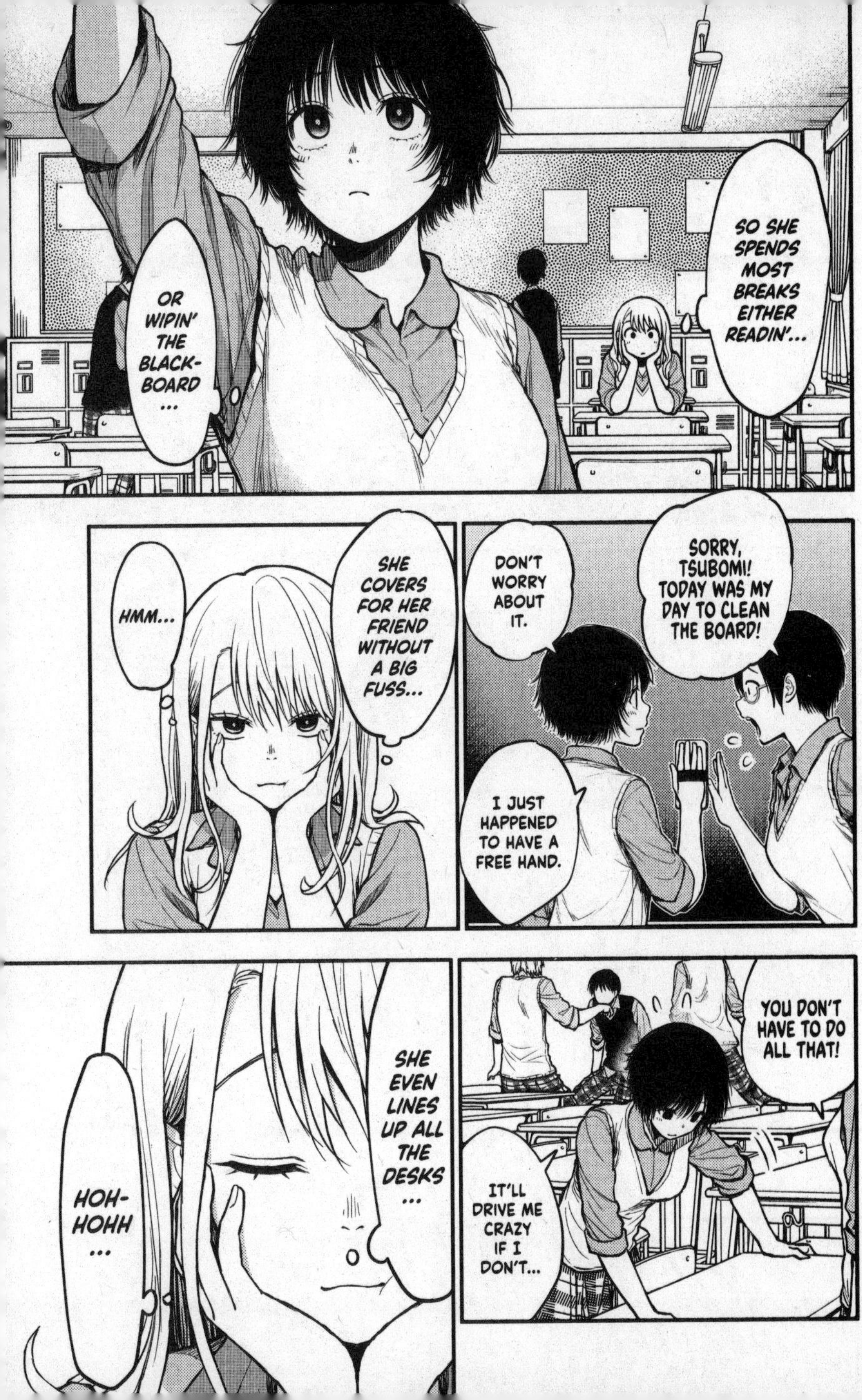
SO SHE SPENDS MOST BREAKS EITHER READIN'...
OR WIPIN' THE BLACK-BOARD...
SORRY, TSUBOMI! TODAY WAS MY DAY TO CLEAN THE BOARD!
DON'T WORRY ABOUT IT.
I JUST HAPPENED TO HAVE A FREE HAND.
SHE COVERS FOR HER FRIEND WITHOUT A BIG FUSS...
HMM...
YOU DON'T HAVE TO DO ALL THAT!
IT'LL DRIVE ME CRAZY IF I DON'T...
SHE EVEN LINES UP ALL THE DESKS...
HOH-HOHH...

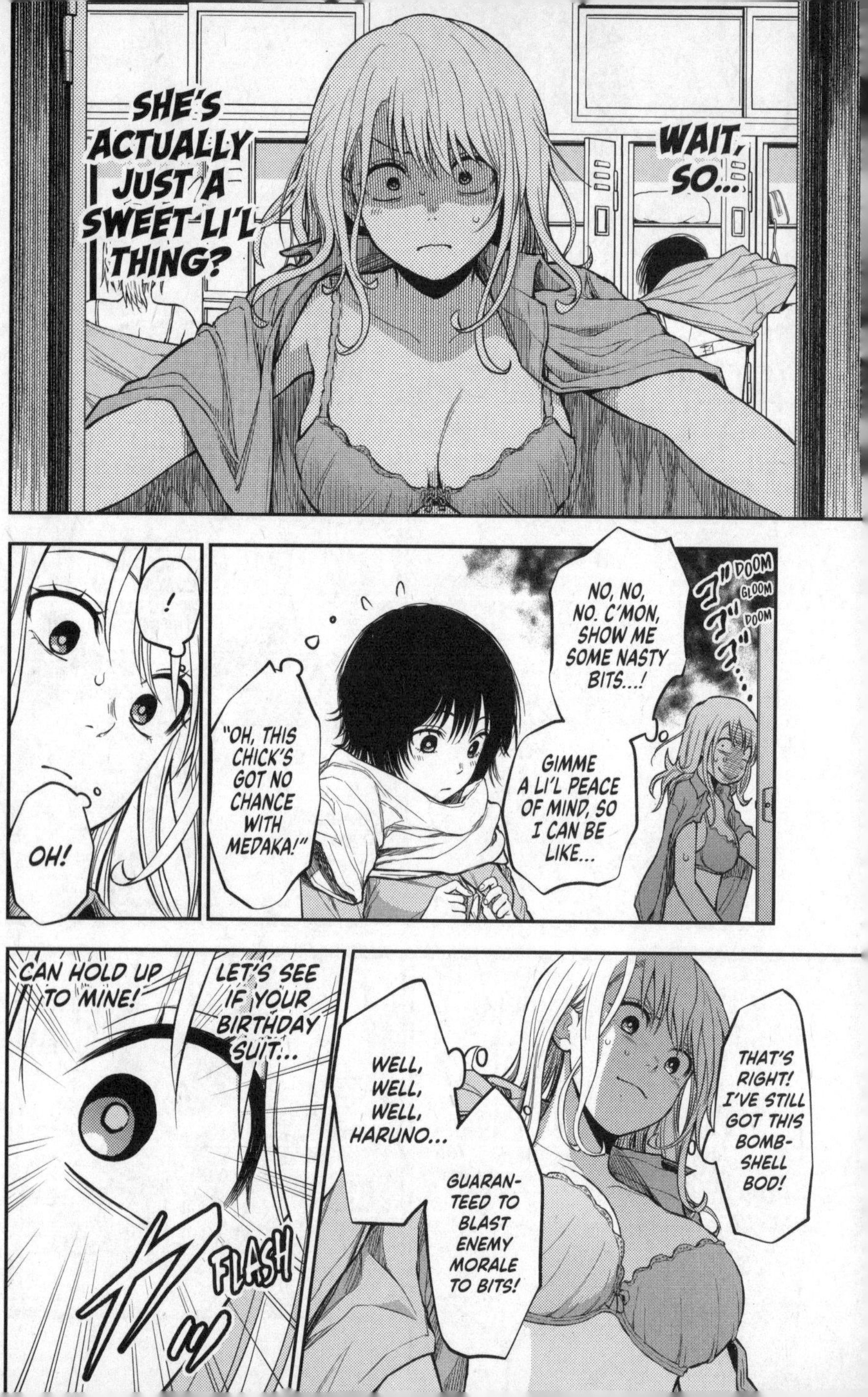
WAIT, SO...
SHE'S ACTUALLY JUST A SWEET LI'L THING?
NO, NO, NO. C'MON, SHOW ME SOME NASTY BITS...!
DOOM GLOOM DOOM
GIMME A LI'L PEACE OF MIND, SO I CAN BE LIKE...
"OH, THIS CHICK'S GOT NO CHANCE WITH MEDAKA!"
!
OH!
THAT'S RIGHT! I'VE STILL GOT THIS BOMB-SHELL BOD!
GUARAN-TEED TO BLAST ENEMY MORALE TO BITS!
WELL, WELL, WELL, HARUNO...
LET'S SEE IF YOUR BIRTHDAY SUIT...
CAN HOLD UP TO MINE!
FLASH

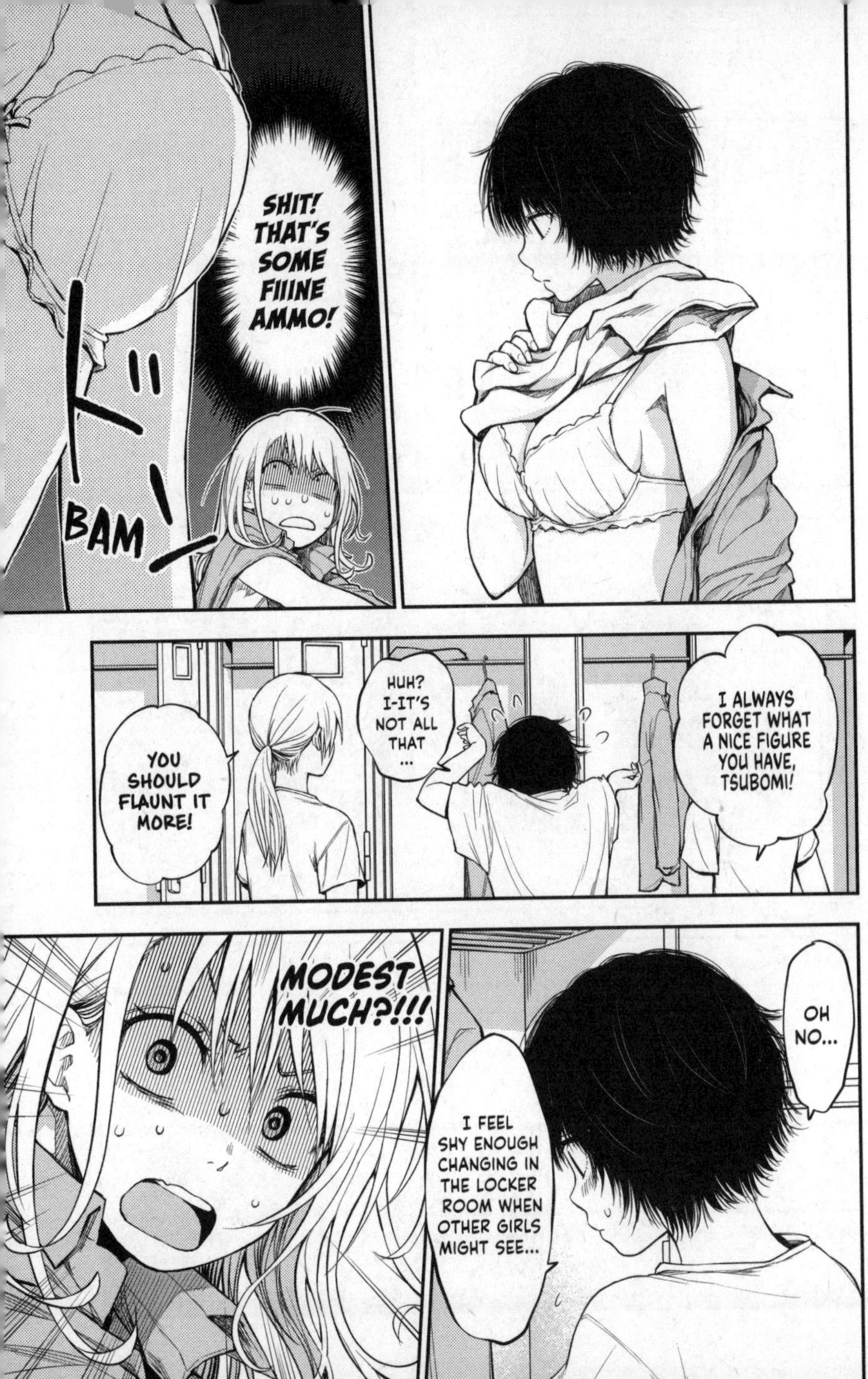
SHIT! THAT'S SOME FIIINE AMMO!
BAM
I ALWAYS FORGET WHAT A NICE FIGURE YOU HAVE, TSUBOMI!
HUH? I-IT'S NOT ALL THAT ...
YOU SHOULD FLAUNT IT MORE!
OH NO...
I FEEL SHY ENOUGH CHANGING IN THE LOCKER ROOM WHEN OTHER GIRLS MIGHT SEE...
MODEST MUCH?!!!

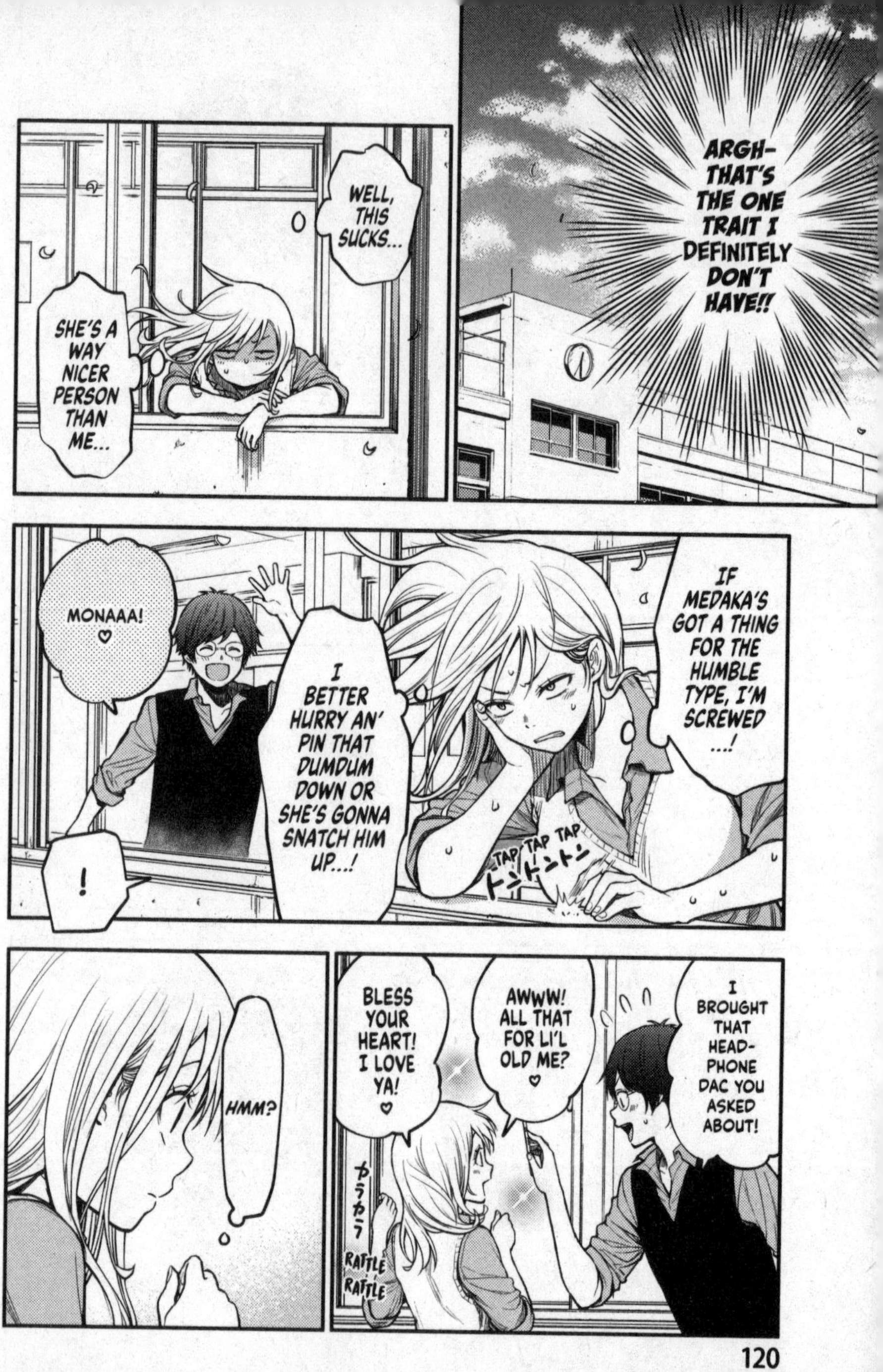
ARGH—THAT'S THE ONE TRAIT I DEFINITELY DON'T HAVE!!
WELL, THIS SUCKS...
SHE'S A WAY NICER PERSON THAN ME...
IF MEDAKA'S GOT A THING FOR THE HUMBLE TYPE, I'M SCREWED ...!
I BETTER HURRY AN' PIN THAT DUMDUM DOWN OR SHE'S GONNA SNATCH HIM UP...!
MONAAA! ♡
TAP TAP TAP
トントントン
!
I BROUGHT THAT HEAD-PHONE DAC YOU ASKED ABOUT!
AWWW! ALL THAT FOR LI'L OLD ME? ♡
BLESS YOUR HEART! I LOVE YA! ♡
カラカラ
RATTLE RATTLE
HMM?

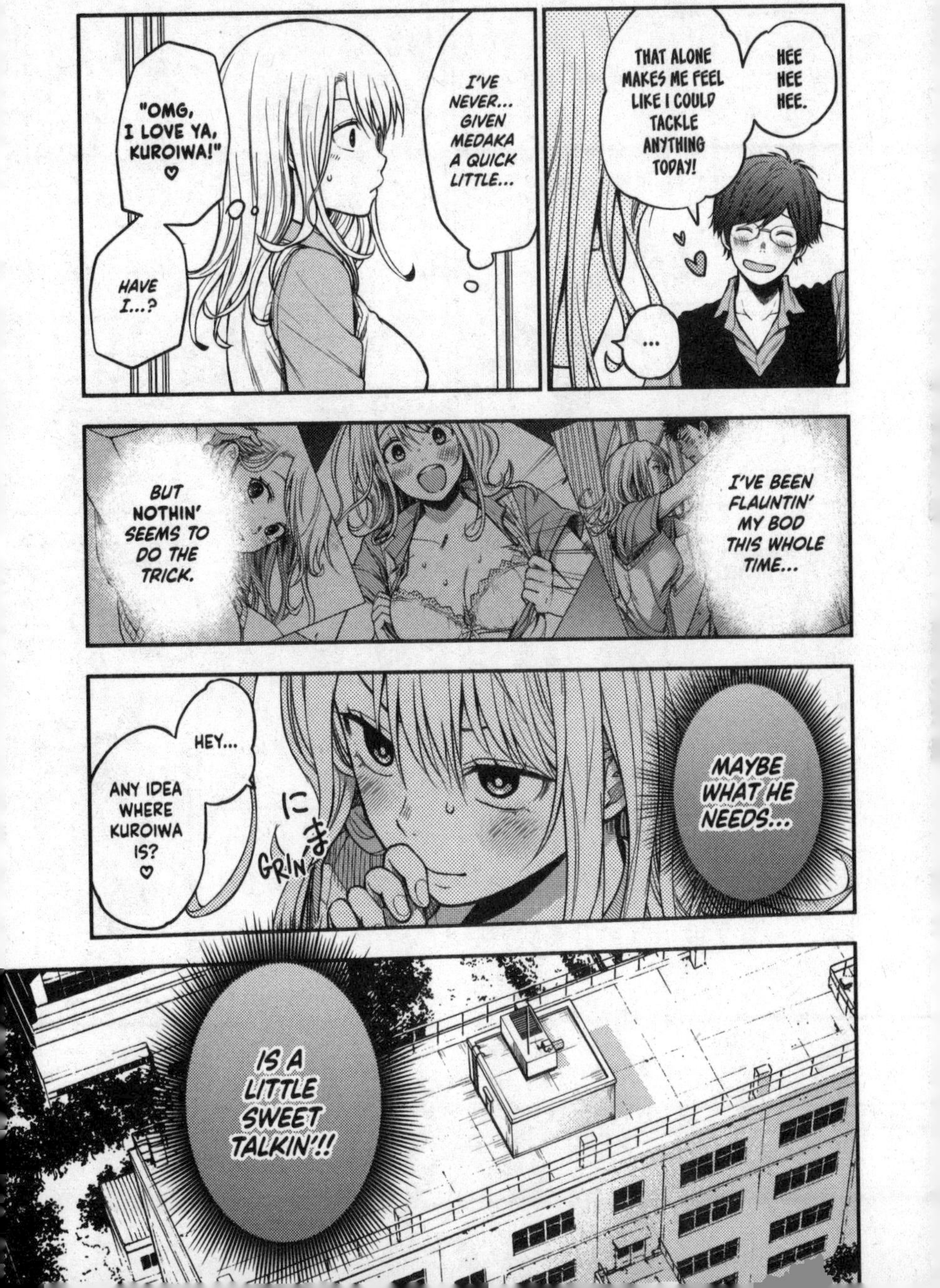
HEE HEE HEE.
THAT ALONE MAKES ME FEEL LIKE I COULD TACKLE ANYTHING TODAY!
...
I'VE NEVER... GIVEN MEDAKA A QUICK LITTLE...
"OMG, I LOVE YA, KUROIWA!" ♡
HAVE I...?
I'VE BEEN FLAUNTIN' MY BOD THIS WHOLE TIME...
BUT NOTHIN' SEEMS TO DO THE TRICK.
MAYBE WHAT HE NEEDS...
にま
GRIN
HEY...
ANY IDEA WHERE KUROIWA IS? ♡
IS A LITTLE SWEET TALKIN'!!

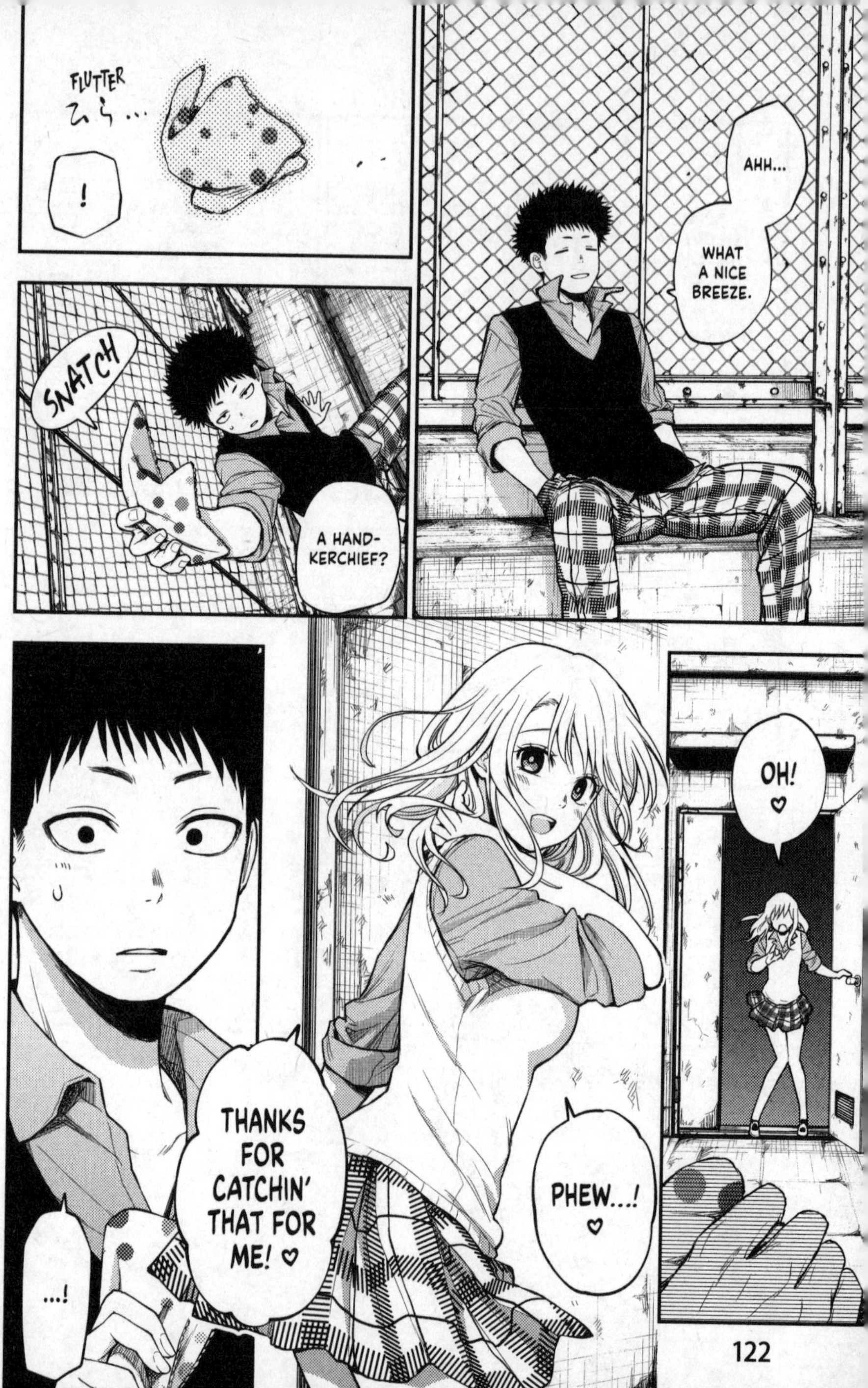
AHH... WHAT A NICE BREEZE.
FLUTTER
ひら...
!
SNATCH
A HAND-KERCHIEF?
OH! ♡
PHEW...! ♡
THANKS FOR CATCHIN' THAT FOR ME! ♡
...!

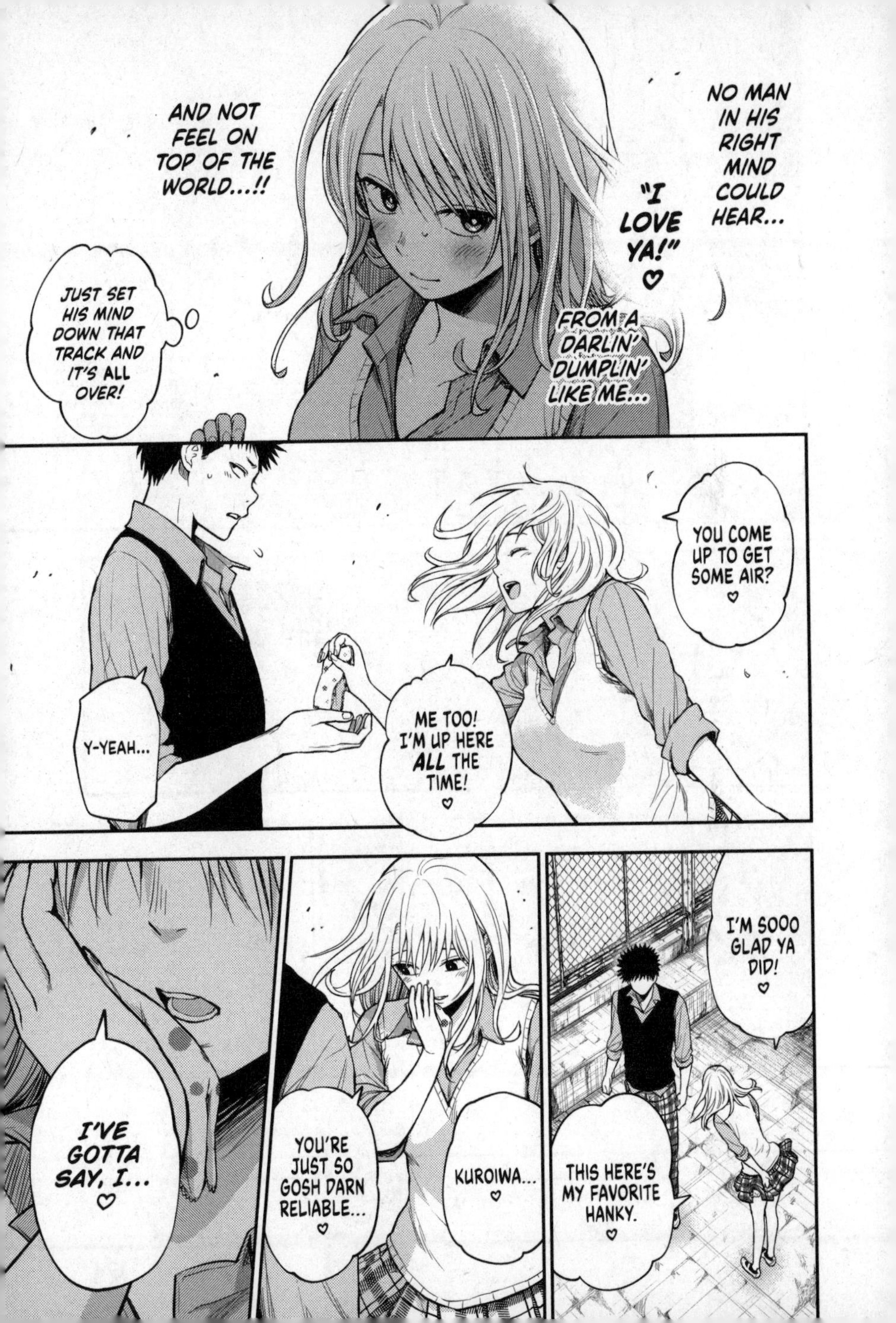
NO MAN IN HIS RIGHT MIND COULD HEAR...
"I LOVE YA!" ♡
FROM A DARLIN' DUMPLIN' LIKE ME...
AND NOT FEEL ON TOP OF THE WORLD...!!
JUST SET HIS MIND DOWN THAT TRACK AND IT'S ALL OVER!
YOU COME UP TO GET SOME AIR? ♡
ME TOO! I'M UP HERE ALL THE TIME! ♡
Y-YEAH...
I'M SOOO GLAD YA DID! ♡
THIS HERE'S MY FAVORITE HANKY. ♡
KUROIWA...
YOU'RE JUST SO GOSH DARN RELIABLE... ♡
I'VE GOTTA SAY, I... ♡

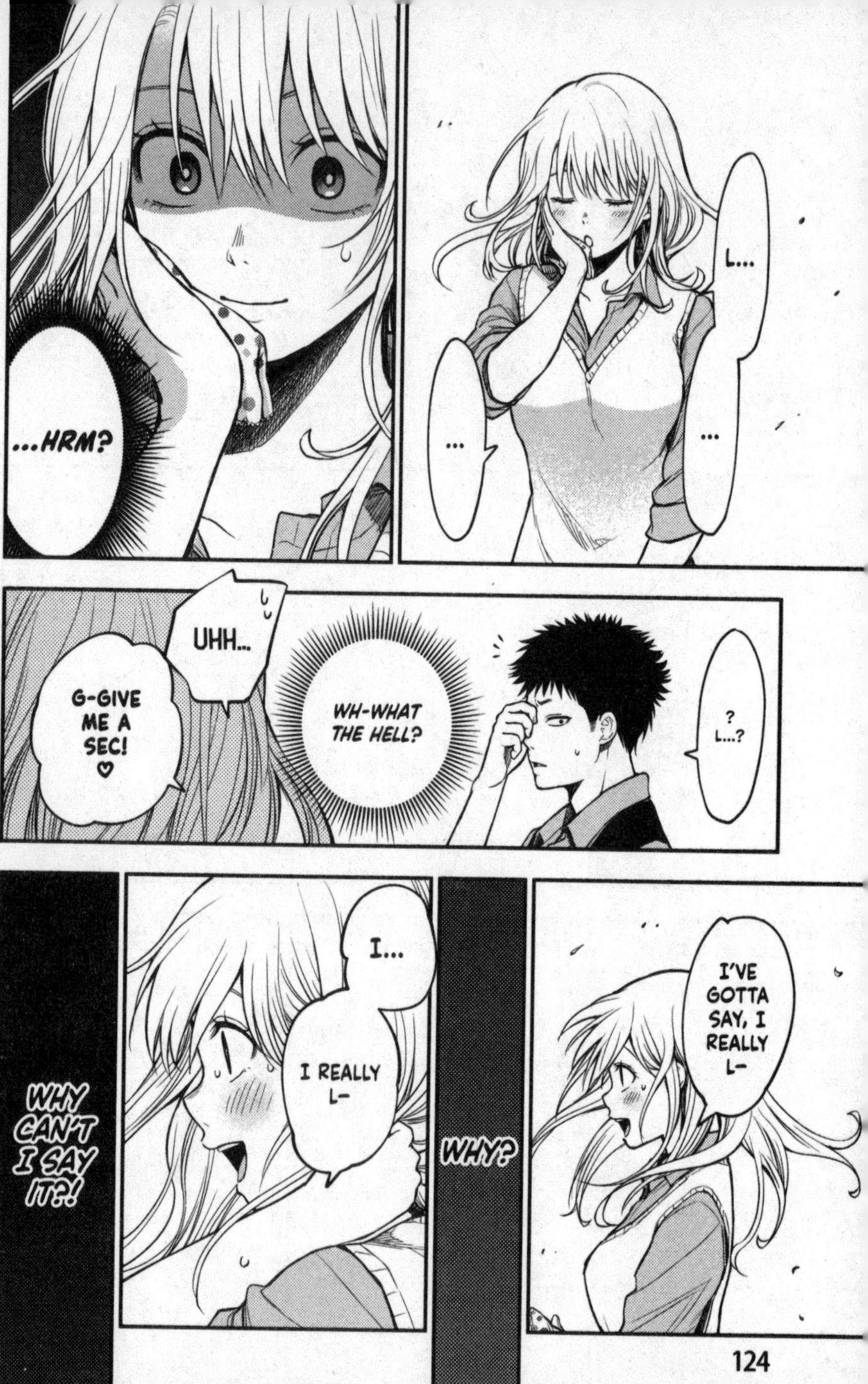
L...
...
...
...HRM?
?
L...?
WH-WHAT THE HELL?
UHH...
G-GIVE ME A SEC! ♡
I'VE GOTTA SAY, I REALLY L–
WHY?
I...
I REALLY L–
WHY CAN'T I SAY IT?!

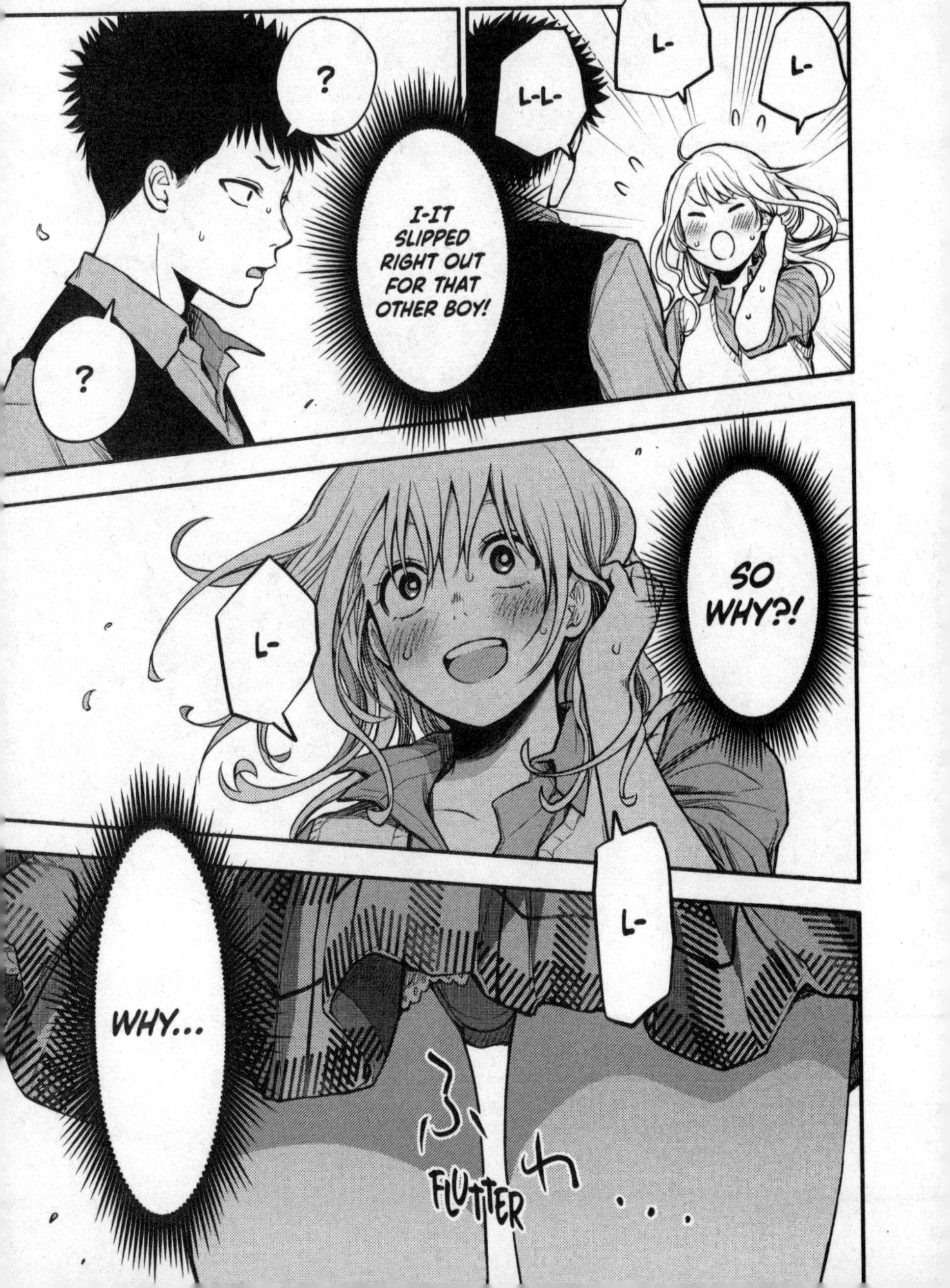
L-
L-
L-L-
I-IT SLIPPED RIGHT OUT FOR THAT OTHER BOY!
?
?
SO WHY?!
L-
L-
WHY...
FLUTTER
...

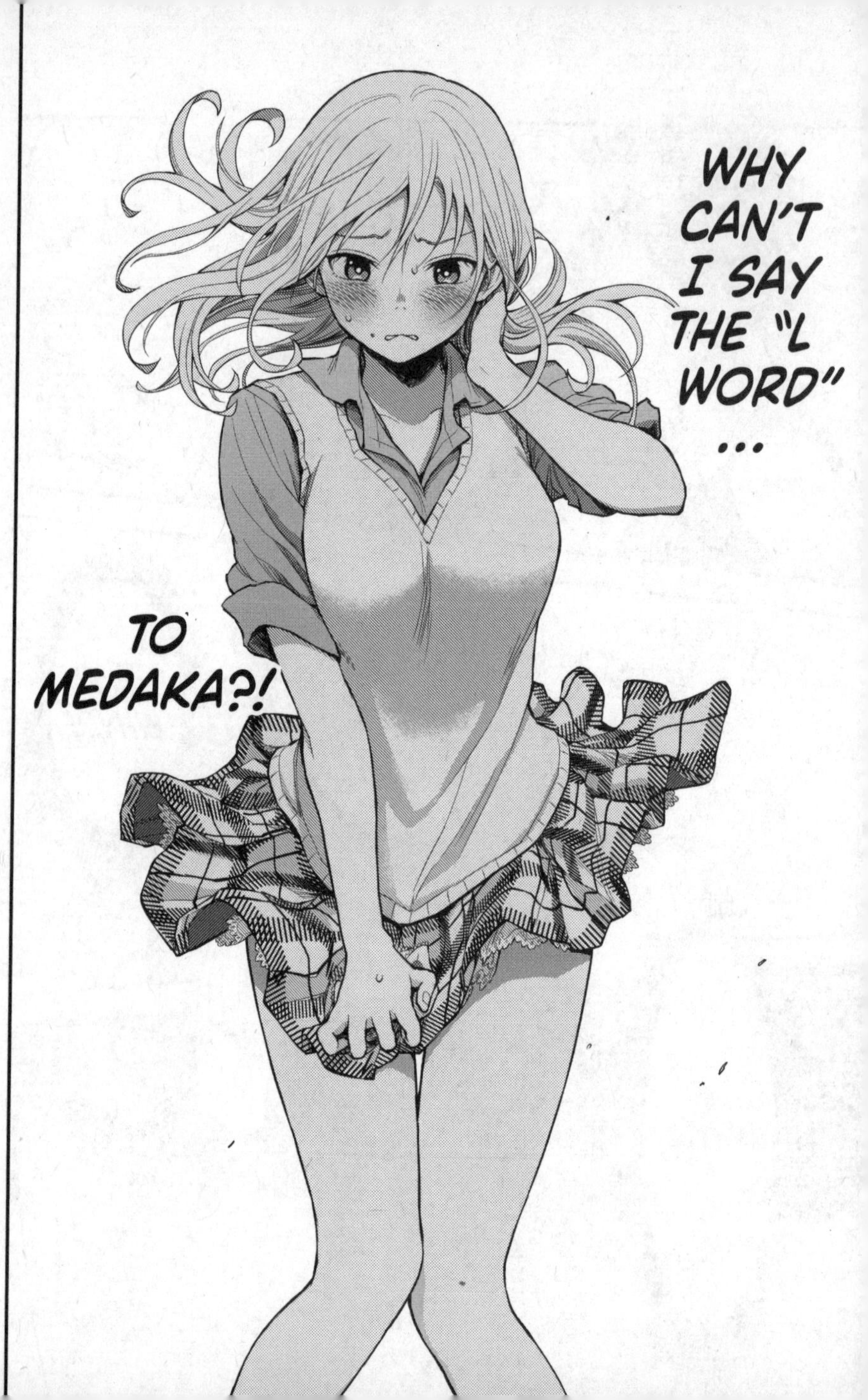
WHY CAN'T I SAY THE "L WORD" ...
TO MEDAKA?!

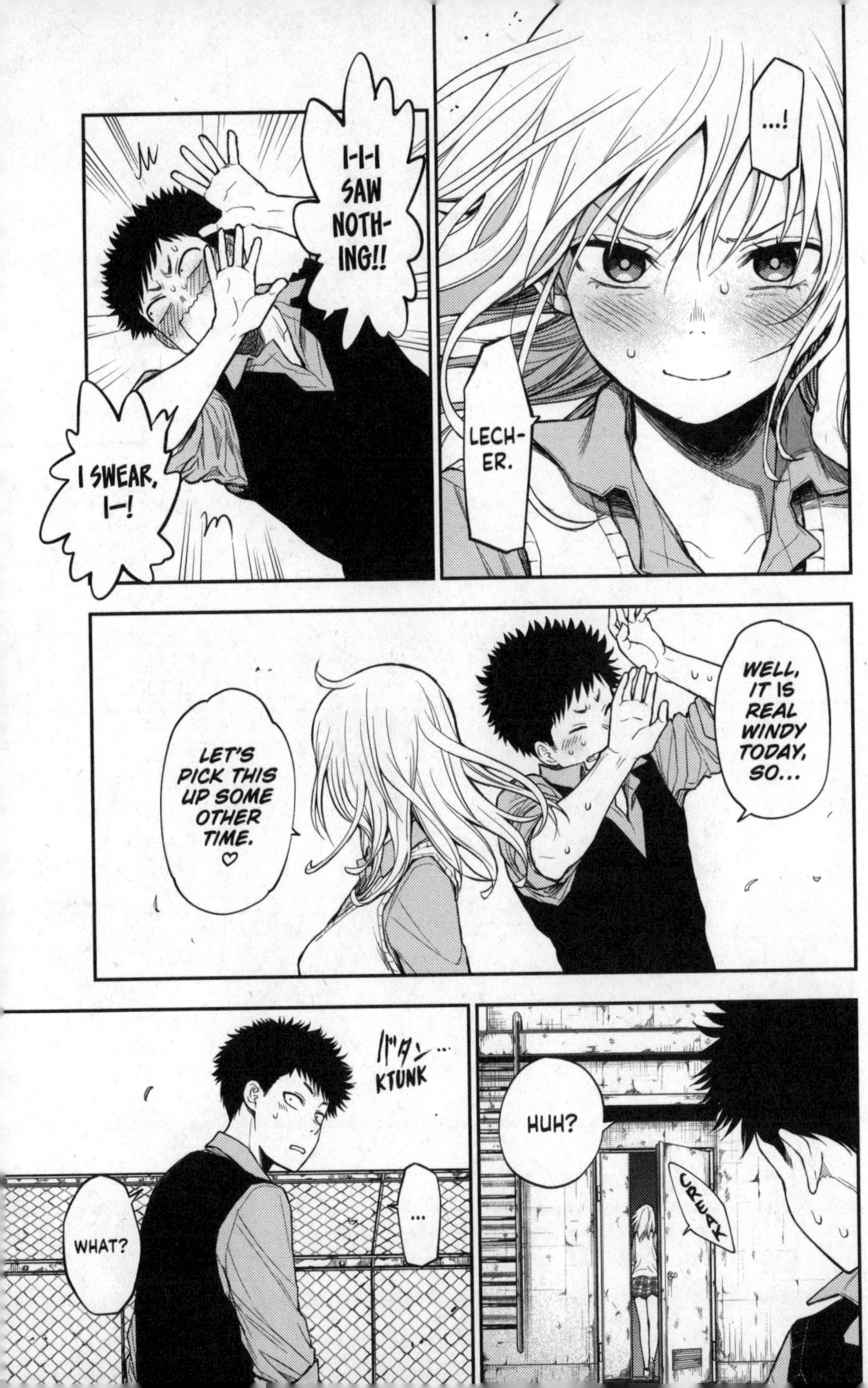
...!
LECHER.
I-I-I SAW NOTHING!!
I SWEAR, I—!
WELL, IT IS REAL WINDY TODAY, SO...
LET'S PICK THIS UP SOME OTHER TIME. ♡
HUH?
CREAK
バタン…
KTUNK
...
WHAT?

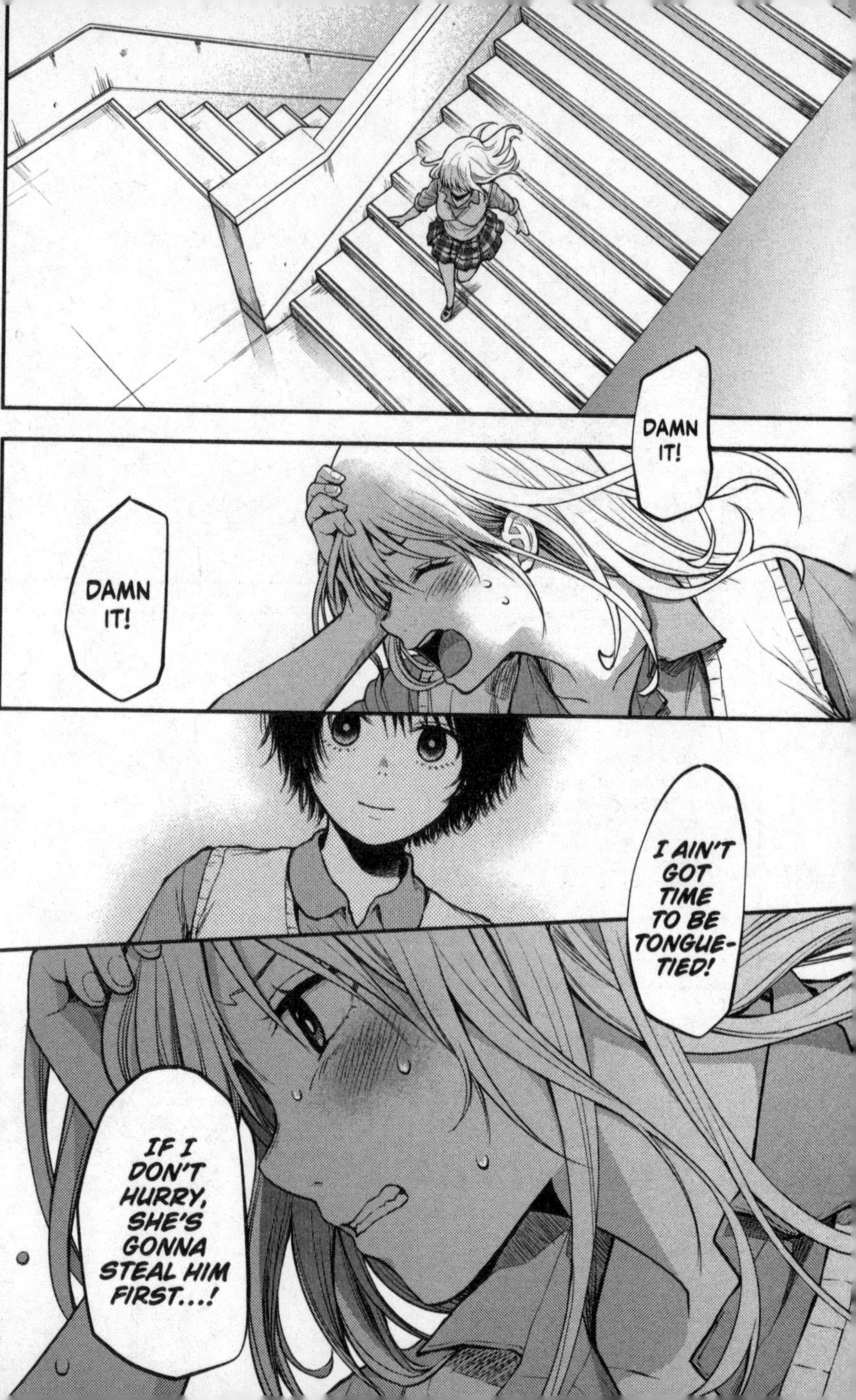
DAMN IT!
DAMN IT!
I AIN'T GOT TIME TO BE TONGUE-TIED!
IF I DON'T HURRY, SHE'S GONNA STEAL HIM FIRST...!

Chapter 7 * That Girl and Her Wallpaper

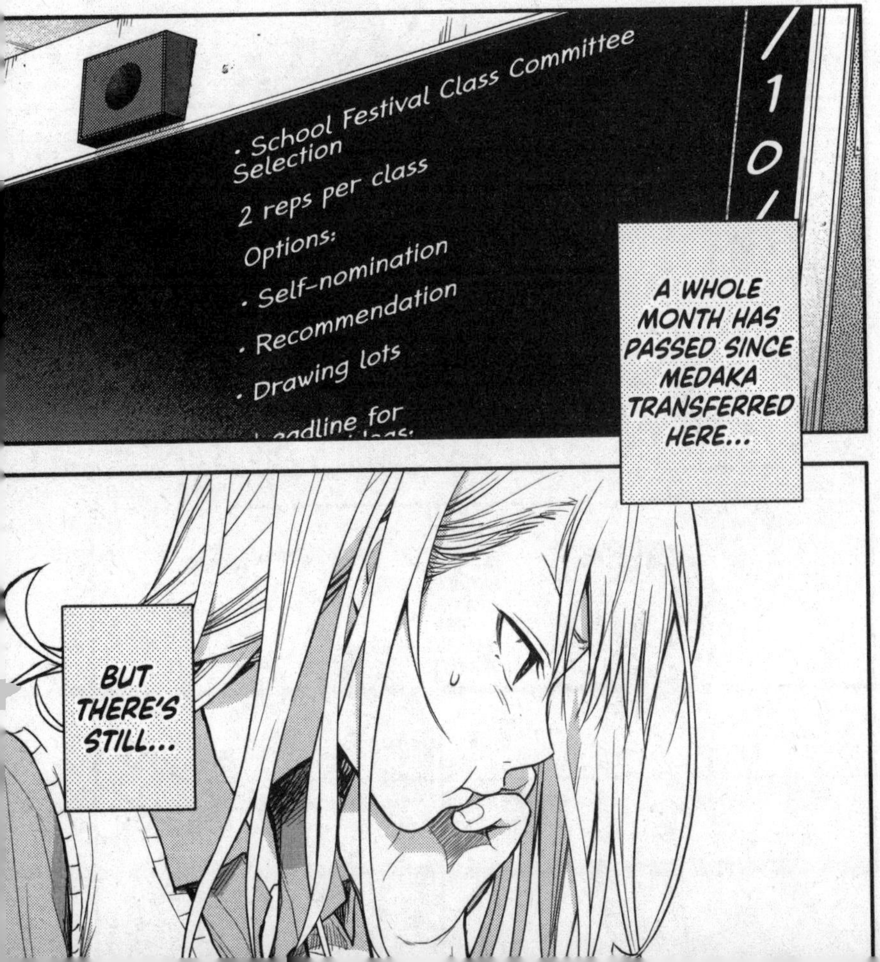
· School Festival Class Committee Selection
2 reps per class
Options:
· Self-nomination
· Recommendation
· Drawing lots
A WHOLE MONTH HAS PASSED SINCE MEDAKA TRANSFERRED HERE...
BUT THERE'S STILL...

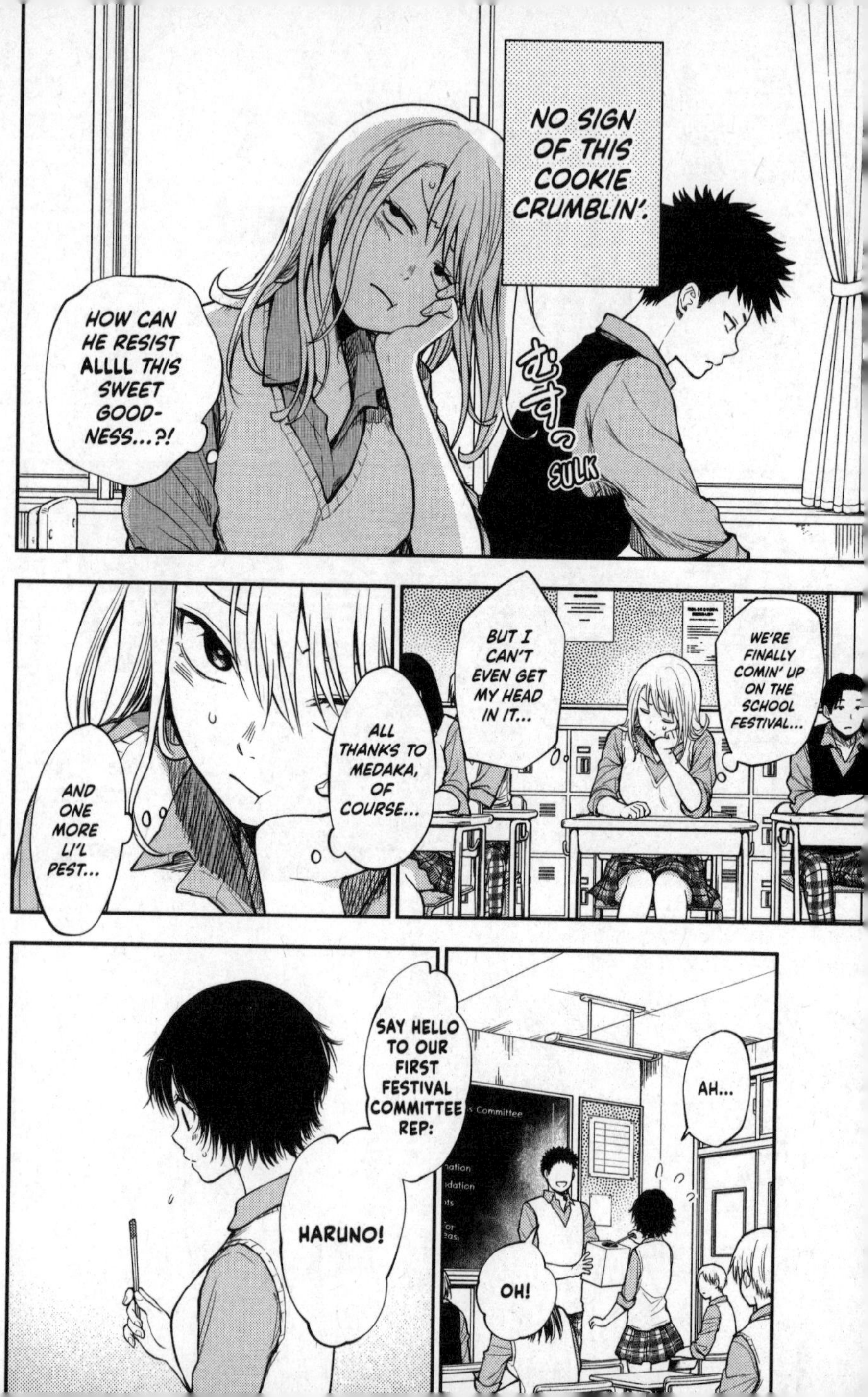
NO SIGN OF THIS COOKIE CRUMBLIN'.
むすっ
SULK
HOW CAN HE RESIST ALLLL THIS SWEET GOOD-NESS...?!
WE'RE FINALLY COMIN' UP ON THE SCHOOL FESTIVAL...
BUT I CAN'T EVEN GET MY HEAD IN IT...
ALL THANKS TO MEDAKA, OF COURSE...
AND ONE MORE LI'L PEST...
AH...
OH!
SAY HELLO TO OUR FIRST FESTIVAL COMMITTEE REP:
HARUNO!

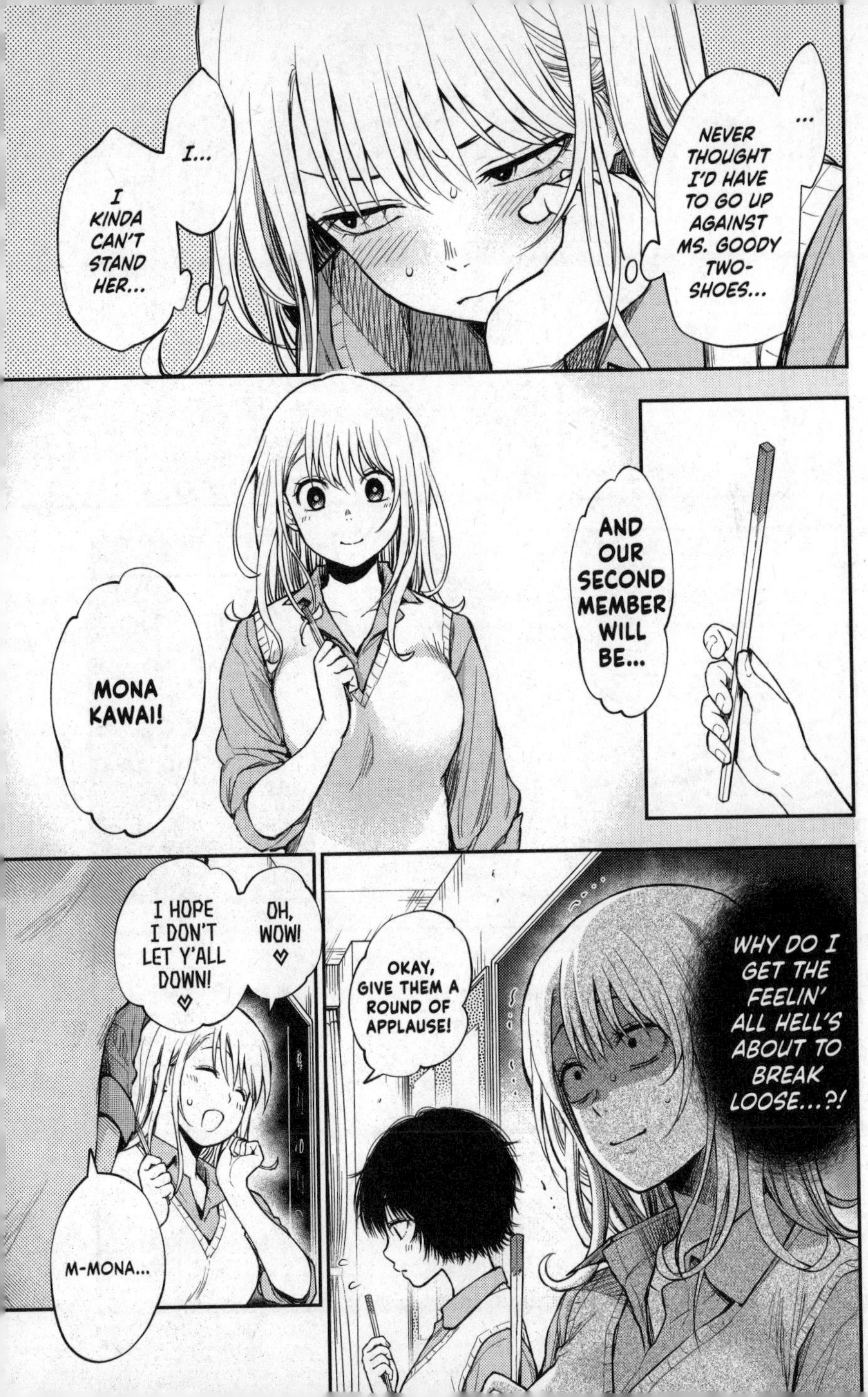
...
NEVER THOUGHT I'D HAVE TO GO UP AGAINST MS. GOODY TWO-SHOES...
I...
I KINDA CAN'T STAND HER...
AND OUR SECOND MEMBER WILL BE...
MONA KAWAI!
WHY DO I GET THE FEELIN' ALL HELL'S ABOUT TO BREAK LOOSE...?!
OKAY, GIVE THEM A ROUND OF APPLAUSE!
OH, WOW! ♥
I HOPE I DON'T LET Y'ALL DOWN! ♥
M-MONA...

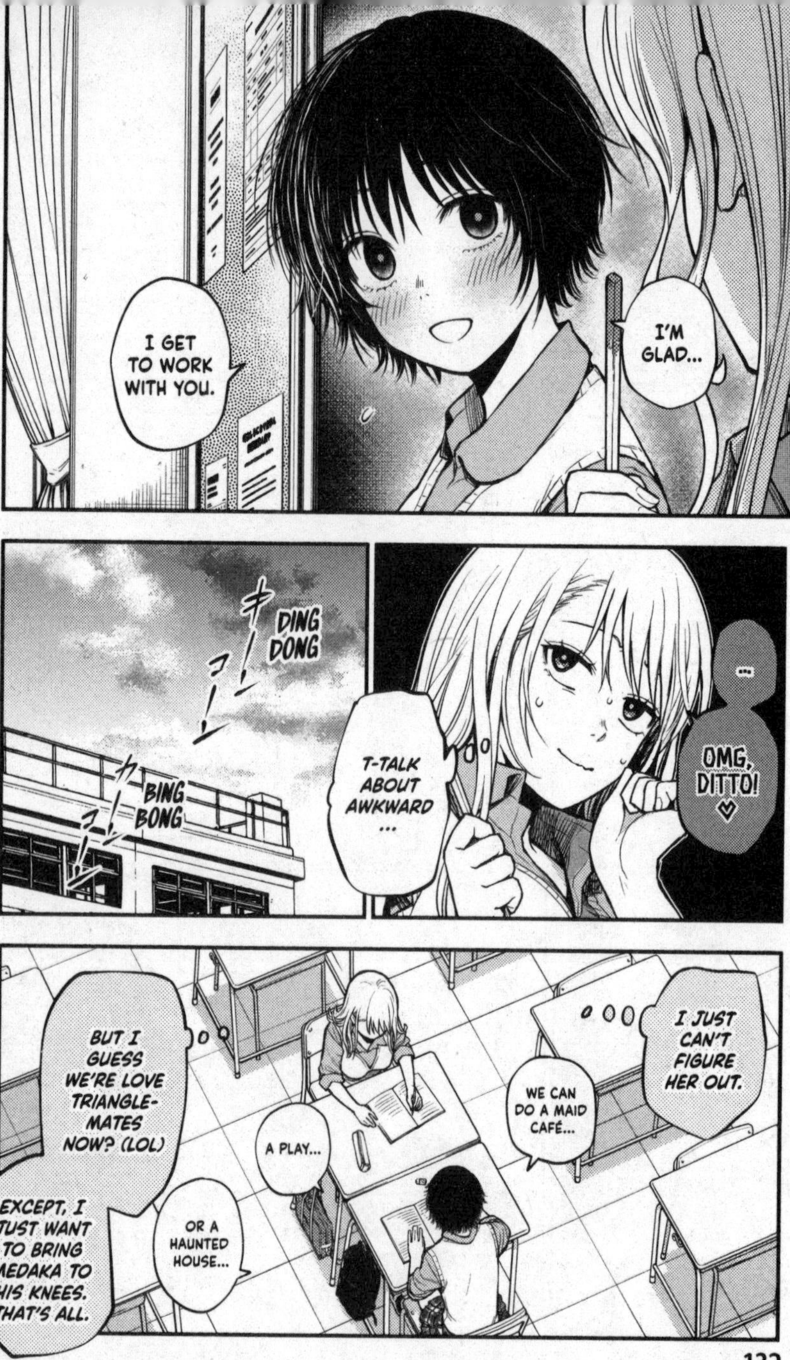
I'M GLAD...
I GET TO WORK WITH YOU.
...
OMG, DITTO! ♥
T-TALK ABOUT AWKWARD ...
DING DONG
BING BONG
I JUST CAN'T FIGURE HER OUT.
BUT I GUESS WE'RE LOVE TRIANGLE-MATES NOW? (LOL)
WE CAN DO A MAID CAFÉ...
A PLAY...
OR A HAUNTED HOUSE...
EXCEPT, I JUST WANT TO BRING MEDAKA TO HIS KNEES. THAT'S ALL.

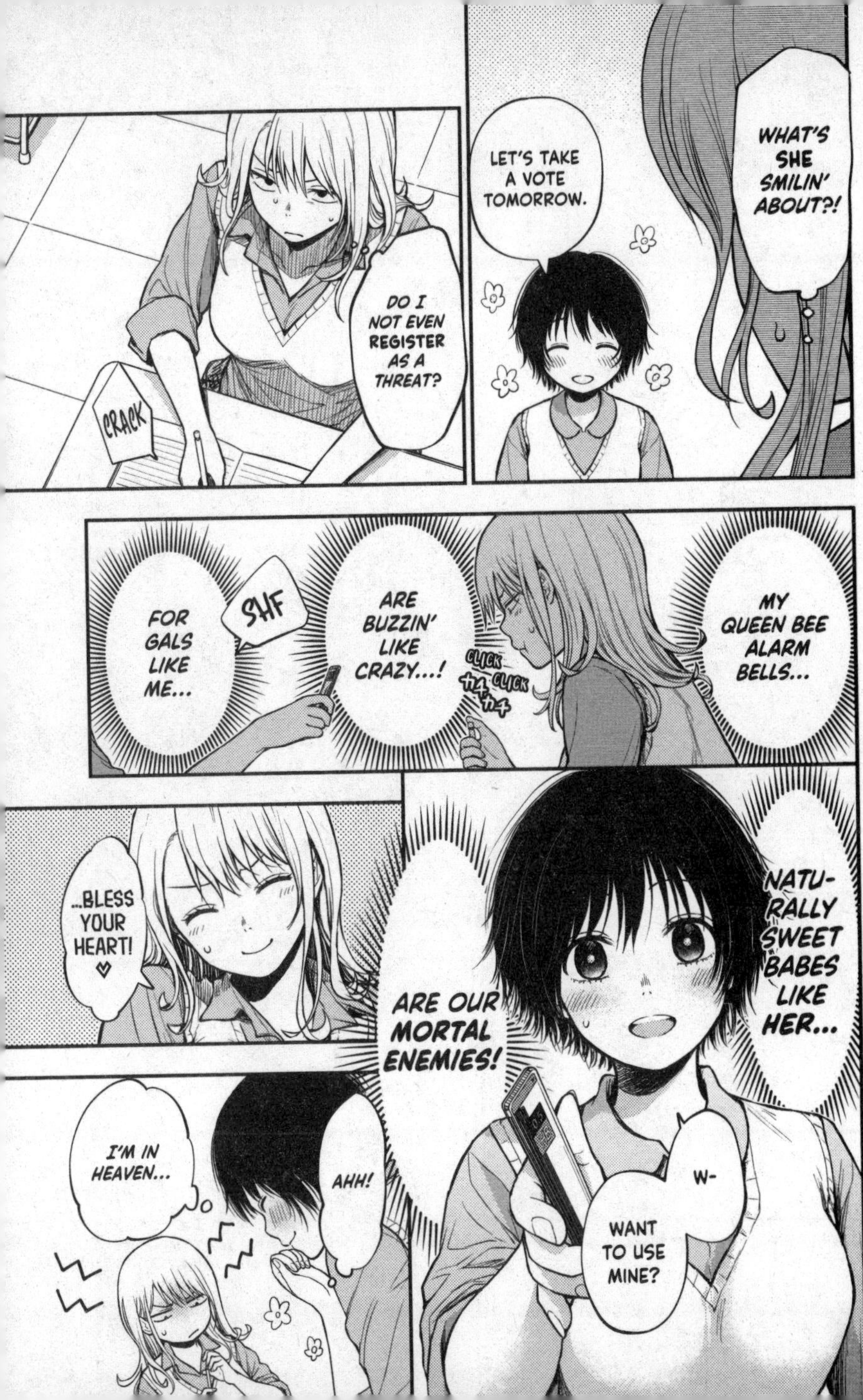
WHAT'S SHE SMILIN' ABOUT?!
LET'S TAKE A VOTE TOMORROW.
DO I NOT EVEN REGISTER AS A THREAT?
CRACK
MY QUEEN BEE ALARM BELLS...
CLICK CLICK
カチカチ
ARE BUZZIN' LIKE CRAZY...!
SHF
FOR GALS LIKE ME...
NATU-RALLY SWEET BABES LIKE HER...
ARE OUR MORTAL ENEMIES!
W-
WANT TO USE MINE?
...BLESS YOUR HEART! ♡
AHH!
I'M IN HEAVEN...

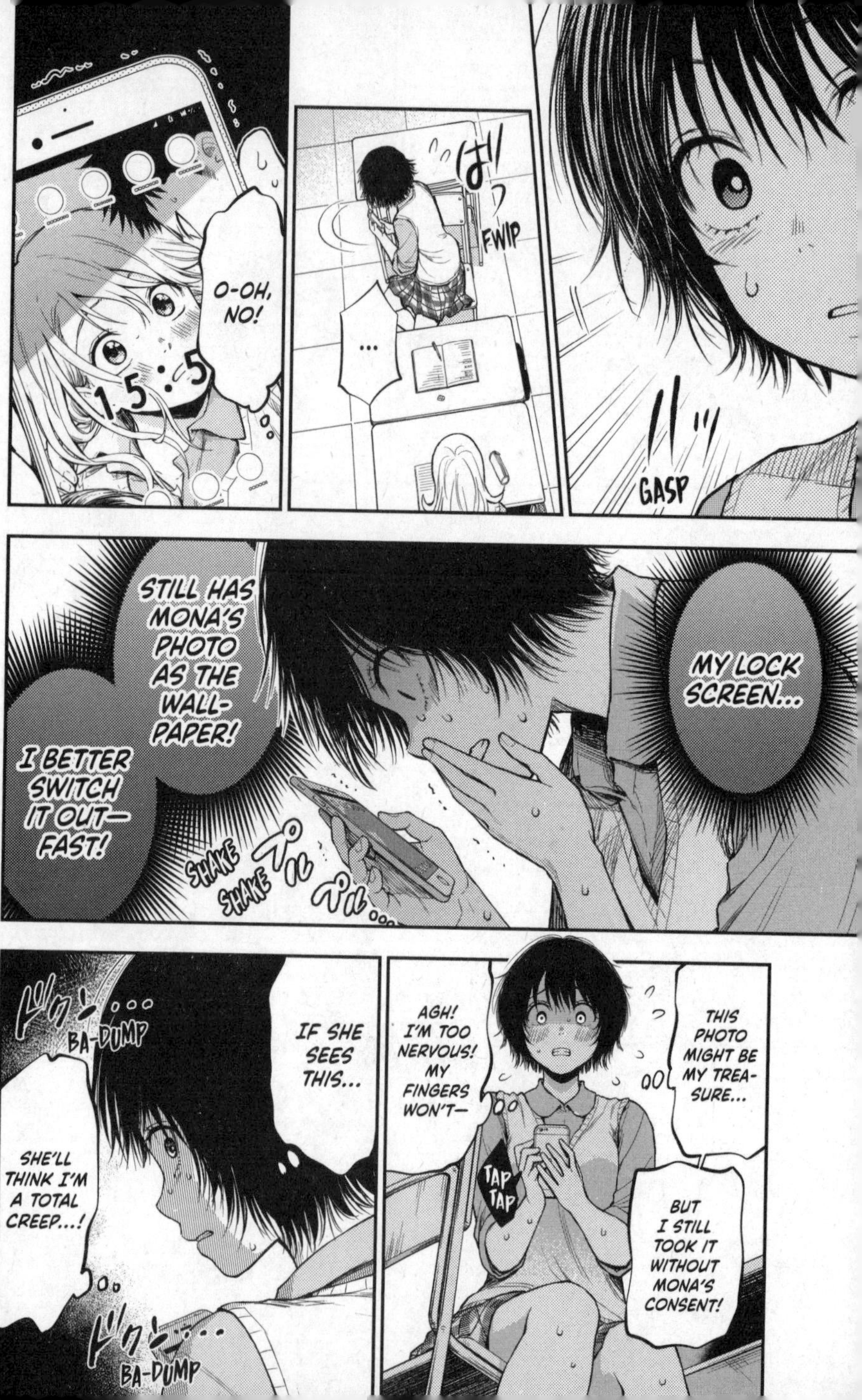
GASP
FWIP
...
O-OH, NO!
15:55
MY LOCK SCREEN...
STILL HAS MONA'S PHOTO AS THE WALL-PAPER!
I BETTER SWITCH IT OUT—FAST!
SHAKE SHAKE
THIS PHOTO MIGHT BE MY TREA-SURE...
BUT I STILL TOOK IT WITHOUT MONA'S CONSENT!
AGH! I'M TOO NERVOUS! MY FINGERS WON'T—
TAP TAP
IF SHE SEES THIS...
BA-DUMP
SHE'LL THINK I'M A TOTAL CREEP...!
BA-DUMP

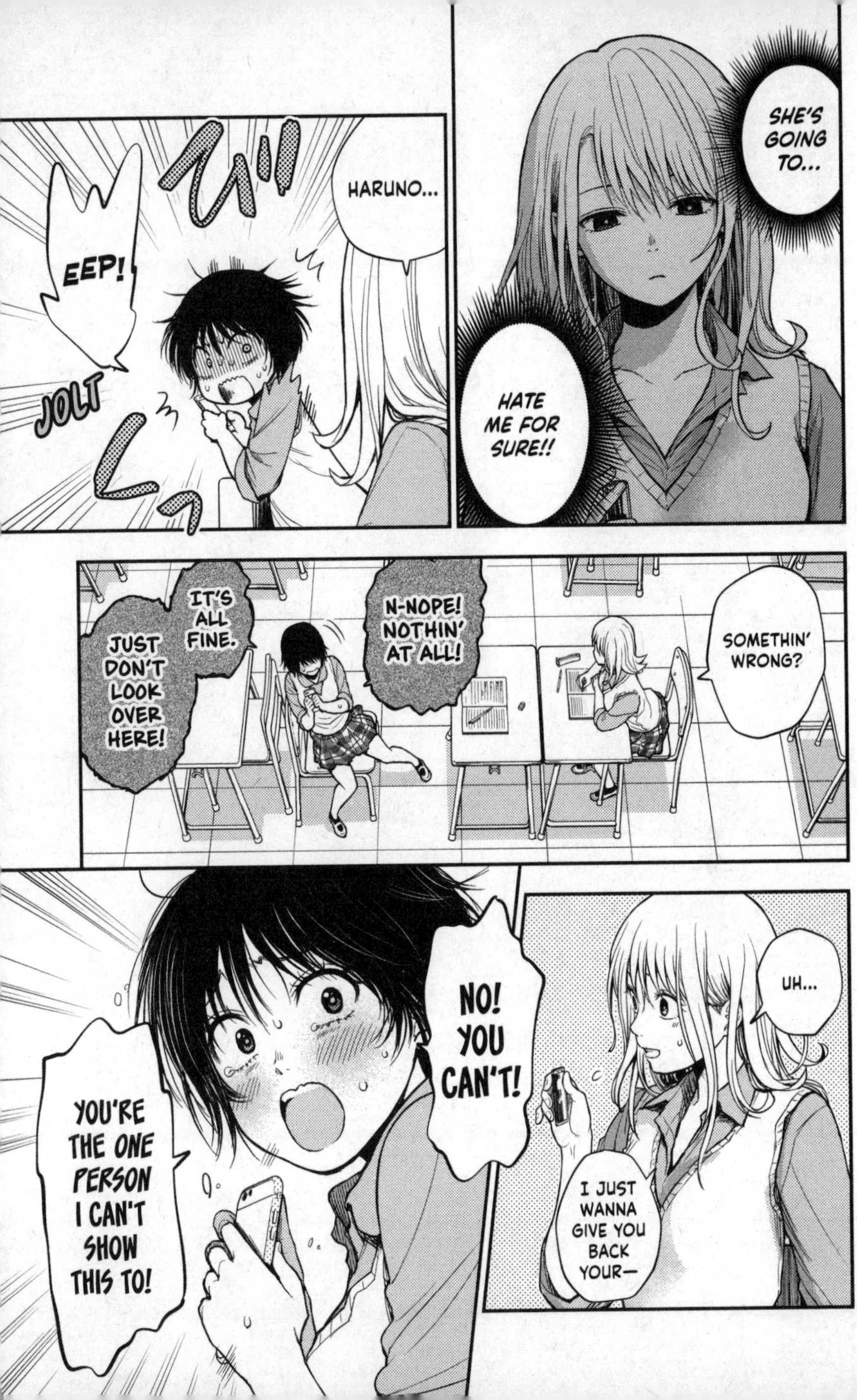
SHE'S GOING TO...
HATE ME FOR SURE!!
HARUNO...
EEP!
JOLT
SOMETHIN' WRONG?
N-NOPE! NOTHIN' AT ALL!
IT'S ALL FINE.
JUST DON'T LOOK OVER HERE!
UH...
I JUST WANNA GIVE YOU BACK YOUR—
NO! YOU CAN'T!
YOU'RE THE ONE PERSON I CAN'T SHOW THIS TO!

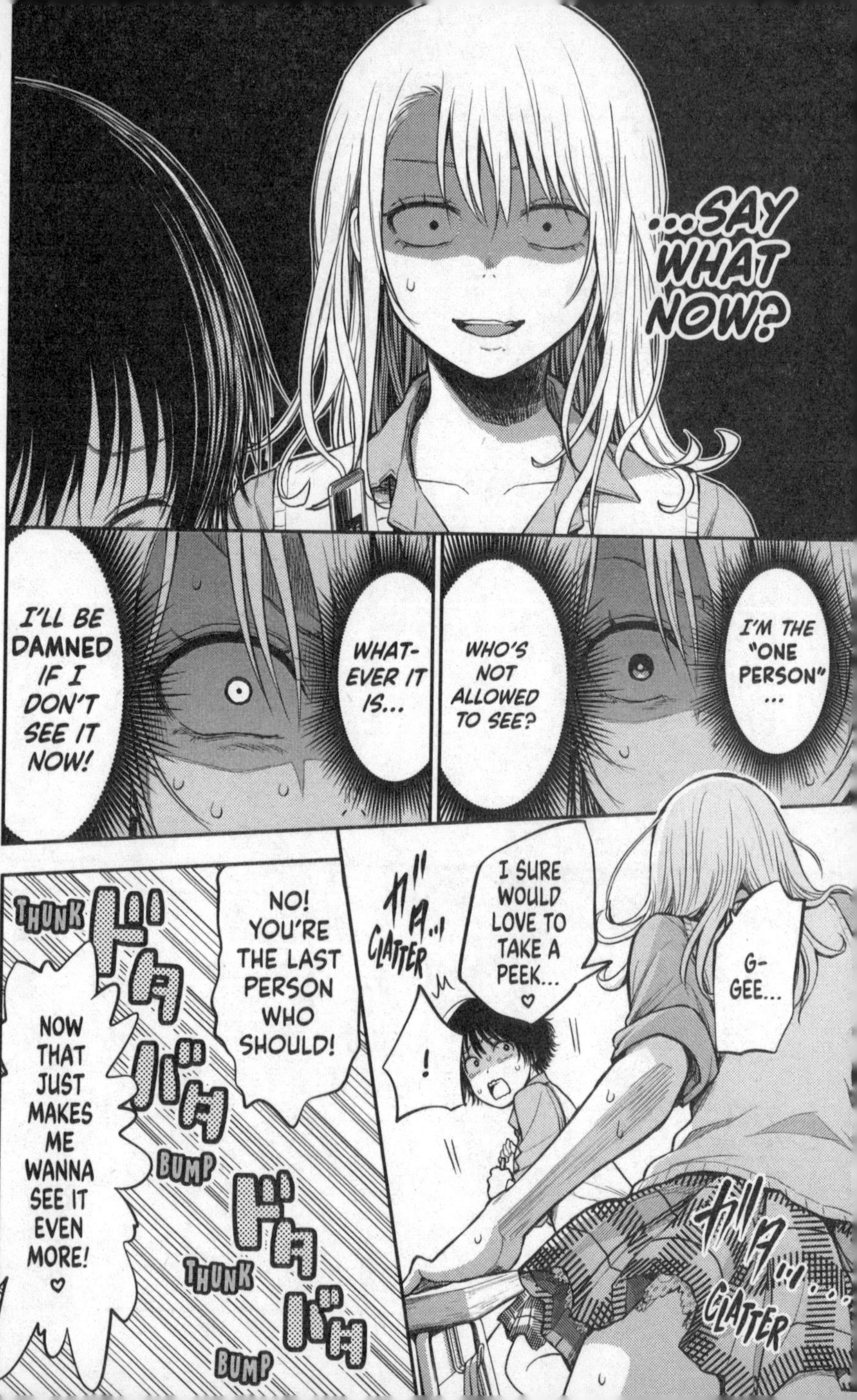
...SAY WHAT NOW?
I'M THE "ONE PERSON"...
WHO'S NOT ALLOWED TO SEE?
WHATEVER IT IS...
I'LL BE DAMNED IF I DON'T SEE IT NOW!
G-GEE...
CLATTER
I SURE WOULD LOVE TO TAKE A PEEK... ♡
!
CLATTER
NO! YOU'RE THE LAST PERSON WHO SHOULD!
THUNK
BUMP
THUNK
BUMP
NOW THAT JUST MAKES ME WANNA SEE IT EVEN MORE! ♡

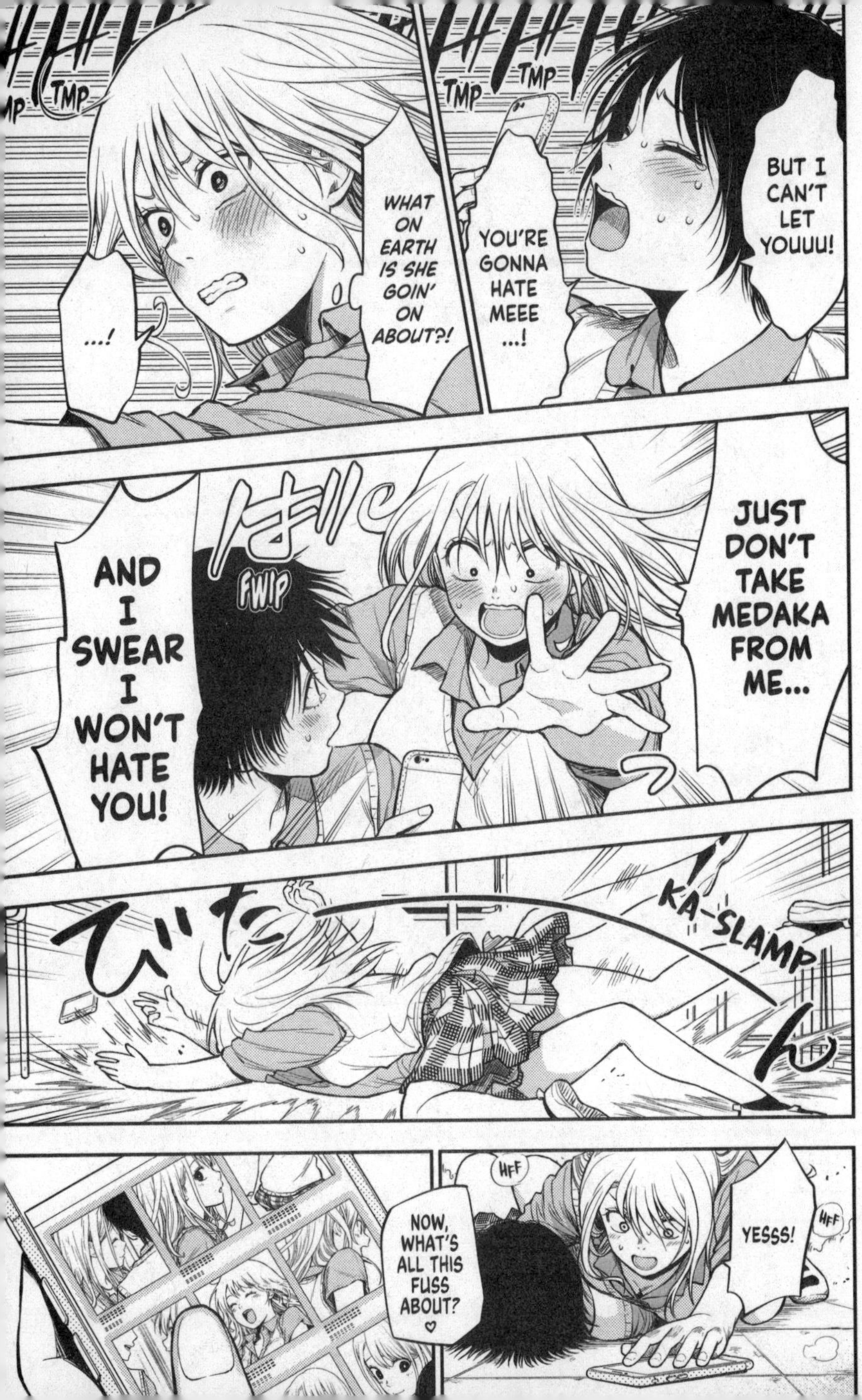
TMP TMP
BUT I CAN'T LET YOUUU!
YOU'RE GONNA HATE MEEE ...!
TMP
WHAT ON EARTH IS SHE GOIN' ON ABOUT?!
...!
JUST DON'T TAKE MEDAKA FROM ME...
FWIP
AND I SWEAR I WON'T HATE YOU!
KA-SLAMP
HFF
YESSS!
HFF
NOW, WHAT'S ALL THIS FUSS ABOUT? ♡

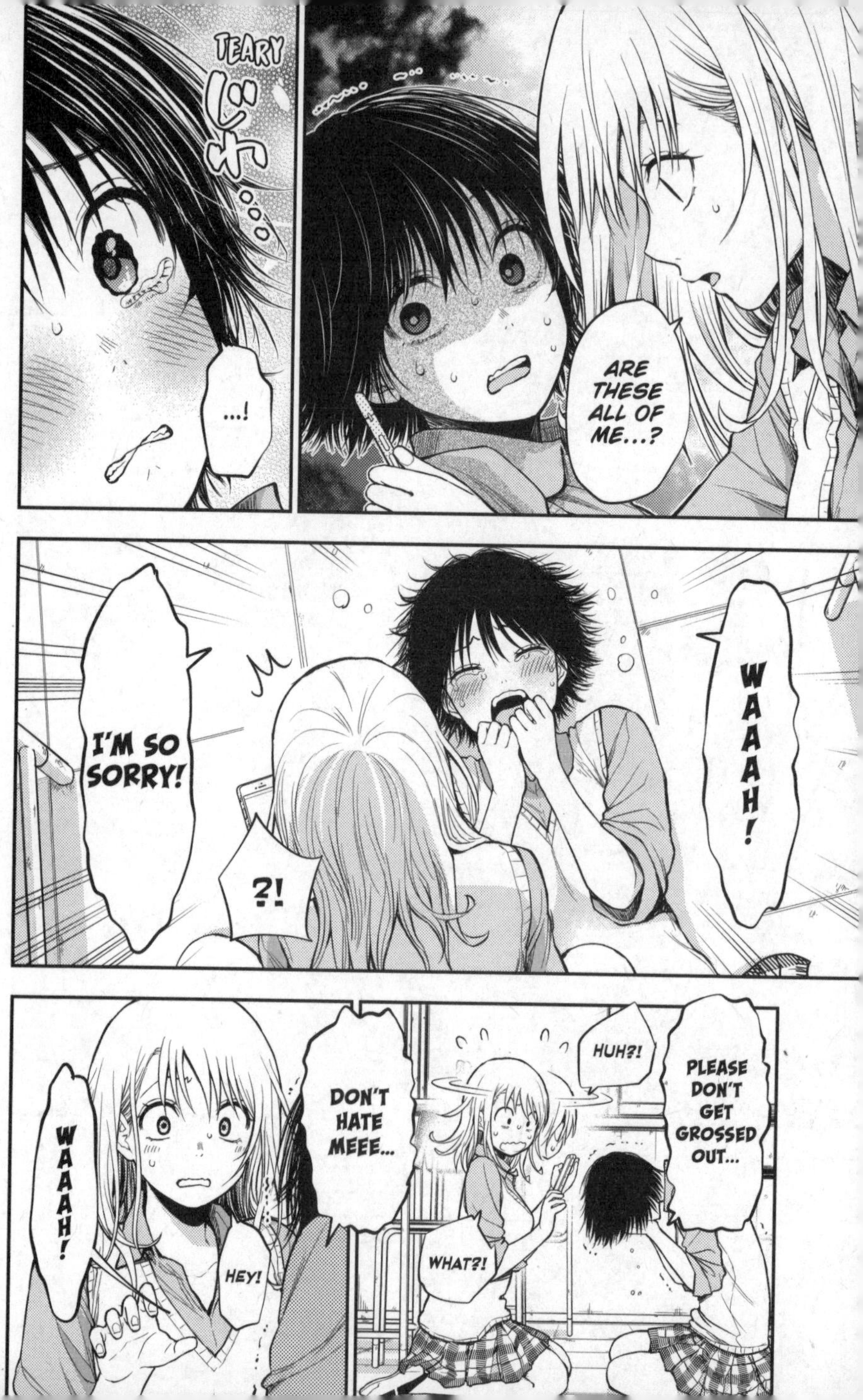
ARE THESE ALL OF ME...?
TEARY
じわ
...!
WAAAAH!
?!
I'M SO SORRY!
PLEASE DON'T GET GROSSED OUT...
HUH?!
WHAT?!
DON'T HATE MEEE...
WAAAAH!
HEY!

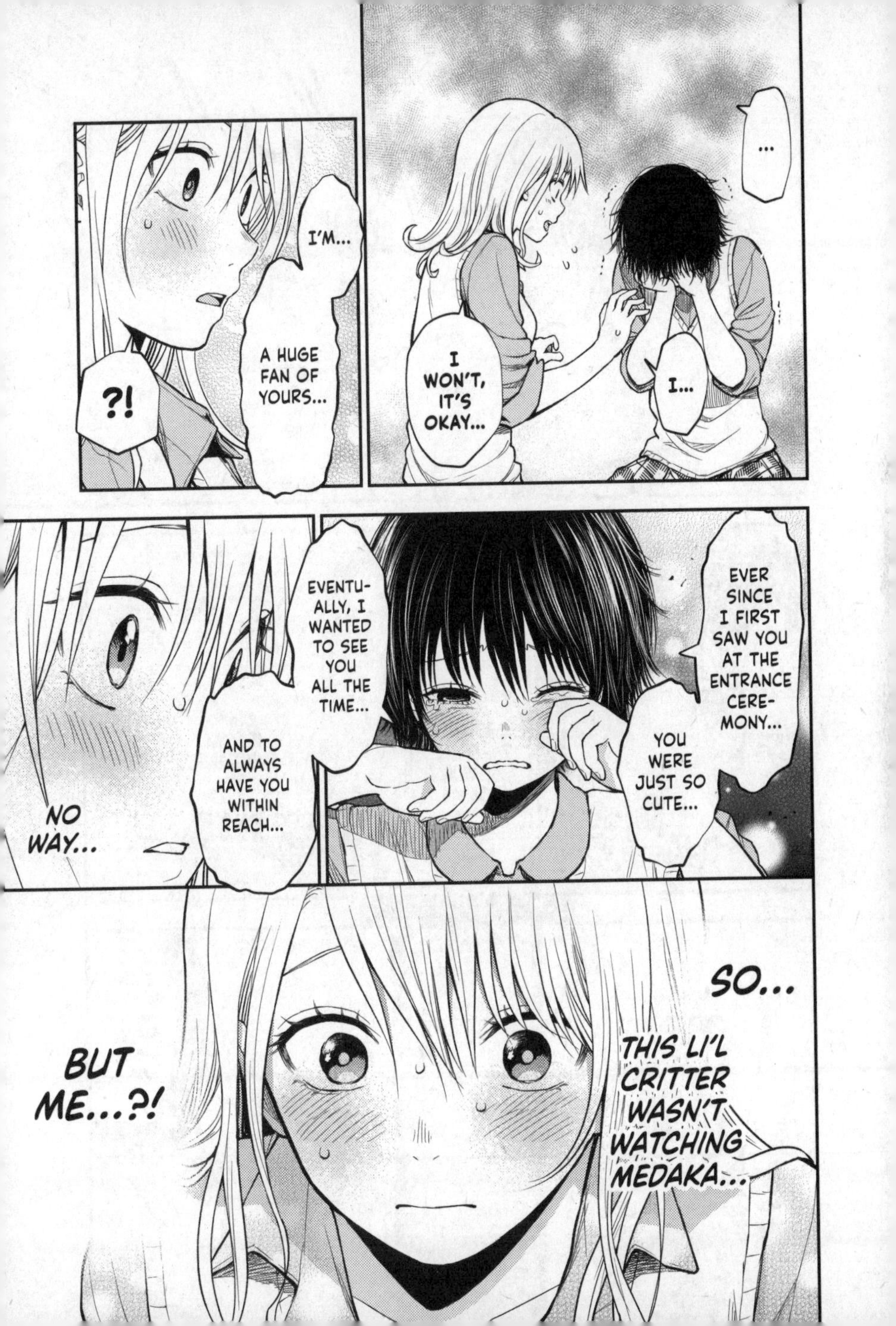
...
I...
I WON'T, IT'S OKAY...
I'M... A HUGE FAN OF YOURS...
?!
EVER SINCE I FIRST SAW YOU AT THE ENTRANCE CERE-MONY...
YOU WERE JUST SO CUTE...
EVENTU-ALLY, I WANTED TO SEE YOU ALL THE TIME...
AND TO ALWAYS HAVE YOU WITHIN REACH...
NO WAY...
SO...
THIS LI'L CRITTER WASN'T WATCHING MEDAKA...
BUT ME...?!

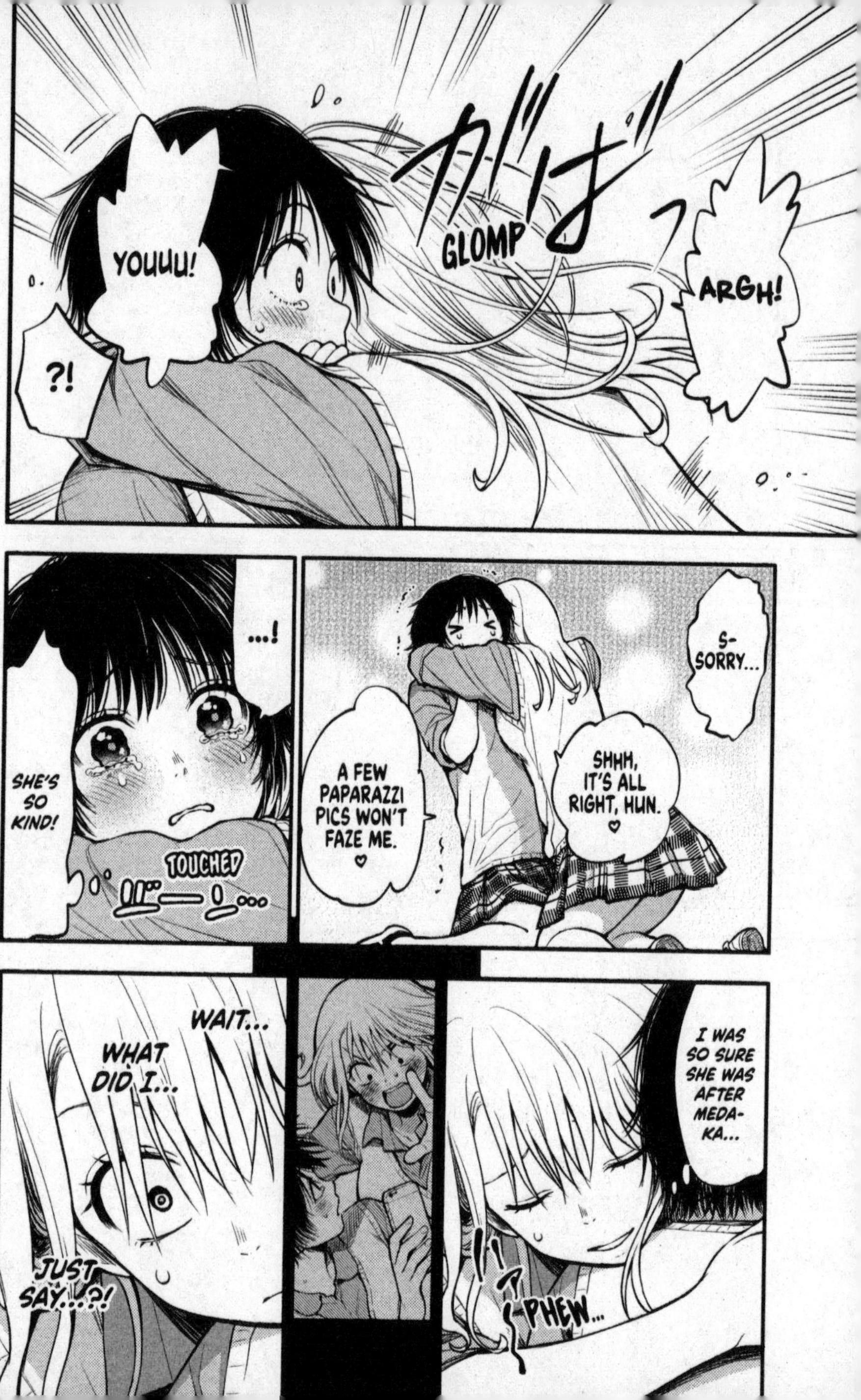
ARGH!
GLOMP
YOUUU!
?!
S-SORRY...
SHHH, IT'S ALL RIGHT, HUN. ♡
A FEW PAPARAZZI PICS WON'T FAZE ME. ♡
...!
SHE'S SO KIND!
TOUCHED
I WAS SO SURE SHE WAS AFTER MEDAKA...
PHEW...
WAIT...
WHAT DID I...
JUST SAY...?!

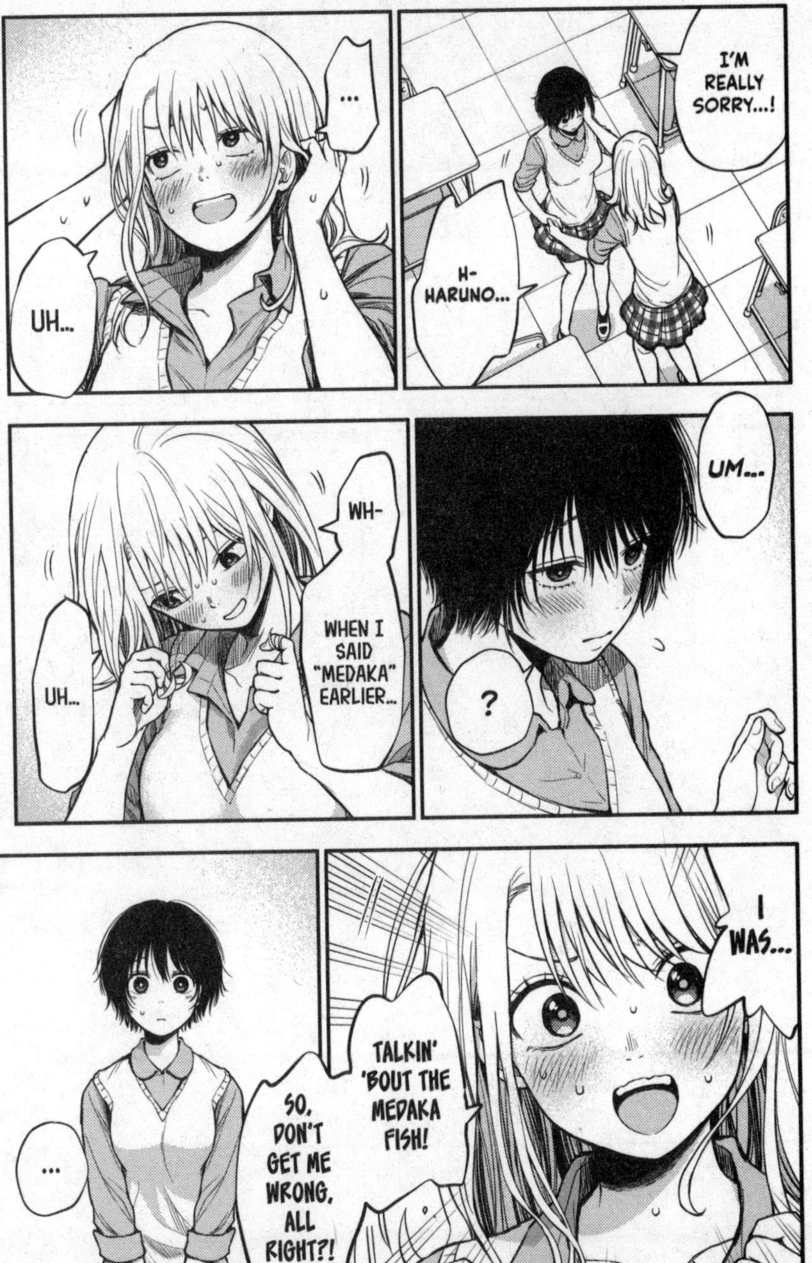
I'M REALLY SORRY...!
H- HARUNO...
...
UH...
UM...
?
WH-
WHEN I SAID "MEDAKA" EARLIER...
UH...
I WAS...
TALKIN' 'BOUT THE MEDAKA FISH!
SO, DON'T GET ME WRONG, ALL RIGHT?!
...

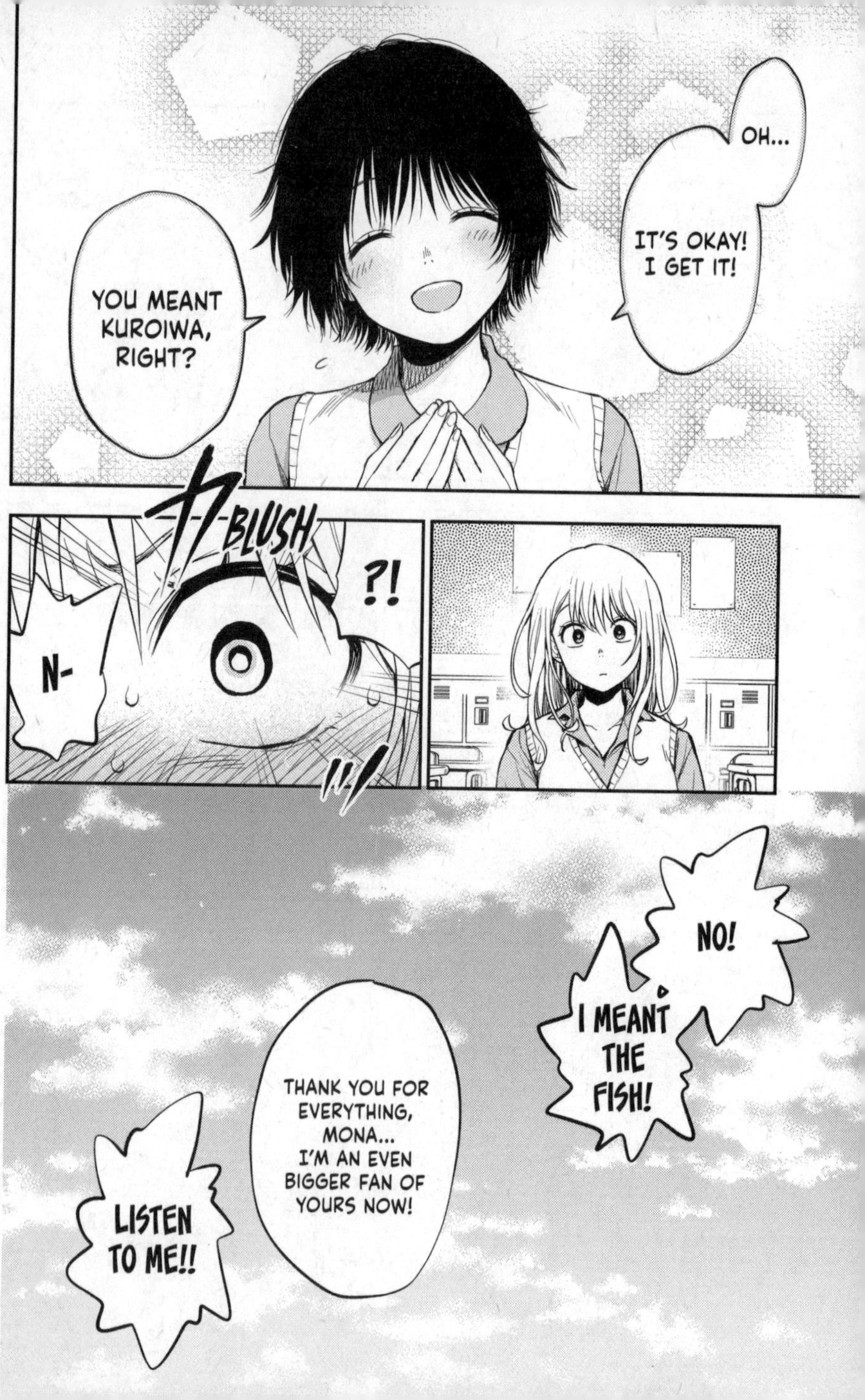
OH...
IT'S OKAY! I GET IT!
YOU MEANT KUROIWA, RIGHT?
BLUSH
?!
N-
NO!
I MEANT THE FISH!
THANK YOU FOR EVERYTHING, MONA... I'M AN EVEN BIGGER FAN OF YOURS NOW!
LISTEN TO ME!!

MONA x TSUBOMI

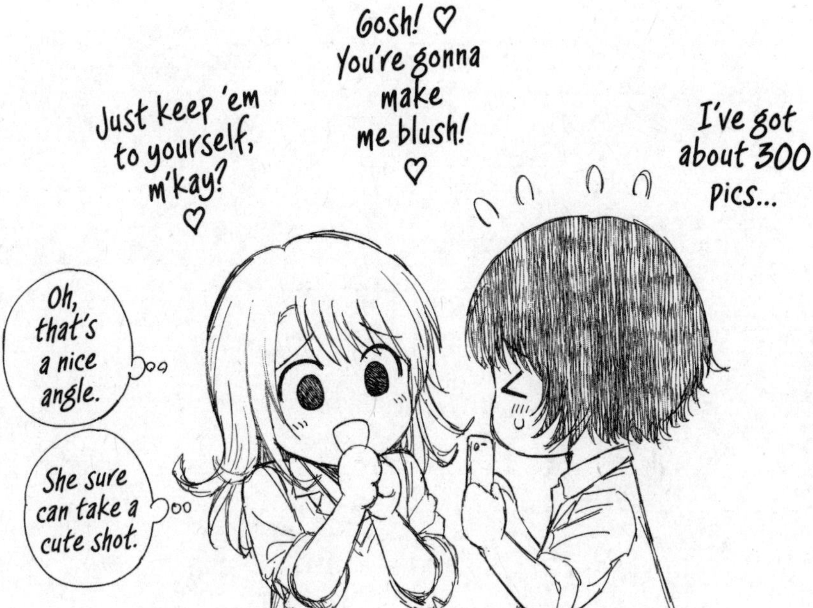
I've got about 300 pics...
Gosh! ♡ You're gonna make me blush! ♡
Just keep 'em to yourself, m'kay? ♡
Oh, that's a nice angle.
She sure can take a cute shot.

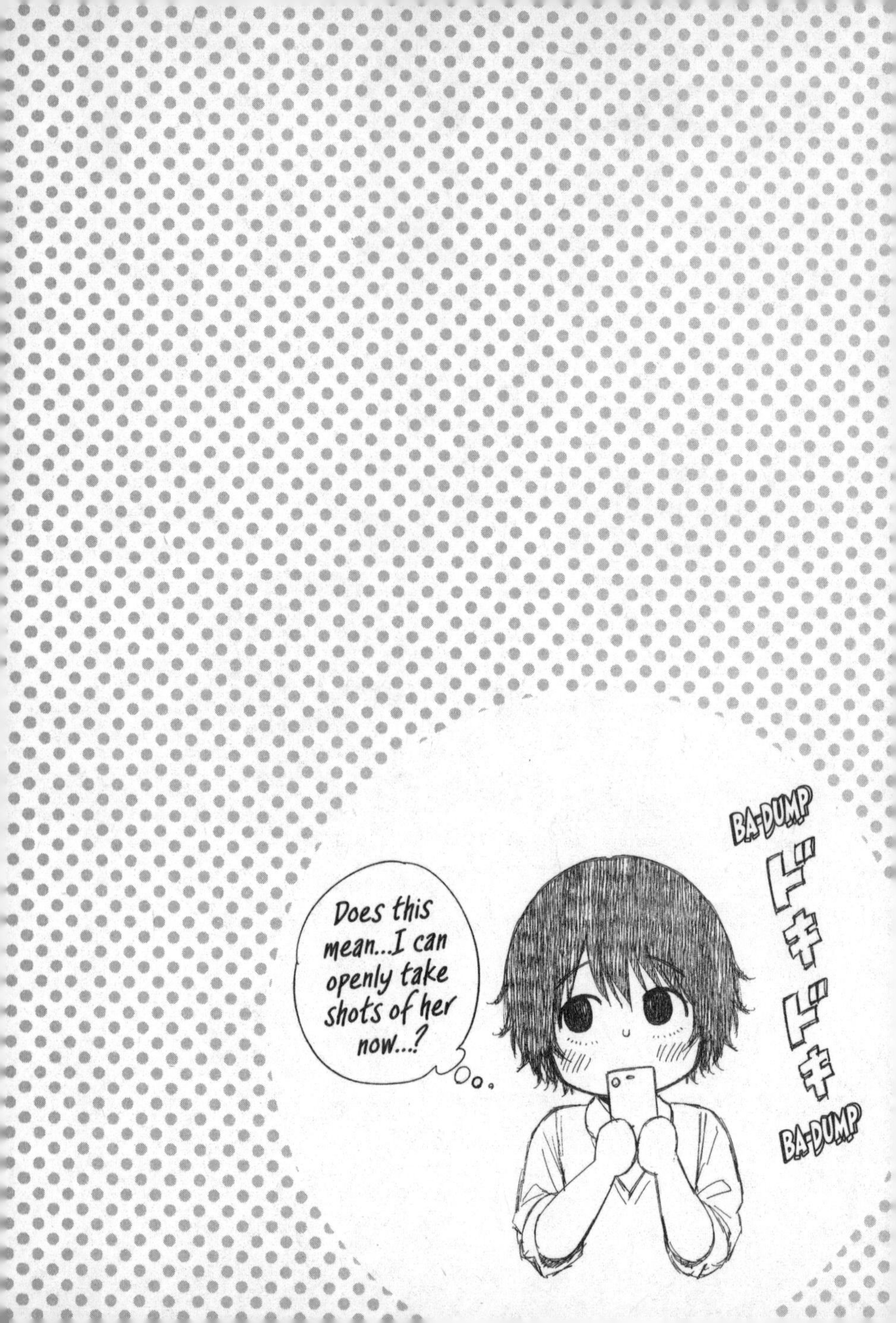
BA-DUMP
ドキドキ
BA-DUMP
Does this mean...I can openly take shots of her now...?

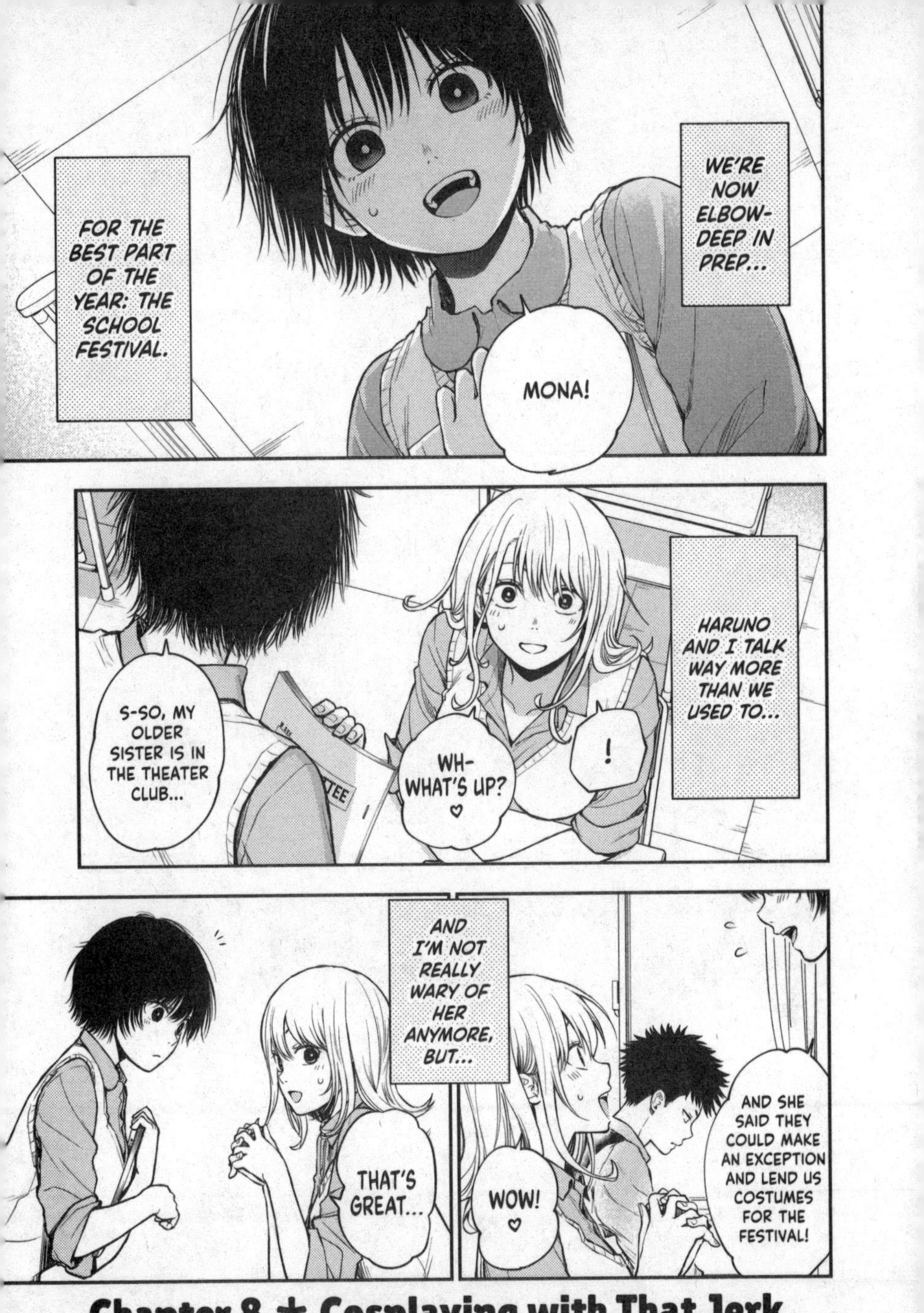
WE'RE NOW ELBOW-DEEP IN PREP...
MONA!
FOR THE BEST PART OF THE YEAR: THE SCHOOL FESTIVAL.
HARUNO AND I TALK WAY MORE THAN WE USED TO...
!
WH-WHAT'S UP? ♡
S-SO, MY OLDER SISTER IS IN THE THEATER CLUB...
AND I'M NOT REALLY WARY OF HER ANYMORE, BUT...
AND SHE SAID THEY COULD MAKE AN EXCEPTION AND LEND US COSTUMES FOR THE FESTIVAL!
WOW! ♡
THAT'S GREAT...

Chapter 8 ★ Cosplaying with That Jerk

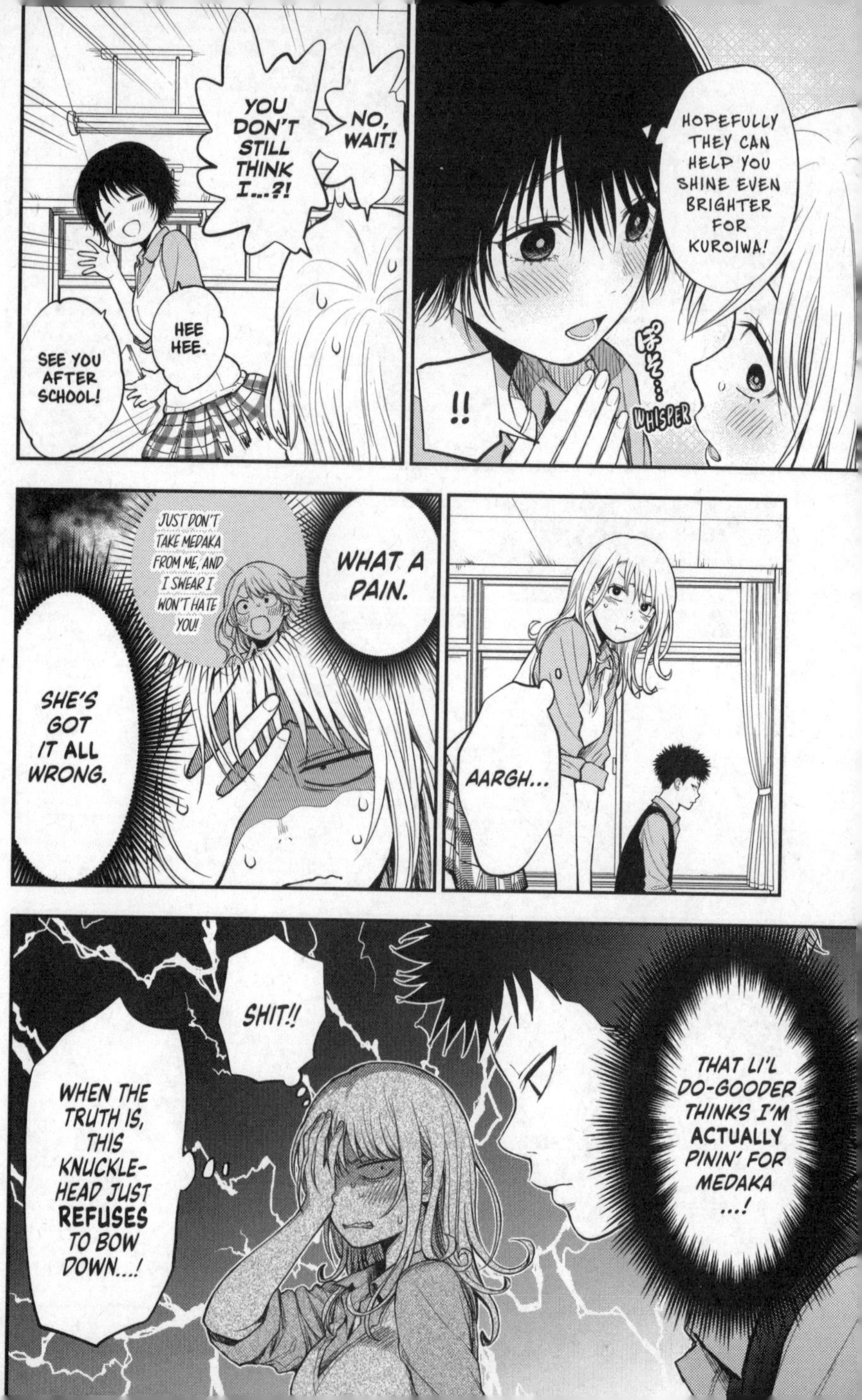
HOPEFULLY THEY CAN HELP YOU SHINE EVEN BRIGHTER FOR KUROIWA!
ぽそ…
WHISPER
!!
NO, WAIT!
YOU DON'T STILL THINK I...?!
HEE HEE.
SEE YOU AFTER SCHOOL!
AARGH...
WHAT A PAIN.
JUST DON'T TAKE MEDAKA FROM ME, AND I SWEAR I WON'T HATE YOU!
SHE'S GOT IT ALL WRONG.
THAT LI'L DO-GOODER THINKS I'M ACTUALLY PININ' FOR MEDAKA ...!
SHIT!!
WHEN THE TRUTH IS, THIS KNUCKLE-HEAD JUST REFUSES TO BOW DOWN...!

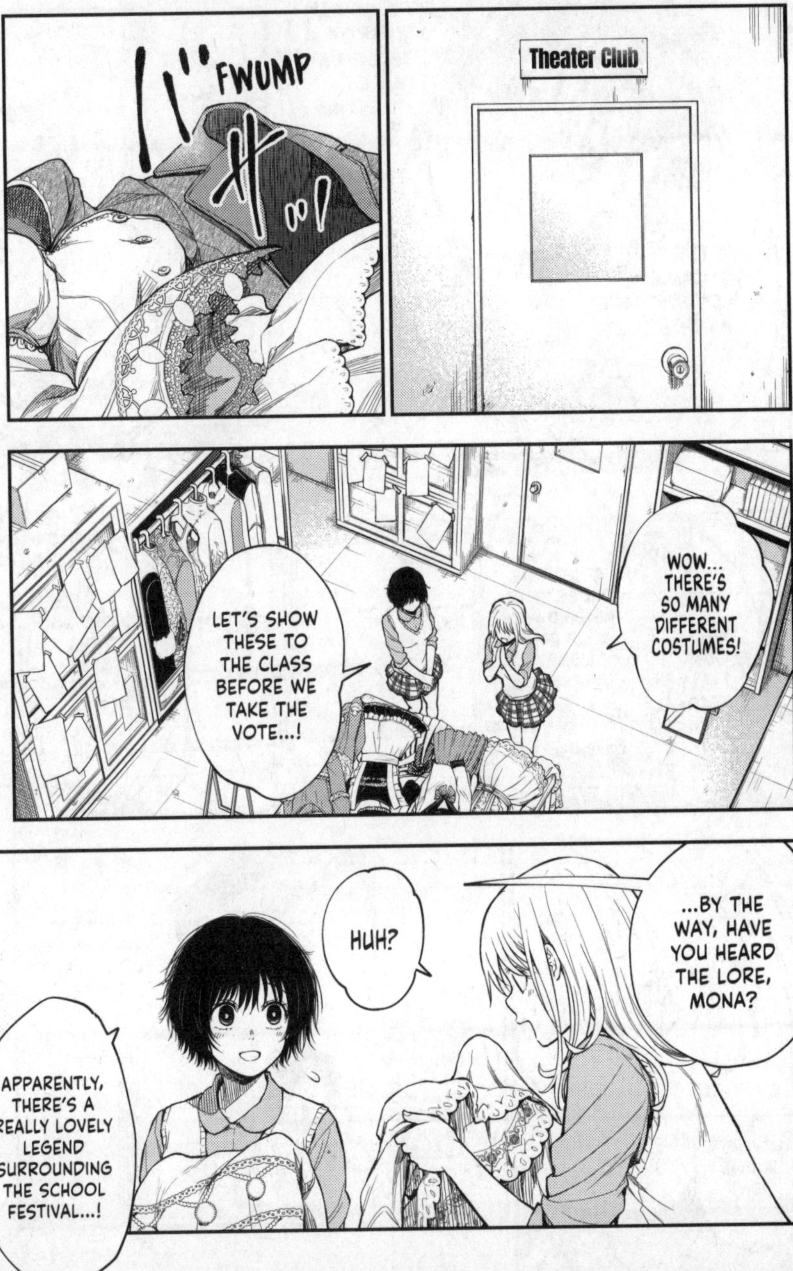
Theater Club
FWUMP
WOW... THERE'S SO MANY DIFFERENT COSTUMES!
LET'S SHOW THESE TO THE CLASS BEFORE WE TAKE THE VOTE...!
...BY THE WAY, HAVE YOU HEARD THE LORE, MONA?
HUH?
APPARENTLY, THERE'S A REALLY LOVELY LEGEND SURROUNDING THE SCHOOL FESTIVAL...!

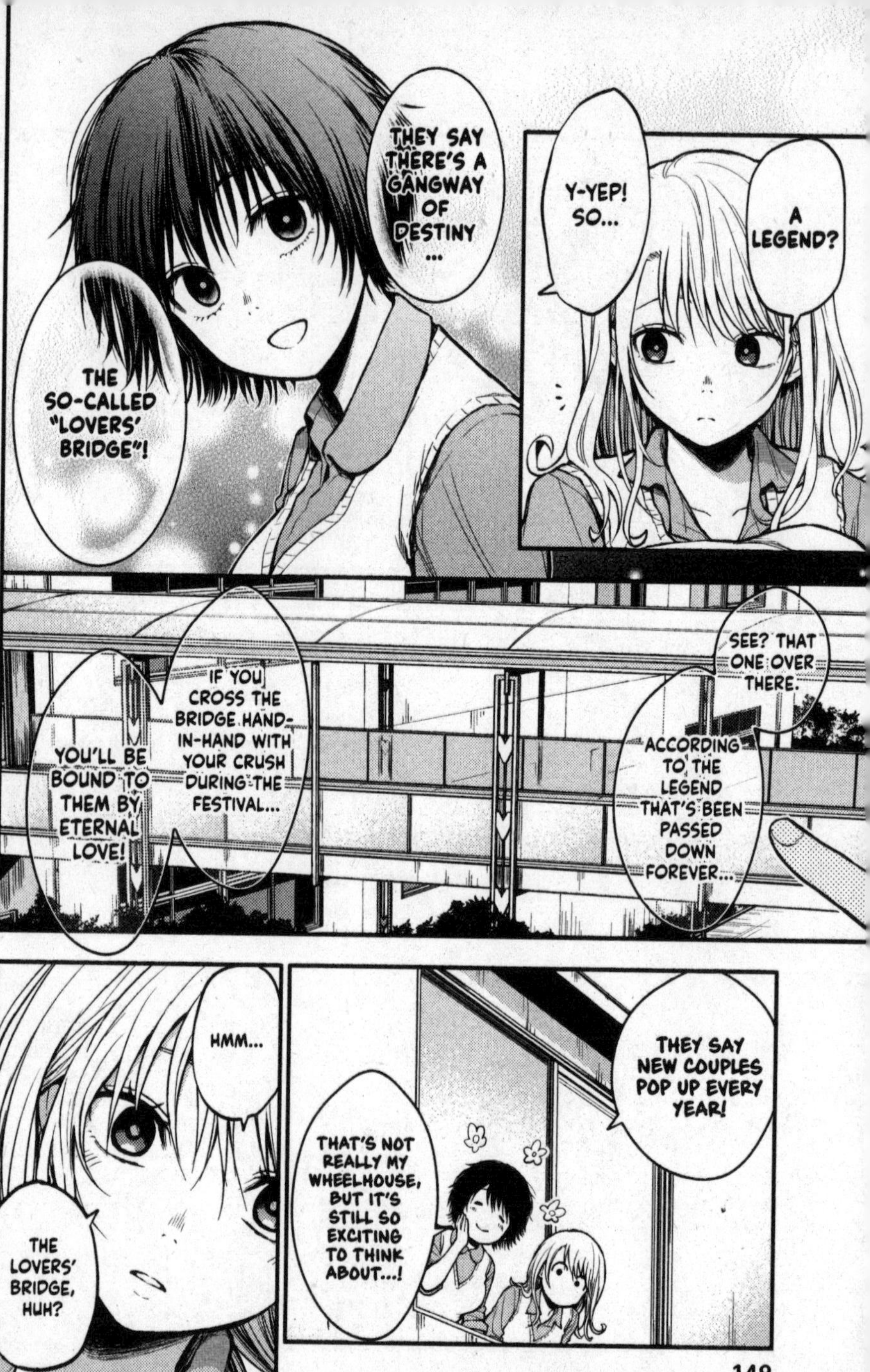
A LEGEND?
Y-YEP! SO...
THEY SAY THERE'S A GANGWAY OF DESTINY ...
THE SO-CALLED "LOVERS' BRIDGE"!
SEE? THAT ONE OVER THERE.
ACCORDING TO THE LEGEND THAT'S BEEN PASSED DOWN FOREVER...
IF YOU CROSS THE BRIDGE HAND-IN-HAND WITH YOUR CRUSH DURING THE FESTIVAL...
YOU'LL BE BOUND TO THEM BY ETERNAL LOVE!
THEY SAY NEW COUPLES POP UP EVERY YEAR!
THAT'S NOT REALLY MY WHEELHOUSE, BUT IT'S STILL SO EXCITING TO THINK ABOUT...!
HMM...
THE LOVERS' BRIDGE, HUH?

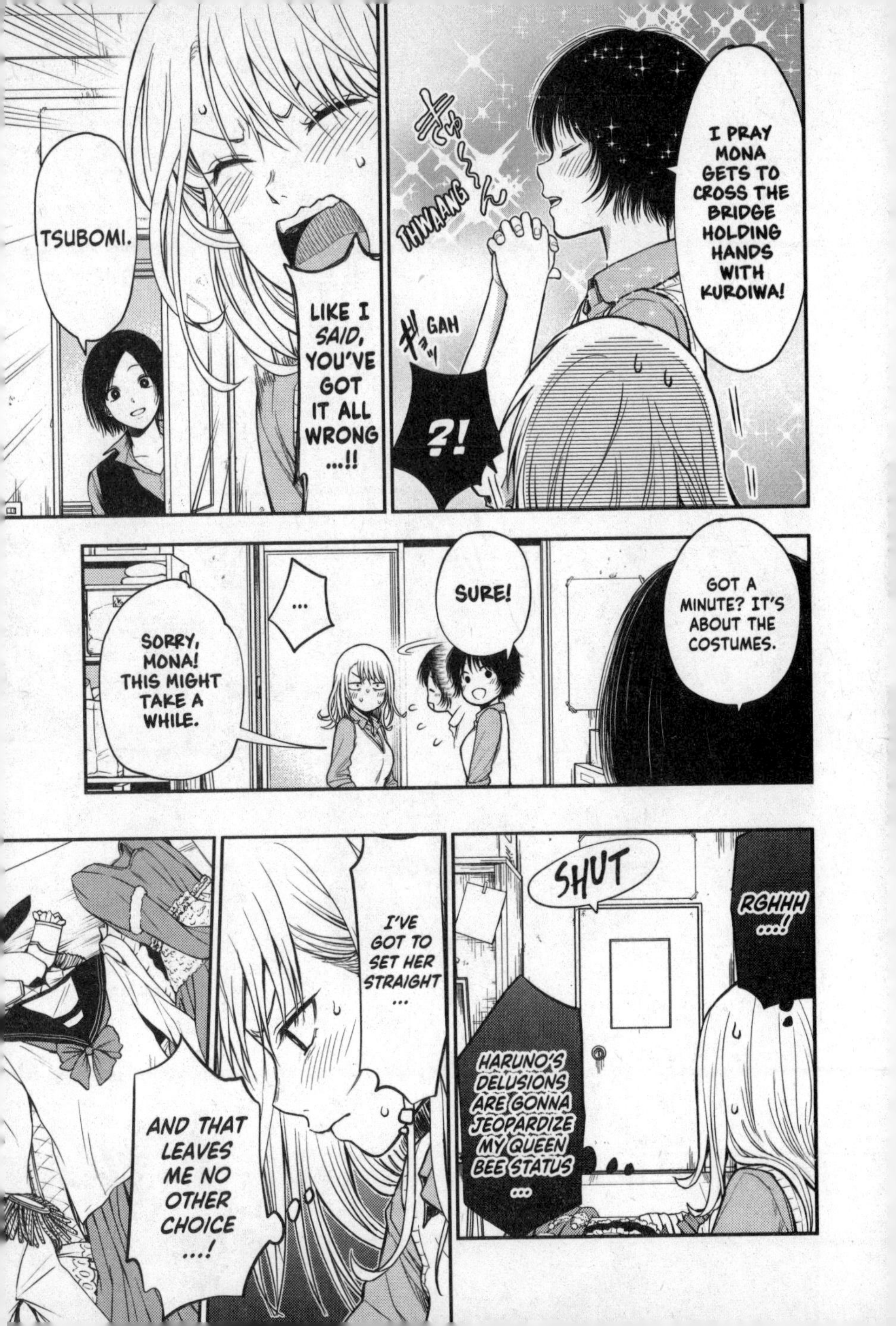
I PRAY MONA GETS TO CROSS THE BRIDGE HOLDING HANDS WITH KUROIWA!
THWAANG
GAH
?!
LIKE I SAID, YOU'VE GOT IT ALL WRONG ...!!
TSUBOMI.
GOT A MINUTE? IT'S ABOUT THE COSTUMES.
SURE!
...
SORRY, MONA! THIS MIGHT TAKE A WHILE.
SHUT
RGHHH ...!
HARUNO'S DELUSIONS ARE GONNA JEOPARDIZE MY QUEEN BEE STATUS ...
I'VE GOT TO SET HER STRAIGHT ...
AND THAT LEAVES ME NO OTHER CHOICE ...!

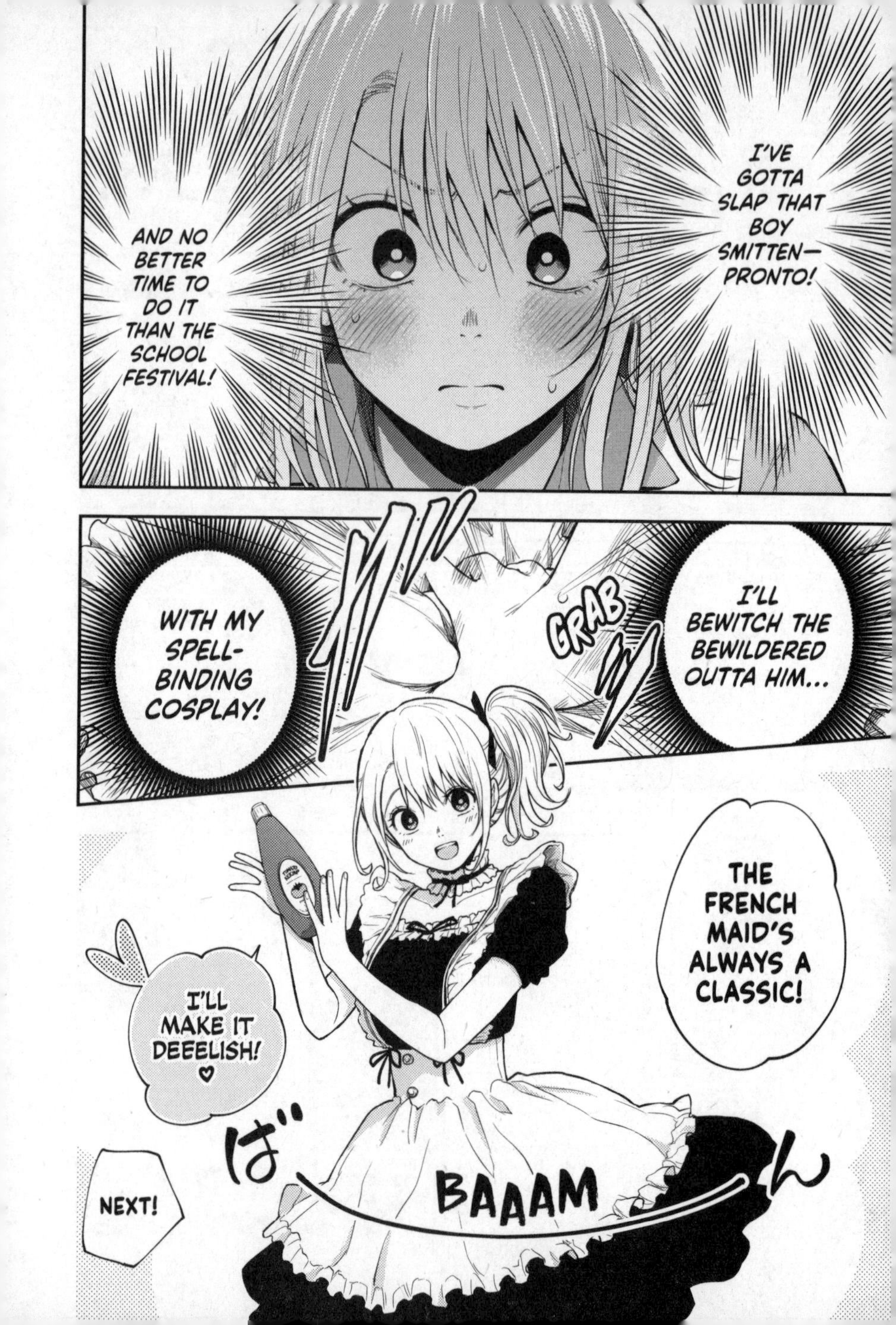
I'VE GOTTA SLAP THAT BOY SMITTEN—PRONTO!
AND NO BETTER TIME TO DO IT THAN THE SCHOOL FESTIVAL!
I'LL BEWITCH THE BEWILDERED OUTTA HIM...
GRAB
WITH MY SPELL-BINDING COSPLAY!
THE FRENCH MAID'S ALWAYS A CLASSIC!
I'LL MAKE IT DEEELISH! ♡
ば
BAAAM
ん
NEXT!

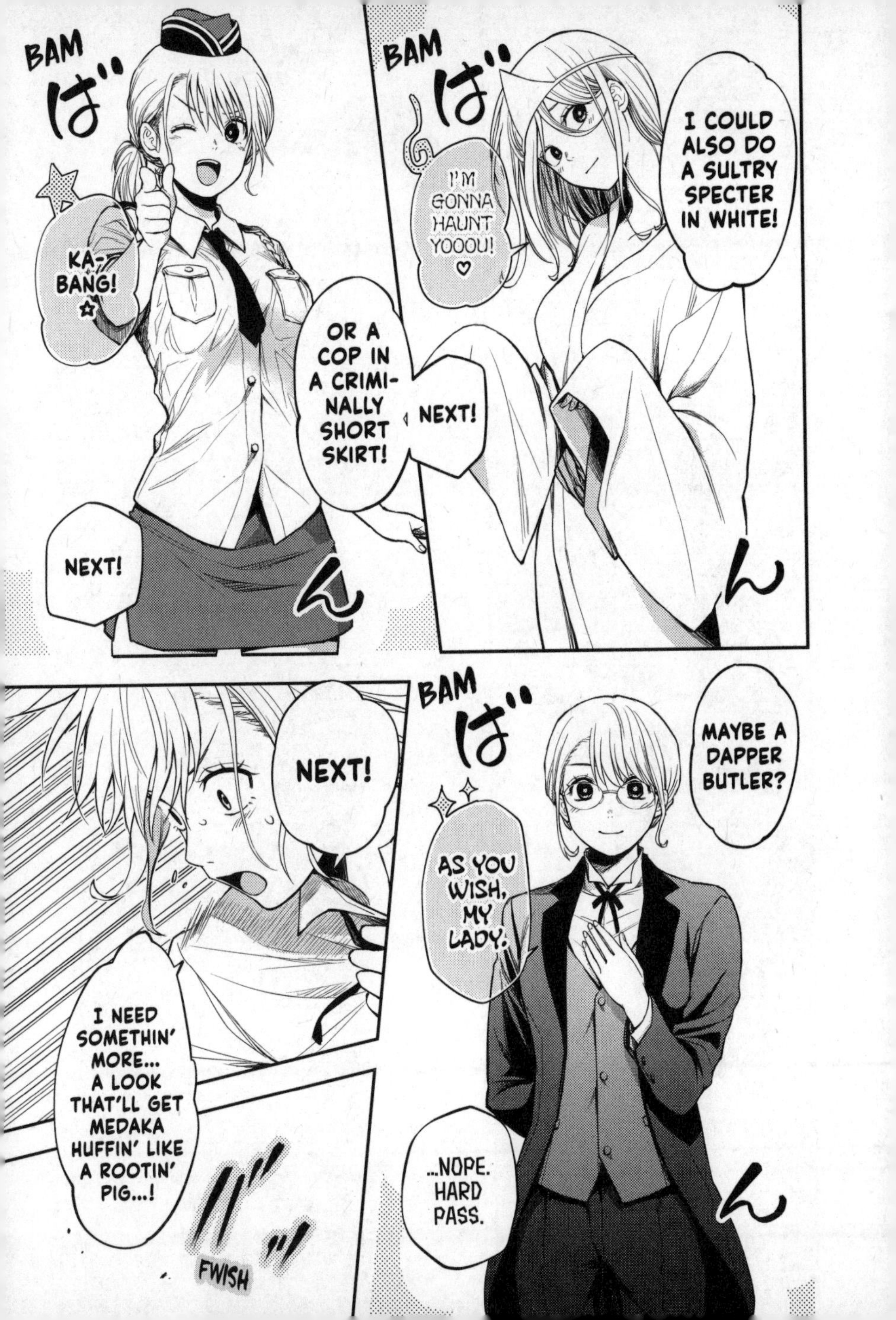
BAM
ば
I COULD ALSO DO A SULTRY SPECTER IN WHITE!
I'M GONNA HAUNT YOOOU! ♡
NEXT!
ん
OR A COP IN A CRIMINALLY SHORT SKIRT!
BAM
ば
KA-BANG! ☆
NEXT!
ん
BAM
ば
MAYBE A DAPPER BUTLER?
AS YOU WISH, MY LADY.
...NOPE. HARD PASS.
ん
NEXT!
I NEED SOMETHIN' MORE... A LOOK THAT'LL GET MEDAKA HUFFIN' LIKE A ROOTIN' PIG...!
FWISH

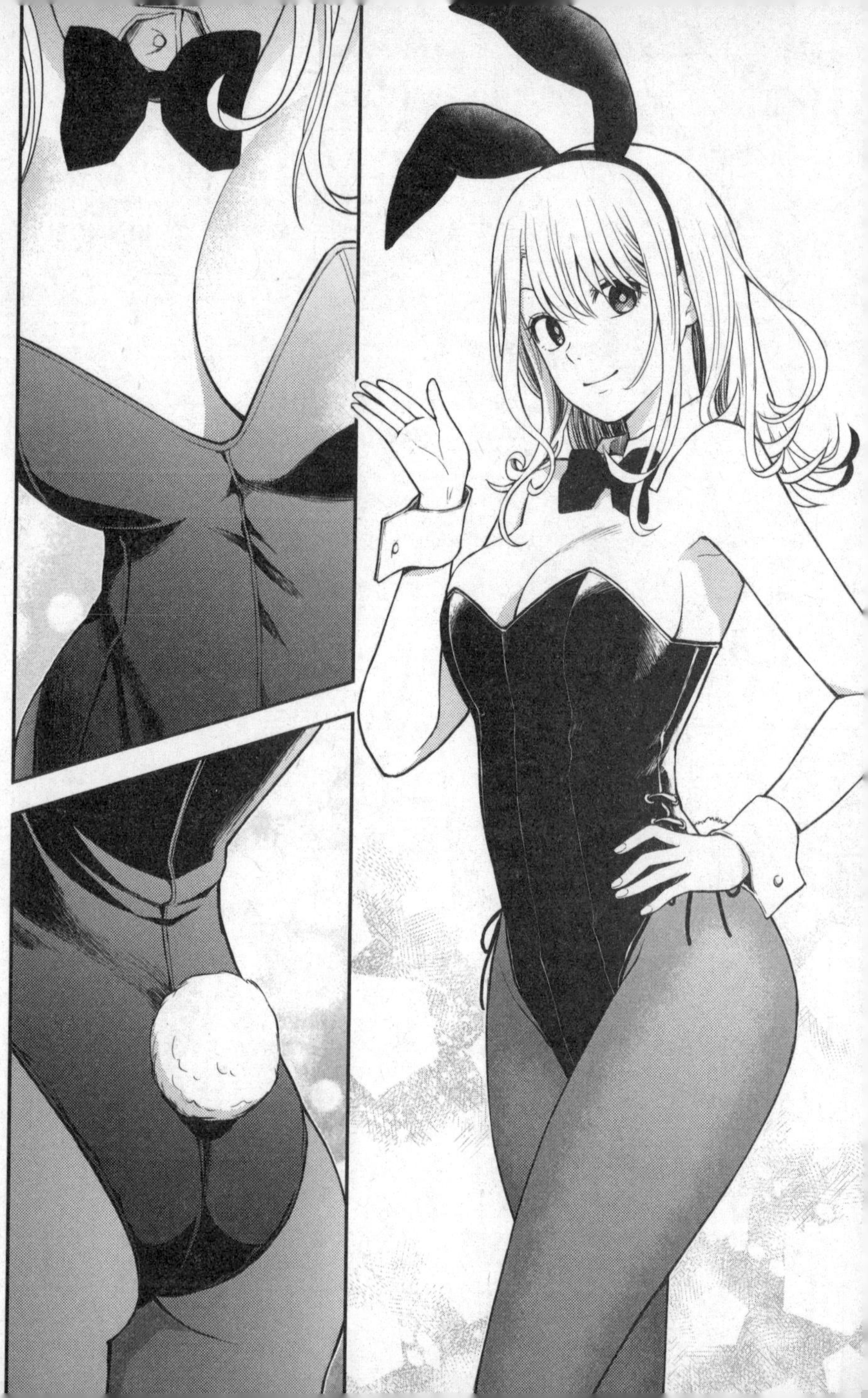

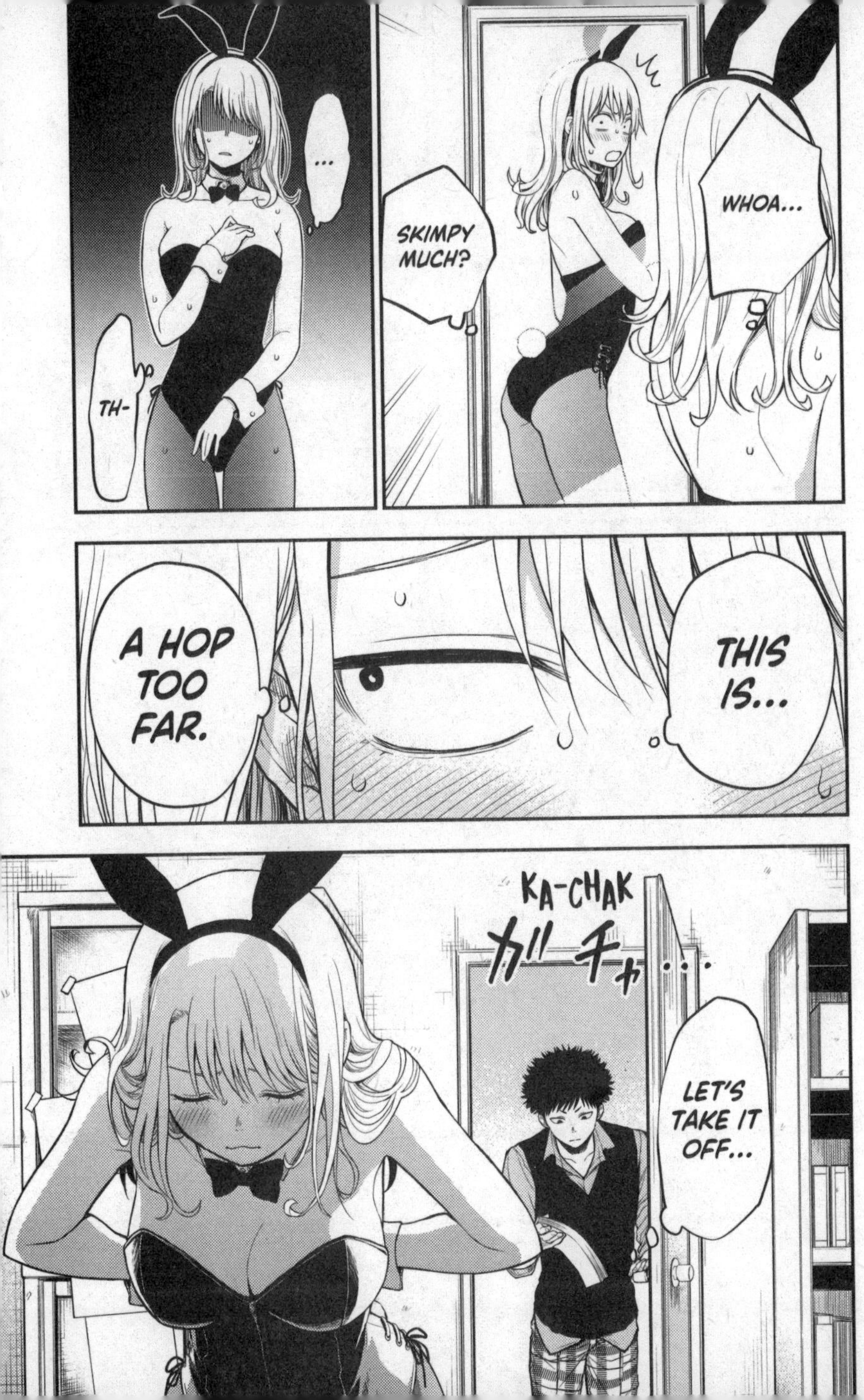
WHOA...
SKIMPY MUCH?
...
TH-
THIS IS...
A HOP TOO FAR.
KA-CHAK
ガチャ...
LET'S TAKE IT OFF...

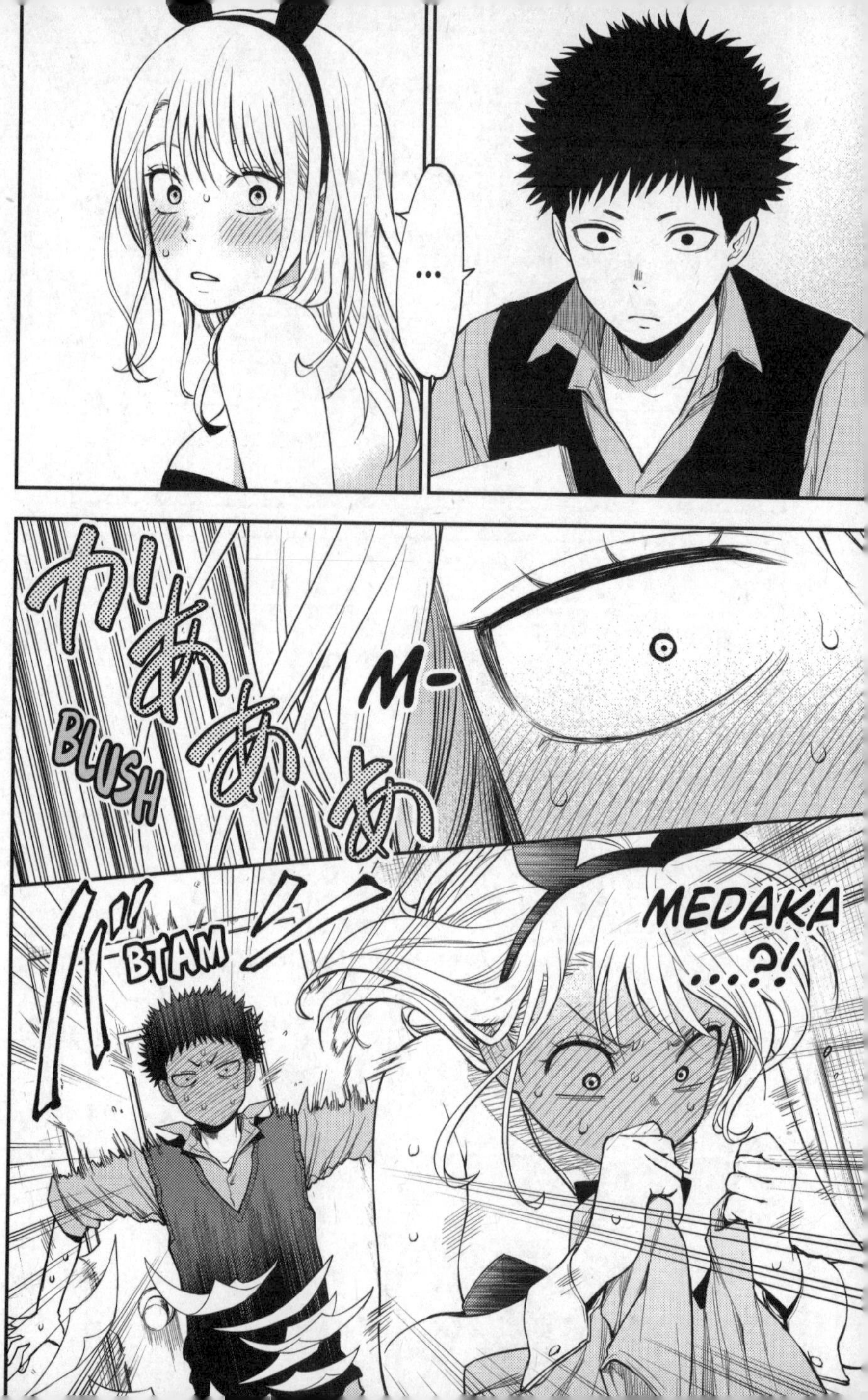
...
M-
わああぁ
BLUSH
MEDAKA ...?!
BTAM

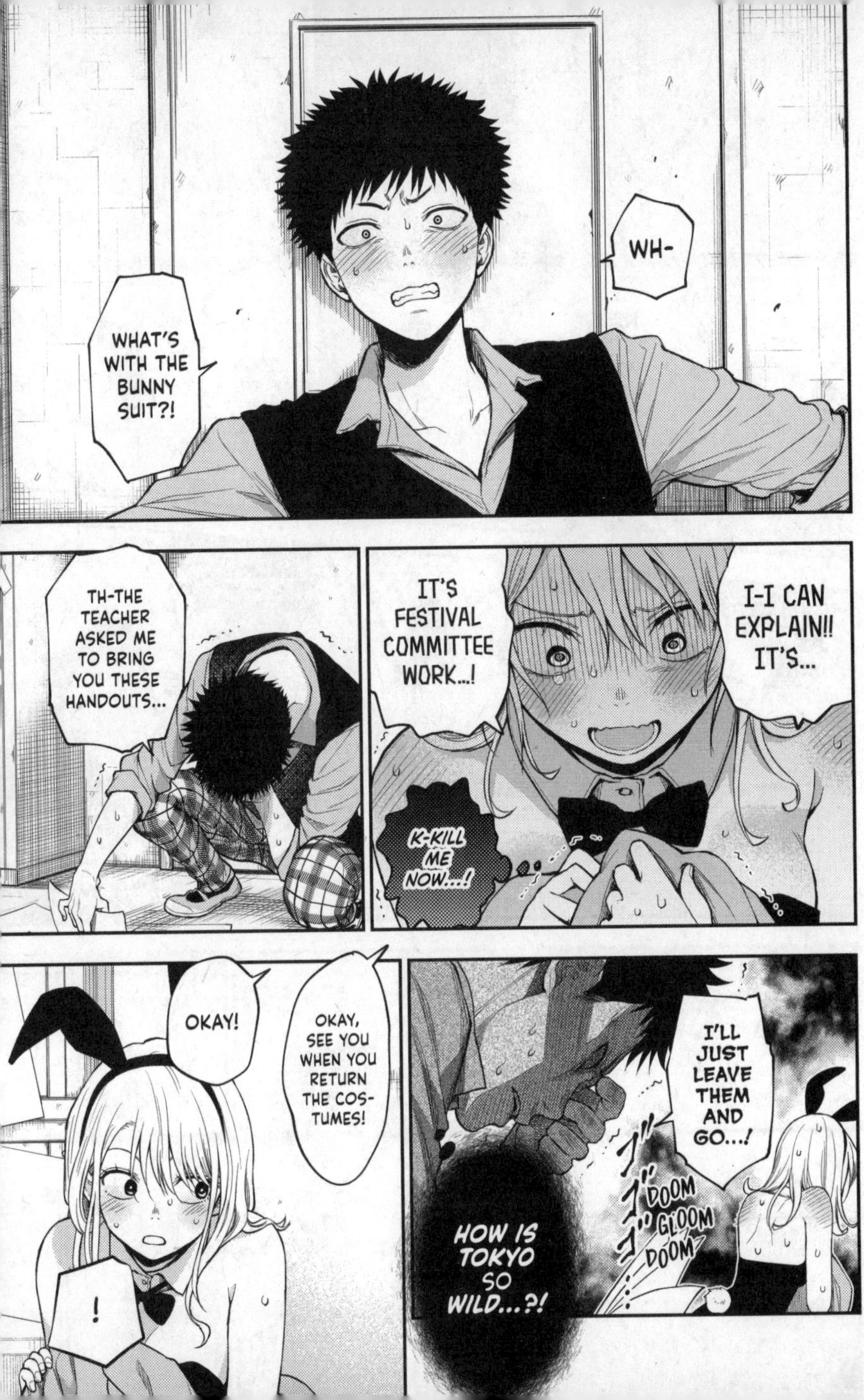
WH-
WHAT'S WITH THE BUNNY SUIT?!
I-I CAN EXPLAIN!! IT'S...
IT'S FESTIVAL COMMITTEE WORK...!
K-KILL ME NOW...!
TH-THE TEACHER ASKED ME TO BRING YOU THESE HANDOUTS...
I'LL JUST LEAVE THEM AND GO...!
DOOM GLOOM DOOM
HOW IS TOKYO SO WILD...?!
OKAY, SEE YOU WHEN YOU RETURN THE COS-TUMES!
OKAY!
!

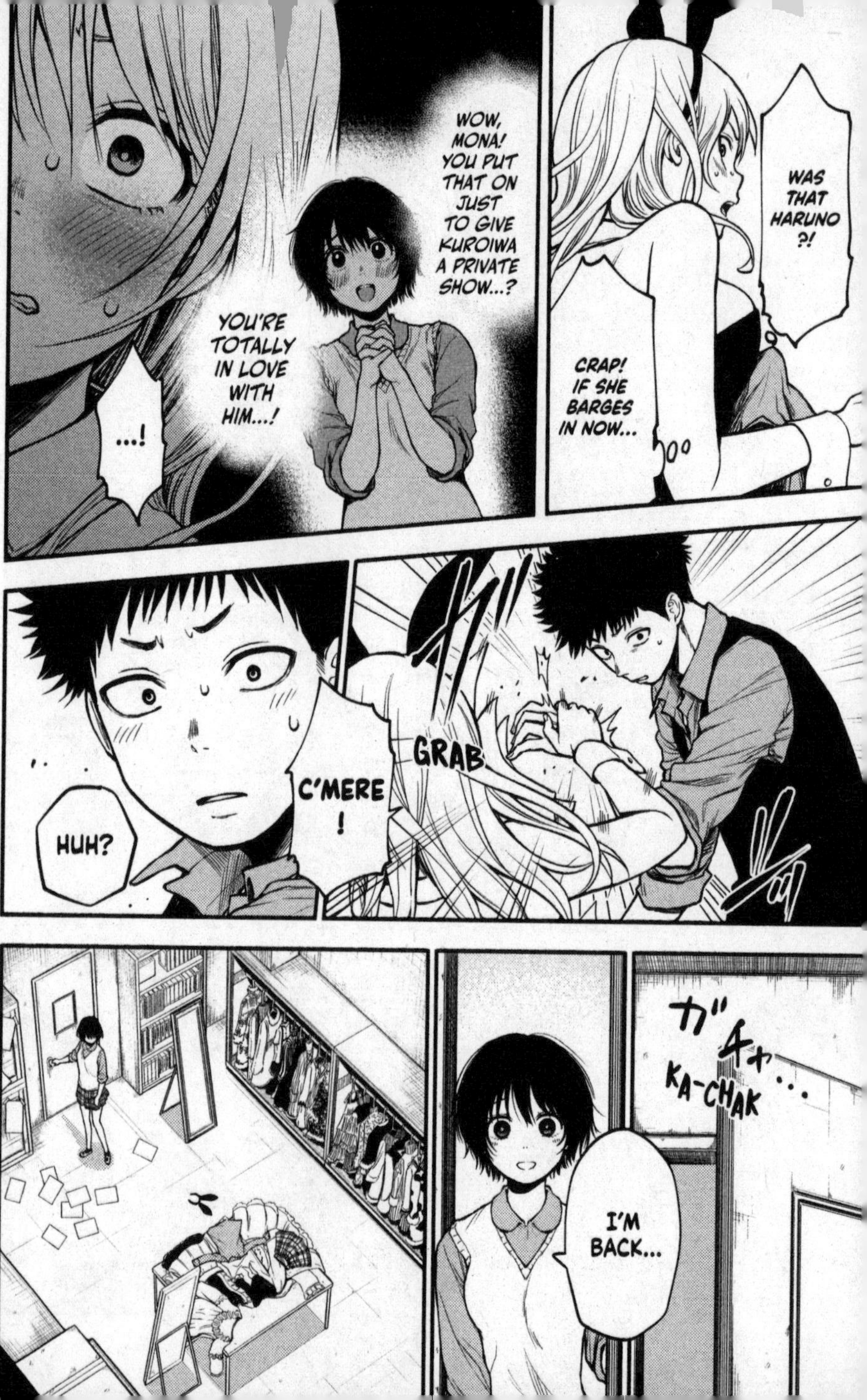
WAS THAT HARUNO ?!
CRAP! IF SHE BARGES IN NOW...
WOW, MONA! YOU PUT THAT ON JUST TO GIVE KUROIWA A PRIVATE SHOW...?
YOU'RE TOTALLY IN LOVE WITH HIM...!
...!
GRAB
C'MERE!
HUH?
ガチャ...
KA-CHAK
I'M BACK...

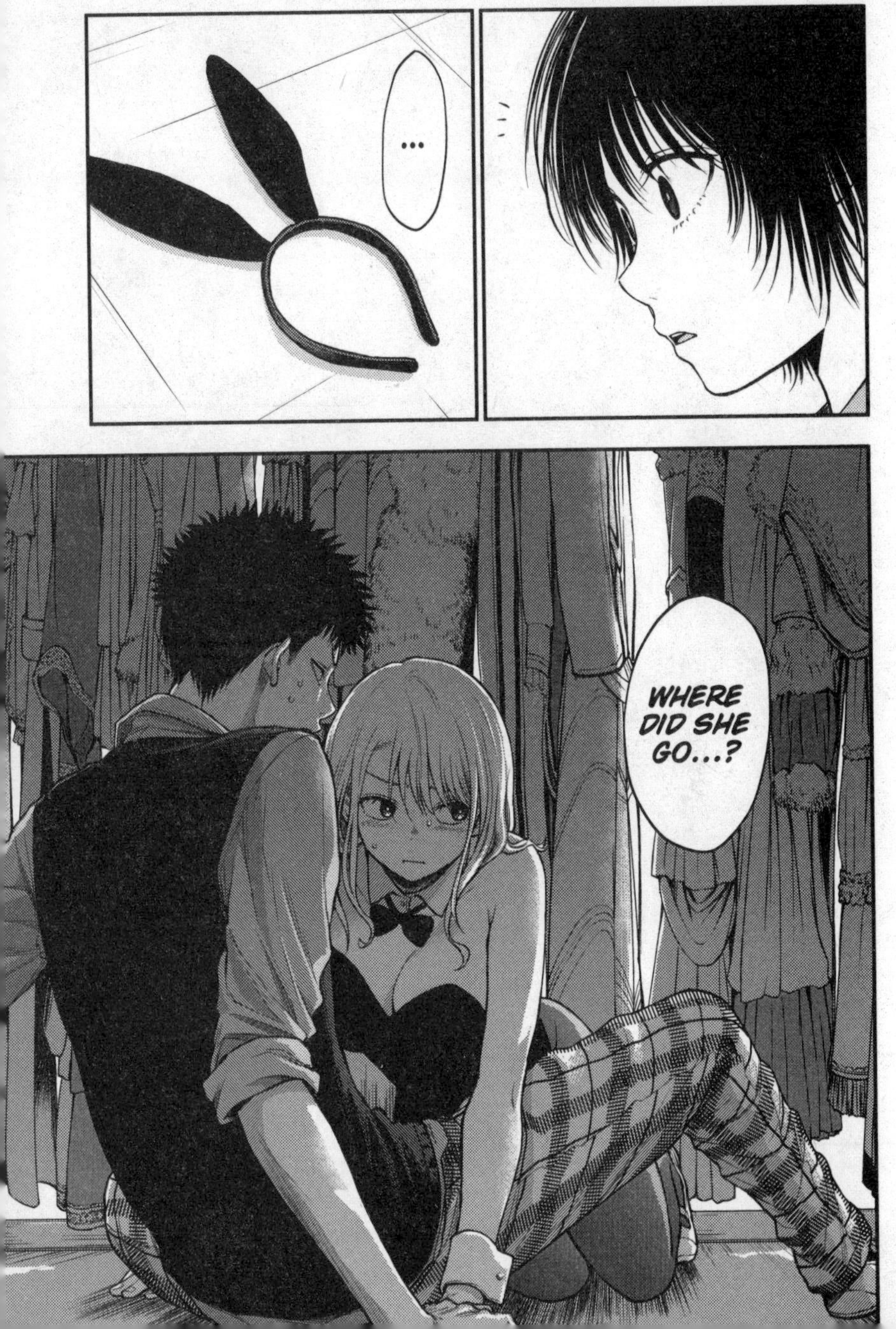
...
WHERE DID SHE GO...?

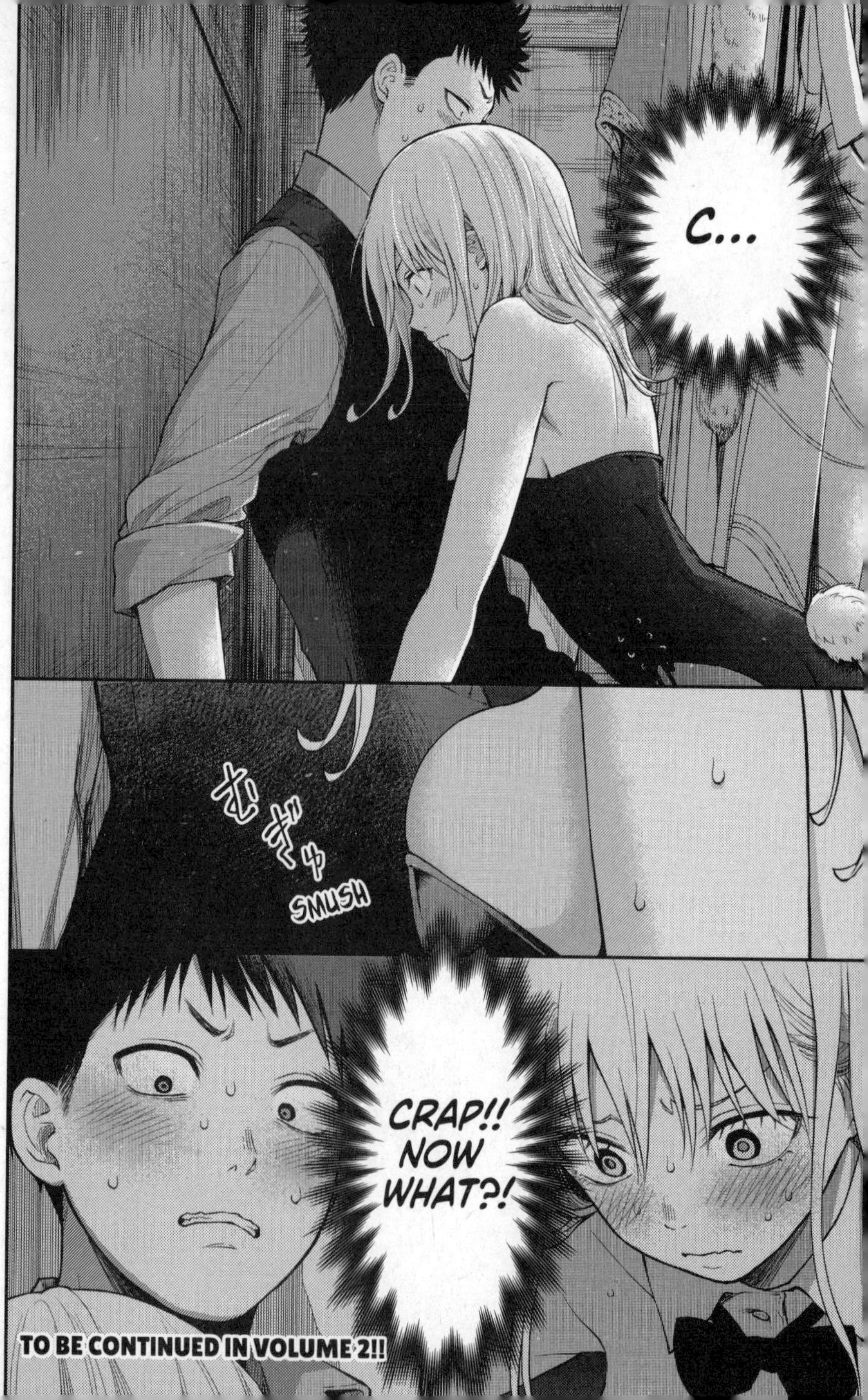
C...
むぎゅ
SMUSH
CRAP!! NOW WHAT?!
TO BE CONTINUED IN VOLUME 2!!

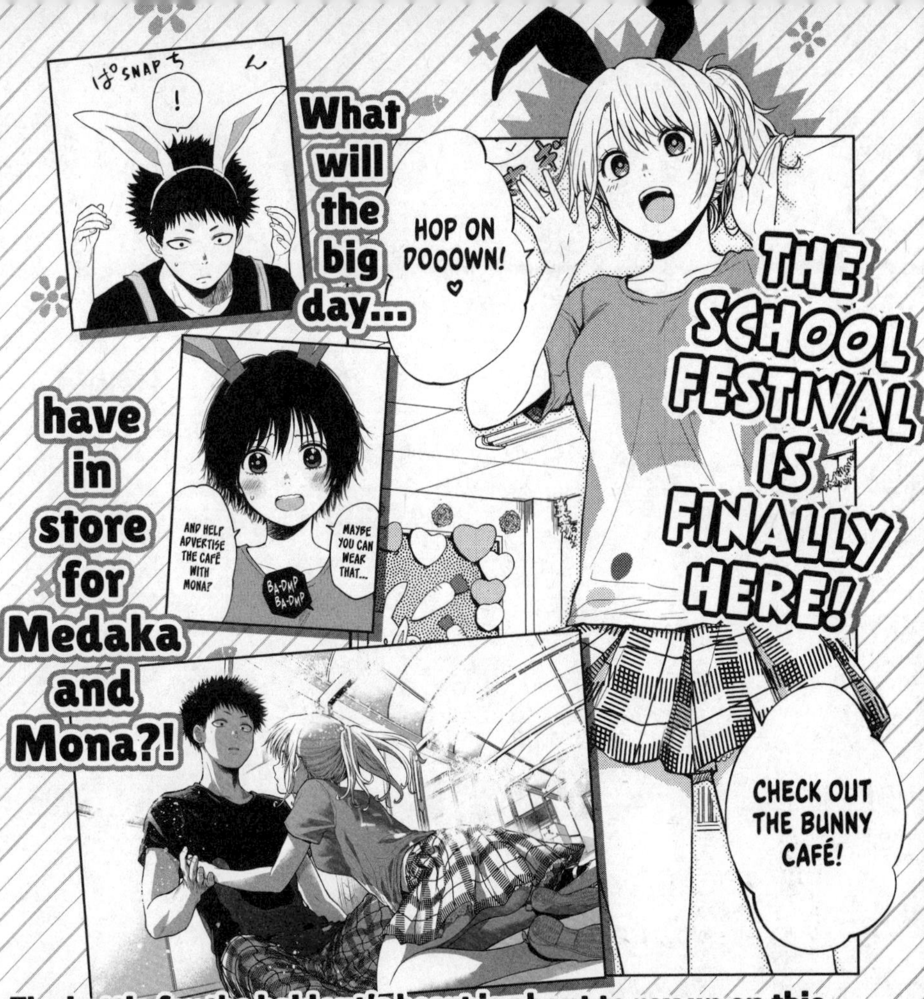
HOP ON DOOOWN! ♡
THE SCHOOL FESTIVAL IS FINALLY HERE!
CHECK OUT THE BUNNY CAFÉ!
ぱSNAPちん
!
What will the big day...
MAYBE YOU CAN WEAR THAT...
AND HELP ADVERTISE THE CAFÉ WITH MONA?
BA-DMP BA-DMP
have in store for Medaka and Mona?!

DON'T TOY WITH ME, MISS NAGATORO

NANASHI

Nagatoro is a cute freshman in high school who loves to toy with her senior classmate (Senpai). Even though Nagatoro tricks Senpai, makes him cry, and teases him, the two of them are hardly ever apart. Do they really like each other as friends? Or are they toying with the idea that they can be something more...? Find out in this rowdy romantic comedy!

VOLUMES 1-14 AVAILABLE NOW!

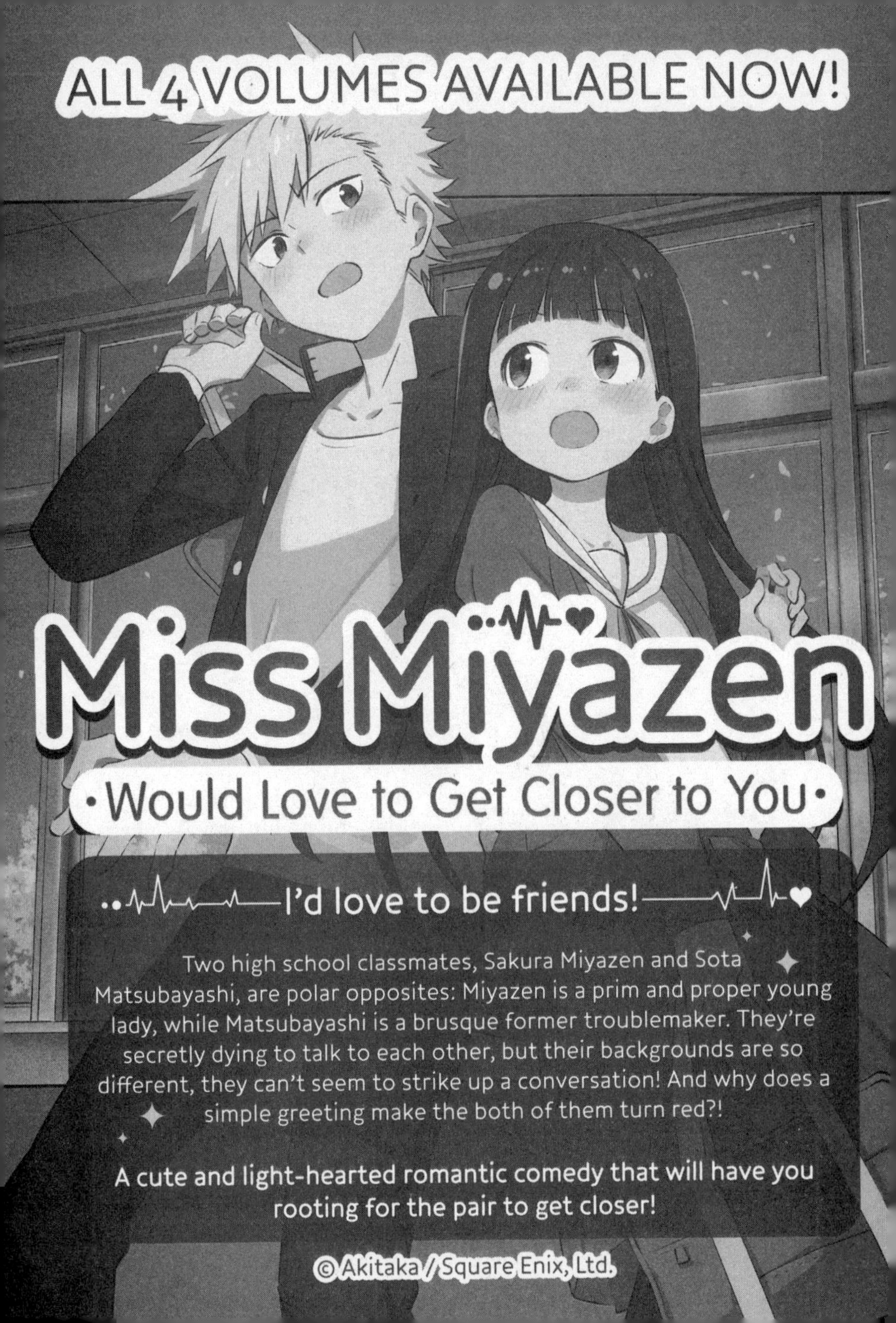
ALL 4 VOLUMES AVAILABLE NOW!
Miss Miyazen
•Would Love to Get Closer to You•
I'd love to be friends!
Two high school classmates, Sakura Miyazen and Sota Matsubayashi, are polar opposites: Miyazen is a prim and proper young lady, while Matsubayashi is a brusque former troublemaker. They're secretly dying to talk to each other, but their backgrounds are so different, they can't seem to strike up a conversation! And why does a simple greeting make the both of them turn red?!
A cute and light-hearted romantic comedy that will have you rooting for the pair to get closer!
© Akitaka / Square Enix, Ltd.

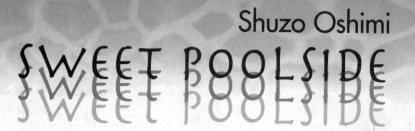

Shuzo Oshimi

SWEET POOLSIDE

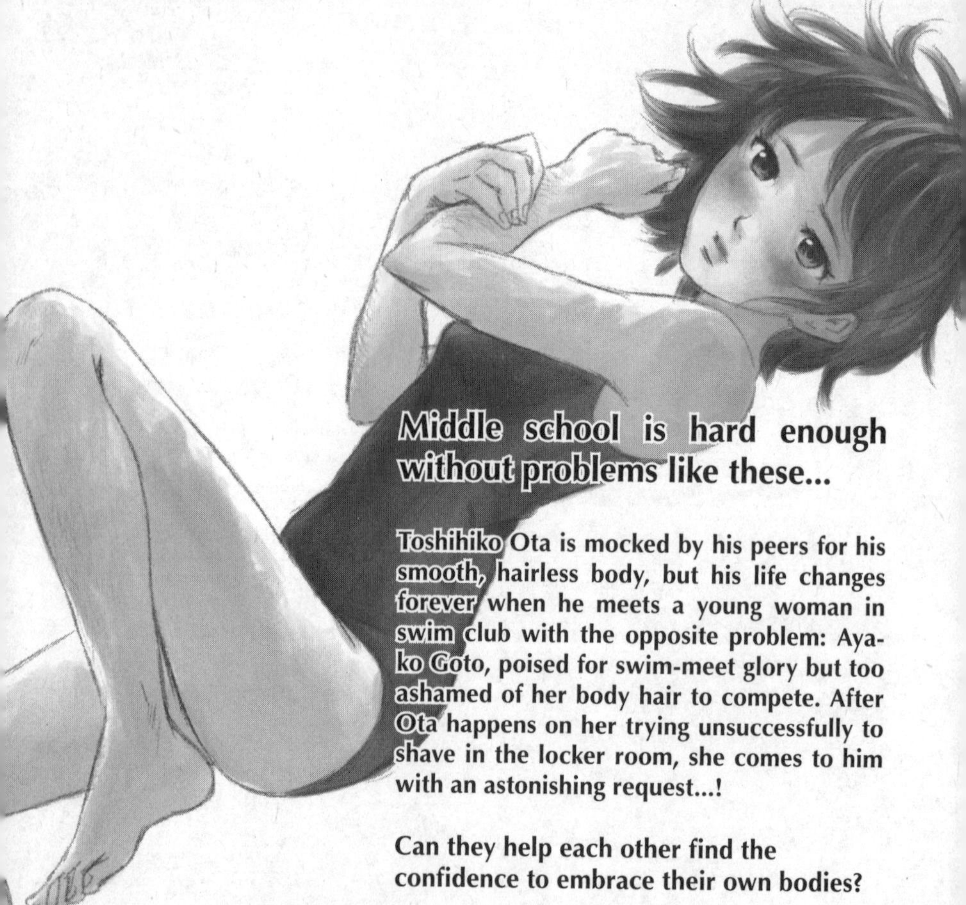

Middle school is hard enough without problems like these...

Toshihiko Ota is mocked by his peers for his smooth, hairless body, but his life changes forever when he meets a young woman in swim club with the opposite problem: Ayako Goto, poised for swim-meet glory but too ashamed of her body hair to compete. After Ota happens on her trying unsuccessfully to shave in the locker room, she comes to him with an astonishing request...!

Can they help each other find the confidence to embrace their own bodies?

Available Now!

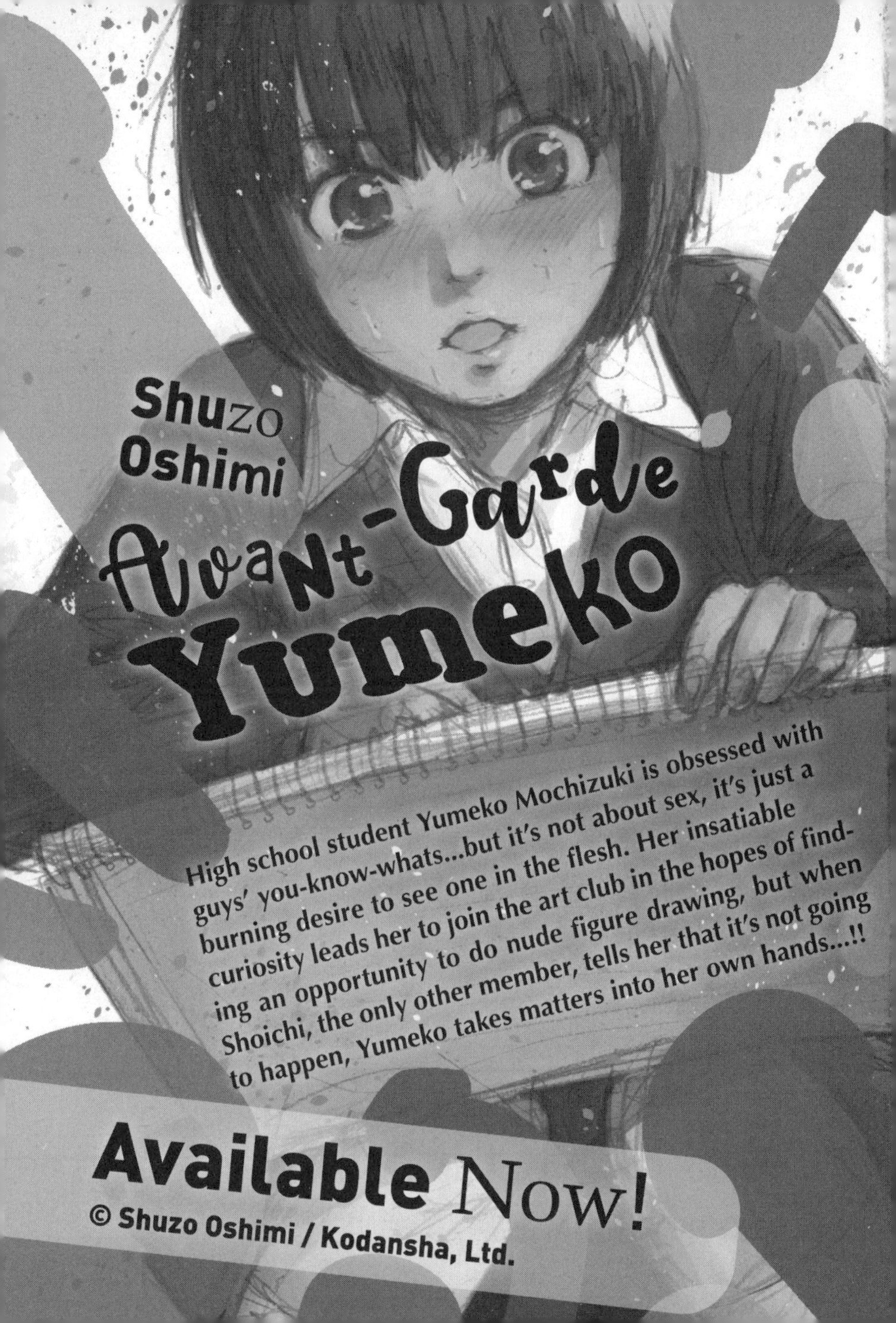
Shuzo Oshimi
Avant-Garde Yumeko
High school student Yumeko Mochizuki is obsessed with guys' you-know-whats...but it's not about sex, it's just a burning desire to see one in the flesh. Her insatiable curiosity leads her to join the art club in the hopes of finding an opportunity to do nude figure drawing, but when Shoichi, the only other member, tells her that it's not going to happen, Yumeko takes matters into her own hands...!!
Available Now!
© Shuzo Oshimi / Kodansha, Ltd.

Medaka Kuroiwa is Impervious to My Charms 1
A VERTICAL Book

Editor (Original Digital): Thalia Sutton
Editor (Print): Alexandra R. McCullough-Garcia
Translation: Anh Kiet Pham Ngo
Production: Risa Cho (print)
          Pei Ann Yeap (print)
Letterer: Arbash Mughal
Proofreading: Kevin Luo (print)
YKS Services LLC/SKY JAPAN, Inc. (original digital)

First published in Japan in 2021 by Kodansha, Ltd., Tokyo
Publication rights for this English edition arranged through Kodansha, Ltd., Tokyo
English language version produced by Kodansha USA Publishing, LLC, 2023

Originally published in Japanese as *Kuroiwa Medaka ni Watashi no Kawaii ga Tsūjinai 1* by Kodansha, Ltd.
Kuroiwa Medaka ni Watashi no Kawaii ga Tsūjinai first serialized in *Weekly Shonen Magazine*, Kodansha, Ltd., 2021-

This is a work of fiction.

ISBN: 978-1-64729-232-4

Printed in the United States of America

First Edition

Kodansha USA Publishing, LLC
451 Park Avenue South
7th Floor
New York, NY 10016
www.kodansha.us

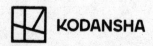

KODANSHA